First Line Management

First Line Management

A practical approach

Diana Bedward
Deputy Dean, Faculty of Management, University of Luton

Christine Rexworthy
Principal Lecturer, Faculty of Management, University of Luton

Carol Blackman
Associate Head, London Management Centre, University of Westminster

Andrew Rothwell
Senior Lecturer, School of Management, University of Derby

Margaret Weaver
Lecturer in Business Studies, Stockport College of Further and Higher Education

Butterworth-Heinemann
Linacre House, Jordan Hill, Oxford OX2 8DP
A division of Reed Educational and Professional Publishing Ltd

ℛ A member of the Reed Elsevier plc group

OXFORD BOSTON JOHANNESBURG
MELBOURNE NEW DELHI SINGAPORE

First published 1997

British Library Cataloguing in Publication Data
First line management: a practical approach
  1. Industrial management   2. Supervisors
  I. Bedward, Diana
  658.3'02

ISBN 0 7506 2799 9

Typeset by Avocet Typeset, Brill, Aylesbury, Bucks
Printed in Great Britain by The Bath Press, Bath

Contents

Preface

First Line Management – A practical approach has been written for existing or aspiring first line or operational managers in all sectors of the economy. Throughout UK organizations there appears to be no consistent use of the terms first line manager, operational manager, supervisor and team leader. However, they all have day-to-day responsibility for staff, they contribute to the production of goods or services, some have financial responsibility, and all manage information.

Chapters in this book reflect these issues, analysing the principles of management which underpin the role, and providing an understanding of the way different organizations are managed. For ease of reference each chapter begins with a set of aims and key concepts.

The emphasis throughout is on the practical application of management. Each chapter contains a set of Activities, which are related to the discussions. Some also contain small relevant case studies. The book is appropriate for students undertaking a Certificate in Management Studies, a Professional Development Certificate, or a Diploma in Management Studies either at the workplace, or at a further or higher education institution. It also provides the broad underpinning knowledge and understanding for the NVQ (level 4) in Management.

Acknowledgements

The authors would like to express their thanks to their colleagues at the Universities of Derby, Luton and Westminster and Stockport College of Further and Higher Education for their assistance in the compilation of this book. They are particularly indebted to them for their cooperation in allowing the reproduction of some lecture notes, handouts and overhead transparencies. The authors acknowledge with gratitude the assistance of the many organizations who have kindly provided relevant material: ACAS; ASM; B & W Associates; BMRB International; Body Shop plc; British Airways; British Gas; BT; Commercial Union; *Daily Telegraph;* Edexcel Foundation; *Guardian; Harvard Business Review; Independent;* IPM; Laura Ashley plc; McDonald's; Mill Hill Missionaries; Mitsubishi Electric UK Ltd; North Yorkshire Health Authority; Pret A Manger; Royal Mail; Sheba; University of Westminster; Welwyn and Hatfield Council.

Whilst every effort has been made to identify the specific sources of such material in order to request permission for their use, in some instances this may not have been possible and the authors apologize unreservedly for any failure in this regard.

1 A manager's responsibilities

Aims

By the end of this chapter, you should be familiar with the different types of organization in the private, public and not-for-profit sectors. You will also have considered the responsibilities and obligations not only of such organizations, but also those of different types of manager in various functional specialisms. In addition, you will have thought about your own experience as a manager – either in the workplace or at home – and conducted a preliminary audit of your existing skills and formulated an action plan.

Key concepts

- Organizations;
- Levels of manager;
- Responsibilities;
- Major functional specialisms;
- Sectors;
- Obligations;
- Managing oneself;
- Self-development;
- Methodical approach;
- Action planning.

Introduction

Before we can begin to discuss the management of organizations, we need to consider just what constitutes an 'organization'. What does it mean to you? To help you, try to identify some of the organizations with which you have been associated and then list the factors which they all have in common. Jot them down and then compare your answer with ours.

Our list includes a school, a university, a charity, a legal practice, a publishing company, a shop, a manufacturing company and a hospital. We decided that they all had a name or title; they had a set of rules or procedures; there was some kind of structure; they had a purpose – perhaps to produce a particular kind of product or service or to raise money; there were people who 'belonged' to the organization either directly as employees or volunteers or indirectly as members or subscribers. All of those factors contributed to a unique organizational 'culture'; the easiest analogy being that of a human 'personality' which you will explore more fully in Chapter 2.

You may have realized already that, in this chapter, we are not just concerned with traditional business organizations such as Marks and Spencer plc or British Gas. We are also concerned with 'public sector' organizations, though the number of these is declining, and also entities known as 'not-for-profit' (NFP) organizations or charities. Another factor which we could have included in our list above is that all types of organization need to be *managed* and there are common, or generic, skills and abilities, coupled with underlying knowledge and understanding, which the managers of any organization need to possess.

The Management Charter Initiative (MCI), based in Russell Square in London, is the lead body for the development of national standards of competence required by managers. Currently, these are available at four levels – Supervisory; First Line; Operational; and Strategic Level for those responsible for deciding upon strategy and its implementation.

At the strategic level of management, the responsibilities of managers are essentially to identify the vision and mission of an organization. This will embrace the purpose of the organization and also its values. The senior management team must then decide on the most effective strategy for the achievement of an organization's objectives. They will need to conduct extensive analysis of both the external and internal environment in which the organization operates in order to decide how best to deploy its resources.

At the next most senior level – the middle or operational level – managers often carry the responsibility for the implementation of strategy; they must monitor the progress and evaluate the processes which the organization is using and provide continuous feedback both to senior managers and also to their colleagues and subordinates.

At first line or supervisory level, the responsibilities of managers are normally for the running of day-to-day activities; they and their people are often the ones who are closest to the organization's customers and clients and they must be constantly anticipating their needs and meeting their expectations. The knowledge and skills required at this level are multi-functional and probably include all or most of the following:

- budgetary control
- health and safety
- employment law
- recruitment and selection
- negotiation
- target setting
- problem solving

- motivation
- assertiveness
- performance review
- time management
- running effective meetings
- team building
- empowerment
- activity monitoring.

This is quite a formidable list, but this book provides advice and assistance on most of them and you will be pointed to more detailed readings where appropriate.

Demands, limitations, choices

Whatever the level of the organization in which you work, you are going to be faced with conflicting *demands*, *limitations* and *choices*. Demands might include minimum levels and standards of work which must be achieved or essential procedures which must be followed; it will also include the demands of your organization's external and internal customers. The limitations may include limited amounts of resources (human, financial, technological) or perhaps lack of skills or abilities. As a result of the conflicting demands and limitations, the manager must make choices and decisions about what work is to be done, the time in which it must happen and the best method to adopt.

Activity 1.1

Write down some of the conflicting demands and limitations which you face in your workplace. Analyse some of the decisions and choices that you have had to make. Would you still make the same decisions now? If they are likely to be different, why should this be so?

Organizational sectors: public, private, voluntary, manufacturing, service

In the UK currently, we have a *working population* – those who are in employment and those who are registered as unemployed – of around 26 million people. In December 1996, the total number of employees was estimated to be 21 674 000 and the estimated figure for the unemployed was 1 977 200 (*Employment News*) the remainder of the working population being self-employed.

Public sector

In the past 15 years, the number of organizations in the *public sector* – those controlled primarily by the government – has declined drastically. Organizations which we typically think of as public sector employers include schools and colleges, universities, hospitals, the Post Office, British Coal, the Civil Service, the armed forces, county councils and local authorities. However, the number of organizations which have been removed from governmental control during the past 15 years and which have been *privatized* is considerable. What does the term 'privatization' mean? Primarily, organizations which had previously provided goods or services as a monopoly or single supplier, have been forced to offer their assets for sale in the form of shares through the Stock Exchange; they have then been restructured to enable competition to occur and their managers have then been accountable to a board of directors elected by the shareholders. If organizations have to compete against one another under *market conditions* – that is without government funds or subsidies, it should encourage their managers to ensure that they are managed as efficiently as possible. Some of the utilities which have been privatized are the water, telephone, electricity and gas industries; others are British Airways and British Airports Authority.

Private sector

There is something of a misnomer here, as Public Limited Companies (PLCs) are contained within the private sector. The easiest way to classify the private sector is to think of it as any organization which is not contained within the public sector as described above! This means it includes not only PLCs, but also private limited companies, partnerships, franchises, cooperatives and sole traders.

Activity 1.2

Prepare brief notes on the advantages and disadvantages of the different types of organization found in the private sector. Make sure that you understand the concept of *limited* liability. This type of information will be contained within most textbooks in the Business Studies section of your local library.

Voluntary sector

Many of the organizations found here have a nucleus of managers to coordinate their activities, but they also rely on the largely unpaid services of people who are prepared to give their time to assist in the promotion of a particular cause. Examples would include organizations like Oxfam, The Samaritans, Save the Children, or the Royal Society for the Prevention of Cruelty to Animals (RSPCA). Frequently these organizations are highly sophisticated and many in the past decade have changed their structures and cultures as a matter of deliberate policy. Just as commercial organizations have had to become increasingly competitive in order to survive, so have those organizations in the voluntary sector. Nowadays, there are so many organizations appealing for funds from members of the public that they have to become highly sophisticated entities to ensure that their cause continues to attract support. Several hundred organizations seek registration as charities with the Charity Commission each week – one of the most significant reasons for application being that, as charities, they are excused tax on their incomes.

Activity 1.3

Read the case study below and then answer the questions below.

CASE STUDY
(from the *Daily Telegraph*, 11 June 1994)
The Duke of Edinburgh (has) called in a speech for a new system of classification in the voluntary sector, with a range of tax concessions according to category. Bodies now regarded as charitable should be ranked by the kind of contribution they make and how far the community rates it as worthwhile, he suggested. Only those bodies which stuck close to the original humanitarian aims of charity law should be allowed full privileges....The voluntary sector is the jewel in the crown of British public life, far more so than in, say, France. It is where a vast army of people, motivated by enthusiasm rather than by money, work to make life better for their follow citizens....There are 170 000 charities registered with the Charity Commissioners, which means 170 000 slightly differing examples of what a charity is....The total turnover of the charity sector is some £17 billion a year, which puts it in the same league as, say, the water or power-generation industry or the GNP of the Republic of Ireland. The rattling collection box is feeding a very big business, which at the top has become increasingly professional

in its managerial and fund-raising skills, while remaining at the bottom, the province of the dedicated amateur.

The fuel in the tank of the charity world is its special tax status. Charities are excused tax on their income. Furthermore, donations to charities are paid from unearned income, which means for every £75 the average tax payer donates, the Inland Revenue refunds a further £25. Companies also enjoy tax breaks on their donations....The Charity Commission has already started to exclude bodies like gun clubs as having aims incompatible with charitable status.

Questions for Activity 1.3

1   How would *you* decide what counts as a charitable organization?
2   What types of organization would you definitely exclude from being charities?
3   If the Duke of Edinburgh's idea was adopted, who do you think should decide on the ranking of charities in terms of how 'worthwhile' they are? Justify your answer.
4   Working with others, see if you can produce a means of categorizing charities according to the contribution that they make to society. Make sure that you are explicit about your criteria.

Manufacturing and service sectors

In July 1996, the number of people employed in manufacturing industries was estimated to be 4 141 000 – about 20 per cent of those currently in work. This is a much smaller number than in recent years. The recession of the early 1980s hit manufacturing industry particularly hard and over three million jobs were lost due to closures of traditional industrial organizations which could no longer compete effectively. The service sector includes organizations in both the public and private sectors. It covers both large organizations such as hospitals, retail chains, schools and colleges, banks and insurance companies, and small organizations providing individual services such as solicitors and accountants, plumbers and hairdressers.

All organizations, from each sector, probably have one thing in common. They have faced unprecedented levels of change in recent years.

Activity 1.4

On separate sheets of paper, write the headings, Hospitals, Schools, Shops, Cars, Information Technology (include more headings if you wish). Now spend 15 minutes listing the ways in which these entities have changed since the beginning of the 1980s. If you are working through this book with a group of fellow students, compare your lists with others. What reasons can you come up with for the changes? What other changes can you foresee over the next 10 years?

Responsibilities

Many organizations employ considerably fewer people than they once did; many employ part-time workers rather than full-time; many have changed their organizational structures, which you will be exploring in Chapter 2.

Just as organizations have changed, so the roles of managers have changed. Many managers at all levels are now expected to assume greater responsibilities and there may no longer be the clear-cut job roles that once existed. However, we can still identify the most frequently encountered *levels* of manager – for example:

- Board of directors: responsible for strategic planning and devising policy
- Chief executive: responsible for overall implementation and coordination of policy
- Senior managers: responsible for implementing policy within *functional* areas such as finance, purchasing, marketing, production, human resource management
- Departmental managers: responsible for allocation of resources (e.g. money, people) and organization of work
- Supervisors: responsible for scheduling and coordination of work
- Team leaders: responsible for allocation and processing of work
- Shop floor workers: responsible for operations

In this example, there are five *levels* between the shop floor workers and the board of directors. Such a structure is referred to as a 'hierarchy'. The tendency for 'tall hierarchies' with many levels of manager is diminishing in favour of 'flatter hierarchies' with fewer levels.

Before going further, consider what the word 'responsibility' means to you – one dictionary definition suggests that it means 'being accountable for one's actions and decisions' (Collins). That is fine as far as it goes, but it raises some interesting questions: who or what are you accountable to? How do you know what your actions and decisions *ought* to be?

Activity 1.5

Write down what you consider your current responsibilities to be. The easiest way to do this may be to consider all the things you have done in the last week. Try to include specific examples of what you consider are your responsibilities to groups such as your friends or family, your work colleagues, your employer (past or present), social or charity groups. How did you decide what constituted your responsibilities? Were they written or implied? When you have done this, try and compare your list with others. What are the similarities or differences? Why should these be so?

Just as you have explicit and implicit responsibilities, so do managers at all levels within different organizations. Their explicit responsibilities will be contained within their Job Description and set out in an individual's Terms and Conditions of employment. However, this is certainly not the whole picture. The pattern in recent years has been for some job descriptions, especially those of managers, to be increasingly vague in defining the exact responsibilities. Why should this be so? One reason is that organizations nowadays have to respond quickly and flexibly to their customers' requirements. Change has become a way of life for many organizations and the nature of the work contained within them may also be changing. In general, organizations are looking for managers and employees who can do a number of jobs – multiskilled is the term most frequently used. They are also looking for their workforces to take on more responsibility for the quality of their work.

For example, at Jaguar cars in the early 1980s, the wage bill for Quality Inspection undertaken at the end of the production line, was 11 per cent of total payroll. When Sir John Egan was recruited to undertake the turnaround of the company, this inspectorate was drastically reduced and responsibility for quality was given firmly to the individual workers on the shop floor. A quality improvement programme was introduced, together with a major training programme, including an 'open learning' scheme whereby any employee of the company could improve their skills and knowledge.

Managers' responsibilities may not always be clearly spelt out. For example, all employees have what are termed 'implied' legal responsibilities – such as not disclosing any confidential information and exercising proper skill and care to ensure the health and safety both of themselves and those with whom they work.

In general we can categorize a manager's responsibilities into those for people, money, results, services, products, information and health and safety. Although the range and depth of responsibility will vary widely according to a manager's level, it is helpful to consider each of the above concepts in a little more detail.

People

One of the best known writers on management is Peter Drucker. His definition of management, made nearly 40 years ago, is still used extensively: 'Getting things done through people'. Although technology has changed the face of most organizations, they still need people if they are to be successful.

Activity 1.6

Read the following extract from the company statement of Mitsubishi Electric UK Ltd and then consider the question below.

Our people are our greatest asset. We would like to build upon this strength through a dynamic working environment where job challenges are successfully met through guidance, encouragement and training as well as our employees' individuality and challenging spirit. We would also like to take full advantage of our cultural diversity through team work, flexibility and mutual understanding. Our success is highly dependent upon the ability of European managers to lead our businesses into the future. We, therefore, must provide the variety of experiences and training necessary to help them succeed in these challenging roles.

Question for activity 1.6

For what reasons do Mitsubishi Electric publish such a statement?

Money

Responsibilities for money can include any of the following: keeping a record of petty-cash transactions; keeping what are termed 'books of prime entry' such as the sales daybook to record total sales, the purchases daybook which provides purchase totals; the returns book where records of credit notes are recorded and the cash book which records all receipts and payments; monitoring the purchase of raw materials; ensuring that budgets are not exceeded; handling wages and salaries; keeping VAT (value added tax) records; calculation of costs; reviewing the cash flow (money in and out of an organization) position to ensure the organization's liquidity; forecasting future financial needs; carrying out investment appraisal and raising money from banks or other sources where necessary.

Services and products

A manager's responsibilities may include the completion of the finished product or the completion of a service. It is more likely though that the manager's responsibilities will extend to a specific part of the operation.

Health and safety

In general, managers have a clear responsibility for providing and promoting health and safety policies; they should ensure that appropriate information from the Health and Safety Executive is displayed and distributed; arrange training as appropriate; keep records and report the occurrence of serious accidents to the appropriate authorities; consult regularly with elected workplace safety representatives; carry out workplace audits and assessment of risks; ensure that where appropriate protective clothing is worn; ensure that machinery is regularly maintained and where there are moving parts such as flywheels, ensure that these are properly guarded; make sure that each employee understands that they have a duty to take reasonable care of themselves and others; ensure that regular fire drills are carried out and that all personnel are aware of fire hazards and action to be taken in the event of a fire or other potential danger.

Information

Before reading on, jot down below all the different types of information that you have encountered in organizations that you have worked for and then compare your list with ours.

Our list included:

- Written – minutes of meetings, letters, memos, reports, procedural manuals, directories, reference books, journals
- Verbal – face-to-face communications, telephone, voice-mail
- Numerical – budgets, petty cash, overtime records, annual accounts
- Graphical – analyses of sales, forecasts of future sales
- Electronic information – databases, spreadsheets, faxes, e-mail

Much more will be said about information in Chapter 8.

Results

All managers are responsible for results of some kind. They may be given specific targets to achieve within a certain period or they may be less precise. Whatever results are required, managers will need to ensure that their teams have a shared understanding of requirements and they will need to monitor, evaluate and provide feedback on the progress that their people are making.

So far, we have not really tried to distinguish between different levels of manager.

Activity 1.7

Before reading on, think of any organization with which you are famil- iar. Write down what you would expect each of the following people to be doing at work: team leader, supervisor, first line manager, middle manager, senior manager.

You probably found it very difficult to make clear distinctions in some of the roles. In general, we suggest that a team leader will prob- ably be leading a small group of perhaps six or eight people – this is known as the 'span of control'. He or she may be responsible for allo- cating their work and ensuring that deadlines are met. A supervisor is likely to be coordinating the work of several team leaders and will be accountable to a line manager – one who has a direct responsibility for a particular aspect of service of production. Depending on the size of the organization, this may be a first line or middle manager. He or she in turn will be responsible to a more senior manager who may be in charge of a department or section.

The range and scope of responsibilities within the context of manage- ment are considerable. At the level of the individual, it refers to the areas within their jobs for which they are accountable or answerable. At the level of the organization, it could refer to corporate responsibility for filing accounts publicly or non-pollution of the environment. It should be noted that within our legal system, a company is held to be a legal entity in its own right and can be prosecuted or sued in its own name. However, an organ- ization's senior managers will be responsible for ensuring that it fulfils its responsibilities.

Corporate responsibilities

Activity 1.8

Reproduced below is the introduction to the Edexcel Foundation (formerly BTEC and London Examinations). Read it through and then consider the following questions

EDUCATIONAL
EXCELLENCE

ED
EXCEL

Introduction
By the Chief Executive Dr Christina Townsend

I am proud to introduce you to Edexcel Foundation, a new and positive force in education.

Edexcel Foundation is the new name for the organisation formed on 24 April 1996 by the merger of BTEC and London Examinations. The name expresses our commitment to educational excellence at a time when the rigour of the assessment system is under scrutiny.

BTEC
London
EXAMINATIONS
EDEXCEL FOUNDATION

Edexcel aims to fulfil the educational needs of students, teachers and employees by providing a wide range of high quality qualifications and support services. These will be developed through research and development and after consultation with our colleagues and stakeholders.

Anticipating the needs arising from the Dearing Report, and employment trends, Edexcel Foundation will develop innovative qualifications and assessment methods to support the changing requirements for knowledge and skills in the workplace of the future. Simplifying solutions and pioneering new combinations of academic, applied and vocational qualifications will be high priorities. At the same time, Edexcel is committed to ensuring that the highest standards of quality are maintained in our qualifications.

Edexcel expects shortly to launch the first product of the merger. Support material which will enable the parallel delivery of Advanced GNVQ and A-Level Business Studies will be introduced as part of a collaborative working programme with a number of our centres, prior to nationwide distribution. Similar projects are in the pipeline.

There are many opportunities ahead and Edexcel intends to be at the forefront of delivering a framework of qualifications to encourage educational excellence at all levels of ability.

Christina Townsend

Figure 1.1

1   How do you think the managing council of Edexcel view their responsibilities in terms of people, money, results, information and services?

2   Thinking of an organization with which you are familiar, how do you think the managing body view their responsibilities? How different are they from Edexcel?

Functional specialisms

In its early days, an organization may be run by one or two people who are able to control and carry out all the activities needed, but once an organization expands, it is usual for them to divide their activities into separate *functions*.

Finance

This area may include overall responsibility for ensuring that there is sufficient money coming into the organization, either from the sale of its products or services, or in the form of donations if it is in the voluntary sector, to enable it to survive and pay its debts. It may employ people to ensure that invoices are sent out on time and ensure that an organization's creditors meet payments due; others may be responsible for the payment of bills for purchases of raw materials and other resources; payment of wages may also be their responsibility. Records will need to be kept of all transactions either manually or electronically. At the end of an organization's financial year, its accounts must be verified and audited and public limited companies will publish their accounts, often in the Annual Report sent to its shareholders, so that their performance can be scrutinized and monitored by any interested party. The finance function may also be responsible for *management accounting* – analysing past performance and forecasting likely future performance, including advising on possible future investments and sources of finance. It will thus have a responsibility for providing considerable information to all sections of the organization. This is likely to be in the form of reports using graphic information, statistics and spreadsheets.

Human resource management

This function used to be more commonly called the *personnel function*. However, its name has changed to reflect its expanding role. The human resources function is normally responsible for recruitment and selection of the workforce, induction of new staff, appraisal systems for reviewing the performance of the workforce and their training and development. Its staff may also have an overall responsibility in health and safety matters. In addition, they will draw up, in conjunction with senior managers, organizational policies on disciplinary and grievance procedures and they will ensure that all staff are supplied with terms and conditions of their employment. You will be able to learn more about this function in Chapter 6.

Operations

Either within this function, or as separate divisions, you will normally find people responsible for the purchase of raw materials, for planning ahead to estimate likely future requirements and controlling levels of stock, for decid-ing on how the work of an organization can be most effectively carried out in terms of the layout of its components and in the scheduling of the differ-ent stages of operation. There may be people specifically responsible for certain aspects of quality – for example in selecting external suppliers who can be relied upon to meet the organization's requirements.

Sales and marketing

This function will be responsible for carrying out market research in order to identify the likely requirements of an organization's customers. Once the products and services have been decided on by an organization's senior managers, the marketing function will work closely with the design and pro-duction teams to ensure their suitability for the target market. They will then ensure that they are advertised and promoted, that their customers know when and where they may be purchased and ensure that their distri-bution runs smoothly.

Project management

Nowadays, an increasing number of organizations are using teams or 'cells' of people, drawn from functions across the organization, to meet the demand for a specific product or service. The advent of technological systems such as 'e-' (electronic) mail enables individuals to communicate their ideas to others almost instantly using either LANS (local area net-works) or WANS (wide area networks). It is thus possible to coordinate dif-ferent activities far more effectively and use people's specialist knowledge and expertise.

Activity 1.9

Provide a description of the responsibilities of two managers with dif-ferent major functional specialisms at different levels within organiza-tions from two different sectors.

The obligations of a manager

This part of the chapter is concerned with the manager's *obligations*, which can be defined as moral or legal requirements. Whilst we can be fairly defi-nite about the latter, it is more difficult to decide what constitutes morals and ethics. In the first section we will explore ethical issues using examples of the kinds of questions faced by some well-known organizations. You will then be invited to consider how you feel about such matters and think of some examples from your own experience where perhaps you faced conflicting priorities and had to decide on how these should be resolved.

Activity 1.10

There are now several organizations operating in the financial services sector which offer investors the opportunity of investing in 'ethical unit trusts and savings schemes'. What kinds of investment do you think would be precluded by such organizations? How do they decide what is 'ethical' and what is not?

The following quotation comes from Anita Roddick, owner of the Body Shop PLC.

> In a society in which politicians no longer lead by example, ethical conduct is unfashionable, and the media does not give people real information on what is happening in the world, what fascinates me is the concept of turning our shops into centres of education. (*Body and Soul*, Anita Roddick, p. 108)

Later on, she discusses the setting up of the Body Shop's Environmental Projects Department.

Activity 1.11

Read the following extract from the same source and then consider the questions which follow:

> In 1986, we (The Body Shop) set up our Environmental Projects Department. Their function is
> - to oversee and co-ordinate our campaigning
> - to ensure that the company's products and practices are environmentally sound
> - to check that everything in our range fulfils our commitment to our customers that Body Shop products do not consume a disproportionate amount of energy during either manufacture or disposal and
> - do not cause unnecessary waste
> - do not use materials from threatened species or threatened environments
> - do not involve cruelty to animals and
> - do not adversely affect other countries, particularly the Third World.

Questions for Activity 1.11

1   Do you agree that organizations such as the Body Shop have a moral obligation to society to campaign on the kinds of issues raised?
2   Do you think that there should be any kind of legal obligation imposed on organizations to publish their position on ethical issues?
3   If so, what types of information should it include?
4   What types of incompatibility can you predict between the requirements for profitability and ethical behaviour in organizations?
5   On what basis can an organization prioritize its obligations?

Ethical questions can lead to lively debate and sometimes considerable conflict. One of the legal issues that has been the subject of such debate for many years has been the question of whether or not certain types of store should be permitted to trade on Sundays. Until quite recently there were severe limitations on the types of product that could be sold. Several large DIY stores have faced prosecution and subsequent fines and injunctions, but complained that the laws were outdated and they were being prevented from meeting their customers' needs. Other organizations campaigned vigorously supporting the idea that Sundays should be preserved as traditional days of rest. Now that new legislation is in force to permit Sunday trading on a large scale, many small shopkeepers feel that their livelihoods will be threatened as the major retailers will attract their traditional customers away to town centres and shopping malls. What do you think about this issue? For example, do you feel that the organizations which previously broke the law and opened on Sundays, operated ethically?

Organizational, individual and personal objectives

Just as organizations have to consider their corporate obligations, so an individual manager may sometimes face potentially conflicting obligations in the workplace. This may be the result of differences in organizational, individual and personal objectives.

Read the following case study and then consider the questions below.

CASE STUDY

Fred Jones has been working in the accounts department of XYZ for fifteen years. He enjoys his work and is loyal and trustworthy as well as efficient in his work. Fred has many interests outside his job and although he was offered the chance to gain further qualifications, he chose not to do so. Julie Smith has recently joined the company as an accounts supervisor. She is a recent graduate and is currently working her way towards becoming a qualified accountant. Tony Newton is the Finance Manager of the department. He is currently under some pressure from the Finance Director to streamline operations and introduce a new computerized system which will be linked up to XYZ's newly acquired subsidiary in Paris.

Questions

1 What do you think are the objectives of Fred, Julie, Tony and the Finance Director?
2 Can you see how their individual objectives may be incompatible with those of others?
3 Can you suggest ways in which each individual's objectives might be reconciled?

In thinking about questions such as this, it is sometimes helpful to use a matrix as shown in Figure 1.2. In the matrix, we have listed some of the possible objectives in the left-hand column and then used asterisks to identify those which are of direct concern to each of the participants.

Activity 1.12

Consider a work-related situation which you have had to face in the past. Consider the range of issues associated with the situation and the other people concerned. Identify your personal objectives in a matrix similar to that above and then identify what you consider were the other objectives of the other individuals concerned and finally those of the organization. Were they compatible? If not, how were they reconciled?

Objectives	Fred	Julie	Tony	Finance Director
Job security	●		●	
Job satisfaction	●	●		
Retain status	●		●	
Demonstrate abilities and absorb new ideas		●		
Improve efficiency of department			●	
Improve information news				●
Cost-effectiveness				●
Co-ordinate international operations				●

Figure 1.2   *XYZ plc*

Legal obligations

Within the workplace a manager will have clear obligations to his or her line manager, colleagues and subordinates and also to himself. One area of particular concern is that of health and safety. Under the Health and Safety at Work Act there is a clear legal obligation on employers to ensure, so far as is reasonably practicable, the health, safety and welfare of all employees while they are at work; in particular, an employer is under an obligation to provide:

- a safe place of work
- safe means of access to the place of work
- a safe system of work
- adequate materials
- competent fellow employees
- protection from unnecessary risk of injury.
- In addition, companies must publish a safety policy, provide adequate instruction and training and establish a safety committee if a union-appointed safety representative asks for one.

The following is an extract from the University of Luton's Statement of General Policy with respect to Health and Safety at work.

Statement of intent

The University accepts its legal and moral obligations to provide a healthy and safe working environment for its staff, students, visitors and contractors, in accordance with the Health and Safety at Work etc. Act 1974 and all other statutes relating to health and safety.

In doing so, it will provide and/or maintain the following:

(a) Plant, equipment, buildings, systems of work and procedures that are safe.

(b) Safe arrangements for the use, handling, storage and transportation of articles and substances.

(c) Adequate information, instruction, training and supervision so as to enable employees to enjoy safe and healthy working practices.

(d) A safe working environment including safe access to and from the area of work.

(e) A healthy working environment with adequate welfare facilities and amenities.

Similarly, employees too have clear obligations. Firstly to take reasonable care of their own health and safety at work and of other persons who may be affected by their acts or omissions and, secondly, to cooperate with their employer in ensuring that the requirements or duties imposed by relevant legislation are complied with. As a result of recent European legislation, there is now an obligation on the part of some managers to undertake, in consultation with representatives of safety committees, health and safety audits and carry out risk assessments and introduce preventative measures where appropriate. The question of health and safety will be considered in more detail in Chapter 3.

A further legal obligation of an employer is that of providing new employees with written terms and conditions of their employment contract. This must set out:

- the names of the employer/employee
- the date of employment/continuous employment
- rate of pay and intervals of payment
- hours of work
- holiday entitlement
- place of work.

Employees may be referred to other documents for details of sickness/sick pay arrangements, pension rights, collective agreements and disciplinary and grievance procedures. However, if employees are referred elsewhere, especially to read collective agreements which apply to them, these must be easily accessible to be read in working hours.

Employers are under an obligation not to discriminate, either directly or indirectly, against individuals on the grounds of sex, race or ethnic origin at any stage, be it at recruitment, in terms and conditions of employment, promotion, training or dismissal.

In recent years, there has been considerable discussion of how organizations can avoid both direct and indirect or unintentional discrimination.

Activity 1.13

Read the following extracts from the *Independent on Sunday* (12 June 1994) and then answer the questions that follow.

Why pregnant often means redundant – Carrie James

Barclays Bank recently made 400 people redundant, but excluded pregnant women and those on maternity leave.

Their equal opportunities manager, Chris Lyles, says: 'Positive discrimination is illegal, but the law does allow a protected group'. He points out that if a whole plant or factory were closed down, there could be no protected group.

Unfortunately, not all employers are as enlightened and ethical as Barclays. Indeed, making women redundant during pregnancy or maternity leave is all too common. The culprits are not just small manufacturing companies whose business has been hammered by the recession. The big law and accounting firms – who arguably should know better – are among the worst offenders. So are publishers – not least those producing magazines promoting women's rights.

Women on maternity leave are easy targets. If a firm can manage without someone for several months, it often concludes it can manage without them permanently. The woman in question is disadvantaged by being out of touch with her work, her colleagues and office politics; she may also be emotionally vulnerable. In short, it is hard for her to put up a fight, and the employer knows it.

It is illegal to make someone redundant selectively and if a woman is singled out because she is pregnant or on maternity leave, that constitutes unfair dismissal. Women are protected by two laws: the Employment Protection (Consolidation) Act and the Sex Discrimination Act. Under the first, the employer has to justify its selection criteria for redundancy. Under the second, the onus is on the woman to prove she has been a victim of discrimination.

The company must offer a woman whose job has become redundant a suitable alternative, if one is available. Moreover, if on returning after having a baby she asks to work part-time, the organization must allow her to do so, unless it can make a very strong case that the job in question cannot be done on a flexible, job-share or part-time basis. If it refuses her request without justifying its case, she may take legal action.

The good news for women is that a spate of recent industrial tribunal cases have found in favour of women who claim to have been unfairly dismissed while on maternity leave. What is more, at the end of last year the upper limit on compensation – which used to be £11 000 was removed. The bad news is that while organizations are getting wise to the perils of selective redundancy, a new and insidious permutation is creeping in. The woman returns to work at the appointed time, but her life is made such hell that she leaves work voluntarily. The company thus avoids costly lawsuits and redundancy payments.

The cost of being unfair to women – Ian Hunter

Twenty four years after British law guaranteed women equal pay for equal work, some believe that equal opportunities legislation has gone too far.

The recent case involving a former Army major, Helen Homewood, illustrates how expensive non-compliance with such legislation can be. Mrs Homewood, who was forced to leave the Army because she was pregnant was awarded a total of £299 851 earlier this year by an industrial tribunal.

The claim followed a High Court decision that the Ministry of Defence's policy of dismissing pregnant women was unfair. Mrs Homewood then claimed sex discrimination. Since last year, awards in such cases are no longer subject to an £11 000 maximum.

Further protection will be in force for all pregnant workers by October. These reforms, contained in the Trade Union Reform and Employment Rights Act (Turera), emanate from the Government's obligations to translate European Directives into domestic legislation. It will become automatically unfair to dismiss an employee because she is pregnant, regardless of her length of service.

Questions for Activity 1.13

1   Why do you think Barclays Bank excluded pregnant women from redundancy?
2   Why do you think positive discrimination is illegal whilst positive action is lawful?
3   Why should it be discriminatory to refuse to allow a woman to work part-time after maternity leave?

Obligations and objectives

CASE STUDY

Jean Smith is the supervisor in charge of a team of seven working in a small metal fabrications company. One of her team members, George Johnson, is an excellent worker, but on a recent occasion Jean discovered that he was not wearing the protective safety goggles provided by the company. When she remonstrated with him, he said the goggles were uncomfortable and that he had only removed them for a few seconds. She has just seen him again removing the goggles in the work area.

Questions

1   What are Jean's obligations in the above situation?
2   To whom does she owe such obligations?
3   How should she handle the situation?
4   What potential conflicts can you see arising?

By now you will have realized that reconciling a manager's personal objectives with those of other colleagues and the organization is not always easy. On occasions, the matter is made more difficult because others' objectives are not sufficiently explicit and even the organization's objectives are sometimes not very clear. People will have different views about what should be a priority for action and where individual loyalties may lie. A particularly useful model for encouraging common commitment towards organizational objectives is that devised by Peter Martin and John Nicholls and reproduced below in Figure 1.3.

As the model shows, there are three major pillars which need to be created:

■   Pillar 1. A sense of belonging to an organization
■   Pillar 2. A sense of excitement in the job
■   Pillar 3. Confidence in management.

Each of the pillars is subdivided and Martin and Nicholls suggest that to achieve Pillar 1, a manager will need to keep people *informed* about an organization's activities, get people *involved* by consulting them wherever possible and giving people the opportunity to *share in the success* of an organization by appropriate reward and recognition schemes. To achieve Pillar 2, the manager must create a sense of *pride* and *trust* by encouraging responsibility and ownership of the quality of products or services, and must create *accountability for results* by delegation of appropriate tasks. To achieve Pillar 3, the manager will need to exert his or her *authority* and show *dedication* and *competence* by setting an example to others and in ensuring the maintenance of appropriate standards.

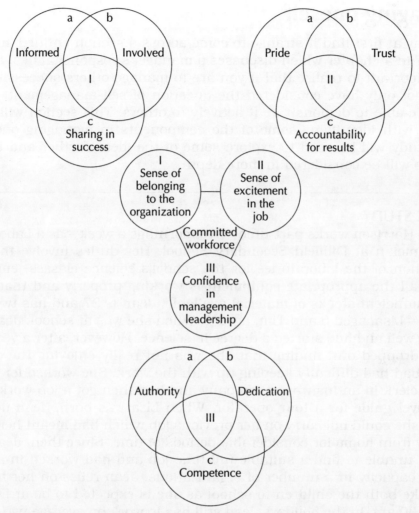

Figure 1.3 (Source: *Creating a Committed Workforce*, P. Martin and J. Nicholls (1987). Published by Institute of Personnel Management, Wimbledon. Reproduced by kind permission.)

Activity 1.14

1 Consider an organization which you have been associated with and, using the above model, decide how it has encouraged the development of commitment within its workforce.

2 Provide an explanation of a manager's obligations to three different parties within an organization together with an identification of possible solutions to potential incompatibilities in obligations. You may be able to draw on your own experience as a manager to provide appropriate material or you may prefer to approach a manager within an organization with which you are familiar and arrange to interview him or her.

Managing oneself

You may at first find it strange to come across a section entitled 'managing oneself' in a chapter which discusses a manager's responsibilities. However, it is important to realize that if you are to manage others successfully, you must not only have considered the question of self-management, but you must be able to demonstrate it actively to others. This section will be concerned with identifying some of the components in managing oneself – a case study will be used to explore some of the ideas further and then key aspects will be considered in more depth.

CASE STUDY

Jean Harrison works part-time – five mornings a week – as a Laboratory Technician at Dillfield Secondary School. Her duties involve the preparation of the laboratories for the school's science classes, ensuring that all the appropriate equipment is working properly and that there are sufficient stocks of material available. Jean is 27 and has two children – Lisa, aged 5 and Tim, aged 4. When she was at school, Jean had done well and had started a degree in science. However, after a year, she had dropped out, finding that she was not really enjoying the course and had had difficulty keeping up with the work. She worked for a year as a clerk in an insurance company and had then got a job working as a travel guide for a tour operator. When Lisa was born, Jean decided that she could not carry on her previous job which had meant her being away from home for considerable periods of time. Since then, Jean had been unable to find a suitable full-time job and had worked in a part-time capacity in a number of organizations. Jean relies on her mother to take both the children to school as she is expected to be at Dillfield by 8.30 am. In the holidays Jean still has to work on average two mornings a week at Dillfield School and she is reliant on her mother and friends, Sue and David, for looking after Lisa and Tim. The job at Dillfield School has been a real eye-opener to Jean. She enjoys her work and she is being partially funded by the school to take an Open University science degree. However, although the course was fine at first, Jean is now finding it difficult to fit in all the work and she is getting more and more behind. Her disappointment at what she sees as her second failure is making her more and more worried. Recently, she has been shouting at the children and resentful of their demands on her time. She has not told the Head of Science at Dillfield School of her problems as she knows that a full-time job is likely to become available in the next few months and she does not want to prejudice her chances of getting the post. To Jean this is particularly important because she is currently struggling to make ends meet and has recently fallen behind with her mortgage payments.

Questions

1   What would you describe as Jean's current commitments?
2   What would you identify as Jean's major problems?
3   What do you think are Jean's objectives?
4   What potential incompatibilities are there between Jean's objectives and those of others?
5   Can you suggest any ways in which Jean might resolve some of her problems?

You probably identified a number of issues here. Jean is clearly facing conflicts in meeting her personal developmental needs, her commitment to her family and the demands of her job. She probably feels that there just aren't enough hours in the day for everything. So the question of managing her time is probably an important issue. However, she cannot manage her time more effectively until she is clear about her priorities. Jean is beginning to show signs of stress and this is clearly another issue that needs to be addressed. However, she probably cannot reduce the level of stress until she has identified and diagnosed some of her problems.

Role mapping

One of the ways which might help Jean see things a little more clearly is by drawing up a Role Map of her relationships with other people. To do this Jean needs to list all the people who she may come into contact with during a typical day. These would perhaps include: Lisa and Tim, Jean's mother, Sue, David, teachers, pupils, head of science, head of school, work colleagues, fellow students, tutor, other friends.

This map shows some of the relationships which may be causing problems both inside and outside work.

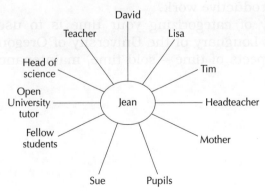

Figure 1.4 *Jean's role map*

In the remainder of this section, we shall be looking at some of the components of self-management, which include managing your time effectively, managing stress, problem solving and decision making.

Activity 1.15

Look at Figure 1.4 and consider the following questions:

1   What do each of these people expect from Jean?
2   How would you prioritize the relationships?
3   Identify the relationships which Jean needs to try to improve.
4   What are the issues which may prevent Jean from improving them?

Draw up your own role map and then spend some time considering the identified relationships. Do you know what your expected role is in each of the relationships? How would you describe your current commitments? Which are the most important and which are potentially conflicting relationships?

Time management

How is it that we never seem to have enough time to do all the things we would like to do? How often have you heard the following types of comment: 'I'd really like to help you on your project, but I have got a hundred and one things to finish first'; 'I'm sorry to break our lunch appointment, but I really must complete this assignment for tomorrow morning'; 'Perhaps we could meet on Wednesday morning in two weeks' time – that's the first free time I have'. According to Peter Drucker, a well-known writer on management issues, time remains the least known, least analysed and least managed of all the factors of productive work.

Another way of categorizing your time is to use the classification developed by Jack Loughary of the University of Oregon. He suggests that there are three aspects of time – sold time, maintenance time and discretionary time.

Activity 1.16

Look at the following items and tick those which you think particularly affect you.

Talk too much	Trying to do everything myself
Poor organization	Low motivation
Can't say 'no'	Poor planning by me
Difficulty in delegating	Jumping to conclusions
Too much information	Failure to identify the real problems
Inconsiderate co-workers	Badly run meetings
Time estimates incorrect	Poorly written communications
Fatigue	Fear of failure
Overlapping responsibilities	Outdated procedures
Poor equipment	Failure to keep relevant people informed
Poor feedback	Failure to set priorities
Putting things off	Lack of daily plan
Others talk too much	Others don't plan
Failure to follow up	Doing too many things at once

Sold time

This is the time that you sell to an employer or, as a student, the time you devote to studying, reading and completing assignments. It involves exchanging your time for money or for a qualification which can be regarded as future money. Sold time extends beyond the actual time spent on specific tasks and includes preparation and travel time.

Activity 1.17: Time management

The first step in managing time effectively is to log all of your activities. Few of us actually realize where all our time goes and it is only when you have a clear idea of how you are using time that you can begin to use it more effectively! Look at Figure 1.5 below and, adapting the times in the left-hand column as appropriate, complete a similar log over the next two or three days. Ignore the letters A, B and C at present. When you have completed several sheets, look back over them and now prioritize your activities in order of importance using the ranking suggested below:

A   These activities are highly valued, important and probably urgent. They may make a significant contribution to the achievement of your objectives.

B   These activities are less highly valued, but are still

important and may contribute towards your objectives. Some of them perhaps could be delegated to
others.

C   The activities in this last category only make a very
limited contribution towards achievement of your
goals and are generally less important.

Look at some of your A and B activities – which are *urgent* – necessary
and top priority – and which are *important* – necessary but could
perhaps wait? Which of your activities fall into the C category? How can
you reduce the time spent on them? Are there any of your current activities where time is wasted? Looking now at the B activities, what
changes can you make in the way these tasks are completed which will
allow you more time to concentrate on those in the A category?

Time	Activity	A	B	C
0700				
0730				
0800				
0830				
0900				
0930				
1000				
1030				
1100				
1130				
1200				
1230				
1300				
1330				
1400				
1430				
1500				
1530				
1600				
1630				
1700				
1730				
1800				
1830				
1900				
1930				
2000				
2030				
2100				
2130				
2200				

Figure 1.5 *Daily time log and analysis*

Maintenance time

This is time spent on keeping things ticking over. It is when you do the things that are necessary to keep yourself going and others who are dependent on you. It therefore includes sleeping and eating.

Discretionary time

This is the time left over for you to spend as you choose, perhaps on hobbies or spending leisure time with friends.

Deciding on the appropriate proportion of each classification is very much an individual matter – for example the needs of a working parent with young children to look after will differ from those of a retired individual. The important thing is that you do spend time considering your use of time! Before we move on to consider other aspects of self-management, here are a few practical techniques of effective time management which you may like to consider:

- Decide to do the most unpleasant job of the day first
- Break down jobs where possible into smaller tasks which may make them less daunting
- If getting started is a problem for you, don't always start at the beginning!
- Tell yourself you're going to do the job
- Set your own deadlines where possible
- Reward yourself at specific stages throughout a task
- Avoid distractions
- Schedule your time for the day ahead according to identified priorities
- Stick to high priority jobs
- Do one job at a time
- Make a list of the advantages of completing a task and the disadvantages of not doing so
- Keep asking 'What is the most effective use of my time now?'

Stress management

Most of us are aware that at different times of our lives, we feel under pressure and perhaps find difficulty in coping with the situations we are faced with. Stress manifests itself in different ways. At extreme levels it can result in quite serious illness such as coronary disease or ulcers. Milder levels can lead to headaches, insomnia and fatigue. The overt signs that tend to be associated with stress include trembling, sweating, stammering, excessive drinking or smoking. The less tangible signs may be loss of appetite, 'but-terflies' in the tummy, and feelings of nausea.

It is important to realize that some stress is quite natural and normal. Indeed, it would be unusual if you did not feel under pressure on certain occasions – for example, the first time you make a speech in public. As indi-viduals, we need to reach certain levels of alertness or arousal to work effect-ively. However, what we also need to be able to recognize are the times when our levels of stress are becoming excessive – for example in the case study at the beginning of this section, we noted that Jean was shouting at her chil-dren, which was perhaps a symptom of the stress she was experiencing. We need to be able to identify the causes of stress and devise ways of coping with it effectively.

In general, let us consider the most likely causes of individual stress. These may include physical sources such as excessive noise or temperature, or perhaps domestic circumstances such as bereavement, a breakdown in personal relationships or financial difficulties. Stress may also be caused by our perceived inabilities to carry out our work effectively.

Activity 1.18

Jot down what you consider to be the most likely causes of stress for you? How do you know when you are suffering from excessive stress?

Dealing with stress

One of the most significant factors in stress management is being able to recognize the symptoms in yourself and in others and where possible having the ability to discuss likely causes and possible solutions. In the workplace, so many changes have occurred in recent years that many employees have found it difficult to cope with the new demands being placed upon them. Uncertainty about their ability to cope is one of the most frequent causes of anxiety, and by clarifying situations stress can be reduced and performance improved. In severe cases of stress, professional counselling or medical assistance may be required, but in less acute situations, actually taking time to diagnose the causes of stress can assist. By carefully choosing friends or colleagues who you trust and who are prepared to listen non-judgementally, you can sometimes identify your own solutions to stressful situations by talking through your difficulties. Alternatively, some people find that completely contrasting activities can assist them to deal positively with stress. For example, taking up a new hobby or perhaps participating in physical sporting activities such as swimming or running can often provide an antidote to stress.

Problem solving and decision making

Sometimes problems can be extremely deceptive – what appears on the surface to be a relatively small problem can in fact turn out to be much larger and much more complex than we first thought.

Activity 1.19

Look at the illustration below in Figure 1.6. How many squares are there?

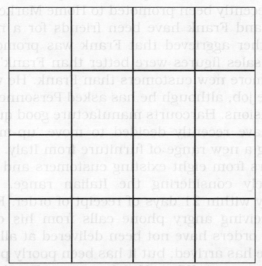

Figure 1.6 *Hidden squares*

Answer: in fact there are 30, but normally relatively few people can 'see' that number. There are 16 individual squares, 1 large one, 9 squares of four blocks each, and 4 squares of 9 blocks each.

One of the most important factors in effective problem solving is to define firstly what the problem is. This is not always as easy as it sounds.

Activity 1.20

Consider the following situation:

You are driving along a dual carriageway in your car. You are scheduled to be at an important meeting in 30 minutes' time. Currently you are approximately 15 minutes from your destination. Suddenly, the engine of your car cuts out and you glide to a halt. *What is your problem? Write down a statement of what you think your problem is.*

In fact you are faced with a series of problems and you need to prioritize the most important. In this case, the first problem you face is the question of your personal safety; the second is the diagnosis of the fault in your car; for example has a distributor lead come loose which you could fix almost instantly or have you run out of petrol? Assuming you can remedy this quickly, you will still be on time for your meeting.

CASE STUDY

Harry Salter is a successful Sales Representative for Harcourt Office Furniture Ltd. He has worked for the company for ten years now and is one of the best salesmen that they have. Harry's Line Manager is Frank Court who has recently been promoted to Home Market Sales Manager. Although Harry and Frank have been friends for a number of years, Harry is still rather aggrieved that Frank was promoted rather than himself. Harry's sales figures were better than Frank's and Harry has also introduced more new customers than Frank. He was not told why he did not get the job, although he has asked Personnel for feedback on two or three occasions. Harcourts manufacture good quality, traditional furniture, but have recently decided to move 'up-market' and have started importing a new range of furniture from Italy. Harry has taken substantial orders from eight existing customers and has several new customers actively considering the Italian range. Harcourts have promised delivery within 21 days of receipt of order. Four weeks later, Harry starts receiving angry phone calls from his customers either saying that their orders have not been delivered at all, or in two cases the new furniture has arrived, but it has been poorly packaged and has been damaged in transit. When Harry contacts Frank, he finds Frank somewhat evasive although he promises to look into the problem. When Harry calls again two days later, Frank replies angrily 'If you keep wasting my time with phone calls, it's no wonder that I do not have time to sort out the problems with the Italian deliveries.' Harry points out that he needs to know exactly when the deliveries are to be made and also what Harcourts are going to do about the damaged furniture. Harry considers that Harcourts are in danger of losing several important customers and also that his own sales commission is in jeopardy. 'That's what you're really worried about' replies Frank, 'It's not the firm's reputation at all that you really care about.' Harry is extremely angry at Frank's comment; he is also worried about Frank's attitude to sorting the matter out. He picks up the phone to complain to the Regional Sales Director, John Egbert. Then he replaces the receiver. 'Am I really being fair to Frank', he asks himself. Frank after all has really been dropped in the deep end. He has had virtually no training for his new job and cannot approach his predecessor for help as he took early retirement due to ill health and has now moved away. Harry begins to wonder instead if any of the other sales representatives are experiencing similar difficulties with Frank and he decides to speak to some of them first.

Questions

1   What would you say are the problems apparent at Harcourt's?
2   What do you suspect might be some of the underlying causes of such problems?
3   What should be done to put matters right and who should do it?
4   What would you do if you were in Harry's position. Justify your decision.

A model of problem solving

The diagram in Figure 1.7 below suggests a model which can be used for systematic and effective problem solving. It starts with the need to recognize and identify that there is a problem and then to diagnose and define exactly what the problem is. This may sound straightforward, but often the really obvious problems are only symptomatic of a deeper-rooted problem which

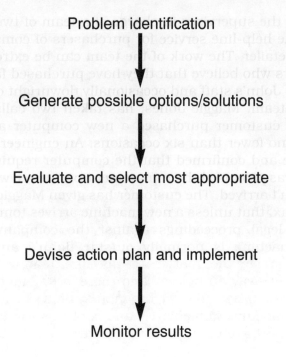

Figure 1.7 *A problem solving model*

is not so easy to identify. So a thorough investigation is usually needed. Only when we have a clear idea of the nature of the problem can we start to come up with possible solutions. We then have to evaluate and choose the most appropriate option, perhaps after an analysis of its particular strengths and weaknesses, and apply it or implement it. However, we still haven't finished – one of the most important features of problem solving is to draw up an action plan for monitoring and measuring the effectiveness of the chosen solution. Has it really solved the problem? How do you know? The process should be iterative – that is, you may need to go back to the beginning of the process if the results are not satisfactory.

Activity 1.21

1　Look back again at the case study concerning Jean Harrison at the beginning of this section. How can the above model be applied to Jean's situation?
2　Now see if you can apply the model to a problem or potential problem which you may face.

CASE STUDY

John Banks is the supervisor in charge of a team of twelve people who run a telephone help-line service for purchasers of computer hardware from a major retailer. The work of the team can be extremely stressful; some customers who believe that they have purchased faulty goods can be very rude to John's staff and occasionally downright offensive. Today one of John's team, Maggie Jones, has taken two calls from an irate customer. The customer purchased a new computer and it has mal-functioned on no fewer than six occasions. An engineer has visited the customer's site and confirmed that the computer requires a particular new part. He was promised the replacement part three weeks previously and it still hasn't arrived. The customer has given Maggie an ultimatum, confirmed by fax, that unless a new machine arrives tomorrow morning, he will issue legal proceedings against the company. Supply of a replacement machine is normally outside John's authority and he would usually refer the matter to his line manager, Fred Lucas. However, Fred is away on holiday and there is no one else available at head office to whom he can refer the matter. John decides to authorize a replacement machine immediately and confirms to the customer that he will arrange for it to be delivered tomorrow morning.

Questions

1. What factors do you think John will have taken into consideration before making his decision?
2. What action do you think John should take now with regard to the customer concerned, Maggie Jones and Fred Lucas?
3. Was John's decision the right one in the circumstances outlined?

Left-brain versus right-brain problem solving

Just as the majority of people tend to be right-handed for writing and drawing, a similar generalization can be made with regard to problem solving! Most people in fact are trained to make more use of the left side of the brain, which is concerned with logical and systematic thought processes, than the right, which is more concerned with what has been termed 'creativity'. Sometimes it is important to use and develop these more imaginative skills. In what circumstances do you think creativity within organizations is particularly important? Can you think of circumstances where a more creative approach would be useful in helping to solve your problems?

Other problem solving models

In addition to some of the models and techniques described, you will find that there are also many others. One of the best known is the *fishbone diagram* whereby the problem is briefly stated at the 'head' of the fish and then the backbone is drawn in with spines and ribs and participants are invited to provide key words which describe the possible causes of the problem. The resulting diagram can be a powerful discussion tool in teasing out all the possible problem areas. Study Figure 1.8 below which depicts a fishbone diagram which identifies some of the possible causes of high absenteeism in a workplace. What additional 'spines' might be added?

An alternative way of identifying possible solutions is to use a *force-field analysis* which identifies the strength of the forces 'for' a particular solution and also the strength of the likely opposing forces. The length of the lines suggests the relative strength of the forces. In Figure 1.9 below we have identified some of the likely forces for and against the idea of implementing regular team meetings to solve communication problems. The aim is either to increase the strength of the forces 'for' or to reduce those 'against'. See if you can add some positive driving forces which could overcome or reduce the negative forces.

One final idea that you might like to apply is the use of a *dif* analysis. This stands for 'difficulty', 'importance' and 'frequency'. Some of the problems we face may be extremely difficult to solve and to do so could take up a disproportionate amount of time and energy. If the problem is not of any real significance and perhaps occurs only very occasionally, then it may be left unresolved for the time being whilst you apply yourself to solving the really important problems which occur most frequently.

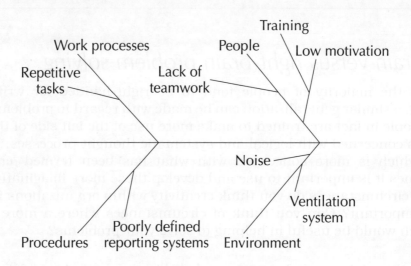

Figure 1.8 *Fishbone diagram*

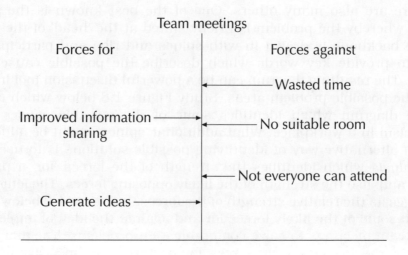

Figure 1.9 *Forcefield analysis*

Activity 1.22

Provide a brief report in which you reflect upon three significant decisions which you have taken during the past year. Analyse how effectively you managed your time, how problems were identified and
solutions implemented. Were you aware of any stress associated with
each situation? How *effectively* did you manage yourself? How would
you handle things differently now?

Practising continuous self-development

In the previous section we examined aspects of managing oneself: now we
need to consider the notion of ongoing development. In recent years, many
organizations have realized the importance of developing the skills of their
employees and have placed an increasing emphasis on training. For some,
the money that they spend on training is no longer regarded just as a cost
to the organization, but as an investment for the future. Organizations have
developed appraisal schemes or performance reviews where their employees
are encouraged to talk with their managers about their personal developmental objectives and their perceived training needs. Sir John Harvey
Jones, retired chairman of ICI said in 1987: 'Increasingly companies will only
survive if they meet the needs of the individuals who serve in them; not just
the question of payment, important as this may be, but people's true inner
needs, which they may even be reluctant to express to themselves.' This
section will be concerned with helping you to evaluate your inner needs and
developing action plans to meet your personal objectives.

Matching individual needs to organizational needs

As well as providing training in specific skills in order to improve workplace
performance, some organizations have adopted the view that employees
should also be supported in undertaking training that is not specifically work
related – the idea being that the 'payback' for the organization will come from
the increased motivation and commitment of the individual. One of the best-
known schemes is that developed by the Ford Motor Company and called the
Employee Development and Assistance Programme (EDAP). In Figure 1.10
below, you can see the range of activities which are on offer to the 8000
employees of the Halewood plant. Although the employee may be required to
contribute part of the cost of training, the company will provide some financial assistance for everyone wishing to participate. Among the benefits identified by the organization are more positive attitudes towards work, attracting
good people to work for them and reduced absenteeism.

Employee Development & Assistance Programme

EDAP CATEGORIES

1. Educational/Academic (GCSE, A Level etc where subject is NOT listed in categories below — exception being Degree course i.e. Arts Foundation).
2. Languages
3. Business Studies/Secretarial/Information Technology (BTEC Business & Finance, Introduction to Computing etc).
4. Music/Performing Arts.
5. Arts/Handicrafts (Painting, Silversmithing, Sewing, Cake Decoration etc).
6. Craft Skills (Bricklaying, Plastering, Woodwork etc).
7. Other Skills (First Aid, Driving, Video, Cookery).
8. Personal Development (Assertiveness Training, Self Defence, Outward Bound etc).
9. Health and Welfare — Physical Activities (Health & Fitness, Aerobics, Keep Fit etc).
10. Health and Welfare — Treatment (Chiropody Clinic, Weightloss etc).
11. Leisure/Sporting (Golf etc).
12. Other (i.e. any course which will not obviously fit into any of the above).

A joint initiative by Ford & the Trade Unions

Figure 1.10

What is self-development?

It is a way of increasing our skills, knowledge and understanding in order to improve personal performance and achieve our personal objectives. It may well involve the ability to transfer newly acquired skills and apply them in different situations. For example, one of the areas you will learn about is leadership, but that knowledge, whilst it may be interesting to you, is really only *useful* when you can apply it to a specific situation. As the concept of self-development suggests, it places the emphasis and responsibility for development on the individual concerned. However, this does not imply that the process is carried out in isolation. Far from it. What you will be encouraged to do in the following sections is diagnose your developmental needs with the help of appropriate people. But before we can really make progress, we need to consider the answers to four basic questions:

- Who am I?
- Where am I now?
- Where do I want to get to?
- How am I going to get there?

Who am I?

You may think you know yourself pretty well, but have you ever stopped to consider how you would describe your personality – that is the features and characteristic ways in which you normally behave?

Activity 1.23

Write a short paragraph describing yourself. For example, are you outgoing, do you enjoy meeting new people, do you like to try out new experiences, or perhaps you consider yourself to be a little shy and somewhat reserved. When you have done this, try to discuss it with someone who you know well and whose judgement you respect. Ask them to say whether or not they agree or disagree with what you have said.

This activity should provide you with some clues as to how other people may see you – which you may find differs considerably from what you would expect. If this turns out to be true in your case, consider why the differences in perception may have occurred.

Where am I now?

To help answer this question it is often helpful to carry out a *skills audit* or self-evaluation of some of our personal skills. Look at the skills listed in Figure 1.11 and complete the matrix in order to start assessing which skills you may already possess and which may need developing.

1   *Decision making*: in the previous section, we considered some of the techniques of effective problem solving and decision making. Think back over some of the decisions you have made recently. Were they sound? Did you try to gather as much relevant infor-

mation as possible? Did you evaluate the alternatives and the consequences for others?

2   *Managing information*: information can include written, verbal, numerical, electronic – the types are almost endless. Consider the decision making situations which you have identified. How well did you handle necessary information? Did you identify all relevant sources? Did you clarify areas which you were unsure of? Did you evaluate the information effectively? Identify two or three recent occasions on which you have been asked to supply information. Who was it for? For what purpose? Could you have presented the information in a more effective way?

3   *Time management*: look back at some of the activities which you carried out in the previous section to identify your abilities here.

4   *Attitudes*: these are very difficult to define – they are not tangible and you cannot 'prove' their existence. Each individual develops his or her attitudes based on their personal values and beliefs. But here you should be evaluating your ability to 'keep an open mind' and trying to be as objective as possible. Again, try to think of some specific instances where perhaps you encountered people with different attitudes from yours – perhaps on controversial political or environmental issues for example. Did you listen to the other person's viewpoint and did you consider their arguments? How did you react to their views? Were you able to put a reasoned argument forward in support of your views or did emotions get in the way? Such issues are very closely linked to the next item.

5   *Empathy*: this concept is concerned with the importance of recognizing that other people may 'see' and 'feel' things very differently from ourselves and being sensitive to other people's needs. What is important to us may not be important to them and vice versa. Empathy is about attempting to look at things from another's viewpoint. It should not be confused with 'sympathy' – it is really more than that. For example, when someone has suffered bereavement, you can sympathize with their grief, but to empathize with them is to consider the totality of their experience.

6   *Self-confidence*: think back to how you felt when you first started in your current job, or if you are completing a management qualification at the present time,

Skill	OK	Need to do more	Possible action
Communication:			
Written, e.g. reports, letters			
Verbal, e.g. presentations			
Listening alertly			
Talking in the group			
Being brief and concise			
Thinking before talking			
Drawing others out			
Observation:			
Being sensitive to others			
Noting possible tensions in groups			
Noting interest level			
Noting who is being left out			
Noting who talks most			
Noting who talks to whom			
Noting reactions to my comments			
Aware of dangers of stereotyping			
Noting when a subject is avoided			
Facing and accepting emotional situations:			
Facing conflict and anger			
Withstanding silence			
Facing disappointment			
Ability to empathize			
Telling others what you feel			
Disagreeing openly and constructively			
Expressing appreciation			
Social relationships:			
Allowing others to have their say			
Standing up for myself			
Encouraging others			
Trusting others			
Keeping promises			
Motivation:			
Awareness of relevant factors			
Recognition of others' needs			
Giving praise			
Encouraging participation			
Showing interest			
Managing information:			
Identifying relevant sources			
Seeking relevant data			
Clarifying issues			
Evaluate information			
Transmit information			
Attitudes:			
Being objective			
Aware of prejudices			
Reaction to others' attitudes			
Keeping emotion in check			
Ability to present a reasoned argument			
Decision making:			
Identifying relevant information			
Evaluating alternatives			
Following through			
Using appropriate models			
Asking for ideas, opinions			
Time management:			
Planning time usage			
Keeping a log			
Reviewing use of time			
General:			
Planning ahead – acting proactively			
Being self-critical			
Able to accept help			
Self-confidence			

Figure 1.11 *Personal skills review*

think how you felt when you started on your studies. What were your fears, concerns or preconceived notions before starting this qualification? Were they related to your level of self-confidence? In what types of situation have you found yourself lacking in confidence? What were the reasons? Were they related to general 'nervousness' or were they due to lack of knowledge or experience?

7   *Motivation*: do you ever stop and identify what motivates you or 'gives you a buzz'? Are you aware how you can improve your levels of motivation? You will read more about motivation in the next chapter but we will also consider it briefly here. In your last job, what aspects of your work provided you with least and most satisfaction? It may help you to think of particular times – or *critical incidents* – when you were particularly happy in your work and also times when you were dissatisfied in your work. What caused you to feel that way? Was the work exciting and challenging? Did you enjoy being part of a team? Earlier this century, a professor of industrial research at the Harvard Business School, Elton Mayo, conducted a series of experiments at the Hawthorne Works of the Western Electric Company in Chicago. His experiments were undertaken to examine the relationship between levels of workplace illumination and work output. The workers were divided into teams, and levels of illumination were varied between the teams and between 'control' groups – ones where the level of lighting remained constant. One might have expected productivity to increase with extra levels of illumination, but the researchers found that productivity also tended to increase within the control groups. The results suggested that what was actually affecting the experimental results was membership of the group itself. The fact that the workers were participating in a team seemed to have an effect on their work and the importance of social relationships at work began to be recognized.

8   *Proactivity*: this is the ability to plan ahead – to anticipate events and prepare accordingly. Consider the following brief case study:

CASE STUDY

Tom Standish is the supervisor of a team of gardeners who manage the grounds of a large stately mansion. Some of his people have been employed in the same positions for many years. It has recently been announced in the local paper that the owners are applying for planning permission to convert part of the extensive grounds into a golf course. Tom telephones the Estate Manager, John Brockley, and asks for an appointment to come and talk to him.

Questions

1   How should Tom plan for the meeting with John?
2   What are the kinds of issues he will want to raise?
3   What action do you think Tom might anticipate taking after the meeting?

What this case is highlighting is Tom's need to act proactively. He has read the article in the paper and realized that his people will be concerned about what is likely to happen to their jobs if planning permission is granted. Tom is anticipating the kinds of questions that he will be asked and seeking answers to as many of them as possible in advance.

Activity 1.24

Can you identify occasions when you could have been more proactive? How might this have helped you to deal more effectively with the identified situations?

9   *Communication*: this is such a large area that in this space we can really only identify certain key aspects. First of all, how would you define communication? We think it is about the conveying or exchanging of information or ideas either by speech, by writing or by signing. Remember that communication is often two-way and we either consciously or unconsciously adjust our communication based on our interpretation of the feedback we receive from others. What would you describe as some of the aims of communication? Perhaps to persuade, to tell, to command, to ask or to argue?

Let us consider oral communication first – possibly a telephone conversation. Because you cannot see the other person, you will not be able to get feedback from the other person's body language – that is their facial expressions or gestures. You will be relying on using language which is appropriate to the receiver – not jargon, unless it is someone who shares your knowledge – as well as your tone of voice and speed of delivery. In written communication, again the language you use must be appropriate to the recipient, and you will also need to use correct grammar, spelling and punctuation. One of the important communication skills that is not always regarded as sufficiently important is the ability to listen. So often, we appear to be listening when in fact we are miles away and possibly thinking about something completely different. It is vitally important to practise 'projective' listening where you really concentrate on the message that the other person is trying to get over to you. Try the following exercise to get a clearer focus on what happens when ineffective listening takes place.

Activity 1.25

To complete this activity, you will need a partner. This could either be a fellow student or a colleague or friend. With your partner, decide who is going to be the speaker and who is to be the listener. If you are the speaker, tell your listener about something that is of interest to you – it may be a hobby, a holiday, your last job. You should take five minutes to do this.

If you are the listener, you must sit passively, *without responding in any way at all*, you must not use words or non-verbal signals. Just sit and listen.

When the speaker has finished (or dries up!) discuss with each other how you felt. If you like, reverse roles, but this time the person who is the listener should *actively* listen – though still without actually speaking. That is, they should maintain eye contact, smile, nod to indicate understanding. You should find the difference quite marked. It is so much easier to describe something to an interested audience!

> ## Activity 1.26
>
> Identify some of your recent experiences of communication. Try to think of situations at work, at home, with people whom you know well and with people who you are not familiar with. They may have involved telephone conversations, letters, formal or informal exchanges. On each occasion consider how effective you were as a communicator. Are there ways in which you would like to improve?

Where do I want to get to?

Having considered some of your personal skills, you now need to be considering your possible career goals. It is increasingly unlikely that you will be staying with a single organization for the duration of your working life. Charles Handy, in many of his books, refers to the notion of portfolio working – where a person works for several different organizations at the same time. Although this may be a long way off, what we can see is the number of full-time jobs decreasing. Individuals need to be continuously developing their skills and talents to ensure their currency and validity.

If you are considering a change of direction, you might approach some of the professional associations in areas of interest to you – for example, the Chartered Institute of Marketing or the Institute of Personnel and Development. The careers section of your local library will have a wide range of publications and addresses from whom you can obtain relevant information. Most professional institutions will be happy to send you their formal published material on appropriate courses, exhibitions and local special events.

You may decide to develop your generic management skills further, possibly culminating in a MBA. Again, research is vital and you should investigate possible future courses as early as possible and talk to those who have undertaken the programme.

How am I going to get there?

Once you have got some ideas of possible future pathways, you need to draw up an appropriate action plan. This may, in fact, be several plans – one for your immediate needs, say over the next term, one perhaps for the next year or so, and one for the longer term of perhaps two or three years. Again, a word of advice. Err on the side of caution and do not be over ambitious. It is very satisfying to be able to complete a small action plan but it can be downright disheartening to only be able to check off a tiny part of a major plan. Set yourself realistic objectives with specific targets and time-scales. A useful acronym to remember in connection with target setting is SMART. This stands for

Specific, Measurable, Achievable, Realistic, Time bound. Targets or objectives should be challenging, but set with these parameters firmly in mind.

Personal learning log

If you are following a particular course, try to get into the habit of keeping a record of your activities on the programme. The purpose of these are really threefold:

1   They will provide a permanent record of the programme.
2   They will help you to *review and reflect* upon your learning, perhaps encouraging you to draw on previous relevant experience or critical incidents which you have encountered and decide how new knowledge might be applied.
3   They will form valuable evidence for inclusion in any portfolio of achievement.

A suggested format for the log sheet is provided below in Figure 1.12 although you may prefer to develop your own.

Title of session: *Date:*

Summary of main areas covered:

Problems encountered:

Action to be taken to solve problems:

Relevance of previous experience:

Assessment of the session's usefulness:

Possible applications in the workplace:

Any further action:

Figure 1.12 *Personal learning log*

Experiential learning

The work of David Kolb and later Peter Honey and Alan Mumford has high-lighted the fact that we all tend to have preferences for different styles of learning. The 'ideal' learning cycle that we should go through is reproduced in Figure 1.13.

From that you will see that a learning experience is not something done in isolation – we first have an experience and then should take the opportunity to review and reflect on what happened. From that we may be able to draw conclusions which means that the next time we encounter a similar event, we may adapt our approach or experiment with a new one. That is why when you complete your learning logs, you should try not only to reflect on what you have learned, but to consider how your knowledge might be applied and also how it might relate to previous experiences. We have suggested that the learning cycle is an 'ideal' approach. However, when faced with new learning situations, we often have a preferred learning style.

Activity 1.27

Look at the following topic areas and then select one for consideration (if you have never learnt any of the topics listed, think of something you have done and use that instead): swimming; tennis; driving a car; foreign language; computing; book-keeping; golf; musical instrument. Chosen topic

- What was it like to be the learner?
- What was good about learning?
- What was bad about learning?
- What did help or could have helped your learning experience?
- What could have happened or did happen to spoil the learning?
- What creates a good learning environment for you?
- How does your learning happen? For example, by experimenting and trial and error? By watching and listening? By memorizing, repeating things over and over? By looking at facts and figures? By working on your own? By getting actively involved? By keeping in the background? Or what?

Try to get others to complete the above activity and when you have finished, form either pairs or small groups and compare notes, looking for similarities and differences. What are the reasons for these?

You will probably find that you have preferred ways of learning and

Honey and Mumford (1989) have characterized the four different types of learner, identified in the learning cycle.

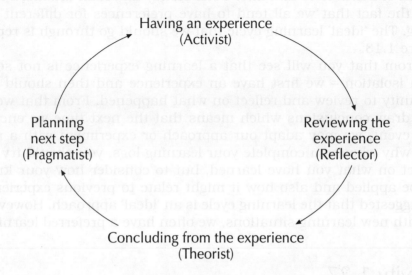

Figure 1.13 *Honey and Mumford's learning cycle*

Activists

■ try anything once
■ tend to revel in short-term crises, firefighting
■ tend to thrive on the challenge of new experiences
■ are relatively bored with implementation and longer-term consolidation
■ constantly involve themselves with other people.

Reflectors

■ like to stand back and review experiences from different perspectives
■ collect data and analyse it before coming to conclusions
■ like to consider all possible angles and implications before making a move
■ tend to be cautious
■ actually enjoy observing other people in action
■ often take a back seat at meetings.

Theorists

■ are keen on basic assumptions, principles, theories, models and systems thinking
■ prize rationality and logic
■ tend to be detached and analytical
■ are unhappy with subjective or ambiguous experiences
■ like to make things tidy and fit them into rational schemes.

Pragmatists

■ positively search out new ideas or techniques which might apply in their situation
■ take the first opportunity to experiment with applications
■ respond to problems and opportunities as a challenge
■ are keen to use ideas from management courses
■ like to get on with things with clear purposes.

It is not suggested that any individual slots neatly into one particular category – merely that individuals often have a tendency to one style rather than others. Which style do you feel is typical of you?

From studying the previous two sections, we hope that you have been helped to look at your present skills, knowledge and abilities and have started to identify opportunities for self-development. You will see in Figure 1.14 a possible format for your action plans (though you should adapt this to meet your individual requirements). The first column will indicate *what* your developmental needs are, the second will outline *how* you propose to meet those needs and the third column will indicate the time span – or *when* the action is to be taken.

Date ....   Number ....

What   How   When   Completed

Figure 1.14 *Action plan*

Make sure that you review your plans regularly and update them. The development of a mentoring relationship, possibly with a workplace colleague, can be beneficial. Mentoring has been the subject of considerable discussion in recent years, but there is no agreed definition of what it actually is! To us, a mentor is someone who is trusted and who will respect whatever confidences you may choose to disclose. Discussions may centre around your programme of study – how to go about completing an assignment or obtaining evidence of competence if you are compiling a personal portfolio for a vocational qualification in management, where you might look for certain types of information. There is also likely to be discussion of any particular difficulties you may be facing – for example finding the necessary time for all your commitments.

The mentor will almost certainly act as a sounding board for your ideas and be able to offer you support through actively listening. If you are currently on a programme of study you may be able to enlist a fellow student to be your mentor.

Activity 1.28

Conduct a personal skills review, after which you should identify your own self-development needs. These should be formulated into an action plan which is reviewed and updated regularly.

Summary

In this opening chapter you have been introduced to a considerable volume of material – some of which may have been familiar to you. You have considered the various types of organization that exist in the public and private sectors – both commercial and also those which are not-for-profit. Coupled with this, you have begun to think about the roles and responsibilities involved in the management of these organizations. Some are explicit, but many are not and we have introduced the importance of the consideration of ethics and values. You have also begun to identify the skills and abilities, some of which you may already possess, which will enable you to manage both yourself and others effectively. Continuous personal and professional development are concepts which every one of us needs to consider if we are to meet the challenges of managing organizations in the future.

References

Buchanan, D. and Huczynski, A. (1985). *Organisational Behaviour: An Introductory Text*. Hemel Hempstead: Prentice Hall.

Martin, P. and Nicholls, J. (1988). *Creating a Committed Workforce*. Wimbledon: Institute of Personnel Management.

Mumford, A. (1989). *Management Development – Strategies for Action*. Wimbledon: Institute of Personnel Management.

Roddick, A. (1991). *Body and Soul*. London: Ebury Press.

2   Managing in organizations

Aims

By the end of this chapter, you should understand different types of organizational structures and how these affect the First Line Managers who work in them. In the first part of the chapter we will consider the structures of various organizations, and the varying responsibilities of managers in their disparate roles. Later on, we will develop some of these ideas further when we look at the culture of organizations, how managers in organizations can deal with change, and the manager's role in motivation, teamwork and leadership.

Key concepts

■ Structures, relationships, systems, influences, span of control;
■ Changes to organizations, causes of change, effect on working relationships;
■ Culture, influences, effects;
■ Motivating individuals and teams, developing teams, the key features of leadership.

Introduction

In this first section we will examine organizational structures, and the effect they have on the managers who work in them, including the role of the manager in different types of organization.

The word 'organization' means 'coordinating activities to achieve an objective'. There are many types of organization in different sectors of the economy.

Activity 2.1

At the start of Chapter 1, you identified a list of different types of organization. What do you think would be their overall objectives?
How might their structures differ?

There are many different types of organization, which exist for a wide variety of purposes. Having an organizational structure helps in the division of work and responsibilities, and from these the work roles and channels of communication flow. We will see later on in this chapter (and others) that many business organizations are becoming much less rigidly structured – flexibility is the key to survival in an uncertain environment, and this is one of the themes that runs through this part of the book.

Organizational structures

Formal organizational relationships and hierarchies

To begin with, let us consider traditional formal organizational structures where individuals will operate within clearly defined parameters, patterns of responsibilities and working relationships. Such organizations are often hierarchies based around formal job grades, and definable relationships that can be mapped on an organization chart, as in the example shown as Figure 2.1.

The relationships within such organizations are often further defined as line, staff and functional relationships – what does this mean?

In line relationships, authority flows vertically down through the structure, such as from a Production Manager to the Production department – the 'departmental' model is frequently encountered in this type of organization. Each person will normally only be responsible to one other person.

Functional relationships apply where specialist staff function in an advisory role, supporting the 'line managers' and their subordinates, and not having direct authority over staff in other departments. The role of the traditional Personnel department (as opposed to the modern Human Resources approach) is a good illustration of a functional relationship.

A 'staff relationship' arises where, for example, a senior member of staff may have a personal assistant. This individual will not normally have direct authority in their own right – they are an extension of their superior.

Finally, the organization chart illustrates some examples of 'lateral relationships' which may exist between people in different departments, which represent day-to-day interactions between individuals at a similar level in the organization which are necessary for the smooth running of the business.

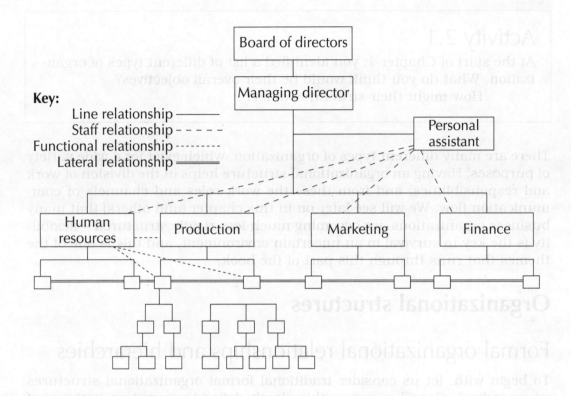

Figure 2.1 *An organization chart*

Traditional structures like this have typified many organizations across a wide range of sectors. They have offered security, career structures, and clear reporting relationships; but could also be cumbersome, prone to conflict between staff and line managers and somewhat inflexible. Such organizations have been prime targets for the 1990s buzzwords such as 'delayering', 'streamlining' and 'downsizing'. We will return to the merits and demerits of designing organizations this way, and the effect they have on their staff, but meanwhile, what alternatives are there?

Matrix organization

The kind of structure described above tends to work well in a permanent organization that exists in a stable environment. Unfortunately for these rigidly structured organizations, uncertainty is very much the norm today, which means a more flexible kind of approach is needed – one way in which this can be achieved is through the use of 'project teams' and a 'matrix organization'.

A project team may be made up of specialists drawn from a number of traditional departments set up to achieve a particular task, such as the introduction of a new product, or the introduction of a new procedure such as an appraisal system. The team has a limited life – when the task has been achieved it is disbanded. An effective project team will have clear objectives and a well-chosen membership.

'Matrix organization' merges the project team approach with traditional structures by adding an extra dimension. Diagrammatically, a matrix organization may appear as in Figure 2.2, where regional markets are used to create an extra dimension to the organization.

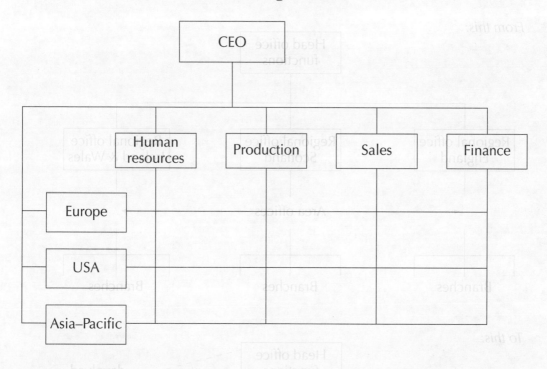

Figure 2.2 *A matrix organization*

Here therefore the functional departments provide a specialist base and an organizational 'home' for the staff, and the lines where the matrix intersects represent cross-functional teams that need to work across traditional departmental boundaries. This is useful where there is a need to involve specialists from a number of areas, where resources need to be shared, or where there is a need for organizational flexibility. There are challenges to this way of working: some staff prefer the stability of traditional departments. There can also be loss of accountability, and lack of clarification of the project manager's authority.

Flat structures

Developments in information technology, the desire to give individuals more autonomy in order to encourage commitment, and the needs for increased cost effectiveness and competitiveness have all helped to drive the trend towards 'flatter' organizational structures. In some organizations this can be identified by a reduction in the number of 'levels' that can be identified between the board of directors and the factory floor. Often this may be a result of 'delayering' – the practice of removing layers of management to produce a leaner organization where communications are facilitated (and costs reduced!).

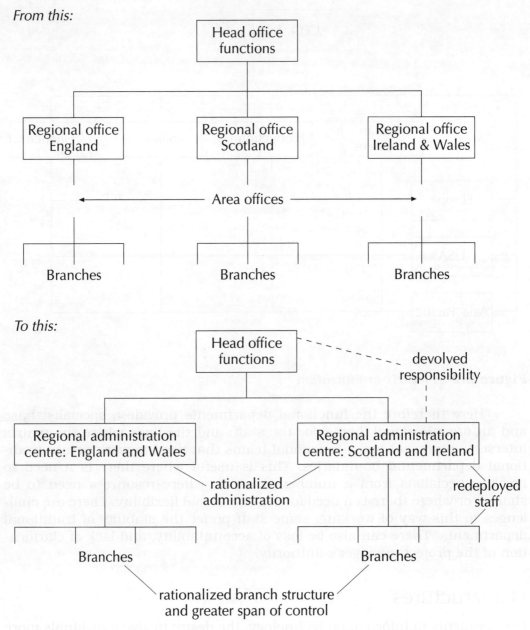

Figure 2.3 *Flattening the structure*

Sometimes the flat structure may be a deeper part of the organizational philosophy – the London company Supremia International has staff organized in 'cells', without formal job titles or structures. Not everyone can cope with working in an organization like this, but individuals in this company were reported to have a lot of responsibility while at the same time operating in a climate of mutual trust. As a disadvantage, flat structures can inhibit the development of future managers as opportunities are reduced. The traditional career paths identifiable in hierarchical organizations are squeezed as the organizational pyramid not only becomes flatter, but also narrower in the middle!

Centralized and decentralized organizations

Why should an organization seek to decentralize its authority structure? Pushing decision making down the line, and 'empowering' individuals and groups was part of the human resource management philosophy of the late 1980s. Sisu-Auto, a Finnish manufacturer of specialist heavy vehicles, adopted this approach with their personnel practices in 1983 when their central group personnel department was disbanded. The practice is not universally successful – *Personnel Management Plus* (April 1992) described how the adoption of this approach in Shell UK had 'diluted the traditional corporate culture which had proved so successful in the past'. In advertising, for example, the message had become fragmented, and different parts of the organization were presenting the company image in different ways.

There can also be pragmatic reasons for centralization. Some years ago, it was not uncommon for branches of domestic banks each to deal with business loans – a very lucrative market, normally dealt with only by the branch managers, with very limited discretionary authority. Rather than rely on a duplicated management structure in each branch, the commercial lending, like many other specialist aspects of banking, was centralized – the high street branches became little more than a satellite 'retail' operation.

Some organizations decentralize for other reasons, and at different levels: the 'Next Steps' report approved by the Conservative government in 1988, recommended that the Civil Service was too big (600 000 staff) and diverse to be managed as a single entity: 'One problem in trying to bind a large and very diverse organization to one central set of rules is that the rules fit no particular part of the organization.'

The devolution of authority went further than this – the 'agencies' which were now formed devolved functions such as personnel management down to line managers. This has brought increasing diversity in personnel practices (such as pay or recruitment), while at the same time restricting labour mobility between the 'agencies'.

Mechanistic and organic systems in organizations

In Scotland, some years ago, Burns and Stalker analysed 20 industrial firms from very different industries, from electronics to engineering to textiles. The study focused on the environments in which the firms operated in terms of their stability and predictability, and the impact this had on their performance. They also identified two very different systems of management practice and organizational structure: the 'mechanistic system' and the 'organic system'. These two systems were extremes of the structures organizations could take on when reacting to technical and commercial change. Burns and Stalker argued that these systems could be planned in to the organization to make the best use of resources, the style being the one best suited to the circumstances. What do these two structures mean?

A *mechanistic structure* is more rigid, and best suited to a stable environment – many characteristics are common to the 'functional organization' described at the start of this chapter. One would expect to find well-defined tasks and procedures, an hierarchical structure, knowledge centred at the top of the hierarchy, an emphasis on vertical reporting relationships, obedience, and loyalty to the organization. The *organic structure* is altogether more suited to changing circumstances. Here, tasks are adjusted and continually redefined, technical knowledge is located throughout the organization, not just at the top, there is a commitment to the common task of the organization; and control, authority and communication operate through a network rather than a hierarchy. Shared belief in the values and the goals of the organization are a key characteristic, which contrast with the 'command' structure of the mechanistic organization.

Activity 2.2

Identify one example from your experience of an organization that fits into each of the categories described above.

Organizational structures, influences and comparisons

What makes organizations the 'shape' and 'size' they are? The number, scale and complexity of organizations and the wide variation in sectors of activity make it impossible to generalize, but it is possible to consider some general themes and trends. Let us consider for example organizations operating in different markets, different sectors of economic activity, or even in different geographical locations. To what extent do these and other factors determine the size, or structure of the organization?

It is often difficult to consider organizations as single, homogenous entities – most organizations are made up of all sorts of different structures rather than having one consistent structure or style throughout. Hence we might find that the structure of the Research and Development department is very different to the Production function, and so on. It follows therefore, that the factors discussed below will affect different organizations in different ways.

Small, medium or large?

In a small organization, there is little need for a structure, or for carefully devised systems and procedures. The owner of a small business will have to interact with only a handful of employees, and the administration may well be handled by just one person. As the business grows, the immediacy of control may well be lost as managers are appointed, and there may well arise a need for consistency of practice or some organization of reporting relationships. Having said that, many small organizations with chaotic administration may well encounter problems, particularly if the 'person Friday' who carried a great deal of the administration in their head leaves! High street banks, for example, use procedures to ensure not only consistency but also financial security, but such procedures can be perceived as restrictive, as inhibiting the free thinker, or as encouraging a 'bureaucratic' (using the term negatively!) mind-set.

Activity 2.3

Identify an example of a small, medium and large organization and then answer the following questions.

1   To what extent are formal procedures used for day-to-day activities?
2   To what extent is there a formal organizational structure, with different 'grades' or levels of staff?
3   How clear is the reporting relationships in these organizations?

The impact of technology

To what extent does the level or type of technology determine the structure of the organization? Today, references to 'technology' tend to produce images of computer-controlled production, or employees in offices sitting at 'workstations' – or even working from home. It can also refer to the type of manufacturing process used, which can have a major impact on an organization.

In an era where the production sector has declined, how have the 'service' organizations been affected by the technology they employ? If employment in the service sector was meant to provide the answer to the decline in manufacturing employment, what does this mean in terms of jobs for the future? And, critically here, what does the impact of technology mean in terms of the structure of organizations and the role of the First Line Manager? There has been an impact on manufacturing organizations, as computer-controlled production processes and so-called 'robot' production techniques have been introduced. The 'delayering' that has taken place in many organizations (although not always attributable to technological advances) has meant that the line of command has grown shorter. Efficiency gains have also had an impact – 'lean' production techniques would probably not have occurred without the corresponding advances in manufacturing technology.

As an illustration, Wickens (*Personnel Management*, July 1993) described the 'lean production' techniques used at Bosch Cardiff, where a high level of process automation was a key part of the equation, and where other features included a flat hierarchy with only five levels, single-status, minimum staffing levels, total personal flexibility, no restrictive job descriptions, and multi-functional teams where the team leaders had a great deal of autonomy.

Ownership of organizations and the link with structure

The process pursued since 1979 of transferring former 'public' undertakings into 'private' hands has brought a more commercial orientation. Local government organizations were perceived by those working in the private sector as over-staffed and inefficient, often indulging the political whims of their ruling councillors, or supporting uneconomic ventures. The contracting-out of former local authority services to private tender has meant the virtual disappearance of some activities from 'within' the structure, although many of the staff employed in the activity concerned may still be the same.

Location and organization structure

What happens when a major business undertaking closes down? The answer, of course, is that the consequences go far beyond the redundancy of the immediate employees. If the area in which the enterprise is located depends heavily on that enterprise, the knock-on effects into other, smaller, businesses can be catastrophic. These may range from direct suppliers to the large firm of, say, raw materials or services; to the local supermarket or corner shop. The fact is that organizations are often heavily interdependent – this can often explain the concentration of similar firms in one area, although this may also be due to historical factors.

National culture

To what extent can differences in organizational arrangements be attributed to the effects of national culture? Can generalizations be made about work organizations in all societies? One view is that organizations in different countries grow in different ways, reflecting patterns in the wider society. For example, British organizations in the past tended to develop a proliferation of specialized managers, which may be a reflection of the narrowly specialized nature of traditional occupational training in the UK, or the influence of the professions, or the enthusiasm that British organizations traditionally had for rigid demarcation of roles.

What is clear is that the advances in technology and communications have made the dispersal of economic activity easier. At the level of the firm there is no longer a necessity for the management function to be in the same place as the production process. This trend has encouraged firms to relocate their manufacturing facilities to lower-cost areas, both in Europe and further afield. Callers to one major UK airline will unknowingly have their booking arrangements dealt with by an administration centre in India!

Reflections on the structure of organizations

What, therefore, can we conclude from the above section as a whole? Firstly, it is far too risky, and the business world is far too uncertain, to say that there is any one 'right way' of designing an organization structure. What is clear is that the rigid hierarchies of the post-war years are a thing of the past. 'Everyone must love change' is one of the maxims of that very modern organization, the Body Shop. Even if we don't always love it, we need to be prepared for it, placing a requirement on organizations to be learning, evolving and aware of their environment.

Managing people

As anyone in any kind of supervisory position will know, it is all very well getting the promotion, having the responsibility, understanding the job – the hard part is managing the people! However, making this happen can take a little time, and will require a great deal of care. What are the factors we need to consider?

Span of control

Clearly no manager should be responsible for more people than he or she can control effectively, and this will vary depending on the nature of the work situation. Professional staff may work in small teams of three or four whilst groups of 12–15 or more would commonly be found in some production industries. A further issue is the span of control when temporary or part-time staff are involved (see Chapter 6 on flexible employment), where the continuity implicit with full-time permanent staff is lost.

At this point it may be worth remembering that it is the way in which the manager balances all the tasks described in this section that will make them a 'good manager'. Blake and Mouton's managerial grid is described later, but it should be noted that the high-scoring managers on the grid showed a concern for both people and production. Later on, when we consider management styles in different types of situations, we will meet the 'contingency' argument – the need for a different style in a range of situations.

Questions

1 What are Line, Staff and Functional relationships in the context of the structure of organizations?
2 In what context might a 'matrix organization' be appropriate?
3 How might a company justify 'delayering'?
4 What are the respective merits of centralized and decentralized organizations?
5 What are 'mechanistic' and 'organic' systems of organization?
6 What is meant by 'span of control'?

Why does change arise in organizations?

In this section we will consider why changes are made to organizations, the ways in which these changes manifest themselves, and the impact that these changes are likely to have on the role of the manager and working relationships. Why is 'change' such an important topic? Consider the following quotation:

> Most of us have a vague 'feeling' that things are moving faster. Doctors and executives alike complain that they cannot keep up with the latest developments in their fields. Hardly a meeting or conference takes place today without some ritualistic oratory about 'the challenge of change'. Among many there is an uneasy mood – a suspicion that

> change is out of control.
> (Alvin Toffler, *Future Shock*)

When was this written – 1993? – 1994? Toffler's book was in fact published in 1970, but even then there was an awareness that the pace of change was increasing. While structural changes in the economy were becoming evident by 1970, could we really have anticipated the advances in computer and communications technology which we now take for granted, and their impact on business? And can we really know what will be coming at us over the next 25 years? The answer, of course, is that we can predict some of what may happen, and hope that our organization is flexible enough to deal with those changes which have a shorter time-scale. Business planning has become a science in itself – strategic management theory is no longer just the realm of the senior executive or the MBA graduate.

Activity 2.4

Write down as many reasons as you can why the pace of change is said to be increasing. What effect will these have on two organizations with which you are familiar and the people who work in them? How will the role of the First Line Manager be affected?

Why should organizations need to change?

One answer is of course that change simply cannot be avoided – it is an inevitable part of everyday life. Accepting that it is inevitable, it can to some extent be planned for, in the short, medium and long term. Because of the integrated nature of business activities, these changes cannot be considered in isolation, and may have influences inside and outside the organization. We know from what we have considered already that many of the external influences on organizations can generate a need for change. Sometimes, the change may be driven from within, and sometimes, the influences may overlap. No single change is an isolated event, and change can be discontinuous – unpredictable in its pace, and its occurrence. For those who wish to read further in this area, they are referred to some of Charles Handy's recent works such as *The Empty Raincoat* or *The Age of Unreason*.

Any of the following may be change factors:

- restructuring
- delayering
- 'lean production'
- cost reduction
- the flexible use of labour

- just-in-time inventory management
- impact of global competition
- political change
- changes in ownership
- organizational ethos and culture.

How do the above factors manifest themselves and what is the impact on the role of the First Line Manager? Generally the effect will be to place more responsibility at the first-line level, sometimes 'empowering' managers to have more independence of action and to handle devolved responsibility.

What happens when the whole culture of an organization changes? The notion of 'culture' is discussed in some detail below, for now, it is perhaps sufficient to consider that it is a company's unique way of doing things that contributes to its success, and which helps differentiate it from its competitors.

In some organizations, increased importance has been attached to the Quality of Working Life (sometimes referred to as QWL), focusing on how people's needs and expectations are satisfied through work. The goals of QWL therefore are to enhance organizational effectiveness through providing more challenging, satisfying jobs; through involving people throughout the organization; and through perceiving people as assets rather than costs. QWL-based organizational change may well require changes in management style – particularly:

- Providing a vision and communicating it
- Encouraging effective teamwork and cooperation
- Encouraging the free flow of ideas and initiatives
- Developing subordinates rather than rigidly controlling them
- Providing more flexible, less authoritarian work structures.

QWL is facilitated by the 'flatter' kind of organizational structure, and by structuring around particular products or customers, rather than hierarchical 'control' systems. The Advisory, Conciliation and Arbitration Service, ACAS, who have an excellent handbook on the subject, recommend that the introduction of QWL should be as participative a process as possible.

Activity 2.5

If an organization is seeking to introduce a major change into the workplace (such as the QWL philosophy), what benefits would making the process 'as participative as possible' bring?

Efficiency and the high-performance organization

'Quality', 'Quality Assurance', 'Total Quality' became buzzwords in the 1980s – it wasn't that they had not existed before, what was new was their widespread application and the organizational changes that went with them. These were more than just good intentions, they were total philosophies that permeated the organizations concerned. In the more competitive business environment, organizations looked carefully at their production systems. Quality standards increasingly became the norm, not just in engineering, but in a much wider range of organizations, and applied across the whole organization. Production methods became more precise, efficient and controlled, and were constantly improved. Alongside this, new forms of work organization were incorporated, based on flexibility of skills and the breaking down of traditional demarcations. Automation and robotics became more widespread, and their adoption no longer gave organizations an automatic competitive advantage.

Nor was the process confined to manufacturing. Banks and other financial sector institutions, which had always been enthusiasts of 'organization and methods' techniques, embraced the networked technologies, changing their structures and their whole way of working. Such changes meant efficiency gains, of course, and also some losses in what were previously considered to be the ultimate in secure careers.

Leaner organizations emerged, although not without some bruising experiences of the change process. Incorporating a 'change culture' into what had been organizations that had traditionally offered secure, lifelong employment was never going to be easy. What was now certain was that the concept of the 'job for life' was a thing of the past. More recently, 'business process re-engineering' has been widely criticized, not least by some of its original proponents – there has been a widespread feeling that rather than aiming for 'lean' organization, a 'copycat' approach meant that many jobs have been lost unnecessarily, with a consequential decline in customer service provision.

Activity 2.6

Identify the main changes you would expect to see in business, organizations and society by the year 2010. You may wish to categorize these changes under certain headings, such as 'Society and the Community', 'The Family', 'Government and Politics', 'The Environment', 'European and International issues' and 'Business and Organizations'.

Changes in organizations and structures

In the UK we tend to believe that we have suffered badly in recent recessions. In some cases this is certainly true, but on a pan-European scale our problems are relatively small by comparison. In Central and Eastern Europe former state enterprises maintained gross inefficiencies but are now having to face harsh reality. Closer to home, organizations traditionally thought of as secure employers have taken out whole layers of their management hierarchy. Bank employees, who thought they had 'jobs for life' as late as the 1970s have seen widespread redundancies due to a range of factors including merger activity.

But what of those organizations that are pursuing expansionary policies? It is often likely that the new employment opportunities will be in part-time, temporary employment, or in parts of the world where labour costs are low.

Teams and groups in the change process

As part of a successful change implementation programme, it is vital to identify those individuals and groups who will be most affected by the change, and to consider what form these effects will take. Who will be affected and will the effects be positive or negative? At this point the support of those people who tend to shape, and often express the views of the workforce becomes of paramount importance. These 'opinion formers' may not be in any sort of supervisory position but, as many organizational behaviour researchers have established, the 'informal' groupings and structures within organizations can have a very significant effect on the way people behave and therefore what actually happens. Consider the 'stakeholders' in the situation – those people who have an interest in the outcome of the change. They may include unions, departments or sections within the organization, managers, shareholders, and so on. How do their objectives match or mismatch with the likely outcomes of the changes planned? Clearly some kind of anticipation strategy may well identify those areas that require action, and may even give some idea as to how the implementation of change may be tackled.

CASE STUDY: TARRAGON ENGINEERING LIMITED

Tarragon Engineering are an engineering company. The company is split into two divisions, as below.

1 *Heating and ventilation systems.* This division manufactures air purification, heating and air-conditioning systems to order for factories, offices and shops. It is a very specialized field, and the order book is almost empty due to the lack of building development which has had a

---

cumulative effect over the last few years, and the general recession in the building industry. The division is housed in an old factory in one of the more rundown parts of the city.

2 *Fabrication*. This division makes a variety of products, normally in a large batch at a time, ranging from rucksack frames to car cycle carriers. They had enjoyed a steady increase in demand during the 1980s by tapping into the lucrative 'leisure' market, and have managed to remain competitive even in the difficult trading conditions of the 1990s. Their spacious and well-equipped factory is situated on a 'green-field' site east of the city. There is also a suite of offices which houses all the main Tarragon administrative functions on this site.

An organization chart reveals that there is a General Manager with overall control of each of the two divisions. A sales manager at each of the two manufacturing sites who directs that particular sales effort, aided by representatives and also a member of the clerical support staff, who reports to the Office Manager. Also reporting to the Office Manager are an accounts clerk and a clerk/typist. The Works Manager, although responsible for much of the design work, is assisted by design draughtsmen who are highly trained specialists in their field. Apart from the foremen and production operatives of various skill levels, there is also a storeman attached to each division who acts as an HGV driver. This structure has been in existence since the company was founded in the early 1970s, but internal problems have made it clear that change is needed.

The Board of Directors have agreed that the heating and ventilation side of the business should be run down, or closed altogether, allowing new investment in the fabrication side of the business which has a potentially larger market. They believe that a streamlined company on one site would be able to remain competitive for several years. Various proposals have been made, such as:

1   Early retirement for all employees over 60, with full pension rights.
2   Retraining for all employees who are to be retained.
3   Redundancy packages above the statutory minimum.

These proposals have met with hostility from the union, which has proved to be a source of disappointment for the board.

The profitability of the firm has been impeded in the past by the fact that they have not really updated their clerical and administrative systems, nor have they really grasped the use of computer-based design. They do have some word processors, but these are due for replacement. Staffing is a problem in some areas, such as the combined post of driver/storeman. Often this person is off-site for long periods (driving) and the other staff cannot find items in the stores. The MD has approved plans to buy a new computer system and feels that the time is right for a thorough review of the organization's structure. He feels that the company has not really made the most of potential business opportunities, and has made no impact so far in European markets. The staff however do not welcome the proposed changes.

Activity 2.7

Consider the options that face Tarragon Engineering. You may find it helpful to construct an organization chart as the starting point for your investigation. If you think it is appropriate, draw out a revised organization chart, following the closure of the heating and ventilation division. In any event, you should devise a new structure, with updated job titles which reflect appropriate changes in the company, and systems of the company.

What other methods will you use to ensure that the company enjoys success in the future?

Involving your staff

So far, we have considered change in the organizational context as something which may be driven by pressures in the external environment, or which may be the result of decisions made at managerial level. There has been brief consideration of involving the 'opinion formers' in the organization, but really if change is to succeed then a consideration of the effects on, and involvement of, the workforce at grass-roots level is crucial. We are after all talking about fundamental changes to the way in which people work, and to their whole lives. Look again at your solution to the 'Tarragon' case study above – we may well be asking the employees to take on new responsibilities, you may be making changes to the decision-making processes, to accountability relationships and the ways in which problems are dealt with on a day-to-day level. You will almost certainly have suggested that some employees face compulsory redundancy – in reality a crushing blow that wrecks careers and aspirations, and causes a great deal of suffering. Surely the best way to deal with change is to try to involve the people who are actually doing the job?

To some extent, we have hinted at the solution to this scenario already. At the start of this section, the 'Quality of Working Life' (QWL) approach was briefly described as an approach to changing the working ethos of an organization. 'Quality Circles' – a group of volunteers engaged in a process of suggesting improvements to existing products and services – can be a key element of the QWL approach in that they give workers the chance to get involved with the organization of the jobs that they do. Here, the view that the employees are a resource that can make an active contribution to decision-making processes provides the opportunity for a degree of self-determination and the application of problem solving skills that more traditional approaches to, say, the management of a production environment may not allow.

Many organizations have experimented with quality circles, with varying degrees of success. Genuine authority needs to be vested in group members, with sound suggestions acted on, and a managerial acceptance of responsibility for action where this is required. They will only succeed in an environment that genuinely accepts the contribution that they can make – simply 'bolting them on' to an existing structural framework will give the impression that the organization is simply paying lip-service to the idea, with a corresponding effect on the motivation and consequent level of interest of the members.

Activity 2.8

Conduct a media search using indexes such as ANBAR and the British Humanities index to locate news items about Quality Circles.
How are they described?
How would you see the role of the First Line Manager in this context?

One of the more widely documented 'team' approaches to the production environment came from Sweden, and Volvo's Kalmar plant, which opened in 1974. The 'dock assembly' process, where a team of employees assembled the whole car, was hailed in the 1970s as the worker-friendly manufacturing technique of the future, and many people still believe that Volvo make cars this way. In fact, the original form of 'dock assembly' only lasted a few years. Originally introduced as a measure to address the perceived difficulty Swedes had with production-line working, the technique was found to cause material supply problems (due to the increasing number of model variants) and problems with the production flow. The employees didn't enjoy working this way – it was found to be stressful in some cases. Absenteeism had also remained high. Volvo returned to line-based assembly, but with tasks organized on a team basis.

However, the story does not end there. Believing the material supply issues to be the key to the problem, the Volvo plant at Uddevalla returned to a form of dock assembly. Teams of eight to ten 'car builders' undertook the final assembly of four cars per shift, with the materials supply problems being addressed by a separate materials centre where components were stored and subassemblies made. The teams were responsible for much of their own training, maintenance, planning, selection and tooling. Each team had a spokesperson, who assigned work, guided the team, planned and reported, led discussions and resolved problems, and the role of spokesperson was rotated on a regular basis. There are flaws in the system: assembly time per car can be sixteen hours, compared with ten hours or fewer in the better European plants. Additionally, the multi-skilled nature of the work meant that when labour turnover was high, different team members could be at different points of learning the job, which could cause frustration in a situation where there was a high degree of interdependence. A high degree of 'post-build' rectification work was also found to be necessary.

What can be learned from this example? Firstly, as we have found before, ideas such as team approaches are not simply a recipe for success. As we know, all organizations are different, even if the products or industry may be the same, and the approach may well need to be 'debugged' in a particular situation if it is be successful. Sometimes there may be a merit in a limited application of the team approach. Staying in Scandinavia, the Rautaruukki steel plant in Hämeenlinna, Finland, has improved safety and housekeeping in the workplace by giving teams of employees control over their physical work areas. These 'Tuttava' or 'Work Safety Teams' do not, however, control the production process – the continuous nature of steel production to some extent precludes this. Once again, therefore, we find it is a case of taking the principle, and adapting it in a way that suits the organizational situation.

Activity 2.9

What do you think would be the key aspects of the role of the First Line Manager in the 'dock assembly' process? How would this differ from the situation on a production line? What particular demands would be placed on the job holder?

'Tell me...'

Sometimes 'good communications' are quoted as being a way in which to enhance the effectiveness of an organization. This is fine as an idea, but needs elaboration if it is to be applied in the context of organizational change. People need to be informed. The less people know about any plans for change, the more scope there is for speculation and rumour, the greater the potential for a negative groundswell of opinion to develop, and the greater the potential for resistance to change. Never underestimate the power of rumours – what is surprising is the willingness that individuals will have to pass on sometimes quite fantastic stories, potentially with damaging consequences.

How therefore should one manage communications? Firstly, communication is considerably more effective if people are addressed in person – memos, or notices are too easily ignored, impersonal, and can be seen as representing a sign of weakness. Secondly, the communications should be truthful. There is nothing that will delight the dissenting voices more than watching 'the management' dig a big hole and throw themselves in it.

Even though it may take time, the employees affected by the change should also be given the opportunity to raise their concerns and ask questions – at least matters will then be brought out into the open, and can be addressed, hopefully providing some reassurance, and minimizing the element of speculation. The aim overall is to get people to understand why the change is necessary, to see ways in which they may benefit from it, and to begin to secure their commitment to it.

Managers' roles

What of the roles of the managers in organizations that have been through the change process? Sometimes employees may suddenly find themselves with new 'managerial' responsibilities they did not have before. In the NHS trusts, for example, medical professionals have now taken on a more 'managerial' role and, as a response, West Dorset Hospital provide a two-day introductory course in management skills for their consultants. The personnel department also runs in-house courses on assertiveness, time management, managing people, and so on. Here is an example of one organization that has been subjected to structural and cultural change but is taking positive steps to help staff members cope with this. With over one million employees, the NHS was the largest single employer in the UK – the scale of training activity required to impart management skills to all those staff who need them cannot be underestimated.

Change and working relationships

As cited in some of the above examples, the effectiveness of the change implementation process has been enhanced by involving people – by getting them to take responsibility for themselves and their work – rather than simply being told what to do in a 'control' type of manager–subordinate relationship.

CASE STUDY: ANGLOBANK (UK)

In the following activity you are to take on the role of a member of a group of management trainees working in the head office personnel department of AngloBank PLC, who are a major high street bank in the UK, although they are actually owned by First City Western, an American banking group. AngloBank have branches in most major towns and cities, reflecting the distribution of branches that existed in the days before two older UK banks merged to form the pre-takeover AngloBank organization. There wasn't really a great deal of rationalization until the bank came into American ownership, at which point a team of consultants were brought in by First City Western with the aim of producing a 'leaner and fitter' organization.

The consultants were very thorough in their approach – after their report was accepted by the parent company last year, the structure, systems and staffing of the UK company was 'redefined', which in practice meant:

- Closing one third of the existing branches, especially those where there was duplication within a local area.
- Delayering – which meant taking out many of the branches managerial staff (in practice, removing two job grades), and centralizing many of these functions into new regional administrative centres and 'corporate business units'.
- A new corporate image and staff uniforms.
- An increased emphasis on part-time staffing, with a 'core' of permanent, full-time employees.
- Closing down the loss-making 'house loan' arm of the company, and integrating these activities into the branch operations.
- A redundancy programme, with compulsory redundancies for 20 per cent of the staff across the organization over a two-year period.
- Extended opening hours, with a new 'flexible rota' system to include cover for weekend working.
- A new computer system, with the aim of producing a faster response to customer queries and more efficient transaction processing.

Six months into the change programme, the consultants have conducted a 'Customer Satisfaction Survey', which indicates that the Bank's customers are very unhappy with the levels of service they are now receiving. There was a great deal of loyalty to the old branch structure, and business and personal account closures have reached serious proportions. One key problem has been the loss of personal contact as staff have been reallocated around the branches in their area.

There are also problems within the staffing itself. All the job positions earmarked for redundancy have now been identified, and although there isn't a real problem with staff turnover among the full-time staff, the company has found it difficult to retain the part-time staff on the new contracts. Some 'exit interviews' have been carried out, which have pointed to poor morale, a lack of team spirit, a tense working environment, and difficulties with the new systems as causes for concern.

The consultants feel that a local solution (i.e. developed in the UK) may be appropriate, and have asked your team to investigate the situation and to make recommendations for future action. They have made some recommendations of their own, which they have asked you to consider, including:

- A system of incentive payments based on customer feedback.
- Branch bonuses, based on targets such as the number of new accounts opened.
- Scrapping the uniforms, and reviewing the company image.
- The introduction of an employee 'empowerment programme', where staff are given greater control over rotas, opening hours and local marketing initiatives.

Activity 2.10

You are required to:

1 Analyse the situation on the basis of the information given, and identify what you see as the key problem areas. Are there any others you can infer, based on what other UK banks have experienced in recent years?
2 Evaluate the recommendations given, and suggest recommendations of your own.
3 Produce an action plan for the next two years to address the problems you have identified, making reference to appropriate theoretical approaches, and how these can be applied.

Organization culture: 'It's the way we do things here'

In this section we will consider those aspects unique to organizations that make some of them more successful than others, the intangible yet all pervasive ways of doing things, or sets of shared values that set them apart, that inform their decisions about their structure and style. We know that employee attitudes and behaviour are influenced by the characteristics of the organization they work for, as well as a recognition that there are many different types of organizations! As Handy (1986) put it:

> organizations are as different and varied as the nations of the world. They have differing cultures – sets of values and norms and beliefs – reflected in different structures and systems. And the cultures are affected by the events of the past and by the climate of the present, by the technology of the type of work, by their aims and by the type of people that work in them.

Fowler (1993) offered a further definition of 'culture' as:

> an amalgam of the effect of employee attitudes, behaviour, and effectiveness of values (the qualities and characteristics the organization considers important), structures (how work and employees are differentiated and grouped), systems and procedures (how work is done and conduct regulated), style (particularly how managers behave), customs (the informal practices that develop over time), and beliefs and myths (the ideas and stories that grow up about the organization).

Activity 2.11

Consider organizations with which you are familiar. What are the immediate, visible or tangible manifestations of their culture that you can identify, based on the above definitions? How do you think this 'culture' affects the people who work there, particularly the role of the First Line Manager?

What kinds of organizational culture can we identify?

Bureaucratic cultures

Here, the organization would be typified by a logical and rational structure, with specialist functions each focusing on their own particular area. Handy called this kind of organization a role culture, and described the structure as being analogous to a Greek temple (see Figure 2.4), with the 'pillars' representing the functional specialisms, and the senior management represented by the pediment on top.

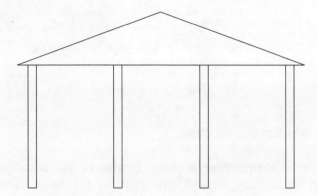

Figure 2.4 *Handy's role culture*

In this kind of organizational culture, if the 'pillars' follow the clearly defined systems and procedures, the result will be as planned. Personal power is frowned upon in this kind of culture. Because there is a clear hierarchy with unambiguous reporting relationships, communications tend to follow through the chain of command. Obviously Handy was describing a 'pure' form of bureaucracy, but principles such as these have served many organizations well for many years. Where the environment is stable, where the product life is a long one, or where the organization could control the environment, then organizations like this have been very successful.

However, this 'culture' does have some drawbacks, which are inextricably linked to their organization and style. For some individuals, they may have offered security and predictability, a lifetime of employment with a steady climb up the hierarchy to some kind of career pinnacle as one approached retirement age. For others, they could be frustrating, rule bound and inflexible, constraining the free thinker or independently minded, restrictive to those 'more interested in results than methods'. Handy referred to 'low calibre people resources' – the 'jobsworth', the person who is content to do their job to the letter or less. They can be slow to perceive the need for change and slower still to respond to it, which is clearly a problem in a dynamic business environment.

Autocratic cultures

Handy called this a 'power' culture, and described it as being typically found in small, entrepreneurial organizations. Diagramatically, he represented this as a web (see Figure 2.5).

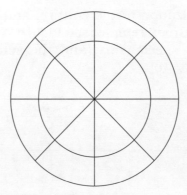

Figure 2.5 *Handy's power culture*

Here, the one power source at the centre of the 'web' is dominant. This may be typified by a family business, run by an autocratic MD, although there are some larger organizations which can provide examples of this, including some in the trade union movement and politics. An organization like this may well have few rules and procedures, and few of the other characteristics of the 'bureaucratic' organizational form. The autocratic leader will exercise control by selecting key individuals, either through heredity or patronage, who will do their bidding. Further control will be exercised by the control of financial resources (and the delegation of this control) and sometimes through personal charisma. Decisions are taken on balance of influence (i.e. 'because I say so') rather than on the basis of logic and rationality. Such organizations may well have strong leadership, and can respond quickly to environmental changes – after all, there is only one person making the significant decisions. This however is also their main weakness. If the 'centre' makes poor decisions, or if the organization grows so large that the person at the centre can no longer control it, then organizations like this may fail. They can be a tough environment for their managers and supervisors too, as they are unlikely to have much say in the direction the organization takes, but will have a great deal expected of them. If these individuals are in key positions and decide to leave, this can have a significant effect – the 'centre' may rely on them more than was perhaps realized!

Democratic cultures

There are two of Handy's cultural models that can be said to be more democratic – his 'task' culture, and the 'person' culture. The task culture could also be called the 'project team' approach, which according to Handy, 'seeks to bring together the appropriate resources, the right people at the right level of the organization, and lets them get on with it.'

Here, there is less emphasis on individual power, and more on the autonomy of the team and the shared influence of its members. This culture attempts to unify the individual with the objectives of the organization through teamwork, where the team members will often cross strict functional boundaries. Team membership is based on expertise, and the life of the team may only be as long as the project they are engaged in. Diagramatically, such organizations can best be described as a net, or a matrix (see Figure 2.6).

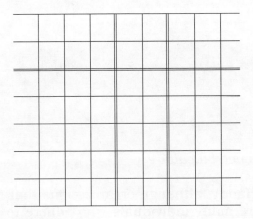

Figure 2.6 *Handy's task culture*

Some of the strands of the net can be observed to be thicker than others – these are the stronger lines of communication, and where they intersect is where the loci of power and influence can be found. Such organizations can be flexible and adaptable, they may have cohesive teams, and will function well in an unstable environment where a rapid response may be required. On the other hand, they may prove to be difficult to control – few things can be more difficult than managing a group of diverse professionals. One manager in this situation described his job as like 'trying to herd cats!'

Handy's fourth cultural model is relatively unusual and uncommon: the 'person' culture. In its pure form, it is little more than a collection of individuals who find it more convenient to work together or to share office space: Handy quotes 'Barristers' chambers, architects partnerships, hippie communes' among others, as examples. There is minimal structure, and Handy represented this diagramatically as a 'cluster of stars' (see Figure 2.7).

One organization that approximated to this model was a wholefood cooperative that existed in the East Midlands in the 1980s. Here, no single person was in overall charge, and a genuine attempt was made to run the organization by consensus decision making and the rotation of roles. Control of an organization like this is impossible except by mutual consent – the examples of the professional practices given earlier can perhaps cope with this culture because of the nature of the membership – as professionals, self-interest is served by the professional practice rather than the bureaucratic need for individual power. Even so, these organizations can turn quite easily into a task culture, or often a power or role culture – individual egos can often get in the way of democratic principles!

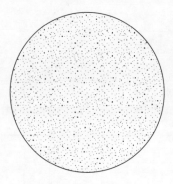

Figure 2.7 *Handy's person culture*

According to Handy, although organizations that follow this form are uncommon, there are many individuals who adhere to this value set even though they may work in quite a different culture. Handy quotes specialists in large organizations, such as hospital consultants, university professors or local government architects – the organization is simply a vehicle to pursue their own career.

Activity 2.12

Can you identify organizations who fit the cultural types described above? What are the characteristics of the organizations you have identified that fit them to the above cultural types?

Now, using the organizations you have identified as examples, identify the strengths and weaknesses of each of these organizational types, from both an employee's and an employer's or senior manager's point of view. Comment on the role of the First Line Manager in each case.

What are the factors which influence organization culture?

While the above classifications are useful, they are nevertheless descriptive, and for our understanding of them to be meaningful we need to consider where they have come from and what are the factors that have influenced the development of a particular culture within an individual organization.

One important determinant of the organization's culture may be the work practices that prevail within it. At a simple level, this can relate to the level of technology involved in a manufacturing operation or the tradition of teamwork in a traditional industry such as coal mining. Alternatively, it may be that a recognition of the need to change a key aspect of the operation, such as customer service, may be recognized as having elements of a necessary cultural change allied to a need to change working practices.

The words 'change' and 'culture' are almost synonymous in management literature – could it be that the organization first thinks about the culture when it is in a period of change? In a modern example, Fairbarns and Jennings (1994) described the way that the culture of SmithKline Beecham was monitored through a process they called 'culture tapping' – the company was seeking to change the culture from a 'keep your head down' mentality to an environment of involvement and proactivity. In this case, the change coincided with the merger of two factories, and a series of questionnaires was used not just to monitor employee feedback to the changes, but also to enhance the feelings of 'empowerment' that the employees may have. Was the process a success?

> over the past three years the site has become more team-orientated. People now work happily in multi-functional groups and are generally more comfortable in their team relationships. People feel more free to influence their own destinies.

To what extent do workplace communications determine the culture of an organization? The answer to this probably lies in an analysis of the kind of communication networks that exist in an organization, bearing in mind Handy's view that 'If there is one general law of communication it is that we never communicate as effectively as we think we do.'

For example,

- Do communications tend to be channelled through the formal hierarchy?
- Do communication networks focus on individual expertise, functioning in multi-disciplinary groups across the organization?
- Is communication one-way or two-way?

To what extent does corporate image influence organizational culture? Consider, for example, the Body Shop – not just the high street stores, which are franchise operations, but also the main manufacturing unit at Littlehampton. The product image influences the company ethos that is projected through the retail stores, and is of an egalitarian, environmentally friendly organization, where the views and contributions of individuals are valued.

Consider the link between the corporate image of organizations you have worked for, even on a part-time basis, and the culture of the organization. To what extent do you feel this relationship is of a cause-and-effect nature?

Questions

1   Imagine a manager is about to introduce a major change into the workplace. What are the merits and demerits of the following communication methods?
    ■ posters placed around the workplace
    ■ mass meetings of the whole workforce together
    ■ small group meetings with time for discussion and feedback.

2   What does the following statement mean to you? 'The quality of decision making in Japanese organizations is a result of the time taken to reach those decisions.'

At the start of this section we referred to employee attitudes and values as an element of culture. Staff morale can sometimes be inferred from the level of staff turnover, and if this is occurring shortly after initial employment then a problem, possibly with the culture, may be inferred. Many people joining a new organization are enthusiastic and keen to do a good job, yet many organizations manage to kill off that enthusiasm within a few months. The following extract is adapted from a description of her organization by a student who did a work placement in local government:

> The atmosphere in the department was quite formal. The impression I got was that people were not content with the services supplied nor with their position in the organization. There was not much discussion unless it was on a business level. People did not lunch together but went home or to the main shopping arcade nearby. A canteen is provided with subsidized prices but when I went, people ate individually. Some of my colleagues complained about the lack of atmosphere in the organization, which had been badly affected by the redundancies made earlier in the year. Some people felt that they were expected to do the work of two or three people now. The pay rises that had been promised had still not appeared, and the benefits package was uninviting. Because of the redundancies, the managerial roles had been altered, and some people now felt inferior to their previous position in the organization.

> To some extent the way people felt was influenced by the 'new town' in which the borough council was located – it is characterless, and facilities are poor. Three of the people I worked with are now leaving the council because of the lack of job satisfaction, and are actually leaving the town as well.

Obviously this is a description of an organization deeply traumatized by recent upheavals, but nevertheless serves as an illustration of how the 'climate' of the organization – the way people feel about being there – can be affected by the culture and vice versa.

What are the effects of culture on organizations?

Having considered the different organizational cultures that can be found, and the factors that influence them, what are the effects of culture on organizations?

For example, a clear relationship can be inferred between organization culture and the structure of the organization. Put simply, it has been common for larger organizations to have more formal structures with separate departments and division of labour, and possibly with multi-site operations. This may affect the nature of the communications in the organization, and will have implications for the management and coordination of the various sub-units. In this way, a 'power' culture in a smaller firm may well turn into a 'role' culture following mergers, acquisitions or expansion.

The values of the organization may also be influenced by the culture. Here the 'values' may be the ethical nature of the decisions that underpin their long-term goals and objectives – 'culture' and 'values' are difficult to separate in many instances. For example, does the organization value long-term survival, or is the emphasis on growth and development? Is the organization a risk-avoider or a risk-taker? What is the attitude of the organization to environmental and social issues? What is the attitude of the organization to the development of its staff?

The following extract describes McDonald's philosophy, and how this impacts on training – although the size of this particular organization is also significant.

> Every day it serves over 28 million people through 14 000 outlets in 70 countries. Just in the UK one million people eat there every day.
>
> McDonald's says these staggering statistics could not have been achieved without putting constant change and training at the heart of the business.
>
> The philosophy of McDonald's is all about getting better than we are today; improving things for tomorrow. The total commitment to training is something which historically has been of paramount importance to the company.

Activity 2.13

Do you think these ideals are realized in practice? How would the company's values affect the role of the First Line Manager in a McDonald's restaurant?

The importance of culture

Time and time again studies have shown that successful organizations have a strong culture. Even more than this, if the employees of the organization take that culture on board, if it is directed towards the marketplace, and if it encourages dynamism, flexibility and a positive organizational style then it is likely to enhance success. For the First Line Manager, culture is a key determinant of the nature of organizational relationships in all directions – although this will of course in itself depend on the nature of the organizational culture and structure!

Activity 2.14

In this activity, you are required to investigate one particular organization of your choice which fits each of Handy's four 'culture' types: Power, Role, Task and Person. You are to provide:

1   A description of the structure of the organization – a chart may be useful. You should also identify the sector of economic activity that the organization fits into, the technology employed, and the organization of the staff.

2   A statement of the goals of the organization. This may be a mission statement, or in the case of a small organization, you may need to interview the owner or manager.

3   A description of the main internal communication methods employed in the organization.

4   A comparison (where possible) of the role of the First Line Manager in each of the organizations.

Motivating individuals and teams

Why is it that some individuals strive to reach extraordinary goals? What is it that enables an athlete or a classical musician to endure years of training, with no guarantee of wealth or fame? What pushes people to work hard, or strive to succeed in their careers? The study of what we call 'motivation' seeks to explain why people behave in a certain way, even though they may encounter problems, and why they will work willingly and well. Through understanding this we hope that we may be able to manage our staff more effectively, to get the best out of them, and to get them to give their best effort for the organization. What are the characteristics of motivation that we need to understand so that we can achieve this?

One definition of motivation is:

> some driving force within individuals by which they attempt to achieve some goal in order to fulfil some need or expectation.
> (Mullins, 1993)

Needs and expectations

What, therefore, are the needs and expectations that individuals are striving to fulfil? One way is to categorize them into intrinsic or extrinsic motivation.

Extrinsic motivation relates to 'tangible' rewards such as pay, promotion, having a pleasant office, and so on. This may not be within the individual's control.

Intrinsic motivation relates to inner rewards such as using one's abilities to the full, receiving recognition, and being well treated at work. These are things that can be determined by the behaviour of the individual.

Mullins (1993) suggests the following as a broad threefold classification for the motivation to work:

- *Economic rewards*: pay, security – the instrumental orientation to work.
- *Intrinsic satisfaction*: the work itself, interest in the job, personal growth and development – the personal orientation to work.
- *Social relationships*: friendships, status, affiliation, group work – the relational orientation to work.

Individuals will 'mix and match' these different sets of needs and expectations, which will determine their motivation to work and ultimately their performance. For example, some individuals will trade off high pay for a social environment in which they are happy to work, while others may be prepared to miss out on their social relationships in order to secure a higher standard of living.

Activity 2.15

What are your own 'bundle of motivators?' What is it that encourages you to work hard? Are these the same bundle of motivators that would drive you to do well in sport? Is there any difference?

The Scientific Management school of thought, principally based on the work of F. W. Taylor, focused on economic needs motivation. Here it was believed that individuals would be motivated by getting high wages through working in the most efficient way possible. With no ceiling on the pay available, the motivational effect was limited only by the individual's ability to work.

The Human Relations writers considered a wider range of needs than simply economic reward. They found that the social needs of people at work are also important, giving us the social concept of motivation.

The Contingency theorists took the view that there are many variables that influence motivation – organizations, and the people that work in them, differ greatly – the complex person concept of motivation.

We will consider some of the theories that look at the things that actually motivate people at work, and also some of the ways in which the process of motivation can take place.

One of the Human Relations approaches is Maslow's hierarchy of needs. Abraham Maslow looked at individual motivation based on the premise that human needs can be considered as a hierarchy, through five levels: from the low-level physiological needs, through safety needs, the need to belong, esteem needs, and the need for self-fulfilment (which he called self-actualization), the latter being the highest level. This is often illustrated as a pyramid, as in Figure 2.8, illustrating that as the lower level needs are satisfied, people aspire to higher things, and thus may potentially progress up the hierarchy.

How can Maslow's psychological theory be applied to people at work? Starting at the lowest level:

- Basic human physiological needs relate to what is necessary to keep the body functioning – oxygen, food and water. The basic psychological contract for work is that we go to work and expect to get paid for doing so – this is the least we can expect from the job. Here, at this basic level, we may find a student's vacation work –

never mind the poor working conditions, the short-term nature of the job, or the boring, repetitive nature of the tasks involved – that overdraft needs to be paid off!

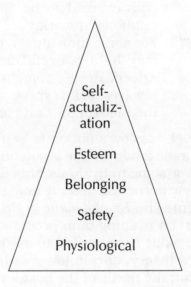

Figure: 2.8 *Maslow's hierarchy of needs*

■ At the next level, human needs, according to Maslow, relate to personal safety, freedom from danger, and so on. In terms of work, the next most basic expectation we may have of the work situation is perhaps security of tenure, the ability to be able to rely on the job as providing some continuing means of support. It still doesn't have to be interesting work, there may still be no status involved, we don't have to get on with the people we work with, but the job is there and it is secure. The *Employment in Britain* survey (1992), carried out by the Policy Studies Institute, revealed that 40 per cent of the respondents nominated job security as an essential factor in choosing a job. At another level, the feeling of a loss of personal safety seriously undermines confidence in society, law and order.

■ The need for belonging, often referred to as love needs or social needs, relates to that basic human need to be with other people and to be liked. Few people prefer isolation to human company, and the membership of a cohesive working group can be a very powerful factor in individual motivation. The survey quoted above found that the most satisfying jobs were those involving other people, and jobs involving caring for people scored the highest. Seventy-one per cent of respondents claimed to be 'highly satisfied' with their social relations at work.

■ For some individuals, the need for status or promotion may be a powerful influence. This is the role of the esteem needs, sometimes called the 'ego' needs. This involves self-respect, as well as self-confidence, and the motivation that comes from a developing career.

At the highest level, Maslow's notion of 'self-actualization' means the development and full realization of one's potential, 'making it', getting to where you want to go. For some individuals, this may not necessarily mean reaching the top of their particular tree, it may mean a feeling of inner satisfaction and fulfilment. The *Employment in Britain* study found that a greater emphasis was put on training than promotion by respondents – giving them as employees the skills they needed to do their jobs well.

In Maslow's theory, once a lower order need is satisfied, it no longer acts as a motivator, the needs of the next level then come into the arena and act as the motivating influence. Maslow also made it clear that the hierarchy is not necessarily in a fixed order, although it may seem to imply this – thus explaining the motivation of the religious devotee, for example, who is prepared to forego material satisfaction for what they see as a higher reward.

How relevant is Maslow's theory to today's work situation? How relevant too, is it to the work of a First Line Manager? Consider the following observations:

1   Many people achieve satisfaction through non-work activities – or through activities that simulate work. This is particularly significant in an era of restricted work opportunities for many people. Voluntary work, running sports clubs, orientation towards the family, can all affect the overall package of individual motivation.

2   Traditional approaches to motivation are often based on the idea that promotion and the career ladder are there as a motivational factor. One major issue for organizations at present is how to continue to motivate their staff when the promise of future promotion no longer exists, due to the removal of traditional hierarchies through 'delayering'.

3   Promotion where it does exist does not necessarily assume greater security – it is not uncommon for

senior executives to be on fixed-term contracts, and the fear of failure can be a very real concern for the newly promoted manager.

4   At times of uncertainty, people may value the relative safety of a stable, though bureaucratic environment, particularly as they approach retirement.

5   Responsibility and autonomy are nevertheless very important motivators for many individuals in the work situation.

ST JOSEPH FIND US MEN!

JOB DESCRIPTION:
Foreign Missionary Priests (Catholic). Prepared to spend their lives (one way or the other) for God and his people.

QUALIFICATIONS:
Academic – negotiable – of sound mind and limb. Prepared to be lonely, sick and misunderstood. Impervious to praise and hatred. Age 17–30.

SALARY:
£97 a month and as much as you can eat (usually).

PROMOTION PROSPECTS:
We try to ensure that ambitious people are not promoted.

TRAINING:
Long! (years and years!) in Dublin, London and Africa.

If you're afraid you might be our man, write to me:
Father John Doran MHM, St Peter's Vocations Centre, Freshfield,

---

Figure 2.9 *Higher rewards? Higher order needs taking precedence over lower levels (by kind permission of Mill Hill Missionaries)*

Maslow himself recognized some of the limitations of his theory and did not actually intend it to be applied to the work situation. It is nevertheless a useful starting point for a consideration of what motivates people at work, and made a very significant impact on the study of work motivation overall. For the First Line Manager, it can help us to understand the motivational forces affecting members of our team, and through attempting to meet their needs aim to enhance commitment and performance.

Activity 2.16

Try to apply Maslow's theory to your own work or personal situation. Do you think that it is an effective way of looking at an individual's set of motivators? What are its drawbacks? For the First Line Manager managing a team of staff, do you agree with the observations as to how this can practically be applied?

Herzberg's two-factor theory

Frederick Herzberg's major contribution to our understanding of work motivation arose out of a study of two hundred engineers and accountants representing a cross section of Pittsburg industry. His subjects were asked to describe times when they felt good or bad about their jobs, and the responses were classified to determine which events had led to job satisfaction or job dissatisfaction. The result was his 'motivation-hygiene' theory of motivation, based on the notion that there were two sets of factors affecting motivation at work.

One of the sets of factors identified by Herzberg can motivate the individual to higher levels of performance, and are related to the content of the job. These are called 'motivators' or 'satisfiers'. They include:

A sense of achievement
Recognition
Responsibility
The nature of the work
Promotion prospects and advancement
Personal growth
Achievement

The second set of factors, if absent, cause dissatisfaction. They are concerned with the context of work and are external to the job itself. These are called 'hygiene factors', 'maintenance factors' or 'dissatisfiers'. These include:

Salary
Job security
Company policy and administration
Relationships with other workers
Relationships with supervisors

Working conditions

Herzberg's research had concluded that motivation and dissatisfaction are caused by different factors at work and, importantly, are applied in different ways. If the 'hygiene factors' are satisfactory, they will not necessarily motivate the individual to work any harder, they will simply prevent dissatisfaction. Giving someone a pleasant office or a pay rise will not produce higher performance, it will simply 'maintain' the individual in their job, although they may stimulate loyalty.

To get people to give their best effort, organizations need to focus on the 'motivators'. This may be achieved through what is called 'job enrichment' – adding to the job to enhance the motivating factors. This does not mean simply adding one boring task to an already boring job – that will simply produce work overload and is likely to cause stress. Job enrichment refers to what is called 'vertical job loading', where opportunities for learning, achievement, advancement and growth are designed into the job.

There have been criticisms of Herzberg's work, one being that it paid insufficient attention to individual differences and preferences, and another being that many jobs do not really give the scope for many of the 'motivators' to be present anyway – for many employees work may simply be a 'means to an end'.

Is Herzberg's theory relevant today? ACAS, in their handbook *Effective Organisations*, which outlines the 'QWL' or 'Quality of Working Life' philosophy believed so:

> Factors which satisfy people at work are essentially different from those which cause dissatisfaction. Individual motivation and therefore greater efficiency can be enhanced by attention to the design of jobs and work organisation.

Vroom's expectancy theory

Vroom's work was based on the idea that people have a preferred outcome to their actions, and will direct their efforts according to what they hope to get out of it. Vroom called the feeling for a particular outcome the 'valence' – the anticipated satisfaction that will be gained from a particular outcome. People also attach probabilities to the likelihood of success from a particular course of action – Vroom called this 'expectancy'. The combination of these two things will affect the person's motivation for a certain form of behaviour. What is the significance of this in the work situation?

Some organizations give their employees the opportunity to get a bonus if they work hard. The problem is, according to Vroom's theory, the employees will only work hard for the bonus if they think it is worth it and achievable. If it is too difficult, for example because the target is set unrealistically high, the bonus will have no motivating effect. Similarly, providing the potential for an individual to advance their career through promotion will not automatically encourage people to work harder – they may decide it isn't worth it because of the stress or the extra workload involved.

The importance of expectancy theory is that it serves as a reminder that organizations need to think about rewards and motivators, including:

- The way individual performance is measured – clear, fair and consistent procedures will be needed.
- Establishing a clear link between effort/performance and rewards, and getting employees to understand that link.
- Recognizing what are appropriate rewards – do the employees think they are important?
- Recognizing the importance of the intervening factors which can also affect performance, such as development and training, and support facilities.

Generally, however, expectancy theory recognizes factors that had been missing from some of the earlier approaches. Individuals do think about the amount of energy and effort they are going to put into their work, and make conscious decisions about how they do their work as a result. For the First Line Manager, the issue is that not all of the above are under our influence, and we are going to need to draw from a range of approaches to get real commitment from the individuals and teams we work with.

Motivational techniques

Having considered some of the theoretical approaches, and some of the motivational factors that can be applied to the work situation, it is now appropriate to consider some of the practical approaches that organizations have taken to increase levels of employee motivation.

Dealing with boredom: job enlargement and job rotation

Earlier in this chapter, we mentioned the work of F. W. Taylor and the 'scientific management' school. When these principles were applied to job design, one of the consequences was that tasks were broken down so far that the jobs that people ended up doing were very boring and repetitive, which had an adverse effect on the rate of output, and affected employee morale to the extent that quality suffered and absenteeism increased. This initially produced even tighter controls on the work – if employees weren't working effectively the solution was to monitor them even more closely. In the 1950s managers began to explore other solutions to this problem, such as:

- Job rotation: where operators were switched from task to task at regular intervals.
- Job enlargement: tasks were combined to broaden the scope of the job that an individual performed.

These principles did have some effect, and have been used up to the present day – bank clerks on lower graded jobs in the 1970s and 1980s were rotated around the job roles attached to their particular grade, sometimes on a weekly basis. The problem was that the control aspect was still there, as every aspect of the job was still checked and double-checked by those on higher job grades. This solution also did not address the key aspect of alienation that arose out of the technology being employed, where clerical employees in the banks were often little more than machine minders, or in the automated jobs in factory production lines.

Looking on the positive side, job rotation did take some of the monotony out of boring jobs, and had the added benefit of making employees more flexible. It does not cost the organization very much, and meant that employees could understand the full range of job roles at any particular level of the organization, which was useful when they moved on to a supervisory level themselves.

Activity 2.17

What are the potential problems of job rotation? What demands would a system of rotating job roles place on the First Line Manager?

Job enlargement can be used where individuals can achieve such a level of proficiency in a job that they can easily cope with extra tasks which are added in to their role to add variety. There are problems with this approach as well, however, for example where an employee leaves or moves on and another inherits the 'enlarged' job. It will be necessary at that stage to reconsider the allocation of work to ensure that the new job incumbent is not immediately faced with unrealistic expectations of the work they are expected to perform. Individuals who have held a particular job role for a long time may have acquired extra responsibilities which they could cope with simply because of the high level of proficiency they had achieved. Even then, adding to their range of tasks can be just as much a source of potential stress, but tempting when the organization is short-handed and individuals may be perceived as capable of dealing with more.

Questions

- Is it job enlargement or just a bigger job?
- Do you agree with the view that people are working a lot harder these days?
- Why is it that employees in the UK work the longest hours in the European Union? Can it be justified on the grounds of job enlargement?

An alternative to simply providing more work of the same sort is job enrichment. Here, as we have seen earlier, Herzberg's 'motivators' can be built into the job to enhance the responsibilities, to provide the chance to do a higher level of work through delegation, and thereby to provide additional opportunities for recognition, and the chance to prove oneself for promotion. This was the idea behind the organization of the 'dock assembly' work units that Volvo attempted, which are described earlier in this chapter. Other ways of enriching jobs may include:

Client relationships: letting employees make personal contact with others within and outside the organization. This may also have benefits in terms of customer care, and 'ownership' of particular customer contacts.

Vertical loading: giving employees responsibility for jobs normally allocated to supervisors, such as the discretion to participate in work scheduling, training, planning and allocating work, determining work breaks, or quality checks – the 'quality circle' principle is a dimension of this approach, as is the notion of 'empowerment' of employees.

'Take the money': financial incentives and performance-related pay

Surely though, we all work for the money? Why are so many employees paid on a performance-related basis? This may only be a proportion of the total remuneration package, but surely it has a motivating effect? It is certainly the case that in many traditional industries (knitwear, footwear, hosiery, for example) there is an enduring tradition of some form of piecework and that, for many senior managers, even the senior management of educational establishments, there may be a performance-related element to their pay package. The *Employment in Britain* study reported that 27 per cent of the respondents were receiving some form of incentive payment, although the proportion of incentive pay to total pay was low, with only 31 per cent of those on incentives receiving 10 per cent or more. The survey reported that fringe benefits were rated low in motivational importance but did have an effect on recruitment and retention – in other words, they are hygiene factors. Occupational pensions were rated as the most important benefit, influencing 10 per cent of employees to take a job, and 15 per cent to remain in their present job. The effect of measures such as incentives and premium pay on general levels of satisfaction with salary levels was found to be negligible.

Activity 2.18
Do you agree with the conclusions of this survey? Can you offer an explanation for these results?

The retention factor can be very important, however. Traditionally, many employees in the financial services sector have benefited from attractive financial arrangements for house purchase or personal loans – the downside of this is that the employee can become 'locked in' to that particular organization due to the financial burden of the removal of these benefits on leaving. In Chapter 6, the notion of 'cafeteria compensation' is discussed, where the employee is able to choose from a range of incentive options to suit their own circumstances and preferences. It would be interesting to consider whether this has a greater motivating effect, rather than simply preventing dissatisfaction.

Activity 2.19

What are the financial benefits enjoyed by employees of financial services organizations and banks at the present time? Are these likely to be motivators, or hygiene factors?

'Speak to me': the role of employee feedback

If an organization wants to encourage and motivate its employees, why not ask them how this should be done? After all, most people have opinions about their job and the organization they work for, so why not tap into these? This section focuses on the role of listening, encouraging, and talking to individuals and teams as part of the manager's armoury of techniques for enhancing employee motivation. This isn't the only potential payoff – finding out how the staff feel can be very valuable for any organization that is about to embark on a major change programme. The use of team briefings or individual feedback may be appropriate in some circumstances, but can depend on the politics of the organization and rely on there being an 'open' culture. Other methods can include telephone hotlines or employee discussion groups.

The link with formal appraisal processes should not be overlooked – an appraisal should provide the opportunity for a constructive discussion about performance and development, and provide a way of looking forward, agreeing objectives and setting targets for the next cycle. An appraisal discussion in itself can motivate, not simply by the fact that the employee will value the discussion *per se*, but also because it is a major opportunity to:

- Identify individual strengths and weaknesses, training needs and 'blocks' to performance both individual and organizational.
- The opportunity to assess and jointly review promotion potential and possible career pathways.

■ Obtain feedback from employees 'on the ground' about organization policies, practices, the quality of supervision and the organizational climate.

Although some appraisal systems are linked in to performance-related pay, their emphasis here is as a developmental tool, and it is important not to overlook these aspects in the situation where the apparent focus may be appraisal-related pay. Ideally the aims should be to create career plans which are about personal growth as well as personal review; and where necessary consider career tracks that may encompass lateral moves to expand learning and competence as well as upward promotion.

Talking with teams

One of the key aspects of the 'Quality of Working Life' approach that has been referred to above is joint problem solving, the aim being to encourage a much higher level of employee involvement than would traditionally be the case. These can be:

■ A temporary task force or project team made up of people from across the organization
■ A 'diagonal sliced' team, to represent different levels
■ 'Kaizan' meetings – meetings concerned with continuous improvement
■ Quality circles.

The key point is that, whether working individually or in groups, employees value a degree of self-determination. This is not the same as abdicating from managerial responsibility and simply leaving them to get on with it – it is about recognizing the strength of the cohesive working group and using that as a resource to develop the organization and motivate the staff.

Mentoring

In this approach, individuals, possibly new entrants to an organization on a management development programme, have identified for them an established member of the staff who acts as a key resource in their development. The role can take on a variety of forms: the individual should be able to approach their mentor, impartially and without any fears about their relative experience, to facilitate their individual development in a supportive way. The mentor may well be a point of reference for the individual in terms of their own personal development, or for day-to-day operational matters. However the role is defined, the aim should be to minimize the alienating effects of 'newness' to an organization, to secure the individual commitment and motivation, and to facilitate the new staff member's effective contribution with as little delay as possible. The mentor role may be identified for up to twelve months in the case where it is used for new staff, or may be an ongoing programme.

Activity 2.20

Imagine you are a new First Line Manager in an organization of your choice. You have been told an established member of staff is to act as your 'mentor'. What kinds of skills and personal qualities would you want this person to have, and what kinds of things would you expect to discuss with them?

Training, coaching and team building

The key features of teamwork

So far, motivation and development have largely been discussed in the context of the individual, with only passing references to the role of teams in organizations. The following section focuses on the key features of team-work, and the contribution that teams can make. Firstly, let us consider exactly what it is that we call a team, and the responsibilities of their members:

- A team may be a collection of individuals assembled for a specific purpose.
- The responsibilities within that team will include having someone to steer it, promote the group, ensure that things get done, and promote harmony.
- A 'real-time' team on the other hand may be an existing work group composed of people who are existing post-holders in a section or department, or a management team in an organization. In this situation they won't have been assembled on the basis of their ability to work together as the team will have evolved over time, and development may be necessary to achieve effectiveness.

Why should an organization have a team to perform a specific task? It may be, for example, that the problem to be addressed needs a variety of points of view, expertise in different areas, or may simply be too big for one person to handle by themselves. Teams aren't a new idea – cave paintings show humans working together in hunting groups, with specialists, leaders and followers just like today's organizational teams. All of these teams need what has been called 'synergy': that the whole is more effective than the sum of the individual members, trust, and the ability to work towards an identified goal. In practice, great care needs to be exercised in the formation and operation of the team if this is to be realized, and if they are already established, sometimes we can't have much influence on their initial formation and makeup anyway. Even so, teams are likely to produce more usable ideas than individuals – the idea will have been through a process of evaluation through discussion.

So what are the characteristics of the individual team members in a working group? Certainly, some people will be 'leaders' and some will be 'followers', but we will discuss these contributions further below. The team will need to balance 'task orientation' – the single-minded dedication to getting the job done – with 'people orientation' – the ability to meet the needs of its members. In existing teams, there may also be job roles that are defined by function in the organization, relationships determined by the informal interactions between the members, and seniorities, particularly significant in hierarchical organizations. If we are looking for a 'good team member', however, it is likely to be someone who can be adaptable and flexible to fill a variety of roles, as well as showing restraint when required – listening skills are at least as important as the contributions of individuals.

The size of teams

It is likely that you will have experienced a good deal of group work. What happens when you are working in a large group, say of ten people? The answer is of course that some individuals may well use this as the opportunity for a 'free ride' – to sit back and let the others do the work, either because they are lazy, or because they are too shy to speak out in a larger gathering. A group of this size will need organizing in some way – it is unlikely to function effectively if simply left to sort matters out for itself. On the positive side, a larger group is likely to have a greater diversity of talent and skill. What about your experiences of working in small groups, say of up to four people? When one person is absent, the effectiveness of the group is reduced by a greater extent, and such groups can become unstable in times of crisis. It is generally recognized that the ideal group will have between five and seven members – this is likely to reduce the possibility of overlapping responsibilities, while still giving each member their own 'territory', and a reasonable division of labour.

The dynamics of teams

Dr Meredith Belbin carried out research into the functioning of management teams, based largely on his work at the Administrative Staff College, Henley, and his book, *Management Teams, Why they Succeed or Fail* has been considered a 'bible' for team builders. He believed that all members of management teams have two roles: one is the functional or job role they bring to the team with them, the second is less formal and relates to their individual contribution to what is going on in the team. Belbin's belief was that different people can contribute different attributes to a team, and it is the range of different attributes that makes the team effective. In his initial research, Belbin identified eight of these secondary roles, which he found to be present in the most successful teams.

Chair: Not always the 'official' chair, respected by the team, not necessarily that creative, but moves the team towards a solution

Team worker: Supports other people, good listener, somewhat indecisive, mediates, socially orientated

Shaper: Highly strung, outgoing and dynamic, intolerant of vague ideas, impatient, can be provoked, dominant, the task leader

Plant: The most creative and intelligent member, the 'ideas' person, can be introverted, and may not communicate well

Resource investigator: Extrovert, good communicator, good for external contacts, good negotiator, but can quickly get bored with new ideas

Company worker: Practical organiser, dutiful, self-controlled and well disciplined, can put ideas into practice, but may find flexibility is difficult, and may not respond well to unproven ideas

Completer/finisher: Orderly, conscientious, likes to do a job well, great strength of character, good attention to detail, good at meeting deadlines

Monitor/evaluator: Analytical, intelligent, evaluates problems, sober and prudent, critical thinker, may well find themselves in conflict with the 'plant'

Figure 2.10 *Belbin's team roles*

If the 'full set' of roles is not present, the team will be weakened. According to Belbin this was most important where the team were involved in dealing with rapid change, and a team operating in a more stable environment could get by without the full set of roles. Similarly, if there are too many of one type of role, then failure would result: imagine a team made up of 'plants' for example – they'd have lots of ideas and argue a great deal, but would probably never agree on the solution! In small groups, members may have to take on more than one role.

Belbin's categories should not be seen as cast in stone – today, individuals need to be flexible. In any case, in his original research, 30 per cent of the individuals tested didn't fall clearly into any one of the eight types –

either because their contribution was limited, or because they had a mixture of the characteristics identified. Identifying roles like this is useful where the teams can be selected, or where we are able to analyse an existing team, but 'real-time' teams are chosen on the basis of function, and the team membership may come and go. Even so, it is important to consider the compatibility of skills – managers can tend to 'select in their own image' which may produce an imbalance of roles.

Activity 2.21

Consider each of the team roles identified above: which one do you consider most closely fits your characteristics when working in your groups? Then do the same for the other members of the group you normally work with, and compare your results.

Sometimes, the techniques of the sports field can be applied to the development of teams and individuals in the workplace. Coaching, in the sports context, can take on a range of guises, from being 'boss-centred', to the 'empowering' approach. The sports analogy is a useful one, but in business, employees may have an advantage over the sports person – if the 'coach' is their manager then the manager is generally out there on the playing field with them!

Coaching in the work context is not new. It means using work as an opportunity to help employees to learn, constructively criticizing and giving feedback, building on ideas, suggesting alternatives. One useful vehicle for coaching can be an operational situation such as the need to develop a new product, tackled as a problem-solving project by staff who would not normally have the opportunity to do so. If successful, the staff will learn something, while at the same time solving the problem. A lot of 'internal consultancy' can be done by people working on organizational problems, needs and opportunities, and they may produce better solutions than an external consultant who will cost a great deal more.

The motivational effect of training is very important, of course, but is not always a good enough reason in itself to justify training expenditure, particularly considering the cost of 'buying in' from external training providers. The organization needs to benefit from these activities as a whole. 'Cascade' networks can provide the opportunity to tap into the buzz of motivation, to give the organization as a whole the chance to maximize the benefits of such activities, to disseminate good practice and stimulate ideas. We can't send everyone for a residential team building course – but we can tap into the learning experiences!

Team building

In recent years, 'outdoor development' training courses, or 'action learning', aimed at team building and developing teamwork skills, have become a popular part of many management development programmes. Many have participated in such activities, and private training consultancies can charge hundreds or even thousands of pounds for the experience! Is it worth it? Why should an organization ask those who may no longer be at the height of physical fitness to abseil, conduct navigation exercises, or attempt to construct the solution to a problem using logs, ropes and buckets of water.

Firstly, they can be linked in to the Belbin typology described above and, although in practice a much shorter exercise than a residential course can be used to get people to revert to type (as opposed to playing the role they think the organization wants to see), putting someone in a situation where they have to confront unfamiliar pressures can be very effective. Problem solving exercises, used well, can test the individual's communication skills, and may bring a realization of necessary modifications in their own management style. There have been many criticisms of such courses, however, and a certain amount of media attention has focused on the confrontational style adopted on some programmes – some have raised questions about the ethics of such programmes as well as concerns for safety. In addition, 'realization' can be uncomfortable, especially if the emergent leader is not actually the boss back at the office! Debriefing the exercise and giving the participants full opportunity to give and receive feedback is crucial – as well as following it up some time later to evaluate the benefits of the exercise back at the workplace.

Activity 2.22

This activity aims to give you the opportunity to devise team-building activities. Devise an activity, intended to last up to one hour, which should provide the opportunity for participants to explore their own contributions to teamwork. The activity may take place outdoors or indoors, but you must consider the safety of the participants, and secondly use the resources available. How should the debrief be conducted?

Questions for Activity 2.22

1 What have you learned from participating in this activity?

2 What is the value of such activities to management training and development, and team building?

3 Reflecting on your identification of the group against Belbin's typologies – do you still agree with your original decision?

Participation, and descriptive feedback

Practical, successful teams are often said to be characterized by animated interactions, and a positive emphasis on participation and consultation. From the above activity, the importance of the debriefing session should not be underestimated – it isn't just a case of doing the exercise, then, 'so, that was that, what do we do next?'. The really important part is to consider what we may have learned from the exercise and to build on this for the future. Sports teams have used this kind of 'descriptive feedback' to good effect, such as after an important match reviewing what happened at crucial points, who did what and why. Participants are simply invited to say what they noticed about the behaviour of others in a non-judgemental kind of way. From this open discussion, consideration can be given to how future game plans can be modified to take account of the learning experiences. Obviously an important part of this process is the ability of individuals to handle constructive criticism in a positive way – 'taking it on the chin' can be difficult where fragile managerial egos may be involved!

It may also be useful to observe groups at work, possibly undertaking an activity such as the one described above, and to attempt to analyse their interactions in terms of the participation of the different group members. This can then be used as a basis for consideration of the strengths and weaknesses of the team members.

Commitment

One of the starting points for some developmental exercises has been to 'leave all baggage at the door'. What does this mean? So far, an assumption has been made that the team members will either participate in the task, or sit it out. Sometimes, however, members may bring hidden agendas with them, nothing to do with the function of the group, and which may include:

- Trying to impress the boss
- Protecting self-interest
- Scoring points off other people
- Covering up mistakes or inadequacies
- Deliberately disrupting the activity just for the heck of it.

It is necessary to establish a scenario where the group either quickly recognizes this and kicks it into touch, or preferably develops a framework where good ideas can be nurtured in a climate of openness and mutual trust.

Very few people function totally independently in the workplace. Even if some individuals try to, it is likely that they are missing out on the benefits of teamwork, and the team is losing out on their potential contribution. In an uncertain and fast-moving environment, where the risks of bad decision making are very high, the effectiveness of a team becomes even more crucial. There are negative outcomes that can arise in groups and teams: the phenomenon of 'groupthink' for example, where putting too high an emphasis on consensus can lead to poor decision making. This is why it is important to consider not only the roles that arise in teams, but the way in which the team operates and the way in which they can be managed. A crucial part of team operation is the role of the leader, which is considered in more detail in the following section.

Questions

1 Define extrinsic and intrinsic motivation.
2 Outline the main differences between the scientific management and human relations approaches to motivation at work.
3 How would you define 'self-actualization'?
4 What is the difference between a hygiene factor and a motivator?
5 How does expectancy theory differ from other approaches?
6 What is 'descriptive feedback'?
7 You have been asked to be a 'mentor' to a new colleague – what would you expect this role to involve?
8 If someone was described as a 'shaper', how would you expect them to behave in a team situation?
9 What is meant by 'groupthink', and what problems can it bring?
10 What problems would you, as a First Line Manager, expect to find in managing a group of fifteen people?

Take me to your leader

'Good leaders are born not made' has been a motto that has served many organizations – and the self-interest of those in charge of them – very well for many years, but is it true? Are there innate characteristics that mean that some individuals are, as one humorist put it 'doomed to succeed' and will always rise to the fore? In this section we will look at some of the key features of leadership, and use this as a basis for a consideration of some styles of management. Throughout, we will consider the importance of the personal qualities of the leader.

Certainly the traditional view was that individuals from a certain social class or educational background possessed some innate advantage

that suited them to the leadership role. 'Trait theories' of leadership identified qualities such as self-assurance, initiative, intelligence, or the ability to
rise above a situation and take a global view. Obviously these attributes are
useful, but they are not the whole story. Trait theories were popular up to
the 1950s, but the emergence of a more democratic culture and the breakdown of traditional social barriers undermined the belief in the 'officer corps'
or 'bred to lead' school of thought – attention focused instead on the style
the leader adopted, and how this affected the behaviour of subordinates: the
'style theories'.

Activity 2.23

Identify and list the functions of a leader in an organization. What do
they do that sets them apart from their colleagues?

How does this differ from the functions of a manager that you
identified earlier?

What kind of things have you identified? To generalize, it is likely that many
of them will be to do with a two-way relationship. Leadership has been
described as where: 'one person influences the behaviour of other people.'

It isn't therefore just one person telling others what to do – it is a
much more dynamic process than that. Leaders can be distinguished from
managers by their approach: managers will tend to rely on the strategy,
structure and systems (sometimes called the 'hard s's'); leaders will consider
these but tend towards the style, staff, skills and shared values (or the soft
s's). Nevertheless a distinction can be drawn between formal and informal
leadership, and the way in which they operate in organizations.

Activity 2.24

Can you identify the 'best leader' and the 'worst leader' you have
encountered in a work situation? What were the characteristics of each,
for example in terms of their personal qualities, or their relationships
with others, or the way they approached the job? Try to identify one
similar situation which allows you to compare their approaches.

'Formal leadership' is much more likely to be role-driven – the legiti-
macy of the leader arises through their position in the hierarchy. This is the
model of the traditional organization, such as a family firm, where the
owner/manager is perceived as having a natural right to be 'in charge' – but
that doesn't necessarily make them a leader! Similarly, in bureaucratic

organizations, there is a legal-rational authority which stems from the individual's position in the hierarchy – a bank manager may be a good example of this – but again, they aren't necessarily a leader. Formal leaders may tend towards what is called 'directive behaviour', where they rely on set goals and objectives, defined roles, planning, organization, evaluation and checking.

'Informal leadership' is more likely to occur when the followers believe in the personal qualities of the leader – vision, strength of personality and the ability to inspire others. Many great sporting personalities fit this description – but equally well this kind of leadership may arise out of the informal structure of the organization. The danger is, that this can be a very powerful counterculture, and can, if it does not share the values of the organization, prove to be a very disruptive influence, and it is one reason why we have considered the team-building aspects to be so important. The informal leader is more likely to have a participative style, and may positively reinforce the formal leader's role by encouraging their peers, help with the provision of information, and assist groups or teams reach decisions or targets.

Activity 2.25

Consider the sporting leaders with whom you may be familiar. What are their personal qualities that make them successful? How could these qualities be applied in a workplace situation? What conclusions can you draw?

Leadership, power and authority

While we have considered the influence that formal and informal leaders may have, it is important to remember that the leader–follower relationship may also have a basis in a power relationship, which to a large extent depends on the way that the subordinate perceives this relationship. French and Raven (1968) identified five sources of power on which the influence of the leader is based:

1   *Reward power:* is based on the subordinate's perception that the leader can obtain resources and rewards for their followers, and may include bonuses, promotions, recognition, or the allocation of more favourable work.

2   *Coercive power:* is based on fear – the subordinate's perception that the leader has the ability to punish, and is the opposite of reward power. 'Punishments' could include public humiliation such as ridicule in meetings, withdrawal of support, allocation of undesirable work;

or, if the leader's role permits, more formal sanctions such as disciplinary action. Bullying (which is what coercive power can manifest itself as) has at last been recognized as a serious problem in the workplace, and will be discussed later in this chapter.

3   *Legitimate power:* this is based on the subordinate's perception of the leader's role in the organization – it is 'position' power arising out of the position in the hierarchy.

4   *Referent power:* this is based on the subordinate's identification with the leader, either by the subordinates respect for the leader, or by shared values or common interests, which may not necessarily be work-related.

5   *Expert power:* this is based on professional credibility, and the follower's perception of the leader's competence.

It is important to note the emphasis on the 'subordinate's perception' – if they don't believe in the leader's ability to control rewards or punishments, for example, then the leader will have no power. These five types of power are related and one may also affect another. A leader who resorts to coercive power, for example, may lose the referent power over their subordinates – the relationship will be based on fear rather than respect.

Activity 2.26

Identify examples of the above from your own experience. Can you draw any conclusions about how the situation came to be that way?

Empowerment

Variously described as one of the most overused buzzwords of the 1990s, or a way of getting rid of people, empowerment is in fact a radical departure from conventional management theory based on the premise not of 'control'-centred leadership, but of getting individuals to take more responsibility for themselves and their actions at work. The following case study describes how 'empowerment' was used in two organizations: Harvester Restaurants and Ciba-UK.

CASE STUDY: IS THIS EMPOWERMENT?

The two companies took quite different approaches: at Harvester, every restaurant 'branch' lost a layer of management, leaving the branch manager to work with a 'coach' who takes care of training and some personnel issues – everyone else is a team member. Everyone has one or more 'accountabilities' which may include recruitment, work rotas or tracking sales, which are allocated at weekly team meetings. Outputs are awarded on the basis of merit badges, and include a bonus scheme or special designations – such as 'team expert' or 'associate' – which, at the time, applied to only six out of the 2000 workforce. The branch manager spends more time on marketing and external liaison, as well as acting as a facilitator – it wasn't easy for chefs to accept that they were now responsible for ordering their own stock or dealing with customer complaints. This probably couldn't have been achieved without the tight structure – every restaurant runs on the same basis and works within the same framework.

Ciba-UK took a different approach – their teams do not have to comply with any centrally dictated structure or way of working, and within a factory each part of it may have a different approach. The responsibility for problem solving is put clearly onto the front-line workforce, but there are no new job titles. The relationship has changed though: 'as in other empowered workplaces, the supervisor no longer commands and checks: he or she coaches, discusses and assesses training needs.'

Analyse and compare the two approaches. Which do you think would be the most successful in the long run?

So is 'empowerment' just a buzzword? In the context of what we have discussed above it is clear that there are advantages in tapping into the strengths of the workforce, of breaking down traditional 'control' structures, and of giving people at work more responsibility for themselves and what they do.

Management styles

So far in this chapter we have explored approaches to motivation, considered the importance of teamwork, and examined the key features of leadership. Throughout, reference has been made from time to time to the 'manager's style'. This refers to the way that managers behave in the workplace, and how this behaviour affects their subordinates and teams. In this section we will look at various styles of leadership:

Autocratic
Democratic
Laissez-faire
Task orientated
People orientated

– through an examination of the work of some of the main theorists in this area. Firstly, what do these styles of leadership mean?

The *autocratic* style is manager-centred, that is, interactions among subordinates tend to be towards the manager. The manager will structure the work situation for their employees, and tell them what to do. The manager alone exercises decision-making authority, and will determine goals, targets, rewards and punishments. This style can have advantages – if the manager is the kindly, benevolent type, they will be very pleasant to work for, and will ensure that everyone knows exactly what to do. Some employees do prefer a more directive approach. The leader themselves will feel 'in control', and will be able to exercise rapid decision making. By definition, however, an autocrat can also be coercive, achieving results by 'management by fear'. Note that some managers may adopt both approaches but with different subordinates! Favouritism and bullying are not unknown in the workplace. Autocratic leadership can also create a 'dependency culture' – without the leader there to tell them what to do, the employees can be unfocused and aimless. Many managers in Central and Eastern Europe have found their new self-determination particularly difficult to handle.

The *democratic* style is group-centred – the team is the focus of power, and the manager is seen as one of the team, or 'first among equals'. The leadership functions are shared with the group – the empowerment situation. The manager can tap into the resources of the group, and values their contributions. In turn, the group members are motivated, and feel respected and valued. On the negative side, delegation can be problematic if the leader does not agree with the subordinate's approach, and also decision making can take longer.

The *laissez-faire* manager leaves employees to work on their own if they seem to be working well, and does not interfere. This is not the same as abdicating responsibility, and is a perfectly legitimate style of leadership. The members of the group have a good deal of autonomy over their day-to-day work, and value the independence that they are given, especially if they are technical specialists or professionals. There can be problems however – the fact that the leader is not omnipresent may cause the staff to question whether the leader is needed at all, and a counterculture may develop. Additionally, some staff members may attempt to take advantage of the trust relationship that is implicit here.

Lickert's systems' of management

Rensis Lickert was an American social psychologist and consultant who carried out research on the effectiveness of different styles of management, and particularly the need for an alternative to the classical approach. He found that low-performing departments in organizations tended to be job-centred, that is that the supervisors concentrated on keeping their subordinates busy on prescribed tasks. Supervisors with high performing departments, on the other hand, were those where the focus was employee-centred, and where the supervisors allowed maximum participation in decision making.

Lickert summarized his research into four systems of management:

System 1: is the exploitative authoritative type, where supervisors use fear and threats, and most of the communication is downward.

System 2: is the benevolent authoritative or paternalistic type, where rewards are used to motivate, but strict control is still exercised. Delegation may occasionally be used, but information flowing upward is restricted to what the boss wants to hear.

System 3: is the consultative type, where the communication is more two-way, but the boss will still retain the right to make the final decision, rewards are used, and some punishments where appropriate.

System 4: is called participative group management. Here, there is total group participation, and decision making by consensus. Superiors and subordinates are very close psychologically. Decision making throughout the organization is through a series of overlapping groups, with each group linked to the rest of the organization by key individuals (called 'linking pins') who are members of more than one group.

Lickert considered that 'System 4' management was ideal for a profitable and caring company. However, that is something of an over-generalization, and tough, technologically competent managers with tightly controlled systems and procedures can achieve high output – it is a case of deciding what is appropriate for the situation.

Activity 2.27

Identify real-life examples of organizations where the approach taken fits Lickert's systems of management? How would this particularly affect the role of the First Line Manager?

McGregor's theories X and Y

Douglas McGregor was an American professor of management. He examined the assumptions that managers make about human behaviour, and how this manifested itself as the management style. He described two extreme styles, which he called 'Theory X' and 'Theory Y'.

Theory X was based on the classical concepts of coordination and control. The assumptions made about human motivation are:

- The average human being dislikes work and will avoid it if they can.
- Most people must therefore be coerced, directed, controlled or offered incentives if they are to put in even an adequate effort.
- The average human being prefers to be directed, wishes to avoid responsibility, has little ambition, and wants security above all.

Theory Y was based on premises similar to Lickert's 'System 4' management style. Here, the assumptions made about motivation are:

- That the expenditure of physical and mental effort in work is as natural as play or rest. Ordinary people do not inherently dislike work, whether it is seen as a reward or punishment depends on the conditions.
- People do not have to be subjected to external control – they can exercise self-direction and self-control.
- The best motivator that can be offered is the opportunity to satisfy the individual's self-actualizing needs.
- The average human being learns, under the right conditions, not only to seek but also to accept responsibility.
- People could contribute far more than they do, and their potential isn't being fully used.

Obviously McGregor's 'X and Y' are extremes – most managers fall somewhere between the two. McGregor did consider that given the choice, most managers would tend towards 'theory X', and employees towards 'theory Y', although again it must be said that some employees actually prefer a directive approach.

Activity 2.28

Consider the following roles and situations. Which of the above styles of leadership do you feel would be appropriate in each case, and why? In each situation, you will need to consider:

1 Who is the manager likely to be?
2 What are the external influences on the group?
3 What are the organizational influences on the group?

- A hockey team playing in a Saturday league
- A group of soldiers in a combat situation
- A group of engineers and designers preparing a Formula 1 racing car for the next season
- A group of students planning an exchange visit to France
- A group of conservation volunteers rebuilding a mountain path
- A group of staff in a restaurant laying-out for a banquet

Task orientation and people orientation

What your discussion should produce is the fact that the situation that the team finds itself in can affect the style of management adopted. In some of the above circumstances the teams would be under pressure from external influences – the sponsors of the motor racing team, for example. In that case the team would be under considerable pressure to have the car ready and competitive by the start of the new season, and this in turn would tend to result in what is called a 'task-orientated approach'. At least one of the other groups exists mainly to serve the interests of the people in it – they will have some element of 'task orientation', but will also seek primarily to fulfil their own needs.

Contingency theories of leadership

Many studies have also looked at the interaction of the variables affecting the leadership situation, and the leader's behaviour – contingency theories are based on the belief that there is no one style of leadership appropriate to all situations.

Fiedler's theory of leadership effectiveness considered the relationship of the leader–member relations, the task structure and the leader's position power (from strong to weak in each case), to the style adopted. When the situation was unfavourable, that is the leader–member relations poor, the task unstructured and the leader's position power weak, then a task-orientated leader with a directive, controlling style would be more effective. Where the situation was favourable, a participative approach could then be successful. Fiedler therefore suggested that the leadership style would vary as the favourability of the situation changed.

Taking the idea a little further, Tannenbaum and Schmidt suggested that the highly-controlling and highly participative styles were actually the two ends of a continuum of leadership style. They identified seven key points along this scale, as shown in Figure 2.11.

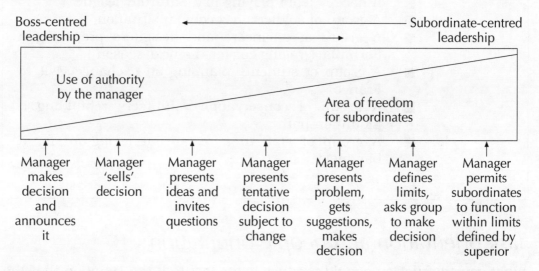

Figure 2.11 *Tannenbaum and Schmidt: from manager to subordinate-centred leadership.* Reprinted by permission of *Harvard Business Review* (an exhibit). From 'How to choose a leadership pattern' by Robert Tannenbaum and Warren H. Schmidt, May–June 1973. Copyright © 1973 by the President and Fellows of Harvard College; all rights reserved.

In fact, the seven points here over-simplify the situation, because this is in fact a continuous scale, and the manager can accept a mixture of direction or involvement at any point along it. The main point that the scale is intended to illustrate is that as one increases, the other decreases.

Tannenbaum and Schmidt suggested that three forces would influence the leader's choice of style:

1 *Forces in the manager*: these would include the manager's beliefs and inclinations, the confidence in subordinates, and the manager's tolerance of uncertainty.

2 *Forces in the subordinate*: these would include the strength of their need for independence, their tolerance of uncertainty, their expectation of the leadership style, their ability to tackle problems, and their effectiveness as a group.

3 *Forces in the situation*: the organizational climate, the pressure of time, the pressures in the manager's job, and the problem itself – whether it was technical or judgemental in nature.

They also considered forces lying outside the organization, and the scope of, for example, employees and managers to change the boundaries of their area of activity.

The role of the manager in motivating, teamwork and leading

So far we have considered the factors that influence employee motivation, techniques for motivating, teamwork, leadership and management styles. 'Management', however, is about applying things to the real world, and in this section we will consider the relationships between the topic areas discussed so far, and the role of the manager in motivating, teamwork and leading.

'The feelgood factor'

What can managers do to get employees to feel good about themselves, their work and the organization they work for? The job that the individual does is a key element – job satisfaction has been referred to from time to time in this chapter, and although it is often quoted as being desirable, is actually quite hard to define. The following headings give a clue as to the scope of the subject – some of the things that we understand to make up job satisfaction are things that the manager can influence:

- *People* factors – such as colleague relationships, networking and informal links in the organization.
- Some *situational* factors – such as the style of leadership, the nature of supervision, and to some extent the working conditions.
- Some *personal* factors – such as the learning and development undertaken by the individual.

There are several factors that make up job satisfaction which a First Line Manager (as opposed to a strategic manager) would find difficult to influence, however. These will include:

- Many *personal* factors – personality, education, intelligence, ability, marital status, personal relationships and the general orientation to work.
- Many *situational* factors – size, structure, procedures, custom and practice, the nature of the work, technology, organization.
- Some *cultural* factors – underlying attitudes, beliefs and values.
- *Environmental* factors – economic, social, technical

and government influences, which can include the 'atmosphere' in society generally – hence the 'feelgood' factor.

What is important to recognize is where the manager can influence events, where a major change programme is required, and what we just have to adapt to!

Personal development is about facilitating the learning, growth and potential of individuals, and is far more than merely job-specific training. Continuous and lifelong learning should become the norm, rather than the post-school 'shot in the arm' training that has too often been the case. This means updating skills as well as acquiring new ones, and training people to be multi-skilled to cope with change. One way to support this process in the workplace is through an appraisal system that focuses on personal development needs. This provides the opportunity to create career plans that include work experience, as well as job goals and personal development. In this 'personal development' process, therefore, the manager is taking on the role of counsellor and facilitator, and possibly a mentor as well. In this way, it may also be possible to identify training needs for groups of employees as well as individuals, and to set up structured training activities, such as in time management, or team leadership skills.

Interpreting and meeting objectives and targets

In spite of the many theories of motivation, and numerous different approaches to leadership, it is difficult to achieve Lickert's 'System 4' in practice, where there is both job satisfaction and a high concern for people, and productivity.

- For individuals – can we motivate them through performance-related pay, promotion or job enrichment?
- For groups – can we give them more autonomy for meeting targets or managing resources?
- For organizations – how can we get individuals to identify with the goals and culture of the organization, through, for example, encouraging a culture of long service, job rotation, and 'single status'.

Activity 2.29

To what extent are the three aims stated above compatible with the prevalent styles of management you have encountered? Can organizations afford to encourage a culture as described above, when 'downsizing' is so prevalent? What do organizations stand to gain from managing this way?

What is the role of the manager in all of this? Put simply, the manager is the one who creates the environment for these things to happen, and who helps the employee interpret the objectives of the organization – either individually or for groups, or through communicating the cultural values of the organization to the employee, and reinforcing these. That is why the role of the First Line Manager is so crucial.

Getting the best from our people – commitment and enthusiasm

Above, we talked about the link between training, personal development and job satisfaction. There are other benefits to developing employees, such as:

- *Enhanced skills*: employees who are skilled, or multi-skilled, have the opportunity to fill a greater variety of roles and make a better input, as well as helping their career development.
- *Commitment*: if employers invest in their employees, they will value this – the payoff should be enhanced retention. Training is not a hygiene factor. It will also improve their confidence in the employer – there is a lot of fear and uncertainty in the workplace these days!
- *Contributing to the team* and not feeling 'second best' against their colleagues. Meeting individual development needs will improve employees self-confidence.
- *Building morale* (and healing wounds!).

Confidence, morale, and the contribution of individuals are important factors in the workplace. It may be, for example, that as a manager you may 'inherit' a situation where individuals are discouraged from contributing because of your predecessor's style – how can you deal with this? Consider the following case study:

CASE STUDY: SPARKS ELECTRICAL

June has just taken over as Branch Manager of the 'Sparks Electrical' store in a city in the North of England – a major promotion, and her first managerial role. In this branch, there are twelve full-time staff and a large number of part-timers. Most of the full-time staff have been with the organization less than two years. June's predecessor, Dave, is being moved on to a role in Head Office, although she understands that this isn't exactly a promotion. Before Dave left, she worked alongside him for a week to ease her transition into her new post, but she has found that the experience actually raised more fears than it allayed – in fact, some of the things that she is finding out about Dave's style of management have given her grave cause for concern.

One particular case concerns Alan, who is one of the longer serving members of staff. He has some supervisory responsibility for one small part of the store and really should have progressed beyond his present role by now. What really concerned June was the way that Dave treated Alan – in the weekly staff meeting anything that Alan said was immediately ridiculed by Dave, even though they were potentially quite reasonable contributions. Dave has also been monitoring Alan's work very closely for the past twelve months, with a daily report-back which none of the other section heads are required to do. Apparently there was a mistake in the pricing arrangements in last year's summer sale which involved some financial loss to the company. To some extent this may have been due to poor communications from Head Office – the same thing happened in two other stores – but Alan took the blame for it, and Dave hasn't let the matter rest since. Looking at Alan's personnel file, the written warning that he received at the time is just about to go 'out of date', and there are no records of any problems since.

Alan is a very hard working and conscientious individual, and he has clearly found Dave's approach very distressing. He has taken to working late to make sure that everything is absolutely 'first-rate' on his section, which it was anyway as he does his job very well – the problem is that he has become used to Dave giving him a dressing-down, often in public, for the smallest thing, real or imagined. To a lesser extent, Dave applies a similar approach to all the staff, with the exception of two men of his own age who are also golfing friends out of work hours. At lunchtimes, these three eat in Dave's office with the door closed. Informally, June has asked Dave about Alan, and questioned him as to his treatment of Alan. Dave actually took this quite well (June was very tactful!), and said:

'Well, you've done a management course – haven't you heard of 'bounce-back' theory? You see, if Alan's any good he'll be able to 'bounce back' all by himself!'

June was disappointed that Dave treated the whole thing so frivolously, especially when it seemed to be having such a serious effect on Alan. The situation is having an impact on staff relations generally – June has noticed that compared to other stores, the 'atmosphere' is quite different here, although the sales performance of the branch is actually very good, due in no small way to the geographical location in a thriving new retail park.

On the last day of her week 'shadowing' Dave, June noticed Alan sitting in a corner of the staff rest room with his head in his hands, and a few minutes later going in to see Dave for his daily report-back session.

> **Question**
>
> From Monday, the situation will be in June's hands. What can she do to restore morale in this branch generally, and to address the situation with Alan in particular? How should she approach the matter of managing Dave's 'golf chums'. What practical solutions can you suggest?
>
> At company level, what are the implications of this case?

Summary

Now that you have read this chapter, it is hoped that you will have gained an appreciation of the importance of motivation, teamwork and leadership. Some of the earlier writers on organizational behaviour fell into the trap of being too prescriptive, and the consequence was that their theories became less and less applicable in a changing world. That is never more true than today – and it is now largely accepted that 'contingency' approaches, a 'flexible' workforce and 'the flexible firm' are more relevant and dynamic models of the workplace.

We hope that you will have gained an appreciation of organization structures, and how these affect the people who manage in them. We have looked at how change arises in organizations and some of the strategies for managing its effects. The importance of organizational culture has been considered and its impact on the role of the First Line Manager. We have also considered the all-important role of the First Line Manager in motivating individuals and teams, and in stepping beyond the managerial function to show leadership skills.

Attention is now focusing on the future of work – ideas explored in a limited way earlier in this chapter and also in Chapter 6, which include homeworking and teleworking, and exploring the potential of the 'information superhighway'. Books and articles that talk of 'the end of work as we know it', the growing body of knowledge some people call 'chaos theory' – all indicate significant changes in the patterns of our working lives. Whatever the outcome, it will be a challenging time for the First Line Manager, and the skills and knowledge we have considered in this chapter will be tested as never before.

References

Advisory, Conciliation and Arbitration Service (ACAS) (1991). *Advisory Booklet No. 16: Effective Organisations – The People Factor*.

Belbin, R. M. (1981). *Management Teams, Why they Succeed or Fail*. London: Heinemann.

Bott, K. and Hill, J. (1994). Change agents lead the way. *Personnel Management*, August, 24–28.

Civil Service Commission (1988). *The Next Step*. London: HMSO.

Corby, S. (1993). One more step for the Civil Service. *Personnel Management*, August, 30–31.

Fairbarns, J. and Jennings, G. (1994). Tapping employee attitudes on a programme of change. *Personnel Management*, March, 38–43.

Handy, C. (1986). *Understanding Organisations*. Harmondsworth: Penguin.

Huczynski, A. and Buchanan, D. (1991). *Organisational Behaviour: An Introductory Text*, 2nd edn. Prentice Hall.

Jones, A. (1993). A new culture in the showroom. *Personnel Management Plus*, June, 20–21.

Mayo, A. (1992). A framework for career management. *Personnel Management*, February, 36–39.

Mullins, L. J. (1996). *Management and Organisational Behaviour*, 4th edn. London: Pitman.

Pickard, J. (1992). Shell UK pulls responsibility back to the centre. *Personnel Management Plus*, April, **3**, 1.

Pickard, J. (1993). The real meaning of empowerment. *Personnel Management*, November, 28–33.

Policy Studies Institute (1992). *Employment in Britain*.

Pugh, D. S., Hickson, D. J. and Hinings, C. R. (1988). *Writers on Organisations*. Harmondsworth: Penguin.

Tannenbaum, R. and Schmidt, W. (1973). How to choose a leadership pattern. *Harvard Business Review*, May–June.

Toffler, A. (1970). *Future Shock*. Bodley Head.

Wibberley, M. (1993). Does lean necessarily equal mean? *Personnel Management*, July, 32–35.

Wickens, P. (1993). Steering the middle road to car production. *Personnel Management*, June, 34–38.

3 The production and delivery of services and products

Aims

The aim of this chapter is to explore the tools and techniques available to managers to design and provide services and products which meet customers needs.

By the end of this chapter you will:

- Understand factors affecting the operations processes to produce or provide services and products.
- Know about the various methods, tools and techniques used to plan and schedule work in the operations process.
- Be aware of the factors influencing efficient purchasing and stock control.
- Understand the methods of managing queues in service and product production and delivery.
- Be aware of the regulatory framework for protection of the consumer and health and safety of the workforce.
- Understand the causes of interruption to supply or production and the need for contingency planning.
- Understand the link between quality assurance and customer satisfaction.

Key concepts

- Types of operations process for products and services;
- Links between design and customer satisfaction;

■   Methods of planning and scheduling for the production of products and services;
■   Methods of organizing operations, allocating work and scheduling;
■   Purchasing and stock-control issues;
■   Managing queues;
■   Regulatory framework for consumer protection and health and safety of workforce;
■   Quality assurance and control;
■   Monitoring and improving products and services.

Introduction

Operations management concerns the transformation of material and other resources into goods and services. This applies equally to the production of products, normally associated with manufacturing industries, and to those services concerned, for example, with health care or local authorities.

The role of the operations manager includes design, planning, monitoring and control. This covers a large number of specialisms, not all of which will be related to the technical background or direct experience of the manager.

Operations managers can find themselves faced with the task of managing a wide range of staff, from technically qualified researchers, designers, engineers and scientists, to clerical, administrative and professional staff and the operators, storekeepers and delivery staff.

The operations manager must understand the importance of quality in services and products and the need to relate that to customer requirements and expectations. The design aspects may cover the design of the product or service, packaging, costing, determining the method of production or service delivery, factory or workplace layout. Planning and organization of operations includes scheduling and allocating the work, purchasing the materials and components, stock control, managing the day-to-day operations process, maintenance, inspection and quality control.

The process is completed by monitoring and controlling activities and offering feedback to the research and development, design and planning sections.

These operational functions are required for all organizations, and apply equally to manufacturing, service and not-for-profit organizations. Increasingly, organizations are using their information technology to assist in these processes.

Planning for services and products

Operations management is concerned with designing, planning and monitoring the production and delivery of products and service packages. This covers not only the physical and tangible elements, but also the actions necessary to deliver the package to the next stage of the distribution chain, or to install the product for the user, offer after-sales service, or help the customer to consume or experience the service or product.

Services range from the provision of transport, retail outlets and restaurants, to entertainment either directly, as in theatres and cinemas, or indirectly as at leisure centres or discos – where the customer has to participate in making the experience. Other cases where the customers are part of the service process include travelling, having a haircut, or beauty treatment. In other cases the customer is not involved but the service is done to their property – car servicing, window cleaning, gardening design, drain clearances and repairs.

The service package may include physical items which are a tangible aspect of the service – the insurance policy, the food in a meal, the lotions used in facial treatments or the programme at the theatre. There will also be the environment in which the transaction or service takes place – the restaurant or bar, the leisure centre, the cinema. The atmospheres and furnishings are an important part of the service. Ancillary facilities may be important such as the number and cleanliness of toilet facilities provided at a theatre or museum, or snack facilities in a museum. In the Musée D'Orsay in Paris, the tea rooms are furnished like part of the museum, with a painted fresco ceiling and a quartet playing chamber music – all adding to the atmosphere of the break for tea and making it part of the outing. There will also be the personal contact: the attitude of the receptionist, or the person in the box office. All these issues, and more, contribute to the whole service package and will affect existing and potential customers.

In terms of products it is not just the physical and functional element of the product, but also the packaging and the aesthetic appeal of the finished item. All these need to be considered in the design, installation and after-sales service. The product should continue selling for you after it has been bought. You want customers to retain a pleasant experience and memory of the product or service and recommend it or your organization to others.

Services cannot normally be stored for future usage and, therefore, there can be immediate feedback of the success or otherwise of the service. In the not-for-profit sector, the consideration of how the recipient receives, understands and values the service is important. In charities the difficult problem is often to decide what the service package is and who the customers are – the ultimate end-users and beneficiaries – or the people who supply the funds – or both these groups.

Links with other organizational departments

It is important that the planning and control of operations is integrated with the organization's objectives and also its planning and control processes.

One of the main resources for the operations department will be the workforce. There should be a close relationship with the Human Resource

Department of the organization. The acquisition and use of resources in plant, equipment, materials, components and stock will have an impact on the financing of the organization, both for investment and cash-flow purposes, and the operations department must liaise with those responsible for financial management.

The relationship with marketing and sales is particularly important in understanding and meeting customer needs. It is the concern of the marketing department to feed back information from the marketplace about customer needs, expectations of quality, the quantities required, and when and where these will be delivered. They will also help to feed back new ideas to the design teams, in order to help them meet the perceived needs of customers.

While the operations department has long-term concerns about capacity and development, maintenance, trained and skilled labour and product and service development, in the short term the planning must be concerned with how to meet the stated demand (forecasts and known orders) for products and services within these limits.

Setting objectives

The effective management of operations, as with all other management functions, requires that specific measurable objectives are set with given times within which they must be achieved. This enables the manager to measure performance, to see if operations have been carried out effectively and efficiently.

To be *efficient*, the production processes for products and services must operate to standards set within the constraints of cost, time and quality standards. To be *effective* in meeting its mission statements the organization must produce products and services which satisfy the customers.

There is a cautionary tale of an organization which boasted of its fine filing cabinets that were so well designed and engineered that you could drop them from a fourth-floor window and they would still be in one piece when they hit the ground ... but when was the last time you needed to throw your filing cabinets out of the window?

Producing a quality product is not enough, the products must also meet identified customer needs.

Managing the organization of services and products

Types of processes and the implications for operations control

This section looks at the types of operating processes in manufacturing products and delivering services.

Manufacturing processes

There are three types of process in manufacturing operations: job, batch and flow; although many operations use a combination of these types. The main factor that determines the choice of process is the volume of production and potential demand. A *job* production process usually produces single units, *batch* processes are used to produce volumes between two and several hundreds, while *flow* processes are used for the mass production of thousands of units. These are discussed in more detail later in the chapter.

Service processes

With some services, production and consumption of the service often occur at the same time. This means that the service cannot be made and stored. There are often tangible and physical aspects to a service which can be manufactured or bought in, and the operations processes for these can be managed using the same processes as above, normally job or batch processes. The final assembly of the service, however, is often in the presence, and often with the participation of the customer.

In service operations the activities are divided into 'front office' and 'back room' tasks. The front office is visible, and is where contact with the customer takes place, while the back room is where normal operational processes occur. The server – customer interface may be face to face, by telephone, or by a machine such as an automatic cash dispenser.

The server at the point of contact may have to undertake several roles. For example an assistant in a shoe shop has to:

- Be the receptionist making the first contact
- Diagnose the needs of the customer, e.g. shoe size, type of shoe, colour, etc.
- Offer alternatives to satisfy the customer's needs
- Sometimes encourage further sales such as shoe polish

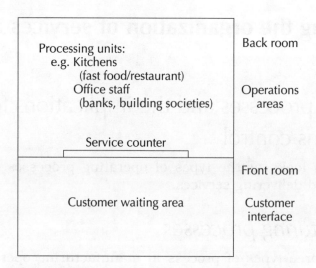

In some service outlets the 'back room' operations are made visible to the customer. Sometimes this may lead to a sense of frustration for customers if they are waiting in a queue and they can see staff who seem not to be fully occupied.

Figure 3.1 *Front room / back room service operations*

■ Invoice and collect payment
■ Update the stock control system.

In service operations, the provider of the service in the 'front office' has to be closely involved with the quality of the service delivered. There will also need to be a quality assurance process at the interface between the front office and back room. The operations manager has to ensure that the back-room activities produce the physical and tangible aspects of the service package to quality standards, as well as managing the ephemeral and intangible aspects of the customer interaction in the front office.

Job or unit production

This involves making a product or service to order rather than producing stock where sales may be made later to customers, as yet unidentified. It usually involves specialized or customized items where the order will not be repeated, at least not for a long time, when the specifications may have altered to a small or large degree.

The range of operations included in the job category includes large projects requiring a dedicated project team as well as smaller one-off products or services. The large-scale projects include those where the product cannot be moved after completion, and has to be built or finished on site. Examples include civil engineering projects such as bridges or transport systems, construction projects, defence and aerospace products, or the building and installation of machinery for complex processes. These activities use a project-management approach.

Service examples include the planning, organizing and management of special events, some of which may occur annually such as exhibitions – the Motor Show or Ideal Home Exhibition, a concert series or a promotional event.

On a smaller scale, it may include one-off specialist projects or consultancy contracts or event management. Examples here include designing and printing a one-off sales brochure, providing packaging for awkward or non-standard size goods; haute couture and other hand-made clothing or products; tailor-made training programmes or customized computer software programmes.

The organization is providing a product or service which may be uniquely tailored to the customer's needs. The customer is usually involved in the project development from the design stage.

The problems for the organization in adopting a job process are those discussed for project management, considered later in this chapter. While the project team may be using the same skills for each job, it faces a new challenge each time. This requires an adaptable and flexible use of staff and equipment.

The organization may not be able to benefit from bulk purchasing and economies of scale. However, while the team develops experience in a range of activities and situations, if demand drops it may be difficult to reallocate specialized staff or equipment. This may result in higher unit costs.

As jobs are made to order, it may be difficult to schedule activities and workloads until future business is confirmed.

Batch production

In this process, used for larger volumes of units, up to several hundred at a time, the operations are broken down into a number of tasks and a 'batch' lot of items are passed through one operation process before starting the next activity. As an item finishes one activity it waits as part-finished stock until all the items in the batch have been through that stage of the process. This may be achieved by moving the batch through a series of processing machines, or by resetting the same machine to undertake a separate task.

Batch processing can be used for processes such as printing or machining, including turning, milling, grinding and drilling. Services such as computer analysis and tabulation, data processing and marketing research analysis may use a batch process.

The operations management problems associated with batch processing include the short-term scheduling, loading, sequencing and routing of batches through the various process and equipment. For operations where the machines need to be reset between batches, an important aspect in the layout and design of the process is to minimize set-up times for the machines between batches. Increasingly this is done by sophisticated equipment controlled by computer.

Various process layouts have been designed to schedule routing of batches through the various stages. In some cases the items are returned to a central point to wait before being allocated to the next process; in other cases the goods are moved physically to another part of the plant where the next series of operations take place, so that the part-finished goods and sub-assemblies progress through the plant smoothly.

Flow, line or mass production

This process involves the movement of items through all the stages of the process without stopping at each stage to wait for the batch to be completed or machines reset. This process tends to be used for high volume manufacturing, for example of consumer durables and vehicles.

In its extreme stage of development it can become *continuous processing* where the plant is designed to run non-stop over 24 hours because of the high levels of automation. At this stage the staff take on a monitoring role rather than active participation in the processing activities, such as in the processing of chemicals, natural gas or petroleum products.

In designing the layout for line processing, activities are divided into tasks of equal length. This maintains the smooth progress of items through the process. Subassemblies are moved around the plant between processes automatically, using mechanical means such as conveyor belts or overhead transport systems.

If one part of the line fails, the whole process has to stop. It is therefore important to ensure the timely arrival of sufficient raw materials, parts and suitably trained staff to operate the line. Interruptions to the process due to machine failure must be avoided. Planned and preventative maintenance of equipment is vital.

As the process flows through the plant without waiting periods, there should be no build-up of part-finished goods as in batch production and no need for storage space in the process. The aim is to have minimum interruptions to the line, but if demand falls there could be an excessive build-up of finished goods instead.

Computer-controlled processing systems

As with the planning of production purposes, computer programmes can be used to tackle complex activities.

Flexible manufacturing systems (FMS) – these rely heavily on computer control at all stages of the process to plan, route parts, control machines and materials flow, transport parts between machines/processes, to give instructions to the operator (human or robot) and maintain a database for monitoring and control purposes.

The system is operated automatically with minimal intervention by operators. It can deal with a number of processes for a range of products using *computer numerical control* (CNC) machine tools, which may be loaded or unloaded by robots or humans.

The main benefits of this system are better utilization of machines, steady flow of production and flexibility in operations. There are lower set-up times between processes when the activity is changed as this can be done automatically by the computer. The computer plans the best schedule to maintain high machine utilization, and less queuing of parts and stocks. Machines can be readily reprogrammed to take on different tasks, allowing immediate changes to avoid bottlenecks, overcome machine breakdowns or interruptions and update the design of products. This allows more certain delivery dates and the ability to react quickly to changes in market demand.

Robotics – with the increase in computer controlled processes there is a need for machines that can be programmed to undertake the heavier, repetitive and more unpleasant aspects of some tasks. Robots are programmable machines that can replicate some of the movements of humans.

Robots are used where heavy items need to be handled, and where the working environment is hazardous or unpleasant. They are ideal for working long, non-stop shifts at unsociable hours, where tasks are simple and repetitive or where quality is important and work must be consistent and to high tolerance levels. Their reliability and non-stop working can improve control of operations and reduce costs.

Robots can be static or mobile and vary from inflexible mechanical devices which proceed with a given task until instructed to stop, to 'intelligent' or 'sensor controlled' machines which can be programmed to choose an appropriate action in response to a set of external stimuli. These may be provided by physical touch, computer or robot vision or changes in environment such as moisture or temperature.

Cellular manufacturing – the use of 'cells' or small groups of machines. These work autonomously to process a group of parts or assemblies. The processing of the unit is completed as far as possible within the cell before it moves on to the next cell, assembly point or stock-holding centre. This system is widely used in the manufacture and assembly of cars and computing equipment. Robots may be used to load the machines and transport goods between cells, with minimum aid and monitoring by humans. Quality control, through inspection and corrective actions, will normally be handled within the cell.

An important implication in the use of cells is the changing role of the human workforce, requiring a flexible approach to the tasks which need to be undertaken in the cell, together with a commitment to achieving targets and concern for reaching quality standards. Workers work in teams with the 'foreman' becoming the 'team leader'. Staff training is needed both for developing multi-skill workers with the new technical skills and for changing attitudes to develop motivation and the interpersonal skills needed in teams.

Project management

Many operations processes contain a project as part of the process and these, as for self-contained projects, may require to be managed independently of the overall process. The project manager needs to manage and control the project often from start to finish.

The manager may, as part of a team, be concerned with assessing the feasibility of the project, estimating costs, and planning the schedule. Supplies and resources need to be identified and acquired. During the work the project manager will monitor and control the activities and appraise the performance of the team. Priorities must be established, critical activities identified and potential problems and difficulties anticipated.

Historically project management used to be found in the construction industry, however, it is now growing across many industries. The responsibilities of the project manager may cover all stages of the project and he/she needs a variety of management skills as well as a professional or technical speciality.

The design of products and services

In developing products and services they must be designed to meet the needs of the customer. The design team needs to consider hygiene and motivator factors in developing the product/service specification.

The *hygiene factors* are the physical attributes. These have to be there although they alone are unlikely to encourage the customer to choose that brand of product or service. If they are not included the customers may choose an alternative brand that does have them. The *motivator factors* are those that make this product/service the one they notice and want to buy or use.

Customers, in buying products or services, choose a mix of features, advantages and benefits that help them solve a problem and satisfy needs. Customers do not buy products, they buy solutions!

In designing new products and services, the marketing research stage is not just about establishing market size, but also about finding out how the customer wants to use the product. If you have a list of guidelines that can take your consumer through these stages, it can help you to define what they are looking for, and their needs and wants. Then the creative talents in the design team can start to turn it into something that is unique to your brand.

The actual design, including the technical skills and creativity of design plus where it will be positioned in the market place (given competitive offers), is the task for the design team. This also needs consideration of the cost of producing the product, the quality, the market size and the time-scale, as well as the competitive offers.

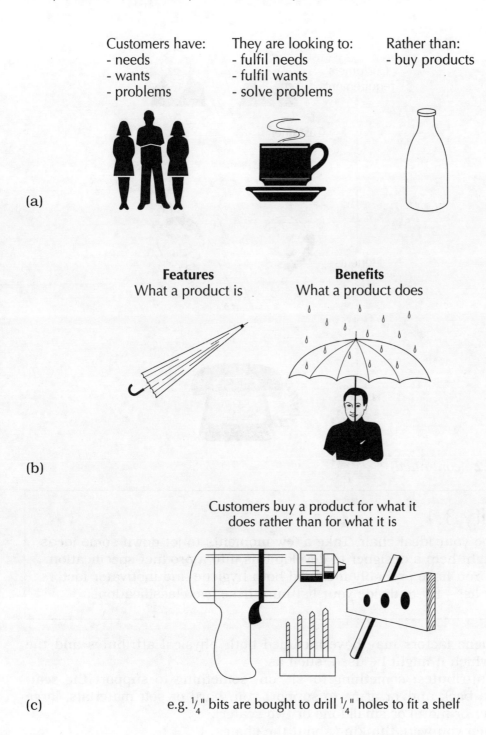

Figure 3.2 *What do customers buy?*

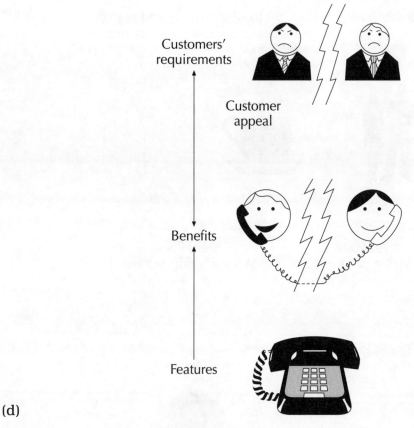

(d)

Figure 3.2 *(continued)*

Activity 3.1

Describe your ideal chair. Take a few moments to jot down some ideas that might help a designer to develop this into a product specification.

You have probably included both hygiene and motivator factors in your list – try to divide your list into these two classifications.

Your hygiene factors may have included both physical attributes and the ways in which it might be used, such as:

Physical attributes: something to 'sit' on, something to support the seat, possibly a back and/or arms to support you, hard or soft materials, large (two seater or more) or small (one or two seater).

When you were thinking about the chair:

- How did you see it being used?
- What was the purpose you had in mind?
- Was it to be used in an office for work or a home study perhaps?

■ Would it be used at a table?
■ Was it a chair for relaxing?
■ Who did you envisage using it?
■ Where?
■ How often?

All these considerations will have implications for the design and position of the product or service in the target market.

What about the motivators? What would make it really stand out in your mind above competing products? – shape? modernity? traditional/outrageous? Was it modern or traditional, unusual or conventional in style? See Figure 3.3.

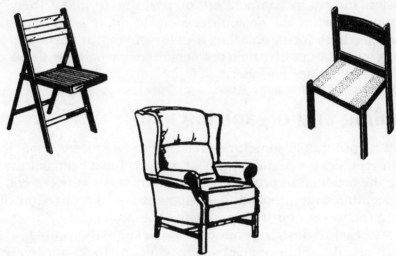

Figure 3.3 *Design a chair*

Research and development

This may be part of the design department or a separate department in its own right. It is normally concerned with looking at the technical development of materials and products and their implications for the organization's products and services.

In *'pure research'* the team explores 'state-of-the-art' issues, hoping to make breakthroughs which further scientific knowledge but are not immediately transferable to products or services. Sometimes research of this nature is supported by the government, or an industry syndicate. Organizations may sponsor original research at universities. However, this can sometimes lead to tension between the organization's need to maintain a competitive edge in converting breakthroughs into commercial products and the pressure on academics to publish their results.

'Applied research' could be a new way of solving a problem leading to a new product or improving a current range of products or services. Copying

and adapting competitive ideas is known as the 'me too' approach. This is often a less expensive option, providing an alternative for a product or service that already has a developed market rather than entering on the risk and expense of developing a market from scratch. When a completely new product is launched it involves educating consumers on what the product will do to help them, and convincing the distribution channels that there will be a demand if they take and promote the new product. Applied research is expected to provide results with immediate commercial applications.

Make or buy decisions

The decision to buy in components or parts or to make them within the organization is part of the design decision. In making this decision the or-ganization needs to focus on what it does; buying in parts where they are less able to control quality, delivery schedules or achieve the economies of scale achieved by other suppliers.

Scheduling and organizing work

The planning process is sometimes referred to as *process engineering*. Once the design specifications and quality standards have been set the process of designing the production process for the products or services can start. This involves deciding which tools and equipment are to be used in the process, scheduling the work, and then managing the project.

A successful design produces a package that gives a fast stock turnover. It should not become obsolete while in stock, nor require frequent changes in machine operations or design modifications. It should use as many standardized components as possible and be simple to process within the given standards of tolerance.

In order to plan, the manager needs to be able to forecast the require-ment for supplies of raw materials and components so that stocks are held to a minimum. The process should be planned to ensure a constant supply of finished goods or services in line with forecast demand levels and minimum operating costs.

Services need to be delivered quickly, on demand and with a minimum wait for customers. The service needs to conform to appropriate safety and quality standards, in an appropriate setting, but without allo-cating too many expensive resources. This is the skill of managing queues. It is a compromise between efficient use of the service providers and the acceptable waiting time for clients. We shall consider queues later in this chapter.

Forecasting demand

Forecasting methods use experience of previous events to predict likely future demand, by using mathematical models to extrapolate past trends, making the assumption that what has happened in the past will continue, if the factors that have influenced it continue. Judgement enters the forecasting process in estimating how far those factors and the resulting trends will continue in the same manner or, if they change, the degree and direction of the change. The complex forecasting models now available on computers can compare and interrelate large amounts of complex data and many variables to give a best, worst and probable estimate of future demand.

To forecast demand for products or services, the organization collects information from a variety of sources, both from published sources and market-research surveys. These are discussed in more detail in Chapter 4.

Short-term forecasts are concerned with detailed estimates for the near future, be that the next few weeks, months or a year. The operational manager can then schedule the production of products or staff needed to provide services. These forecasts are made within the context of *long-term forecasts* which look forward to factors expected to influence demand over longer periods of

---

Activity 3.2

Make a list of all the short-term planning which you think needs to be done to manage the day-to-day activities of a hospital ward.

Now think of the long-term planning needed to run the same ward. Which of these can be determined and which are uncertainties?

---

time and the investment in resources needed to meet these changes.

Your first list probably includes:

- Resources available – staff, beds, materials, drugs
- Number of patients
- Medical condition of patients
- Expected number of new patients
- Expected number of discharges
- Unexpected new patients – emergency admissions.

Your long-term list could include:

- Future demographic changes in the catchment area
- New treatments
- New drugs
- New materials

■   Changes in patterns of disease
■   Changes in funding methodology
■   Changes in the political climate
■   Changes in government policy
■   A change of government.

The demographic changes in the catchment area can be predicted reasonably, but changes in the external environment may not be so easy to predict.

Long-term forecasting

Long-term forecasts of demand and the factors likely to affect it are important in terms of developing and designing operations processes.

Scenario planning was developed in the 1970s by Shell UK. It is a
strategic process which considers alternative ways of dealing with changes
in external factors which affect their business. It includes political stability,
economic developments within their home countries and in developing
economies, international trade movements and barriers, exchange rates,
technological developments, exploration for oil fields and many other
factors. This technique has been widely adopted within organizations to help
develop contingency plans for future activities and investment.

Contingency planning involves thinking through and developing plans
to cope with conditions and events which may not happen, but which, if
they do, could have serious consequences for the organization and the way
it operates. In the broadest scenarios, these events are linked to a change in
investment and directions for the organization, and may occur gradually.
Elsewhere in the operations of the organization, there need to be contingency plans to deal with short- and medium-term events and those which
can have sudden and potentially serious effects on tactical operations plans.

Activity 3.3

Think about your own work, or an activity which you undertake regularly. List the tasks that need to be done tomorrow (short term), and
within the next month (medium term). What information would be
needed in planning these activities? How does your list differ for the
short- and medium-term activities? What information might be collected about things which will affect your work over the next five years?

Planning and scheduling tools

Gantt charts

This tool is a form of bar chart on a time-scale which can be used to compare *actual* progress with *forecast* progress. They were devised by H. L. Gantt (1861–1919) who worked in the area of statistical production control. The charts were devised for making simultaneous comparisons of the progress of several activities. See Figure 3.4(a).

Network analysis

Network analysis is used to plan, schedule, coordinate and control the work throughout the project. It is a representation in diagram form of all the activities in a project or process, and shows all the interconnecting links between events from the start to the finish of the project, showing the time needed to complete each stage. It can be used to determine the *critical path* of a project – that is the quickest time in which the entire project can be completed. Although network analysis can be conducted manually for more simple projects, usually a computer programme is essential.

Network analysis can be used for planning operations in any situation where a number of activities have to be completed within a specified time frame. This can include activities such as planning and constructing new facilities, installing new equipment, introducing new products or controlling sub-contract work.

Where the duration of activities can be estimated, network analysis becomes a useful tool which aids the planning process. It is not appropriate for those activities within the organization where there is no clear time horizon or it is difficult to predict the length of each stage, such as research and development activities.

It can be used to schedule resources, define work schedules, and monitor progress. Purchasing and stockholding can be scheduled at the appropriate time to reduce stocks held by an organization. It can also identify those tasks which are essential or critical to overall time-keeping and meeting deadlines. Potential problem areas are identified in advance and can be monitored more closely, or allocated extra resources or staff in time to avoid delays.

All the activities needed to produce the product or service have to be identified, with their most likely completion times. The inter-relationship between these activities must be defined – which ones have to be completed before others can start. This shows the order in which work has to be completed and areas where the completion date might be brought forward, by allocating more resources to critical or lengthy tasks. It indicates which tasks are less critical in timing than others, which may be batched together for processing when resources or equipment are available, or interrupted for work on more crucial areas. See Figure 3.4(a).

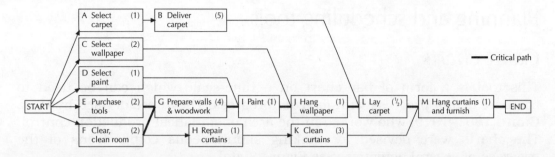

In network analysis the project needs to have a recognizable start and finish point. In this example it starts with the decision to redecorate and finishes when the room is ready for occupation again.

The project is then broken up into a series of activities of differing lengths, some of which need to be completed before others can start. The time needed to complete each activity is estimated. The network is then built as a logical sequence of events, showing those activities which need to be performed in a planned sequence, and those which can be undertaken simultaneously.

The time for each task is added to the diagram and the minimum time required to complete the project identified. The activities which take longest to complete before the next stage can start are the 'critical activities' and the critical path is the series that needs to be completed without interruption or waiting times to complete the project in the shortest time.

Each activity is placed on a node, and the duration, in days added.

Paths	Activity	Duration	
E/F–G–I–J–L–M	Decorating	$9\frac{1}{2}$ days	Critical path
A–B–L	Carpet delivery	$7\frac{1}{2}$ days	
F–H–K	Curtain cleaning and repair	7 days	

The critical path, is the decorating activities as this is longer than the others, and has to be done in sequence. However, as both the other paths involve outside agencies (carpet supplier, dry cleaners), if either of these activities take longer than schedule, the critical path can change. If, for example, the carpet delivery or curtain cleaning takes longer, the critical path will change.

Another problem may arise because the carpet is ready for delivery on Day 6 but it not due to be fitted until Day 8 and decorating will not be completed until the end of Day 7. This could cause storage problems so you might choose to start this activity later, or ask the supplier to delay delivery until Day 8 when the other activities will have been completed.

When planning and allocating resources to a project, it is important that the critical activities are carried out on schedule; if they are delayed it will delay the final completion time of the project. You will observe that some non-critical activities can start later than others and the project can still be completed on time. You may also choose to shorten the critical path, perhaps by asking a friend to help with the decorating (allocating more resources) and thus finishing the decorating activities ahead of schedule.

In this way you can look at a network and decide when the crucial times are for progress chasing, where there is slack in the network and when you might need to allocate more resources. The network shown above can also be shown as a Gantt chart. While the network is extremely useful for planning purposes, many managers find a Gantt chart easier to monitor work in progress.

— activity
– – 'float' days (spare days in hand)

Figure 3.4a *Critical path analysis example – decorating the spare bedroom*

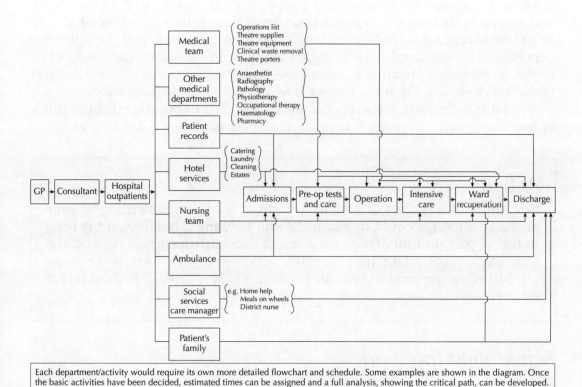

Each department/activity would require its own more detailed flowchart and schedule. Some examples are shown in the diagram. Once the basic activities have been decided, estimated times can be assigned and a full analysis, showing the critical path, can be developed.

Figure 3.4b *Flow chart showing complexity of activities to be scheduled for one patient from referral to discharge.* Source: based on an initial outline by Rhonda Morgan, North Yorkshire Health Authority.

In this way network analysis can be used to plan and schedule future work. It can then also be used in day-to-day operations to see where emergencies might occur, or where staff or materials can be reallocated in case of shortages.

Activity 3.4

Think of the activities which need to be planned in a hospital from the time the letter is sent to notify the patient of the date of the operation to their discharge. List the activities which you think might be involved and see if you can determine the critical path. This will involve deciding which activities have to be completed before the next stage can happen and which can run concurrently.

Your list will probably have covered administrative and nursing activities, admission, pre-operation tests and post-operation care as well as the 'hotel' services and other supply departments. Apart from nursing and medical staff in the ward and operating theatre, you may also have included the following departments: radiography, pathology, haematology, physiotherapy and occupational therapy, pharmacy, supplies, ambulance, porters, records and social services. See Figure 3.4(b) for how the critical path might look.

If this is the critical path to get one patient to the operating theatre, think of how much more complex it is to plan the operations for a day or a week.

Activity 3.5

Now think of a project or activity you do at work, or something in your personal life. This could be planning and booking a holiday and getting to the airport on time. Draw up a list of the activities involved, add the time each stage might take, identify which activities have to be completed before the next stage can happen. Draw a critical path diagram for your activity.

Scheduling the work

This involves sequencing, determining the order in which tasks will be undertaken. It determines start and finish times for each order or batch and allocates resources to the tasks. The resources needed in terms of materials, components, machinery and staff have to be assessed. The method of scheduling may differ for one-off jobs and projects, and for processes which are making items for stock. In the former the schedule needs to anticipate and control operations so that the delivery deadline is met; in the latter the schedule needs to take into account the optimum usage level of machines and other resources, to maintain an even level of production.

The task of scheduling is more straightforward where demand is known and stable, enabling reasonably accurate forecasts. Where there is uncertainty about the level or timing of demand for products and services, the problem of capacity planning becomes more difficult to detail in advance. It needs a higher degree of flexibility and shorter scheduling timetables to enable the organization to react to changes.

Capacity planning

The operations manager aims to match the level of operations with the level of demand. This needs to consider the trade-off between costs, standards and service levels. It is important in the manufacture of products not to achieve constant production schedules at the cost of building up large stocks which may later need to be discounted or deemed obsolete. In service industries capacity management is vital as the service cannot usually be stored, especially when the customer participates in the service!

Capacity planning requires decisions on the timing and level of demand for products and services and how these can be matched with available capacity. In the long term this may affect where the resources or site are to be located and how to cope with fluctuations in demand.

In such cases it is important to identify any patterns in variation. Demand may vary in the short term on a daily basis, for example the variations in demand for food in a restaurant, or the numbers of customers who need to shop during their lunch hour. There may be variations over longer periods, giving rise to predictable patterns such as the seasonal demand in warm weather for beach clothes and ice cream.

Once the pattern has been determined, the operations department has to cope with any variations. The organization might decide that it is more appropriate to vary the capacity available to cope with the peaks, rather than try to influence the demand pattern. Where insufficient capacity is available, the organization may decide to sub-contract some activities rather than to increase its capacity.

There needs to be a trade-off between optimum capacity levels and customer requirements and satisfactions. If other organizations can manage capacity more efficiently, customers may be lost to them.

Vary capacity

- By scheduling more staff for peak periods
- By use of flexible equipment that can be switched from less urgent tasks at short notice
- By using subcontractors to provide materials or part-finished goods to cope with peaks in demand without maintaining your own over capacity at other times
- By sharing capacity with other organizations.

Manage the demand

- By marketing activities, price alterations, advertising
- By developing non-peak demand, mainly from other market segments
- By extending the product or service range to produce complementary products and services to fill times of low capacity
- By allowing stocks to rise in times of low demand to cope with period peak demand
- By introducing a reservation or appointment system for services
- By allowing customers to wait with longer delivery schedules or allowing queues to form.

Figure 3.5 *Managing variations in capacity*

Using computers to improve the quality of operations management

Most planning and control activities were originally undertaken manually, using charts and mathematical formulae. These can now be undertaken by computers. The technological improvements in processing information and using information technology, together with the lower costs of computing facilities, and readily available software packages mean that even small enterprises can use computerized planning and control systems in their operations departments. In larger organizations they have become an essential aid in design, planning and control activities. Computers can be used to help design, allocate resources, give instructions to the workforce and machinery and record all activities. They can take corrective action and order goods.

Modern data processing equipment offers cheap, fast analysis of complex activities and large quantities of data. They can store, manipulate, help to interpret findings and present results. Computers can perform the tedious tasks of processing and presenting vast quantities of data, possibly with fewer errors and in a fraction of the time that the old manual systems took. The manager can have access to better information, leaving more time to concentrate on its interpretation and use in decision making.

As operations become more complex there is greater pressure on operations managers to perform efficiently and effectively to meet predetermined and precise cost and quality targets. This makes the tasks of planning, scheduling and controlling the processes more vital. Speed and accuracy can be critical.

In all areas, computer technology can aid the manager, either using standard packages or customized programmes. The designers, operators and managers need to be trained in the use of the new technology, and require access to helplines in order to overcome technical problems.

PRODUCTION FORECASTS AND ACTUALS

| UNITS PERIOD | PRODUCT A | | | | PRODUCT B | | | |
| | | | CUMULATIVE TOTALS | | | | CUMULATIVE TOTALS | |
	FORECAST	ACTUAL	FORECAST	ACTUAL	FORECAST	ACTUAL	FORECAST	ACTUAL
1	2000	2000	2000	2000	4000	4000	4000	4000
2	2000	2100	4000	4100	4000	3800	8000	7800
3	2000	1700	6000	5800	4200	4200	12200	12000
4	2500	2200	8500	8000	4200	4200	16400	16200
5	2500	2300	11000	10300	4200	4200	20600	20400
6	2500	2500	13500	12800	4000	4200	24600	24600

The analysis allows the operations manager to see if the production output is sufficient overall to meet demand and where corrective action needs to be taken.

Figure 3.6 *Spreadsheet analysis*

At a simple level, standard *spreadsheet packages* can be used as a business tool for planning, budgeting and record keeping. Where spreadsheets are part of an integrated package, they can use the data to make graphs and charts for reports and visual presentations. This makes it easier to analyse and interpret the data. For example, it can analyse and compare outputs for machines, processes or departments, check progress against targets and trends.

Using computers in design

Computer programs are used widely both in the design of products and services and the production of drawings and data for specifications (*computer-aided design* – CAD) and in the design of the tools and manufacturing processes (*computer-aided manufacturing* – CAM) including the design of numerically-controlled machines (*NC machines*), robots and automated materials handling systems.

For more complex systems of operations and production, computers can link the design and production processes directly, with the computer linking the specifications to the programs for the machine tools (CADCAM). This is sometimes known as *computer-aided engineering* (CAE). Some organizations are adopting fully integrated computer-controlled systems, known as *Computer Integrated Manufacturing* (CIM) which integrates all processes by computer program, from design to machine-tool programming to the manufacturing process and quality control.

Using computers to plan and schedule operations

The process of combining the forecast demand and/or known orders into detailed instructions for work schedules, allocating work to resources and routing part-finished goods through the process has been made easier with the advent of affordable computer technology. In planning major projects computers can be used for *network analysis*, and in the daily instructions for materials and parts required, job allocation, scheduling and routing.

Using computers for stock control

Computers can be used to calculate optimum stock levels, monitor the levels of stocks available and then compare the two. They are used to provide information for decisions, to keep records and to issue purchase request forms and other paperwork, thus aiding the operations manager at the various stages of purchasing and stock control.

A *materials planning requirement* (MRP) resources stock-control program can link stock levels and usage to purchasing requirements. It provides information and issues official requisition forms, invoices and information for accounting and control purposes. Thus it provides information for management decisions and accurate stock records.

Purchasing and stock control issues

In an ideal purchasing and stock-control system, forecasts of demand would be accurate, planning would match implementation and goods would arrive at the right time, in the right quantity and of the right quality. As this rarely all happens at once, there is the need for organizations to balance orders for raw materials and components against the rate of usage, and to balance stocks against the cost of holding those stocks. Good analysis and control systems are required, which are frequently computer based.

Stocks can represent over 25 per cent of an organization's assets, so that the management of stock levels and costs is an important part of the operations management task. It is vital that the costs of ordering and holding are kept to a minimum. As always there is a trade-off between efficiency and service levels. The manager has to balance the need to hold stock levels down to control costs against the need to maintain an efficient resource utilization. Stock shortages can cause valuable equipment or other resources to be kept idle and customers' delivery dates may not be met. High or frequent stockout levels or longer delivery schedules may cause loss of distributors' or customers' goodwill. Eventually it may lead to loss of business as the customers turn to alternative sources of supply.

Various departments within the organization will hold different views of the ideal levels of stockholding. The operations departments will require sufficient raw materials and components to allow the smooth processing of items in accordance with planned work schedules without unplanned or undue downtime or idle capacity. Marketing and sales departments will favour a higher level of finished goods and spare parts for immediate sales and delivery without stockouts and loss of goodwill or competitive edge. The concern of the finance departments will be to keep all stocks at the lowest possible level to reduce their impact on cash flow and capital requirements. The ideal stock-control system will try to balance the needs of each department within the organization for adequate stocks where and when required but at the lowest possible level and cost.

Most large retail operations now link their stock control directly to sales of goods through the bar-coding on goods which is recorded at checkouts. It is a detailed system: one of the authors put three different types of mushroom in one bag, all of them the same price, but the checkout assistant had to sort and code them separately, explaining that each type had to be linked to its stock levels for performance analysis and reordering.

Stocks held by an organization include:

- raw materials
- components

- part-finished goods bought in to be processed
- work in progress as part-finished goods
- subassemblies as they move through the processing stages
- finished goods awaiting sale or delivery.

There may also be stocks of tools and consumables used during the processing, spare parts for maintenance or spare parts kept to service customer needs as after-sales service.

Optimum stock management systems

It is important to determine the optimum stock levels. Computer programmes are widely used to control stockholdings and reordering to maintain these levels.

An organizational policy on an acceptable service level for customers will also affect stock levels. This is often referred to as the percentage of sales that can be met from stock rather than back orders. Back orders are those taken when there is no stock available to cover the sale and must be met from current work in progress, usually to an estimated delivery date. Organizations need to determine what level of stockouts is acceptable to customers without losing goodwill and sales.

The costs that the manager has to take into account are:

- re-ordering materials
- holding stocks – an opportunity cost which means cash is tied up in holding stocks when it could be used for other projects which may give more return
- storing stocks – warehousing and handling costs
- stockouts – in terms of downtime causing idle resources, loss of goodwill or sales. These may involve judgement on the part of the manager on the basis of market knowledge and customer feedback.

In managing stock levels, it is important to identify the types of stocks which may be held and the reasons why they occur. The main types of stocks which may occur include:

- raw materials or components
- work in progress
- buffer stocks
- finished goods
- customer and service related stocks.

Raw materials and components awaiting processing

These are goods waiting to enter the process. Here the concern will be to evaluate lead times for delivery from suppliers. *Just-in-time* (JIT) is one process which aims to reduce stocks to a minimum. Low stocks at this stage reflect accurate knowledge of usage rates, a good knowledge of suppliers, delivery lead times and efficient purchasing and progress chasing methods. It relies on accurate information about when and in what quantity the goods are required.

Work in progress stocks

These are stocks which occur during the various stages of the operations, as part-finished goods wait in batch systems between processing points. As one activity finishes the goods wait for the next activity to start. This may be scheduled so that the operator or equipment is used to capacity, with less idle time.

Buffer stocks

Most organizations carry a buffer stock of raw materials and part-finished goods. This is the amount required to cover usage in the time period between ordering new materials and their arrival. This time period is known as the lead time. The manager has to decide how high or low this buffer stock can be. As estimated delivery times get longer, customers may prefer to go to alternative suppliers who can deliver from stock or who quote earlier delivery dates. JIT stock systems aim to operate without the safety net of a buffer stock. Buffer stocks may also be used as a protection against variations in demand and supply.

Finished goods stocks

A fluctuation may occur in demand, either seasonally or due to a temporary change in market conditions, which could lead to a period of inactivity at some stages of the operations process. In order to make better use of resources the decision may be made to continue producing stock to help smooth out the imbalance between production capacity and sales. However, this leads to a build-up of stock waiting to be sold.

A danger here is that the downturn may prove to be permanent, leaving the organization with excessive stocks of finished goods which may become obsolete or spoilt. Changes in market demand need to be evaluated carefully.

Customer and service related stocks

These are stocks that are related not to operational process but to marketing strategies. They may be items kept as spare parts for maintenance or repair of customers' equipment; or as a buffer stock for major customers who require guaranteed level of stocks to protect their own supply needs for a JIT system.

On a short-term basis, promotional campaigns or exhibitions may be expected to lead to an increased demand and stocks may be built up in anticipation. Cooperation is needed with the marketing and sales departments to control the level and timing of such stocks.

Conventional or classical stock control systems rely on estimating the balance between excessive stock and the danger of stockouts.

Classification of stocks

In deciding the method of stock control to be used for different categories of goods, an '*ABC analysis*', based on the Pareto principle, of 20 per cent of the items accounting for 80 per cent of the value, can be used. The aim is to divide all stock items into categories according to the stock value that they represent. A typical evaluation will show that 20 per cent of the items represent 80 per cent of the value of stocks required, these are termed 'A' category items. The next 35 per cent of items will represent 15 per cent of value – 'B' category goods, and the remaining goods (45 per cent) will account for the final 5 per cent of value – 'C' category goods. Once stock items have been classified, an appropriate stock control approach can be adopted.

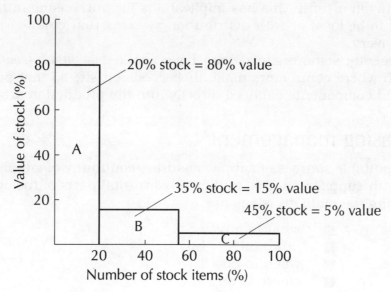

Figure 3.7 *Pareto diagram*

Category A goods carry the highest value and it is important to maintain control of their stock levels. This may be through a *periodic* reorder system. At regular fixed times, the stock level is checked and the quantity that has been used is reordered to bring stocks up to the predetermined optimum level. The time period is set in relation to the usage rate and lead times for delivery so that no stockout will occur.

Category B and C goods account for less value, and may use a *fixed quantity* order system where reordering will occur when a predetermined low level of stock is reached. Order size will be set to bring stocks back to optimum level again.

Just-in-time stock control systems

Just-in-time (JIT) is a system introduced originally in Japan and later adapted for use elsewhere. It aims to minimize stock levels by meeting the requirements of the next stage in the operating process for parts and materials on demand and immediately. It requires good information and control methods and a good relationship with suppliers. It also relies heavily on high levels of quality control in both supplies and processes within the organization.

A JIT system works with zero or the lowest possible stocks, with goods or services being delivered to the point where they are needed in exact quantities at the precise time that they are required. There are no obsolete or inferior materials, there is also no safety margin or buffer stock. Goods are ordered in the exact quantities for the next working period – often a day at a time. This has implications for purchasing in that suppliers have to be local or with distribution systems that enable frequent and rapid delivery.

Recently some organizations have adopted a *'just-in-sequence'* (JIS) approach where contractors make their goods on site so that part-finished goods and components can feed directly into the production process.

Purchasing management

Finding suitable sources of supply, ensuring continuity of supply and negotiating with suppliers on cost and quality are vital parts of the operation. In purchasing the main decisions are:

- what to buy
- how much to buy
- when to buy it
- where to buy it.

The purchasing department then monitors sources of supply to ensure value for money. It is now common to find organizations developing a better relationship with suppliers who become involved at the design stage, which can assist in achieving and maintaining quality standards.

Purchasing may be on contract, by quotation or on an 'as required' basis. Some suppliers may be given a blanket contract to cover a specified time period or to provide all requirements for a particular line or location. While broad levels of demand are agreed, quantities are called down as required. Where deliveries are quick and reliable this allows the organization to reduce its own stockholdings, and is used at extreme levels in just-in-time systems. However, such contracts will normally carry fixed-price agreements.

Quotations against tenders may be used in large-scale and complex projects or in purchasing services. Explicit tender documents are produced and contracts are awarded against set criteria. The purchasing department may oversee the process and make sure that it meets the legal and contract requirements of the organization, but user departments will be closely involved in the selection.

Some organizations operate a 'consignment stock' process. It is similar to a sale-or-return system which offers a cost saving for both the manufacturer and the supplier. The goods are stored, free of charge, on the manufacturer's premises. The organization has assured supplies for the operations process, but they are invoiced at regular intervals only for the amounts used. The quantity and a minimum stock level is agreed, in advance, by the purchasing department, site engineer and supplier. A weekly computer tabulation is produced to show how much has been used and the purchase department raises an order for the amount which has been used to bring it back to the minimum stock level. This is the amount invoiced by the supplier. If required, daily tabulations can show when or if there are any abnormal usage levels which would require special action.

Centralized purchasing and stock systems may be used in larger organizations which operate at scattered sites, such as retail or service organizations. A centralized materials management function will allow bulk buying benefits, and specialization by buyers. It works well where many standardized items or components are used, but is not so suitable for the control of perishable or bulky items or where localized differentiation is required.

Managing queues

Operations managers need to balance the use of resources against the costs incurred. Imbalance can either mean too many resources are used or queues form.

In service industries long queues may lead to customer frustration, loss of goodwill, and eventually, loss of the customer.

In manufacturing industries queues occur when one process is working faster than the next. Here it affects the efficiency and smooth flow of materials and parts through the production process. Machinery stands idle and stock builds up. In motor-car manufacturing a delay or disruption in the paint shop will cause cars to be held after being primed. Too long a delay may mean that the production line has to be stopped as there is insufficient space to hold the queue of cars waiting to be painted.

The operations manager is faced with the questions:

■ How long a queue is acceptable?
■ How should the queue be managed to minimize customer frustration?
■ At what point will customers switch to an alternative supplier?

The mathematical models used in queuing theory are based on:

■ The average processing or serving time.
■ The average time between arrivals of work or customers.

As an illustration consider customers arriving at a supermarket checkout. If one checkout can serve, on average, twenty customers an hour, this gives an average serving time of 3 minutes per customer. It is most unlikely that a customer will arrive at the check-out every 3 minutes. If customers arrive more frequently they will have to queue, less frequently and the checkout assistant will be idle.

There will also be variation in the time taken to serve the customers – after all, 3 minutes is the average time. Have you ever arrived at a supermarket check-out with a basket containing only a few items to find two customers in front of you with trolleys fully loaded with goods? The total time taken to serve all three of you may not exceed 9 minutes, but you probably queued for 8 of them!

The aim of queue management is to balance the service level to the customer with the cost of providing the service.

Activity 3.6

Next time you find yourself in a queue ask yourself:

1   What is causing the queue?
2   Is the wait acceptable?
3   What could be done to shorten it?
4   What are the reactions of other people in the queue?

Figure 3.8 *A queue*

Solving the queuing problem

There are really only two solutions to any queuing problem:

1   Reduce the queue length and/or the waiting time. Some supermarkets promise to open another checkout (unless all are already open) when there are queues of more than two customers. They do this by rescheduling staff from other duties.

In manufacturing a faster processing time can help shorten the queues. This can be achieved by improved technology, more automation, better planned layouts or systems, more staff or better trained staff.

The M25 motorway has a variable speed limit on certain busy sections. This aims to manage the traffic flow and reduce the traffic jams.

2   Manage the queue to make it more acceptable to the customers. Doctors' and dentists' surgeries and hairdressers have always supplied magazines in their waiting areas, and some hospital waiting areas now show videos. Theme parks give estimates of the queuing time for their popular rides, and put on entertainment for the waiting children.

In all queuing situations it is worth involving both the staff and the customers in seeking solutions. Staff then 'own' the problem, and are motivated when they see their ideas and actions leading to improvements. Customer perceptions are important: do they prefer a slow moving short queue to a faster moving long queue, even if the eventual queuing time is the same? At what point will they take their custom elsewhere?

Handling interruptions and contingency planning

Interruptions in the manufacturing or service delivery process disrupt the flow, may cause bottlenecks, loss of production (downtime), late deliveries, customer dissatisfaction or the imposition of penalty clauses. They may be anticipated or occur as an emergency, have short- or long-term effects and result from external or internal interruptions to resources, including supplies, equipment, shortages in staff or appropriate skills.

Contingency plans to overcome interruptions should be included in the overall departmental plans. Short-term interruptions may be tolerated or dealt with by routine reactions, whereas more long-term interruptions may need more radical changes. Plans may cover having alternative sources of supply or standby equipment. For example, in the intensive care ward of a hospital, there will be provision for generators to be used in the event of a failure in the electricity supply, which would cause life-saving machinery to fail. Resources may be diverted from other activities; other methods of production used, involving reworking of materials or goods or sub-contracting work. In extreme cases this could lead to long-term changes in production processes or supplier relationships.

External circumstances are usually beyond the control of the organization, but must nevertheless be anticipated by managers. Late delivery of materials and stock shortages may be caused by problems such as strikes in other industries; disruption in international supply routes caused by adverse climatic conditions, by war or threatened war or unrest; by trade barriers which are temporary or long term. The operations manager needs to monitor such events and gauge their likely duration and the seriousness of the impact on resources for the organization.

Internal interruptions in the supply of resources may be caused by plant and machinery breakdowns; computer malfunctions; stock shortages; problems with stock quality; staff absenteeism, sickness or lateness.

Consumer service organizations, such as water, sewage, electricity, gas and telecommunications companies, need to have emergency repair staff so that disruption to customers' supplies are repaired as rapidly as possible. The manager needs to monitor the availability of staff with appropriate skills. A computer control system can combine a database of the staff, their skills and ability levels to tackle various problems, and their availability. It can also record all information about job times and work done for regular managerial reporting systems. It can then be linked to a graphics package which presents the data in both graph and tabular formats. See Figure 3.9.

SEEK-CALL

DO YOU NEED TO GET THE RIGHT PERSON
TO THE RIGHT PLACE AT THE RIGHT TIME?
DO YOU NEED TO CALL STAFF TO FIX PROBLEMS?
DO YOU NEED TO MANAGE "CALLOUTS" MORE EFFECTIVELY
THEN SEEK-CALL IS YOUR ANSWER

WHAT IS SEEK-CALL?

SEEK-CALL is a modular call manager with 'Point and Click' mouse operation that is simple and fast to operate with a built in telephone dialler. SEEK-CALL has been developed over many years in close co-operation with users to give a practical system suited to your every day requirements.

WHAT DOES IT DO?

SEEK-CALL selects the right person for the job without local knowledge. It keeps track of the progress of the work and records completed work. SEEK-CALL automates rotas, dispenses with complex paper records and copes with the inevitable changes of operational requirements.

FEATURES

- Simple 'Point and Click' mouse operations
- Screen dialling and paging with built in dialler
- Pick sites from displayed listing or code
- Call list automates staff selection
- General phone book with screen dialling
- Speaker gives hands free monitoring
- Three skills for every site
- Staff holiday absences programmable
- Recording to date and time stamped files
- Work records provide management information
- Training minimised with intuitive operation
- Modules allow additional features when required
- System tailored by experienced users
- Proven system from experienced supplier
- Upgrade path to networked systems

SITE SELECTION (site)

Site selection from a 'Pop up' window automatically gives the correct Call List without local knowledge.

SKILL SELECTION (6)

Every site can have three call lists for multi-skill needs, each site can have different lists for flexibility.

CALL LISTS (A to H)

The Call List displays the Callout staff, select the entry then telephone or page by selecting 1, 2 or 3.

SCREEN DIALLING (1 & 2)

All dialling of calls is by 'Point and Click' on the screen with the built in dialler. This speeds up operations and minimises 'Late Night' errors.

STAFF DATABASE

Staff are visible in the staff database display, simply add to the Call List by picking from the listing.
Selecting the entry automatically adds the name to the Call List together with the call information.

BROWN A	KENT C
CHARLES C	MILLER P
EVANS M	NORTON P
HEAL F	PRICE M
JONES RE	REED B

SCREEN PAGING (3)

Tone page by 'Point and Click' or message page from screen or keyboard with message pager module.

PHONE BOOK (F3)

F3 provides a 'Pop up' phone book at any time for those useful telephone or pager numbers using built in dialler.

COMMENTS (5)

Each Call List can have comments to give flexibility for temporary changes, these cancelling on pre-set dates.

UNAVAILABILITY

Pre-programming up to ten entries each person for holidays and training etc. This avoids calls to staff who are unavailable. Entries cancel on pre-set dates.

STAFF DATA

```
Evans M
1st   TEL        123456789   Staff radio call  Radio
2nd   TEL        34567890    Staff comment  A comment
Staff pager/type 1234567/0   Staff record     45
Staff fax        0978546     Staff record currently
Staff default location           unlocked
                 School Lane staff  alloc tasks (0)
Staff grade      WE 222      staff hold tasks (0)
Staff manager    MANAGER
```

Comprehensive staff data with contact numbers and personal comments. Management information can allow sorting of records to the appropriate manager.

TASK TRACKING

```
Enter problem    A PROBLEM ENTRY FIELD
                 TRACK AND RECORD
```

A fault summary may be entered and combined with Task recording to provide records of work and tasks.

TASK RECORDING

Tasks may be recorded and cleared to date and time stamped files. This allows quick operational checks and provides a source of management information.

Figure 3.9 *SEEK system*

```
SMITH A Task 49
Site name      : SEEK
Receive date   : 22-02-94  Allocate date : 22-02-94
Receive time   : 11:53     Allocate time : 11:53
Complete date  :
Complete time  :
Fault report   : ALARM
Clear          :
Clear comment  : ADD A COMMENT TO THE FAULT CLEAR
```

CALL LIST

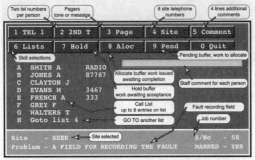

```
1 TEL 1    2 2ND T    3 Page    4 Site    5 Comment
6 Lists    7 Hold     8 Aloc    9 Pend    0 Quit
```

```
A  SMITH A     RADIO
B  JONES A     87767
C  CLAYTON J
D  EVANS M     3467
E  FRENCH A    333
F  GREY F
G  WALTERS T
H  Goto list 4
```

```
Site    - SEEK                        S/No  - 58
Problem - A FIELD FOR RECORDING THE FAULT   MANNED - YES
```

A call list is the centre of operations, all contacts can be made from this screen.
A call list can apply to any number of sites simplifying and speeding data entry.
Up to eight entries on each list with every site offering three call lists for multi-skill requirements.
A GO TO entry allows unlimited continuation to other lists.

WORK RECORDS

Even if Task details are not recorded as above transactions are recorded and can be reviewed at any time.

```
                    Options
1 - Closed log files    4 - Change log files
2 - Telephone log files 5 - Quit
3 - Comment log files
```

All calls and transactions are recorded to Log and telephone files. These are kept for each day. Comment log kept for each month. Change records all data changes. The default daily log file is kept for all transactions and records the following information:

```
REC > 22-02-94  11:57 ENTER PROBLEM TRACK
                           AND RECORD
SITE > SEEK
ALOC > 22-02-94  11:57 SMITH A

COMP > 22-02-94  11:57 CLEAR  A CLEAR COMMENT
```

REC	- Received time	Recorded information
SITE	- Site name	Site or location
ALOC	- Allocated time	Allocated to
COMP	- Completed time	Clear comment

ROTAS (optional)

```
        Rota setup
1 - Change daily rota time
2 - Change weekly rota times
3 - Rotate all weekly rotas
4 - Rotate all daily rotas
5 - Previous menu
```

The Rota module allows automatic Daily or Weekly rotas. The Rota option will then rotate the call lists presenting the correct staff at the top of the displayed Callout list.

We pride ourselves on personal attention and support and we can provide tailored software solutions

Figure 3.9 *(continued)*

OPTIONAL MODULES*

The starter module can be expanded to suit your needs with additional modules as required.

MESSAGE PAGING*

Send pager messages direct from keyboard or from present messages on the screen by using the paging module and built in modem.

ROTAS*

The rota module allows preprogramming of rotas with automatic rotation staff on call lists. Rotas can be daily or preprogrammed from four weekly options.

STAFF QUALIFICATION*

Staff records of skills allows you to allocate work correctly, assist in BS 5750 and aid holiday planning.

SYSTEM CAPACITIES

Sites	2000	Telephone book	150 per
Call lists	1000	(Pop up)	letter (A to Z)
Staff	600	STAFF DATA	
		Telephone	
Staff per call list	8	numbers	2
Skills per site	3	Pager	1
Site Tel numbers	8 per site	Comment	1 line
Site comments	2 lines, timed	Unavailability	10 entries

REPORTS*

Produce management data for reports automatically with analysis of transactions.

Computer Telephony integration

Computer and Telephony integrated systems; Auto Attendant and Voice Mail are available as stand alone systems or linked to Seek configurations.

EXPANSION

'SEEK' systems can provide a comprehensive range of Call and Task managers. These can be existing designs or custom built to your exact requirements. Seek systems range from the SEEK-CALL, stand alone, to custom designed touch screen networked staff and Task management systems, these can be integrated with computer controlled telephony to provide comprehensive control solutions. Our range also includes specialised display boards linked to custom designed software.

SYSTEM REQUIREMENTS

PC	386SX 25 MHZ or better; 4 Meg RAM, 80 Meg Hard disk; 3½ in Floppy, VGA colour monitor; 2 Free expansion slots. Mouse
Telephone	Pulse or tone dialling Direct line or extension
Support	90 days hot line, extendable
Package	Software, Manual, Built in dialler, loud speaker. Modules as required
Optionally	Complete system
Upgrade	Task manager customised systems, Touch screen and networked

B & W ASSOCIATES

DENBI HOUSE, 11 THE WARREN, CHESHAM, BUCKS HP5 2RX
Tel 0494 771325/0707 874494 Fax 0494 785635

Sometimes interruptions are caused by the breakdown of equipment. Regular servicing and maintenance is essential. Occasionally, where a piece of equipment is critical to the production flow, standby equipment may be kept to cover production even if this is at a reduced flow rate while the main equipment is being repaired. Sometimes this will be a general purpose piece of equipment which can normally be used on other non-critical tasks or for spare capacity at peak times. Operations managers have to consider the trade-off between keeping standby equipment in case of emergencies, against costs of downtime on critical operations.

Where new systems are introduced, for example a new computerized payroll programme to replace a manual system, the old and new systems may be run side by side for a short period. This allows any technical difficulties to be corrected and staff to be trained to use the new system within a tolerable error level.

Sometimes an interruption may lead to the production of some items that do not meet quality control levels and there may need to be considerable reworking of items or materials.

Quality assurance and control

Why measure quality?

Quality is a concept that tries to ensure customer satisfaction. Accreditation for an internationally recognized quality standard, such as ISO 9000, may offer a competitive edge or be a requirement in an industry where customers insist on accredited suppliers, which is happening increasingly in Europe.

Quality may be interpreted in different ways by different groups of people – both inside and outside the organization, depending on whether they consider price, cost or value to be most important.

Activity 3.7

Recognizing quality: consider the products or services of your own organization, or one with which you are familiar. How would you define their quality? Do you think that others would give a similar definition?

The *design department* may see a 'quality' product as one where no expense is spared to provide 'good' quality materials and processes, to provide a 'high quality' product which meets its technical specifications in performing the required functions.

The *operations department* may regard a quality product as one that is consistently within the tolerance requirements, with no errors or rejects.

The *finance department* may interpret 'quality products' as those where the product, while fitting the purpose for which it was intended, is produced at the lowest possible cost to provide target contributions to overall profits.

The *customer*, on the other hand, may be looking at 'value for money' – which may not always be the cheapest product available. For some customers this means a low-cost item which performs tolerably well and which will later be discarded. Another customer may see 'quality' as a high-price product which 'looks its price' and will last a lifetime. Still others may be concerned only with appearance but not too concerned if it lasts! This might be the difference between a low cost ball point pen and a high-price fountain pen. Both perform the same basic function – as a tool to write with – but each will carry a different connotation of value in the eyes of the customer. This depends upon need and perceived value, which is discussed further in Chapter 4.

So which of these views of quality is right? Or are all of them right for their own objectives? Must quality always be defined in clear details? The answer is yes – quality can only exist as it relates to the objectives set for that particular product or service for a specified group of customers or users.

The operations definition of quality will cover a number of aspects: the product or service must be fit for its purpose, reliable in use, last for the expected amount of time, be trouble free in operation, and be pleasing to the customer. The delivery of the product or service must meet agreed or promised time schedules, and arrive in the quantity ordered. A quality approach helps to develop a cost-effective operations process which eliminates waste and duplication and reduces the cost of errors.

The operations manager will be concerned with two major categories of quality – conformance and design quality.

Conformance quality refers to the degree to which an item satisfies its technical specification. It may include fitness for the purpose for which it is intended, how well the end product meets its design specification and designed tolerance levels; consistency of output to these standards, product reliability in use and longevity, costing structure, ease and speed of machining, processing or preparation.

Design quality includes all the attributes that will make the item a 'quality' product or service as perceived by the group of customers at whom it is aimed. This may include how well it satisfies the customers' particular requirements (the functions it performs and fitness for purpose); customers perceptions of value for money and price level; product reliability and longevity, ease of installation or use; availability or accessibility (location of service, the need to queue, delivery or ready availability of products and services in a number of outlets); a satisfactory range of functions and characteristics, aesthetic appeal and overall image.

It can be seen that some, but not all, of the aspects of quality are common to both categories. The designer may have to choose between the requirements of the two categories where there is a conflict.

Total Quality Management (TQM)

Total Quality Management has grown out of the work of W. Edward Deming, who introduced Japanese methods in his organization after the Second World War. It entails a wider interpretation of quality management – not just for finished goods inspection but an approach for the entire operations of the organization. Quality becomes the responsibility of every employee from the senior management levels down to the least skilled and, wherever possible, encompasses external organizations including suppliers, contractors and distribution and sales outlets.

The Chartered Institute of Marketing describes it as follows:

> A TQM approach means management must train and motivate staff both to enable and to empower them to take responsibility for their own performance. Everyone has to work to satisfy the needs of the internal and external customers. The focus on internal customers necessitates the breaking down of functional barriers and the improvement of internal communications. The customer must be seen not only to be the external purchaser and end user, but also the internal customer – colleagues and other departments. The next person to handle your work is one of your customers.

The organization incorporates a commitment to quality in its mission statement and strategies adopted, and creates a framework which enables quality to be achieved at all levels and in all activities. This may involve attaining recognition for one of the national or international standards for quality.

Total Quality Management relies on setting up procedures to ensure that quality is planned in advance rather than relying on a post-operation inspection of the quality achieved. It attempts to make sure the output is right and avoids interruptions and costs of failure after the event.

Activity 3.8

Think about an organization with which you are familiar. Does it have a total quality management policy? How could you measure an improvement in quality?

Standards for quality assurance

There are international standards regulated by the International Standards Office which provide a framework against which organizations can judge their own procedures. The original UK standard, BS 5750 was a framework designed to achieve this but it has now been superseded by the International Standard ISO 9000. The standards arose originally from military standards and procedures in engineering inspection and control but have now been extended to include many facets of the organization.

Applying the Standards does not of itself guarantee quality, but allows the organization to consider how to achieve it. It provides a written framework for planning, monitoring and controlling processes in order to introduce best practice.

Quality assurance is the total system needed to assure quality for customers, by showing that the organization is working to set standards in all aspects of its operations. Accreditation for internationally recognized standards goes beyond operations activities and is seen as part of a TQM approach – where everyone within the organization is made aware of quality criteria and procedures.

The framework requires detailed documentation, the preparation of which encourages organizations to identify and evaluate operations and implement improvements. This can lead to more efficient working practices, minimize waste and errors, and help to build team spirit. The ultimate goal is the consistent provision of quality products and services which satisfy customer needs.

There are two main manuals that need to be prepared for registration for ISO 9000. The first covers the quality policy and must include a statement of the organization's intent and commitment to quality. The second manual, on operations procedures, details the procedures to be implemented, those people given authority and responsibility for implementation, the resources available and the arrangements for regular internal audits. It must also indicate how the policy will be communicated to all employees.

Environment management standards are an area of growing importance concerned with managing the quality of the internal and external environment. These too now have their own set of UK and international standards.

Activity 3.9

Environmental issues include looking at 'environmentally friendly' ways of producing products and services. Think what this could mean for an organization with which you are familiar.

Formal quality assurance standards which the organization may introduce in processes and approaches are designed to raise awareness of quality issues amongst all employees. This provides a backdrop of 'quality orientation' within the organization, and needs to be encouraged from the top levels of management.

Standards are also being introduced for staff training within organizations in order to encourage the adoption of best practice for the industry or profession. Investors in people, championed by the Confederation of British Industry, is concerned with the organization's approach to internal communication and training to maintain quality standards. Many professional institutions are encouraging their members to keep themselves up to date through continuing professional development (CPD).

Activity 3.10

Think about a task you do at work, or as a hobby. If you had to write a procedure for controlling the quality of the process and output, what standards could you set to ensure the quality of the outcome and what control processes could you implement to ensure this?

Systems to control quality

Inspection and quality control

Centralized inspection: may be used when specialist test equipment or technical skills are required for inspection purposes. This may be located in one department which undertakes inspection tasks for all materials, part-finished and finished goods throughout the organization.

It can lead to difficulties in selecting the sample for inspection, transporting the items to the central location and the time gap in waiting for results. If processing continues meanwhile, and a fault is found, it may mean that the entire batch needs to be scrapped or reworked. It can also hold up the flow of the process if the goods need to be inspected before they can move onto the next stage.

A more serious disadvantage that can occur with centralized inspection is a change in the attitude of the operatives, who adopt the view that quality is the task of a small specialized section and therefore not their responsibility.

Decentralized inspection can vary from inspectors on the 'shop floor' who test materials and goods during or at points between the processing stages to fully integrated inspection undertaken during the process and monitored by computer programs. The benefit is that problems and variances from standards are identified quickly and can be remedied immediately. The inspectors can be integrated with the work team, and discuss issues of quality on a regular basis.

Achieving quality

Measurement of products which are substandard or rejects for reworking or scrap may occur because of faults in raw materials or components, equipment or operating processes. Standards are set giving the tolerance levels (deviation from specification) and the number of substandard items in a batch that will be accepted. The inspection process then only interrupts the process if that level is exceeded. This might allow, for example, five imperfect items in every hundred, the five items being reworked later, scrapped or sold as seconds.

The ultimate goal is defect-free work based on the notion of zero defects and rejection of 'acceptable' quality levels. An illuminating example comes from an IBM subsidiary based in Ontario who ordered a shipment of components from a Japanese supplier. They specified their acceptable quality level as three defective parts in every 10 000. In a covering letter from the Japanese supplier which accompanied the shipment, they stated how difficult it was to produce the defective parts, saying 'We Japanese have hard time understanding North American business practices. But the three defective parts per 10 000 have been included and are wrapped separately. Hope this pleases.'

Many of the processes or approaches adopted in quality assurance were originally developed in Japanese organizations and have been adapted and developed for use in other types of organizations.

Quality circles

A quality circle is a discussion group of up to twelve staff, normally within the same work area, who meet regularly to identify and find solutions to quality issues. Membership of the group is voluntary and the circle chooses its own problems to discuss. Solutions are presented to management, and if accepted, the group is involved, wherever appropriate, in the implementation and subsequent monitoring.

While originally the groups were formed to look at quality issues, they often expand to looking at a wide variety of work-based problems, and become part of an organization's approach to total quality management.

To be successful they need top-level management commitment, and an atmosphere which indicates that authority, resources and support will be given to implement solutions. Often the team will require initial training in problem definition and decision making, and also support during the ensuing process.

It is important that the rest of the organization is made aware of the existence of the quality circle and what they are trying to achieve. Recognition must also be given widely to any successful solutions that are implemented.

The benefits of circles are improved products, services and processes, consideration of problems and solutions by the employees responsible for implementation, and a more involved and committed workforce. Staff are encouraged to take more responsibility for the smooth operation of the organization.

Some drawbacks are the problems of maintaining commitment and motivation within the group, especially if some suggestions are considered inappropriate for adoption.

Zero defects approach

An approach to quality control and management which aims for a commitment to flawless output – no deviations of standards are expected. This is often adopted as targets for smaller cells and groups who can control their own efforts.

Kaizan systems

Another approach adopted from Japanese systems of management. This is a development of the quality circle approach which is designed to achieve the motivation and involvement of all employees in striving for quality. This approach encourages employees to consider not just the quality standards of what they currently do but to achieve continual improvement. This can be applied to all aspects of the organization and not solely operations control.

Monitoring and improving products and services

Reasons for monitoring activities

Managers need to keep records of activities and prepare reports on operations to feed into the planning and control process. The historic records are used in the planning process to help evaluate how activities have taken place, where problems arose and where savings can be made.

Other records are required for day-to-day management of activities, to identify problem areas and the cause of the problem so that corrective action may be taken as soon as possible. It is also necessary to check progress against targets regularly to enable schedules to be maintained or resources to be reallocated to ensure completion dates are reached.

Records are also required for financial reasons, both for budgetary control and for legally required records for balance sheet purposes.

Aspects to be monitored

Managers collect information during the process to enable them to compare what is being done to achieve intended outputs.

There are two aspects to monitoring operations. In both cases the use of statistical control models and computers are likely as the processes and analysis become more complex.

Performance monitoring

This involves the collection of data on a regular basis throughout the operations process to help monitor progress. The aim is to produce data and record what happens so that managers can identify problems and take corrective action.

Improving products and services

Organizations regularly review their products and services in order to maintain and increase customer satisfaction and sales. This leads to considerations of design to improve the product/service package and re-engineering to improve the processes used.

Obtaining and using feedback

Customer feedback on perceptions of service level, product or service quality is vital to managers. Not only will they be considering this, but they should also be evaluating rival products and services to ensure that they are maintaining a competitive edge. Feedback should be undertaken on a regular basis and include both quantitative and qualitative information. Methods of collecting such data are considered further in Chapter 4.

Process evaluation

The aim is to evaluate whether or not the process has been designed and planned in the best way to achieve target output at lowest cost. This involves defining the processes and how they operate against the objectives and standards. Corrective actions can be designed into the system.

Value analysis

In the effort to satisfy the customer in an economic way, value analysis can be used to look at the components and materials which contribute to a service or product package. The aim is to eliminate unnecessary components or processes, and to remove excessive specification. For example, a company which made printed labels used high-quality adhesives which would survive extremes of temperature and vibration over long periods of time. However, these labels were only being used during the transport and installation of machines – and the longest they would need to survive was six months. In this case, cheaper materials, which did not tolerate such extremes of conditions and did not have such a long life, could be substituted at great saving to the manufacturer. It also allowed them to reduce their price and become more competitive in the marketplace. As a result of reducing quality margins on this product the company actually increased both its market share and profits!

While there is always pressure for the operations manager to keep costs down while increasing efficiency, there may sometimes be a danger of sacrificing quality for low cost. If the customer perceives a reduction in value, even where changes are marginal and do not affect the safe or effective use of the product or service, customers may feel it no longer constitutes value for money and go elsewhere.

Value analysis should be a team activity and include representatives from design, engineering, purchasing, work study, finance and marketing so as to ensure that all aspects of the product or service and its market are considered.

Not all attempts at reducing costs are as successful as that of the label manufacturer. A chocolate manufacturer needed to react to the rapidly rising costs of cocoa due to various climatic and political problems in the producing countries. They thought that the price was the most important factor for customers; 28p was the price that customers had said was reasonable for a treat. They decided to continue to maintain their price but reduce the thickness of the bar to compensate for rising costs. Eventually it became a very thin bar indeed and the customers detected the change. At this stage the product was compared unfavourably by the customers with other chocolate bars and confectionery snacks that were available – even at higher prices. Somehow the thin bar just didn't seem value for money compared with the new chunky competitive products. Customers stopped buying the thin bars, the market share dropped and the manufacturer had to reintroduce the original thicker bar at a higher price.

Work study

Work study includes method study which aims to eliminate unnecessary tasks or duplication in operations, and work measurement which assesses the times taken to do each task and looks for ways in which time (and thus costs) may be saved. Standards can then be introduced, giving a basis for monitoring future performance.

Method study involves defining each task in the process so that duplication of effort or inefficient work practices can be identified and better methods introduced. Once the new methods are introduced, they need to be monitored and measured to assess whether improvements in performance can be maintained.

Work measurement involves the systematic study of each task to establish how long it should take and to set standards which will become yardsticks against which actual performance is then measured. Standards are usually set taking into account the experience and competence of the workforce, using average levels which can reasonably be maintained rather than the times of the most proficient. In some cases work measurement may show that the tasks could be undertaken by a less experienced or skilled workforce, leading to overall cost savings for the organization.

Ergonomics

Ergonomics looks at the working environment and its impact on the workforce. It will consider the design and placement of equipment, machines, control panels and analyse how they may affect the behaviour and efficiency of workers. In design layout, consideration is given to the physical environment where the operations take place, including heating, lighting, ventilation, acoustics and sometimes the colour and aesthetics of the workplace. It is believed that a better working environment, where the layout and equipment is designed to cause the least stress for workers, will ultimately lead to better performance.

Regulatory framework for operations

The regulatory framework includes general UK and European Community regulations and guidelines which relate to the design, manufacture and provision of goods and services, as well as those regulations specific to their own industry or sphere of operations.

There are two major areas of regulations relevant to the manufacture and delivery of products and services, namely the need to protect consumers and users of the products and services, and the health and safety issues concerning the manufacturing or service production activities.

The need to protect customers and users

An organization needs to ensure that the goods and services it produces are of 'merchantable quality'. This means they should not be defective, and are reasonably fit for the purpose for which they are intended, given the state of scientific and technical knowledge when the product or service was first sold. This means that organizations must take care, not only at the design stage but throughout development, to include any new information on safety known to them or in the public domain.

Some of the regulations that affect the design of products, and service organizations that supply and service those products, are given below:

Misrepresentation Act 1967. This seeks to prevent false statements about goods prior to sale which might mislead the purchaser. This applies both to false statements knowingly given (fraudulent misrepresentation) and those which may occur innocently when the seller genuinely believes the statement to be true. Anyone selling goods or services is expected to possess 'expert knowledge' about the items which they are supplying. Buyers may be able to claim compensation to the value of the loss incurred by relying on such false information.

Sale of Goods Act 1979. This requires sellers to supply items that are of merchantable quality and reasonably fit for the intended purpose. Any defects must be pointed out at the time of sale, and the supplier cannot impose any condition of sale that exonerates them from this responsibility.

Supply of Goods and Services Act 1982. This extends protection for the buyer to cover any services offered with products including the installation of goods and equipment. This must be done with care to ensure that they are fit for the purpose and the work is completed within a reasonable time period.

Weights and Measures Act 1985. This requires suppliers to specify correctly the quantities of pre-packaged goods and since 1996, these must be displayed on the packaging in metric values.

Consumer Protection Act 1987. Under this act manufacturers, suppliers and sellers are expected to take all reasonable measures to ensure that goods are safe and that buyers are not misled about the price.

Health and safety in the production and delivery of products and services

The second area of responsibility is the health and safety issues concerned with the operations activities in producing and delivering products and services. This may affect the organization's employees, the general public and damage to the environment.

The basis of these aspects is covered by the Health and Safety at Work Act 1974 under which the employers have a duty to ensure a healthy and safe working environment 'so far as is reasonably practicable'. Employees are also expected to take reasonable care to ensure they do not endanger themselves or others. In general, the Act and Management Regulations are goal setting, in that they set out what has to be achieved but leave the organization to decide how this will be done.

The law requires the employer to employ good management practices and common sense in looking at what the risks are and taking sensible measures to overcome them. The organization has the ultimate responsibility to insist that safety policies are implemented. The degree of risk of a particular job or workplace needs to be balanced against the time, trouble, cost and physical difficulty of taking measures to avoid or reduce the risk.

In the UK, health and safety matters are governed by the Health and Safety Commission (HSC) which provides guidance, Approved Codes of Practice (ACOPs) and regulations:

Guidance: following the actions in the Guidance notes, while not compulsory for employers, helps them to do sufficient to comply with the law. Their aim is to help organizations interpret and comply with EC and UK health and safety law, give technical advice and keep employers up to date as risks and measures change as technology changes. Guidance notes may be general, applying across industry or specific to the problems of an industry.

Approved Codes of Practice: There are some 50 codes in operation currently, and they offer examples of good practice which have a special legal status. If employers choose not to adopt them, they have to show how else they have complied with the law. The codes give advice on how to comply with the law, and examples of terms such as 'reasonably practical', 'suitable' and 'sufficient'.

Regulations: These are laws, approved by parliament, usually made under the Health and Safety at Work Act.

Some risks are so great, or may require such costly control measures, that it may not be appropriate to leave these to the employer's discretion. The regulations identify the risk, and set out the specific action which must be taken by organizations to overcome them.

Where possible, regulations are 'goal setting', allowing organizations to decide how they will achieve the required safety levels. Others are prescriptive, and identify in detail what must be done, and some are absolute and must be done without qualification.

Regulations may apply to all companies, or apply to hazards which are specific to an industry or certain materials. Some activities or substances are so inherently hazardous that they require licensing.

To manage health and safety at work, under the Management of Health and Safety at Work Regulations 1992 (The Management Regulations) employers are required to carry out a risk assessment and take actions on its findings. Organizations employing five or more employees need to have a written health and safety policy which must be brought to the attention of all employees. They must make arrangements for implementing health and safety measures identified in the risk assessment; appoint competent people to implement the arrangements, set up emergency procedures, and provide clear training and instructions for employees.

It is also necessary to ensure that the practices are observed and implemented: procedures are followed; protective clothing is provided and worn wherever necessary; and plant, machinery and equipment are safe and regularly maintained to an adequate standard. In larger organizations there may be a safety committee which includes trade union and employee representatives, which meet regularly to consider health and safety matters which affect employees.

The Health and Safety Commission is the regulator for these aspects, and its operating arm, the Health and Safety Executive, consults with and helps organizations to adopt safe working practices, adapt to changes in technology and interpret regulations passed both by the UK and the European Commission. Their inspectors visit organizations to ensure that they are complying with the regulations. They have a range of pamphlets on safety matters and a telephone helpline for organizations on safety issues.

Summary

In this chapter you should have gained an understanding of the factors affecting the processes used to provide services and products and recognise that these must be carried out in a safe working environment. We have introduced some of the tools and techniques used in planning and scheduling work. For complex operations many of these tools and techniques, and those used for purchasing, are computerized. We briefly looked at queues, why they occur, and what a manager can do to alleviate them. Finally, we looked at the link between quality assurance and customer satisfaction. This links into the topics covered in the next chapter.

Appendix   Some of the regulations which apply generally across the workplace

Since 1987 there has been a substantial body of EU laws incorporated into the UK's statutory provisions. This accelerated in 1992. The Health and Safety at Work etc. Act 1974 remains the principal regulatory provision. However, many more acts are in force. There is an overwhelming body of regulations. Many are purely domestic in origin whilst others are partly EU and domestic. More recently much health and safety secondary legislation has come almost entirely from the EU.

Being aware of the requirements presents the First Line Manager with a major problem. HMSO publish the statutory instruments together with the ACOPs (an approved code of conduct) and Guidance. *Health and Safety Monitor*, a private publishing venture, provides an effective, reliable and critical updating service.

Management of Health and Safety at work Regulations 1992: These regulations require specific procedures to be followed so that the employer can show that they are fulfilling their duty of care effectively. This will be a boon to the employer in checking compliance. It will also be of great benefit to the enforcement authorities. The regulations set out the details of the risk assessment, subsequent action and the need to appoint competent people to implement the measures and for training and information for all employees.

Workplace (Health, Safety and Welfare) Regulations 1992: Every workplace in the land is now subject to a comprehensive set of statutory requirements with which everyone has a duty to comply. These regulations cover a wide range of basic health, safety and welfare issues such as ventilation, heating, lighting, workstations, seating and welfare facilities.

Health and Safety (Display Screen Equipment) Regulations 1992: This sets out requirements for work with visual display units (VDUs).

Personal Protective Equipment (PPE) Regulations 1992: These require employers to provide appropriate protective clothing and equipment for their employees. Organizations must also ensure that they are worn whenever appropriate.

Provision and Use of Work Equipment Regulations (PUWER) 1992: This requires that equipment for use at work, including machinery, is safe. The definition of 'work equipment' in the regulations is very wide and comprehensive. It covers the whole range from single machines such as computers, through assemblies to the complete plant.

'Use' is also widely defined; it means any activity in relation to work equipment including starting, stopping, transporting, repairing, servicing and cleaning. This wide meaning of the word 'use' closes many of the loopholes existing in previous protective legislation.

Manual Handling Operations Regulations 1992: This covers the moving of objects by hand or bodily force in the workplace.

Health and Safety (First Aid) Regulations 1981: This covers requirements for first aid provision.

The Health and Safety Information for Employees Regulations 1989: This requires employers to display a poster telling employees what they need to know about health and safety.

Employer's Liability (Compulsory Insurance) Regulations 1969: This requires employers to take out insurance against accidents and ill health to their employees.

Noise at Work Regulations 1989: This requires employers to take action to protect employees from hearing damage.

Electricity at Work Regulations 1989: This requires people in control of electrical systems to ensure they are safe to use and maintained in a safe condition.

Control of Substances Hazardous To Health Regulations 1994 (COSHH): This requires employers to assess the risks from hazardous substances and take appropriate precautions.

4 Customer relationships

Aims

The aim of this chapter is to consider the organization and its relationships with its customers; how organizations research their markets and identify customer needs; and provide a quality product or service which satisfies those needs.

By the end of this chapter you will:

- Understand why customer relationships are important and how they relate to a marketing and quality orientation.
- Know which sources of information and methods can be used to collect, analyse and interpret data on customer satisfactions.
- Understand how customer satisfaction can be measured and monitored.
- Know how organizations can improve their service standards and customer relationships.

Key concepts

- Customer relationships and the marketing concept;
- How an organization commits itself to improving customer relationships;
- How customer needs are identified using customer and marketing research methods, analysis and interpretation;
- How these needs are satisfied by identifying current levels of service and gaps in performance;
- How organizations can monitor and improve current service levels.

Introduction

Customer relationships refer to the interaction between the organization making a product or supplying a service and the customer chain. This includes customers, clients and users of services, and the members of the distribution chain connecting the provider with the ultimate users – the wholesalers, retailers and agents, buyers and users. Customers can be internal or external to the organization.

Some people may consider 'customers' to refer only to the buyers and users of commercial products, whether they are consumer durables, such as cars, houses, computers, washing machines etc., or fast moving consumer goods (FMCGs) such as fruit juices, foodstuffs, washing powder, cosmetics, stationery.

The word 'customer' refers also to buyers in the business to business markets – companies selling to other companies. This could be:

- Durables: office equipment, machinery, plant and equipment
- Consumables: raw materials, components, stationery, office supplies
- Services: catering, cleaning, consultancy and advice.

In addition, public sector and not-for-profit organizations have redefined their activities in terms of services to their customers. In recent years the concept of 'selling a service', and thus the need for marketing, has become more important in the public sector and not-for-profit organizations. Although they may not always have a tangible end product, they are providing a service for users, for which there is a set of needs and a satisfaction level.

Organizations are adopting a customer approach and using marketing principles to identify their customers, their needs and wants. They can then adjust their services or products to meet those needs.

The importance of customer relationships

In recent years many organizations, including public sector and not-for-profit organizations, have recognized the benefit of developing a marketing orientation. They think about who their customers are and what their wants and needs are. They try to identify the levels of service and quality that their customers demand.

There are mission statements and customer-care promises for the NHS, schools, local authorities, charities and all manner of other organizations. The adoption of the Social Charter and agency status by many public sector service providers, and competitive tendering, mean that the emphasis has changed to concentrating on how they can help meet the needs of their clients, customers and users.

Adopting the marketing concept

The term 'marketing concept' is now widely accepted as an approach where the organization identifies customers and their needs. It then develops and adapts its products and services to match market needs, providing benefit (or profit) to the supplier, user and the consumer channel in between.

The purpose of marketing is to help the organization achieve its strategic purpose and mission, whether that is survival, to make a profit or surplus, to operate within a grant or funding limit or to be prosperity directed. The tasks of marketing include:

- Finding customers and markets.
- Developing or designing products or services to satisfy market or customer needs.
- Adapting and changing what the organization produces or does to meet the market or customer needs.
- To react to the opportunities identified through the application of the marketing mix.

The marketing mix , often known as the 'four Ps', includes:

- The *product or service* offer – branding and packaging
- The *price* of products or services, or the cost to the customer of using the service
- *Place* – channels of distribution including physical distribution, and sometimes warehousing, sales and direct marketing, and
- *Promotion* – advertising, sales promotion, publicity, press releases, public relations and point of sale display.

In addition, any service organization needs to consider a fifth 'P' in *people* as they are the vital component in delivering services. As marketing has become more sophisticated the marketing mix has been extended to include other 'Ps' such as physical events, environment and atmosphere, and politics. The organization chooses the optimum combination of the variables in their marketing mix to meet the customer needs identified in their own market.

The customer-focused organization

An organization that has adopted a marketing (and thus a customer) orientation is one that has the customer and their needs as its focus. Such an organization finds out what the customer wants and attempts to supply that, rather than devising a product or a service that it may believe is of good quality and absolutely necessary. If the product or service does not meet customer needs then the organization will struggle to sell it.

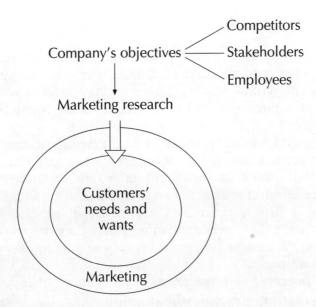

Figure 4.1 *Customer focus*

A customer-focused organization adopts a customer care philosophy and communicates this to all its staff and trains them in good customer care techniques and practices.

To find out what the customer needs and values, the organization will undertake market research. It will decide on criteria to segment the market according to their needs and not for the organization's convenience. It will then target specific groups of customers with a specific product or service offer to suit their needs more closely.

It will also seek to adapt and change the offer to appeal to other and new target groups. It investigates and analyses the competitor's offers and positions its own offer in the most advantageous way. It decides on the critical success factors and amends and adopts its strategies to achieve these.

Perhaps most important of all, it will adopt a marketing strategy that is integrated in all its facets with the organization's mission, objectives and goals and the activities across all departments.

The issues of customer care and quality will be a major consideration at all levels within the organization. Quality targets and standards are concerned with the product or service the customer receives and the level of customer care, not just the efficiency of the organization's internal processes and procedures. The European Union's recent research shows that around 80 per cent of quality programmes do not work successfully because they do not combine quality of processes with quality customer service and customer care programmes.

Customer care and its relation to quality

Since the 1980s there has been an emphasis on quality and excellence in business, and with it increasing attention to customer service. This has reached beyond the realms of the business world to all providers of services, whatever type of service they offer, or whatever the structure of their organization.

As the market becomes more competitive, it becomes necessary to work harder to attract and keep customers – the popular belief is that it costs at least four times as much to get a new customer as to retain a current one. Therefore, it makes sense to build relationships with customers for mutual benefit. The happier they are, or the more closely your product or service offer meets their need, the more likely they are to go on using your products or services and to give good reports of you to others, encouraging them to buy as well.

This has been termed '*relationship marketing*'. It is a development of the original marketing concept which emphasizes the benefit of building long-term relationships with customers and the customer chain. This helps to integrate the ideas of quality, customer service and marketing together to achieve customer satisfaction.

Broadcasting an organization's intentions to employees and customers

It is important that organizations show their commitment to good customer relationships, and their intention to monitor and improve their service to customers. Where an organization has a serious commitment to quality service this is included in the organization's policy and strategy statements, mission statements and operating plans. It will also be reflected in all sales promotions, advertising or publicity campaigns and other communications to prospective and current customers.

Mission statements cover the vision the managers have for the organization – how they see it in the future, the type of organization it should be, the characteristics it wishes to adopt, and the strategies adopted to achieve these goals.

The mission statement and quality intent can then be used in publicity to communicate this to employees and customers. An example of this is the slogan 'Right first time, on time, every time!' used by British Aerospace in all its internal documents.

MEETING LOCAL NEEDS

The Council's Housing strategy for 1996/97 has just been published. The strategy outlines the Council's plans for improving the quality of housing in Welwyn Hatfield, increasing the supply of local affordable homes and meeting local needs. The Housing Department works closely with other Council departments to meet these targets.

KEY COUNCIL TARGETS

- We will regularly monitor the needs of the local community and work to provide new homes either directly or in partnership with other organisations.
- As your landlord, we will provide you with responsive and accessible neighbourhood based housing services which are driven by quality and customer care.
- We will work to improve the condition of the housing stock across the district having particular regard to safety, security, affordable heating and energy efficiency.
- We will encourage new businesses to set up in the community and encourage local businesses to expand to increase the employment opportunities for local people.
- We will ensure that all of our services are accessible to the poorer sections of our community and we will provide services that meet their needs. We will try to help people wherever possible through benefits and advice, training opportunities and generating local employment.
- We will look at the health of the district and examine the contribution the Council can make to address some of the problems that we experience locally.
- We are committed to raising environmental awareness and we will work with the community to encourage positive action to improve the environment.

Figure 4.2 *Welwyn and Hatfield Council statement*

Activity 4.1

You have already considered the company statement of Mitsubishi in Chapter 1 when you looked at its implications for managers. Now look at the statements taken from the policy and public documents of a variety of organizations in Figure 4.3, and ask yourself 'What does this tell me about their attitude to customers?'

The University of Westminster: The mission of the University of Westminster is to be the leading provider in the capital city of a highly accessible portfolio of higher education and associated strategic research.

Welwyn and Hatfield Council 'is committed to providing good quality services at reasonable cost. We aim to satisfy our customers and to ensure everyone is treated fairly and efficiently.'

'**BT**'s mission, our central purpose, is to provide world-class telecommunications and information products and services, and to develop and exploit our networks, at home and overseas, so that we can:

- meet the requirements of our customers,
- sustain growth in the earnings of the group on behalf of our shareholders, and
- make a fitting contribution to the community in which we conduct our business.'

Laura Ashley plc: 'Our mission is to establish an enduring relationship with those who share a love of the special life style that is Laura Ashley. We will act so as to protect the integrity of that relationship and to ensure its long term prosperity.'

British Airways: 'Our mission is to be the best and most successful company in the airline business.'
    However, its goals are more explicit, to be:
- safe and secure
- financially strong
- global leader
- service and value
- customer driven (to excel in anticipating and quickly responding to customer needs and competitor activity)
- good employer
- good neighbour

Figure 4.3 *Examples of mission statements*

Look at the statement from the strategic plan of the University of Westminster in Figure 4.4 and compare it with their mission statement. How do you think they compare? Is the intention in the mission statement matched by the strategic plan?

STRATEGIC PLAN 1992/97

The mission of the University of Westminster is to be the leading provider in the capital city of a high quality accessible portfolio of higher education and associated strategic research.

In achieving this mission the University of Westminster will:

- provide the widest possible access to all those who wish to benefit from its activities
- provide courses structured within national and international credit transfer frameworks ranging from foundation level, certificates, diplomas, degrees to post-graduate and post-experience studies
- provide courses in a comprehensive range of disciplines with flexible modes of attendance to meet the needs of students
- provide a responsive and substantial programme of professional development to meet the needs of individuals and organisations particularly in London and the South East
- build upon its European and International links and experience to provide relevant education and research
- provide opportunities within a multi-disciplinary environment for the development of academic, cultural, recreational, spiritual and social interests of students to enable them to respond to the challenges of life, employment and social change in the twenty-first century
- encourage across the whole institution the further development of research and consultancy in partnership with commerce, industry, the professions and the public sector
- provide for the development of its staff to meet institutional and related personal objectives
- ensure close collaboration with industry, commerce and the professions in the design and delivery of courses and in making the results of research available to the public and private sectors

---

Figure 4.4 *Mission statement – University of Westminster*

> Now consider your own organization or one with which you are familiar. Look at its mission statement. What does it say about the quality and nature of the service it intends to provide?

The development of good customer relationships has become an important consideration for organizations along with the move towards quality in processes, products and services. An organization with a consumer orientation is one that develops its policies, strategies and activities around satisfying identified wants and needs of its customers and users of its products and services.

However, as we shall see, it is important that the organization, in selecting its mission and quality care standards, should discover and reflect real customer needs and then measure its achievements in satisfying those needs.

The identification of customer needs for services or products

The size and nature of markets and types of customer varies enormously, according to the nature of the company or organization and the products or services that they provide. For this reason it is essential that organizations find out as much as they can about their markets. If an organization wishes to adopt a customer orientation, it needs to identify the customer groups and how their needs can be met.

Describing a customer need

There are formal and technical ways of specifying customer needs. This is the specification which links what the customer needs to the product or service offer. The description of the type of product and service needed and what it has to do is called the *performance specification*. This includes those aspects which are vital (customer needs) and those which would be appreciated if included (customer wants) but are not essential. If these wants are excluded it might not prevent the customer buying from you unless they can find them in competitor's products or services.

The performance specification forms the basis of the *design specification* which then describes the type of product and service that needs to be designed. This will include sufficient information for the product and service to meet customer needs at an appropriate price. It will include both tangible and intangible elements and is equally relevant for products or services.

The resulting 'product or service offer' includes the physical and tangible items that form the 'core product or service' together with the services and supplementary items. These refer to packaging, style, image, pre- and post-sales service, which go to make up the 'augmented product or service offer'. Together these provide the 'total experience' designed to meet customer needs.

The tangible elements may include technical details of dimensions (size or weight, etc.); attributes such as taste, sound or colour; the functions it is required to carry out over a particular time-scale, duration or lifestyle and in which conditions (heat or cold, light, vibration, mobility) and tolerances it will operate. It will indicate which of these are critical or merely desirable. For a service it might include other aspects of the environment such as style of seating or decorations. The intangible elements are often equally as important, and are usually described in more subjective terms. These may be described as hard or soft variables.

Hard variables for products, which may be given measurements and tolerance levels include:

> *physical attributes*
> - features and functions required
> - packaging for safety, protection, handling, storage and aesthetics
> - price band and credit options
> - availability of the product or service
> - delivery times
> - tolerance and accuracy levels
> - the accessories which could be added on.

Availability can mean wide availability in many types of outlets or restricted availability in exclusive outlets where more precise information and sales help can be given. Availability can also mean available on demand or after an acceptable waiting period.

A measure of availability is the delivery gap. Are the customers expecting it to be a stock item, available on demand – such as a personal stereo – or is the customer prepared to accept a delivery time of six to eight weeks such as happens with furniture. The quality of service will then be measured by on-time delivery.

The availability of a service may be described as how quickly repairs are carried out, or the duration for which the service is available. For instance does a 24-hour service mean you can access the service day and night, or that a repair will be effected within 24 hours? The important point is how much this matters to the customer.

Soft variables could include:

> - colour
> - taste
> - smell
> - style

■ brand image
■ the status that ownership or consumption implies and if environmentally friendly or recyclable.

For a service the tangible and intangible attributes can be similar to those of products but with the addition of:

■ The *environment*: seating, decorations in waiting areas (in a restaurant, theatre, takeaway, shoe repairs, NHS hospitals and clinics, doctors'/dentists' surgeries); cleanliness, lighting, decoration, suitability, taste, sound level.
■ *Position and facilities*: region, location, ease of access, parking, breadth of service extras or accessories, for example the provision of office facilities in a hotel used by business people.
■ *Consistency of service*: from one encounter to the next.
■ *Perceived quality of service*: including timing – perceived waiting time, degree of choice and the face-to-face delivery of the service and attitudes and friendliness of staff.

One library decided to test the perception that their customers have about the friendliness of the counter staff. The staff made eye contact and smiled at a proportion of the users, and sometimes made a light touch on the hand or arm but didn't speak as they checked out their book; for the rest they made friendly comments but made no eye contact. Overwhelmingly, the users who felt the service had been most friendly and *helpful* were those that had received the touch or eye contact. It is often the small things that make for friendly service and make customers feel satisfied with their purchase or service.

When you are considering product or service specifications, you should try to decide what the basic need that is being satisfied is and what aspects form the augmented product offer. Consider the following examples of products and services and how the basic need is augmented to build a brand image.

In the case of cat food, the basic need could be considered to be the provision of a nutritious and balanced food for the cat. This can be provided in a number of forms – moist canned food, moist foil packed meals and dry biscuits. All come in a variety of flavours, colours, textures and smells. Are these to tempt the cat to eat or for the owner's reassurance?

Once the basic product form is decided, the cat owner has a number of other attributes to consider, including flavours, texture, smell, shelf life, ease of transport and storage, ease of use (such as the ring-pull can) price and brand image. All these items help to make up the augmented product offer.

Beyond the augmented product are the intangible aspects of the brand which help to woo customers to buy a particular type of cat food. The advertisements appeal to owners to provide a quality food to repay the cat for the love and affection that the cat provides – the gourmet approach – it's worth the premium price to show your cat you care!

Sheba (Pedigree Petfoods) have gone further in developing the customer relationship. When cat lovers send for one of their special offers they are asked for their cat's names, ages and birth dates. Thereafter, the cat receives a well wishers card on its birthday and at Christmas – just that little extra to show they care!

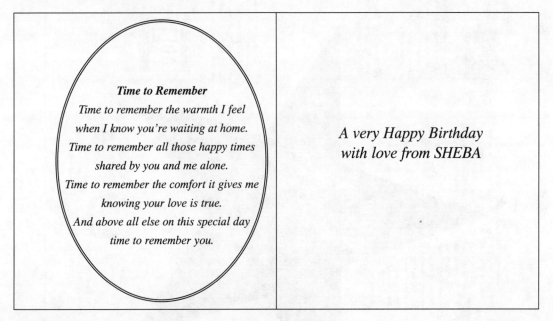

Figure 4.5 *Cat birthday card from Sheba*

The same idea of core and augmented products applies for services. In a restaurant, while the core product may be the food and drink – the basic need is to eat, but often it is a social event so that the augmented product that completes the meal becomes as important as the food and it is this that will make the experience satisfactory or not.

The augmented product will include the quality, taste and aroma of the food; decoration and style of furniture, tableware, napkins and other tangible items; the cleanliness of the cloakrooms and toilet facilities. The atmosphere and style is important as well: lighting, noise, how close the tables are and other physical attributes such as the location of the restaurant, ease of access and parking.

Finally there is the quality of the service and the attitude of the staff. All this will add up to the psychological feeling of well being and a satisfied customer.

Welcome to ★ PRET A MANGER ★ ...a radically fresh approach!

In just nine years our employees' passion and determination have taken us from a single kiosk in South London to a dynamic chain serving millions of customers. This Mission Statement is about our food, our culture and our resolution to provide our customers with exceptional standards at a fair price.

★ At Pret we go to extraordinary lengths to ensure the food we sell is fresh, healthy, natural and of the highest possible quality. Our sandwiches and baguettes are made throughout the day, one by one using unprocessed natural ingredients. We steadfastly avoid obscure chemicals, additives and preservatives commonly found in 'fast food'.

We do not operate a central production factory nor employ mass production techniques. If our sandwiches don't sell out each day, we give them away rather than compromise our standards.

★ Pret A Manger hams are prepared by hand, then roasted in a traditional oven and basted with honey and cloves. The colour, texture and taste of our natural ham is a world apart from the processed and 'pumped' imitation ham most commonly found.

We use only fresh chicken breast (no leg or brown meat), we use strong mature cheddar, our mayonnaises are made with fresh herbs and our lamb comes from an organic farm at Eastbrook in Wiltshire. Our pasta salads are all hand-made using fresh pasta, not the cheaper dried variety.

★ All the eggs we use are free range and come from Martin Pitt's Levetts Farm where there is no routine use of antibiotics, and likewise no chemicals, hormones or artificial yolk colourants are added to the chicken's food.

Pret Tuna is Dolphin Safe and our Scottish Salmon is poached in our shops every day.

OUR MISSION is to create hand made, natural food, avoiding the obscure chemicals, additives and preservatives common to so much of the 'prepared' and 'fast' food on the market today.

★ We were awarded a star by the Egon Ronay 'Just A Bite Guide', where our food was judged to be 'Outstanding', and we thank Harden's Restaurant Guide for the many glowing reviews given to us. Our Heathrow team are thrilled to have received the 'Two Chefs Hats' award.

★ Our delicious Mediterranean Bread, Walnut Bloomer and Sun-dried Tomato Loaf are all baked without preservatives.

chemicals and yeast enhancers commonly used in the baking industry.

★ Giles Dick-Read, our full time coffee expert, chooses only the finest Arabica beans for our famous cappuccinos.

Pret coffee machines grind the beans to order; we do not use the quicker (and cheaper) reservoir machines.

★ 'Power', our freshly pressed carrot juice is part of our range of 100% natural juices. It is full of nutrients and vitamins and unlike the so-called 'health drinks' trendy today it contains no chemicals or additives.

Nine years ago, Colin Lloyd and Kate Cherkoff appeared at our first shop with a sample of their delicious Passion Cake. Using only 100% natural ingredients, no preservatives or artificial flavours, they now produce six varieties of cake for Pret A Manger.

★ Our second 'Helping the Homeless' truck is now on the road. Soon, many, if not all London's hostels for the homeless will be receiving our fresh food free of charge. Thank you to all those who continue to help us with this project and a big thank you to all at Crisis.

OUR THANKS GO TO THE BRITISH SANDWICH ASSOCIATION FOR AWARDING US SANDWICH SHOP OF THE YEAR!!!

★ In a business renowned for being environmentally unfriendly Pret is bucking the trend. We use recycled paper and plastic and have developed an aluminium can recycling scheme. Nearly all our cake packaging is card rather than plastic and we serve our coffee in paper cups rather than the usual non-biodegradable E.P.S variety.

Teamwork, dedication and a product you can trust is what Pret A Manger is all about. On behalf of everyone at Pret, thank you for visiting our shops. If you would like to speak to me or one of my colleagues regarding anything to do with our company please feel free to call on 0171 827 6300.

Thank you.

Julian Metcalfe
CHAIRMAN

PASSIONATE PRET ABOUT FOOD

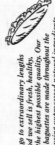

Figure 4.6 *Pret A Manger Service offer*

In a hotel, the basic need for a night's shelter may be covered by a room, bed and bathroom and access to food and drink, but many of the 'extras' have now become expected so that the augmented product has become part of the core product in meeting expectations. The core product includes the location, room and other facilities including parking and ease of access. The accessories and extra facilities, such as a swimming pool, sauna or fitness centre, can be crucial in setting the level of satisfaction. Tea-making facilities and television are now standard items, and the hotels have to make extra effort to provide an augmented product targeted at certain sectors of the market. There may be games and activities for family visitors or fax and computer facilities for business visitors. In some hotels they are making extra efforts to capture the custom of the women travelling on business, and not just by extra security precautions and a hair dryer and ironing board in the room. Some hotels are attempting to make the atmosphere of public areas of the hotel more appropriate for single women travellers so that they can enjoy the facilities without feeling awkward.

Where a product is being manufactured it is accepted that the specification is written in great detail, and often forms part of the contract between organizations. This should be equally important for services operations. Many of these are now being included in charters setting out what the customer can expect.

Activity 4.2

Choose a product and a service that you have bought or experienced recently. The service could be tangible (a meal or visit to a beauty parlour where you can see, taste or feel the service) or intangible (a car service or MOT or perhaps a visit to a solicitors for advice or to swear an oath) where you take on trust the service you are receiving.

Write a specification for these items as if you were ordering them – what features and service levels would you look for?

Now, write down what you actually purchased with a description of its features. Were you satisfied with the purchase? Was there a satisfaction gap between the ideal and the actual? How did you measure this satisfaction – using hard measures (tangible and measurable aspects) or more subjective attributes? Did the promotion that attracted you to the purchase help you? How could it have been better?

Try to rank your reasons for choice in priority order.

When deciding on the product or service offer, the organization also has to consider quality levels. This can mean different things to different customer groups. Some users will see quality as a high status article, which is made of the best materials, which will 'last a lifetime'. Others will be looking for a cheaper version which is adequate to fit the purpose at that time – maybe it is a stopgap item which is not required to last long; maybe it must be able to fulfil a function in difficult conditions but appearance is not an issue.

There are endless combinations of wants and needs – and the organization must ensure that the offer they are making is the right one at that time for the group of customers concerned. This is why marketing is concerned with segmenting and targeting markets, because not everyone has the same needs.

Segmenting and targeting markets

Segmentation of markets is one of the fundamental principles of marketing and essential to building good customer relationships. It is the process whereby the market is divided into relatively homogeneous groups of people who can be deemed to have similar interests, tastes or reasons for choosing, buying or using the product or service in question.

The most quoted criteria used to segment markets are those that can be easily recognized or measured: geographical location, demographic factors (age, sex and life cycle), lifestyle or user benefits. The best criteria are those that are meaningful to the consumer, rather than the most convenient for the organization. The organization might find it convenient to use sales force areas or geographical boundaries to describe markets, but these are not market segments unless the customers in the different geographical areas have significantly different needs. Once you have divided the market into segments of similar needs you must choose which of these is most appropriate for you to approach. See Figure 4.7.

Activity 4.3
Think about the varieties of tea that are available, given different types (Indian, Chinese; green, black), flavours (Darjeeling, Assam, Keemun, Earl Grey, fruits, etc.) and forms (loose leaf, tea bag, single-cup bags, instant tea). How might you segment the market for tea?

The examples given above relate to the product, but you might have chosen segments based upon why the customer is drinking tea, as this might affect the products with which the tea competes. For example, is it for a quick break in the office? The customer probably would like something that is quick and easy to use, probably a single-cup tea bag or instant. To avoid the problem of keeping fresh milk or lemons in the office the customer might choose an instant tea with the whitener included. The main reason for this choice would probably be for convenience. If, on the other hand the tea is being drunk on a social occasion, where there are a group of friends or family and there is plenty of time to brew and enjoy the drink, the customer might choose a speciality leaf tea rather than a product for convenience.

Market segments must be recognizable in terms of a cluster of customer needs, criteria commonly used may include:

Demographic factors (characteristics within the population which may be measured):

Age, sex, income, education level, religion, ethnic origin, nationality, family size, family life cycle (based on children's age and if they still live at home), occupation, language spoken.
A cluster of the above is recognized as socio-economic groups (A, B, C1, C2, D, E: based on income, occupation and family traditions, habits and taste).
Location may be considered if this is reflected in different customer needs for products and services.

Personality factors:

Lifestyle, outlook, personality and character traits, innovators, trend setters, taste makers, followers.
A range of such segment descriptions have been developed, which try to describe the customer's attitude to life and buying behaviour. An attempt to build the customer's profile beyond the basic demographic characteristics.

Buyer behaviour:

benefits sought; brand loyalty; new or repeat purchase; frequency or size of purchase; reason for purchase (own use, gift, special occasion).

Business factors:

Type of organization (commercial, not for profit); type of business; size of organisation; buying style.
Buyers for organizations are buying because of 'derived demand' – to meet the needs of the organization and not those of the individual buyer.

Figure 4.7 *Criteria for segmenting markets*

Activity 4.4

The tea bag has increased its share of the tea market in the UK in the last twenty years. New shapes have been introduced, sometimes for the convenience of the user and sometimes for the producer. Recently, a manufacturer has announced the launch of a triangular shaped tea bag (see Figure 4.8). How would you go about marketing this as a benefit to the customers? Which target market would you choose?

Change brewing for reshaped tea market
Glenda Cooper

Britain's tea-bags turned over a new leaf yesterday as the two biggest companies announced revolutionary concepts to change our drinking habits.

As Brooke Bond launched its pyramid tea-bags, which are meant to produce an infusion as good as loose-leaf tea, its rival Tetley retaliated by disclosing plans for a non-drip bag.

Brooke Bond which makes PG Tips, has spent four years developing the Pyramid, a bag in the shape of a tetrahedron, which allows 50 per cent more room than conventional square or round bags. 'The tests proved that the tetrahedral tea-bag comes closer to allowing the tea to brew like loose tea in a teapot than any other bag,' Brooke Bond said.

The tea-bag, invented in 1953, remained largely unchanged until Tetley introduced its round version in 1989. It is now the dominant shape in Britain, where tea-bags account for 90 per cent of sales, worth £530m a year.

Tetley's non-drip bag is being tested in Australia; plans for a British launch have not been completed. 'It means you'll be able to lift the bag from your cup without spilling it all over your desk,' said Ian Prutton, director of world-wide business development. 'It has two strings with tags which, when they are pulled together, squeeze all the excess liquid out of the bag.'

Brooke Bond says its new bag is 'the first major innovation since the introduction of the square bag in the 1950s to offer genuine taste and brewing benefits.'

Fred Marquis, of the thermo-fluid section at Imperial College, London, tested the bag. 'It tends to naturally float on the surface of the water, allowing the water to flow more freely in and out of the tea-bag. It is this extra movement of tea-leaves which helps the brewing process,' he said.

PG Tips Pyramids are to be launched in south-west England in April and then in the rest of Britain.

Source: Guardian

Figure 4.8

Understanding customer behaviour

To develop good customer relationships it is important to understand why and how customers choose the products and services that they buy or use. In identifying and describing customer needs it is important to know what they are buying and why. The product and augmented product or service is not usually bought for the product itself but to serve a need or satisfy a problem. The examples given before for cat food, restaurants and hotels show that the customers may choose a brand for more reasons than just to satisfy the basic needs.

You need to consider the problem that the customer wants solved and not the product or service that helps them to do this. A factory manager does not buy a forklift truck but a means to move heavy or bulky items around the factory easily and safely. A customer may appear to want to buy a drill and a 3 mm bit, but what they are really buying is the ability to make a 3 mm hole so that they can get on to do the job! A couple may not be buying a coffee but the opportunity to talk in a convivial atmosphere!

Figure 4.9 *The problem may be to find out how customers use your product*

Look for the need that is being satisfied to learn more about how your product or service can more closely fit the need. To do this you need to know a little about the motivation behind the purchase as well as the physical attributes that are needed.

It is important to understand how customers buy as well. How does the customer choose the purchase – what stimulates the need, who else might influence the brand or timing of the purchase?

In every decision there are several decisions to be made these may be reflected by different people who take different roles in the decision, or by one person who takes on all the roles:

Initiator: indicates that there is a need for a product or service

Influencer: adds information or opinions to the decision process

Decider: finally decides on the type of product or service or which supplier to use

Buyer: goes through the physical actions of purchasing the item

User: the person who finally consumes or uses the product.

When you decide to buy a chocolate bar for a snack, you may take on all these roles, although you might be influenced by what your friends tell you is a pleasant snack, or you might be influenced by what is actually available when you get to the counter.

Figure 4.10 *Decision-making units*

Which sort of outlet will the customer go to for the purchase? What sort of evaluation happens before the decision to buy is taken? Do customers buy the product on impulse and later rationalize how well it suits them by reading the advertisements and deciding the image is right? Do they set out a complex matrix of factors and attributes and measure each possible product or brand against this, carefully weighting each attribute for its importance? All of these things happen and it is important to know which is the pattern for your organization's particular product or service. This will help to decide on the most appropriate marketing mix, and which aspects need to be emphasised in building your customer relationships.

Activity 4.5

Think about a product or service that you have bought recently, or where you have been involved in discussions about buying. What role did you take in the purchase decision? What buying process was used? Was it an impulse buy or did you find out about the alternative products on offer first?

Your answer probably depended upon the cost of the item and how frequently you buy this sort of product. If it is a fairly low-priced item that you have bought many times, it is unlikely that the decision-making unit that influenced you was very large, nor that you spent much time making the decision on which one to buy. If on the other hand, you were considering a larger purchase, such as a consumer durable product or a car or holiday, or if it is something that you were buying for the first time, you probably involved more people in the decision by asking their opinions, sought expert opinions and read advertising brochures and information.

The purchase idea:	the need for a product or service is identified, perhaps stimulated by external factors such as an advertisement, or seeing the product in use.
The purchase dimension:	consideration of the type of product characteristics which might fill the need
Information search:	the search for information on products and services and their availability through: – talking to other people – seeking expert opinions – advertisements – brochures – sampling the product
Evaluation of information:	judging the alternative products and brands available against the standards already set
Purchase decisions:	the actual brand chosen may be the result of a rationale comparison, or restricted by availability

The decision process is usually more complex at the first time of buying than for repeat purchases

Figure 4.11 *Stages in the buying process*

Activity 4.6

Consider a purchase made by your organization, perhaps for a computer or printer, for machine tools, or for a new cleaning service. How was the First Line Manager involved in the decision? How large was the decision-making unit? How many people were asked for their opinion? What buying procedures were followed? Is this the same for all purchases or does it vary depending on the size of the order? Is this different because of the scale or because it is an organizational purchase?

Imagine that you were selling this product or service to your own organization. What steps could you have taken to discover what the customer needed? How would you have changed the selling process?

Sources of information

Information about customers and their needs can be collected in a number of ways and from a number of sources, all with different cost and accuracy implications. The aim of collecting information is to help managers in their decision making. Sometimes information is required to be collected on a *continuous* basis so that it can be used to compare trends. An *ad hoc* survey will collect information once rather than regularly, to help with a specific decision or to solve a particular problem.

Before any information is collected, it is important that the reason for obtaining the information is determined. We will return to this issue of defining the problem and setting objectives in the next section, when we discuss the research brief.

There are two main categories of information, usually described as primary and secondary data. *Secondary data* is the information that can be collected from other published sources. This can include statistical information, survey reports or articles. These are published by a variety of organizations including the Government Statistical Service, marketing research organizations, banks, trade associations, trade unions, political parties, trade journals and newspapers.

Primary data is information collected to answer particular questions or to solve specific problems. It is collected directly from the market, from customers or the consumer distribution chain through marketing research surveys. This is often referred to as fieldwork. It can also include feedback from the sales force, distributors and customers.

The data collected may be quantitative or qualitative. *Quantitative information* is data that will answer the question 'how many?' It can be used to describe a market's size and structure and the market shares of the companies in it.

It can tell you how many people are in your market, the number of people who already use or buy your product and those who don't; how many like one brand and how many don't; how many people hold a certain opinion and how many don't.

Qualitative information, on the other hand, deals more in 'why' questions. The opinions and attitudes behind consumer decisions are sought. What do people like about a product or service, how do they rate a particular characteristic and what helps them decide on a purchase?

Together these two questions, 'How many?' and 'Why?' are used to find out more about customer needs and satisfactions. While quantitative data is important in most decisions, it can be incomplete without the supporting qualitative data.

Using secondary information

One way of looking at secondary data is to think of it as 'second-hand' information from other organizations. It can provide a good overview of a topic, or an underpinning of knowledge. However, it has limitations and the information may not quite provide the whole answer for your purposes and may need to be supplemented with primary data from a field survey.

Secondary data can be internal or external to the organization. Internal information comes from the organization's records of production or service, sales, usage patterns, stocks, accounting and financial data and of course its customers or clients.

External data has already been published by other organizations. When evaluating secondary data you need to consider how well it fits your purpose, whether it is sufficiently complete and accurate. The main thing to remember is that it has been collected by some other body, for a particular purpose. This purpose may or may not match your own purpose.

Such information may be out of date. If it was collected some while ago, there may have been further developments in the time between collection and publication. It is also vital to verify the information by cross checking the information with at least one other independent source and to consider if any bias has been introduced by the format of the report or the underlying objectives of the survey.

Desk research is the starting point for most projects and surveys. Most organizations collect it on a regular basis to keep abreast of trends and changes in their market. Often it can provide sufficient information for a decision to be taken. It is a relatively cheap way of collecting information but depends upon the expertise of the researcher to decide what is relevant and to check and match the various pieces of information to give a representative picture.

Despite the pitfalls, there are still many good reasons to use and interpret secondary information, It can:

■ Provide preliminary information for a larger project.
■ Provide background to an unknown industry or market, giving information on the structure and major players.
■ Provide a list of respondents (the sampling frame) for the main field survey.

Desk research can be used to provide:

- General economic background
- Changes in the environment
- Market size and trends
- Market structures
- Profiles of current and potential customers
- Market intelligence and competitor profiles
- Product and price information
- Sampling frames

Figure 4.12 *The uses of desk research*

1 *Go from the general to the particular*
  The less you know about the topic, the more important it is to start with an overview before getting into the detail.
2 *Start with other people's interpretations*
  While there are many sources of hard data collected from primary sources by government and trade associations – at the start see how others have used and interpreted it – rearranged, merged. See what they think it means and then go back to the source data.
3 *Assume it exists in the form in which you want it*
  Always assume you will find the details somewhere, and see how often you are proved right.
4 *Write it down*
  Keep a reference list of sources as you go, and note the sources quoted in the articles – to make sure you are not just looking at lots of different interpretations of a single source of data.
5 *Look for a second independent source to verify the first*
  Never rely on just one source – they may have got it wrong.

(Source: adapted from a presentation by Martin Stoll.)

Figure 4.13 *The rules of desk research*

An example of the types of information which may be used is a survey of the prospects for the London labour market. This showed that London had consistently underperformed in the UK economy in recent years, with many job losses due to the restructuring of organizations. The unemployment rate had reached one of the highest in the UK and long-term unemployment would still be a problem in the near future. All the economic reviews for the area forecast a return to growth in job opportunities with an emphasis on business services, finance, high-tech industries and tourism, and an increase in self-employment of 2 per cent. It also showed an under representation of women and ethnic minority groups in certain occupational areas; 49 per cent of ethnic minority women are economically active compared with 53 per cent of white women. While women in general represent 44 per cent of the UK labour force, they are under represented in the management and administration (32 per cent) and professional (38 per cent) occupations, and for ethnic minority women the proportion is lower (21 per cent ethnic minority males are at managerial level compared with 9 per cent women).

   The survey drew upon information from The London Chamber of Commerce and Industry London Quarterly Economic Report and Survey, 2nd Quarter 1995, LCCI London Economy Research Programme Annual Review, October 1994, London TECs Employer Survey 1994[en]5; Equal Opportunities Commission, Economic Assessments and Reports 1995 for the London TECs (Aztec, CENTEC, SOLOTEC, LETEC, West London TEC, North London TEC); London Research Centre Demographic and Statistical Studies 1995; Equal Opportunities Commission Statistics Department 1994; Labour Force Survey, Spring Quarter 1995; Department of Employment, 1995; Equal Opportunities Commission: Black Women in the Labour Market,1994; Ethnic Minority Women and the Labour Market, 1991 Census analysis.

Figure 4.14 *Secondary data example*

Activity 4.7

There are many different sources of information. Choose a market or topic that you know well or which is relevant to your organization. See how many sources of information are available and how much information you can find out about it from published sources. Try to include at least two internal and two external sources in your list.

First, find out what sources of information are available within your organization (monthly or annual reports, your organization's sales or usage figures for example). Visit your local reference library and list the different types of information available that are relevant to your topic.

You may have found the following type of sources: information and source-books, trade-association materials, trade directories, newspapers, trade press and journal articles, and a wide range of government and other published statistics. There is an Annual Abstract of Statistics which lists where and how often the other statistical surveys are published. You may have come across business monitors, Social Trends, Economic Trends, Population Trends, Family Expenditure Survey, General Household Survey and many more. There are also statistics on the import and export of goods from HM Customs and Excise.

Think about the information you found. How up to date was it? Do you think it gave you a complete picture? Could you verify the main facts from more than one source?

Market intelligence

This may include both secondary and primary data. It is the collection of information about customers (for business-to-business sales) and competitors (to analyse competitive positioning). This is not the stuff of James Bond and industrial espionage but the legitimate collection of information about your competitors from published sources, or comparative data from consumer and channel surveys.

Such information can cover market share, brand images and company performance and intentions. It may encompass financial data from company annual reports which includes a chairperson's statement of what has happened and future intentions as well as financial figures. This can be supported by company financial profiles available from companies such as Dunn and Bradstreet or ratios reports for industries from ICC (Inter Company Comparisons) which gives information on industry sectors about the largest companies, sales and profitability.

Other sources of information are the reports in newspapers and trade journals, trade association gossip, company newsletters and journals. It is essential that such articles are cross referenced as they mainly consist of new stories and do not always give the whole picture.

Organizations have their own sales brochures, advertising and promotional and public relations material. These can provide you with qualitative information about the company culture and values, the image it wishes to promote, whether it is an old-fashioned, steady company or young and dynamic; it will tell you about the products and service it provides, and perhaps its distributors, agents or price range. It may even tell you if they claim to be the market leader!

Activity 4.8

Think about your own organization or one with which you are familiar. See how much information you can find out about it from external published information. If you can discover this, so can your competitors.

Collecting primary data

When desk research indicates that further information is required about a market, customer needs or competitive organizations, it is necessary to collect primary data through a fieldwork survey. There are a number of methods of collecting primary data, each suitable for different purposes and kinds of information, and each with their advantages and disadvantages.

First, it is important to define the problem for which the information is needed as this will affect both the type of data and the method to be used. This leads to the *research brief*.

This involves defining the problem that the research results will help to solve, deciding what information is needed and which method to use to collect it.

All research and every element of a marketing research survey should be governed by the question:

> What *decision* will be made on completion of the research to solve the *problem*? How will this piece of information contribute to that?

1 What is the problem?

2 Is there more than one problem?

3 Which problem should have priority?

4 What are the alternative solutions?

5 Which 'solution' is best?

6 Who will implement the decision?

7 When, where and over how long will the decision be implemented?

8 What are the costs and pay-offs of the decision?

9 How will the outcome be monitored?

10 Is the problem recurrent?

Figure 4.15 *Steps in identifying the problem*

What is the basic problem you are trying to solve?

Problem: sales targets have not been achieved.

What are the symptoms? Are your customers unhappy? How do you recognize this? What symptoms have you seen?

Scenario 1: You are not getting repeat orders from new customers, or customers that you have had for a long time are suddenly not reordering? Have the numbers of complaints increased?

Where is the problem? Maybe your product quality is not up to standard? Maybe your service is not satisfactory?

Survey action: customer satisfaction survey; trade satisfaction survey, sales and customer feedback, investigate quality standards.

Possible solution: improve product, or quality standards for production and service.

Scenario 2: Sales are slowing, sales force feedback about increased difficulty to sell and increased competition.

Survey: competitive intelligence to consider competitive positioning.

Possible solutions: adapt marketing mix and increase promotional spend to meet new competitive activity; develop and improve product and service as appropriate to meet challenge.

Scenario 3: You wish to enter a new market, or develop a new product.

Survey: to investigate gaps in the market, market structure, size and trends, and competitive information.

Possible solutions: develop new product for market gap, or adapt current product to meet identified need in a new market.

The research brief should include a clear statement of the aim of the research – why is the information needed? Is it for sales forecasting and requires accurate sales and demand data? Is it to launch a new product and you need to gather likely reactions of the customers to the new product?

Figure 4.16 *Types of problem and possible research briefs*

CASE STUDY: THE NEWTOWN LEISURE CENTRE

As the manager of a sports centre, you are considering a number of options to build the business up, and wonder if a survey of your current customers will help you to decide what to do.

The Centre offers squash and badminton facilities, a fitness centre and a studio that is hired by local aerobics teachers on an ad-hoc basis for exercise classes. The local authority swimming pool is only 300 metres along the road from you. You are situated on a busy road into the town centre and there are parking restrictions; although there is a public car park (pay and display) on the town side of the swimming pool.

You know that a new leisure centre complex is to be built at the local football ground, which is located a few miles outside the town centre. It will offer a golf driving range, badminton, squash, fitness centre, free parking and a bar and snack bar. The membership will be open to the football club supporters. In reality it is a move to encourage more people to pay a subscription to the football club, but anyone will be able to join even if they don't come to watch the matches.

You have the finance to extend your facilities and you are planning to refurbish the changing-room facilities and can include unisex saunas and whirlpools in the project. With some replanning, you could include a small lounge and a snack bar but you are not sure if you need to include space for a licensed bar. You also have space to build your own car park.

You have just had a call from the principal of the local college, asking if their more advanced students could offer beauty treatments, such as facials and massages, at the sports centre, to gain evidence for their NVQ. The college would provide the equipment and they would give a percentage of the income to the centre. You are considering taking out the current sun-bed facilities as the equipment needs replacing and you are concerned about the reports that sun-beds could be linked to skin cancer. This would make space available for the treatment room.

You wonder if your customers will leave to go to the new football club, where parking is easier and there will be more facilities and longer opening hours (except on match days)? You are about to draw up a research brief for a local marketing research agency.

Questions:

What do you think is the problem? What information do you need to collect?

You will have noticed that there are a number of separate problems that you could identify, such as:

1   Do you want to increase your membership, or get your current customers to spend more time/money with you?
2   Do you need or want to diversify, adding extra activities, and operational considerations? Why and in what direction?
3   What will be the effect of the increased competition on your current customers or on new customers you might hope to attract?

These are major questions, but there are also questions related to the specific services you might add.

1   Is the lack of parking facilities a problem for your customers?
2   Will the provision of a car park increase the use of your centre?
3   Would a free car park be used by swimming pool customers and bring you no extra benefit?
4   Could you do a deal with the local council to share the costs and maintenance?
5   Do current members want any of the extra facilities you could add? Would they attract new members?
6   What would be the operational implications for you: new staff? longer opening hours? new skills for current staff? new regulations on health and hygiene? more insurance?

The answers to some of these questions may be available within the centre already, others will require the manager to interpret data collected, while others could only be answered by talking to your customers.

The phrase 'talking to the customers' is important. It can mean getting feedback, either occasionally or on an ad-hoc basis, or gathering market research from a representative sample of members and possible potential members.

Using feedback from sales staff, the consumer channel and customers

Using feedback involves collecting ideas and opinions from a range of people concerned with your business or operations. One way is to collect regular feedback from your *sales staff* using specially designed forms which they return regularly or by listening to their opinions in monthly or weekly meetings. The sales staff are in contact with the customers directly or through the trade channels. However, they might not always be able to see the wider picture and their feedback must be supported and checked with other sources.

Activity 4.9

Think about your own organization or one with which you are familiar. Which methods does it use to collect feedback from its customers? How does it use this information?

Talking to the customers – choosing the sample

Once you have identified the main problem, set the objectives for the research survey and listed the types of information needed, you must decide how you will collect the information and from whom. It would be time wasting and costly to try to ask the opinion of everyone in your market, especially if you have large numbers of customers. Therefore a small selection of your market is chosen to represent the whole.

The total market from which you choose is called the universe or sampling population, and the selection of people you take from it is the sample. The sampling frame is a list from which you will select the people to be interviewed. It must be up to date, as complete as possible and relevant to the survey.

Selecting a sample that is representative of the universe you are sampling is a difficult and skilled operation. The sample must be adequate in size, and relevant in that it chooses people who will have knowledge and opinions about the subject, or will know about the product or be likely to use it. This requires an understanding of probability theory and sampling methods.

Steps in selecting the sample:

1 Define the universe or population from which you are sampling.
2 Obtain a complete and up-to-date sampling frame.
3 Choose the type of sampling method to be used (random or probability).
4 Decide on the size of the sample.

The main sampling methods are random or probability, although there are variations of each of these. A *random sample* is one governed by the theory of probability and must be chosen according to strict rules. It should guarantee that each and every person in your chosen universe will have one, and only one, chance of being chosen for the sample. A *quota* or *judgemental sample* uses knowledge of the structure of the chosen universe and selects a sample to represent that universe.

If there are a number of groups or segments in the universe who are likely to hold different views, the sample must be chosen to take account of this.

Activity 4.10

A large catering and hospitality organization is considering banning smoking in its restaurants and public houses. It is commissioning a marketing research survey to find out if this would be popular with its current and potential customers and the impact the ban might have on business. Who do you think should be included in the universe for this survey? Which different segments must be considered?

Market research survey methods

The main methods of collecting primary data are:

- Observing what people do
- Setting up an experimental test to see how they react
- Asking what they have done, are doing or are going to do, using questionnaires or checklists.

These methods all have potential for bias in the answers. Bias is a distortion of the true picture, either intentionally or by chance. This may be caused by an inadequate sampling frame which means the sample chosen is not representative of the universe. Major causes of bias are: the willingness or otherwise of the respondent to help; respondents giving you the answers they think you need rather than the truth; and misinformation by intent or by memory failure. This last point is a particular problem for marketing research. Can you remember what brand of toothpaste you bought last month or how many times you ate pizza for lunch in the last four weeks? The questions must be carefully framed to make it easy for the respondent to remember and give accurate answers.

Observation

This is learning about consumer actions by observing what people do, without interfering in their decision-making process. When they are not aware that you are watching or measuring their actions. This reduces the bias as it cannot influence their choice.

One way is to watch how people buy, using video or personal observation. A method which is becoming increasingly popular is the use of mystery shoppers. Researchers act as customers and report on how service staff respond to customers, the quality of service they give, and their general helpfulness. This is used by organizations whose goods or services are available through a large number of managed outlets and who wish to maintain a quality service for customers. This includes transport companies, banks, brewers for their managed public houses, betting shops, supermarkets, and car manufacturers for their distributors.

Another formal method of observing what customers buy is the *retail audit*. A panel of retail outlets is organized by a market-research agency who undertake a stock audit of what is sold at each outlet. The store where the audit is undertaken must be chosen to be representative of the normal outlets for that kind of goods.

The information collected includes the volume of goods sold by brand, and sizes and prices paid. This is done over specific periods and allows the marketing manager to check the *trends of market share and sales*. The information is collected from the stores themselves and therefore the customer is not aware of the research and their choice is not influenced by the market-research method. This type of survey is useful for organizations selling fast-moving consumer goods when a regular and rapid feedback on consumer choice and market share is desirable.

The main disadvantage of observation methods is that they collect quantitative and not qualitative information. Unless you set up a specific method of identifying the customers, you know what is being bought but you do not know who the customers are or why they are choosing those brands.

Activity 4.11

Observation: How much information can be collected through observation? Use observation to write a summary of the marketing mix of a fast-food outlet.

For example, you could describe the product range, prices, decoration, atmosphere, cleanliness, and if customers mainly eat on the site or take the food away. You could observe the outlet at different times of the day and week and decide if there is a pattern of customer demand. You could determine how often there is a queue, how long customers have to wait and how the organization deals with this. You could begin to describe the customers – individuals, families or groups, age, sex.

If you then had to use the information to develop a publicity campaign what else would you need to know that you have not been able to observe?

A hall test may be used to introduce a product to a new segment, to check out that the packaging works, that instructions are clear or that the colour of the packaging is acceptable.

One example of such a test is a company which wanted to take a product which had been used successfully in the industrial sector and sell it to home owners.

The product in question was a glass crack repair kit. It was an adhesive which strengthened the glass pane and had the cosmetic effect of disguising the crack – apparently making it disappear. It was intended for use on large window panes and had to be used relatively soon after the damage and while the crack was still clean. It had been used successfully by industrial users for some years.

When it was decided to launch the product into the consumer market, the first step was to take some questions on a country-wide omnibus survey. This allowed them to reach a wide sample of people at a lower cost than they would have had to spend to reach such a wide sample themselves by a survey of personal interviews. They undertook an 'incidence test': that is they wanted to discover, on average, how many households had broken window panes and what they did about them. They were also asked if they would be willing to take part in further research.

This gave them a sampling frame for the next stage of the research, which was to invite a representative sample into a hall test to see how they used the product.

First, the technique was demonstrated to them, and then they were asked to try it themselves and discuss how easy or difficult it was to use. The final stage was to ask another sample of people to try the product in their own home.

As a result the manufacturer adjusted the packaging and instructions for the product before it was launched in the consumer market, because of the different way in which they approached the task and how the consumer market used the material. For example, a small plastic cup was included to hold the mixed solution, a cotton wool bud to spread it, and a small blade to wipe off the excess dried adhesive.

The problem with tests such as these is that while the group of customers involved with the tests are giving you their opinion of the product at the time, this does not necessarily reflect what their buying behaviour will be once the product is available in the shops.

Figure 4.17 *The glass repair kit – transferring a successful trade product to the consumer market*

Experimentation

It is possible to set up laboratory-type tests with consumers using a product to show how they react to the product and its ease of use. This may be carried out with a number of customers in a central location (a *hall test*, see Figure 4.17) or the customer may be asked to try the item in their home or office for some weeks or months *(placement test)*.

If you have you ever been asked to taste a product – perhaps a drink or a new spread, while shopping but have not then been asked to fill in a questionnaire with your comments, this is not market research but a sales promotion to encourage you to buy the product. It has nothing to do with the collection of information for market research purposes.

For taste tests or placement tests the sample will have been carefully selected to represent their target market. You can be sure they will be asking a wide range of people. Sometimes taste tests are '*blind tests*', where they ask you to try and compare two unnamed products and tell them your opinion of each and which you prefer. They may be testing their product against a major competitor. You may recall the Pepsi Cola taste tests which have been featured in advertisements. This was based upon the findings of a market-research survey taste test.

Sometimes organizations need to test their own new improved product against their regular one. The idea is to see if the consumer can express a preference by taste alone, without the extra information from brand names and promotional images.

Groups and clinics

Group discussions, sometimes called focus groups, bring a group of people together for a short period to answer questions about a particular product or topic. The session is facilitated by an experienced researcher, who will lead the group through a series of topics, and ensure that everyone gets time to think about the product or issue and gets a chance to express their opinions. This may give a richer response when people can hear the views of others and then compare them with, and possibly confirm, their own views. The groups are small, usually eight to ten people at most. While a number of groups are usually undertaken around the country, this can only provide qualitative information and not quantitative, because the sample size will be too small for extrapolation of market sizes and trends.

Questionnaire-based surveys

This involves asking questions using a questionnaire. This is the type of survey people associate most frequently with marketing research. The questionnaire may be used for face-to-face (personal) interviews, by telephone or by mail.

The questionnaire is a set of questions asked in a specific order so that all respondents are asked the same questions, in the same words and in the same order, to avoid bias being introduced by the way the researcher asks the questions. They are used in all large-scale research, where there may be a large number of interviewers, who are not usually involved in the design of the questionnaire or the objectives of the research. It is important, therefore, that the questionnaire offers continuity to the survey.

A *checklist* may be used instead where the sample size is smaller, often in industrial or business-to-business research, or where the subject needs wider discussion of a number of points rather than specific questions. In such cases the interviews may be undertaken by the research executive who has written the checklist and who understands the objectives of the research.

Recently the author was invited to a Television Preview session. It was held in a hotel, there was a large audience and we were shown videos of two test programmes, lasting a half hour each.

The audience was asked to fill in a questionnaire at the beginning, which asked for details of age and occupation and address (for market classification) and they were given a selection of items and asked to choose which ones they would really like to own. An incentive for attending was the chance to win a selection of goodies taken from this list.

After each programme they were asked to fill in a questionnaire about it, to say if they had enjoyed it, which characters and actors and actresses they had liked or disliked, and if they would watch the programme if it were to be screened at a particular time and on a particular day. They were also asked if they would be willing to answer further questions on the telephone (recruiting for a telephone interview).

In between the programmes and in the middle of each video were a series of advertisements 'to make it more like a normal TV programme' the audience was told. A telephone call was made to the members of the audience over the next few days to follow up on these advertisements. It was looking at recall – could we remember which products were advertised, could we describe particular advertisements, had we seen any of those advertisements on the television, and could we confirm whether we had enjoyed either of the programmes?

This was not the only preview meeting they had held. There had been several similar evenings at various locations around the country. Recruitment had been mainly by post to the respondents' homes, using a sample generated from postcode areas. This was supplemented by face-to-face recruitment over the previous two or three days in the shopping centre close to the hotel.

They also collected feedback from the audience on the research company's own performance in welcoming the audience and the organization of the evening.

Figure 4.18 *A television programme hall test*

Face-to-face or personal interviews are an expensive way of collecting data but are often the most effective. In a face-to-face situation the interviewer can achieve rapport with the respondent, build their confidence and willingness to complete the questionnaire, ensure all questions are answered and probe for further information where appropriate. They can also show alternatives and demonstrate the product. The respondent can be asked to show proofs of purchase to back up their stated brand choice. They can be shown lists of choices or phrases to choose from, sometimes to prompt their memory or to narrow down the field of choice.

The disadvantages are that the interviewer may create bias. The respondent may take a dislike to the interviewer or their attitude or might try to guess from their facial expressions and body language which answers they would prefer. Also, there is the cost of the interviewing field force, which will be required to be located across the country, and the time taken to travel to the interview. In a random sample this may require two or three return journeys if the respondent is not in the first time.

A further difficulty is that the interviewers have to be trained how to complete the questionnaire without leading the respondent or influencing their answers. Where questions require the respondent to give an opinion or reason as a response which cannot be recorded by ticking boxes or choosing from a list, the interviewer must take down the response verbatim and not interpret or shorten the reply. In many cases, these days, the interviewers have lap top computers, which save time in editing, coding and transferring the data from paper at a later date. In the case of interviews undertaken overseas, there is the added problem of language and cultural differences both in writing the questionnaire and conducting the interview.

Activity 4.12

Think back to the survey we discussed earlier in this chapter to gather opinions about a ban on smoking in an organization's restaurants and pubs. Try writing the questionnaire for a face-to-face interview. Try to put your questions in a logical order and write them out so that an interviewer could read them out and write down replies.

Have you used mainly closed or open questions? Have you thought about how you will analyse perhaps 200 responses? Read your questions again? Are they clear and unambiguous? Will the questions give you information in a form that you can use to make some decisions? You have probably found that writing a questionnaire is more difficult than it sounds.

Telephone interviews

These are useful as a screening process and for short or exploratory interviews. They may be used to screen from a sampling list, to find out if the respondent is worth visiting for a personal interview or to recruit them for a focus group. Sometimes the interview may be conducted entirely on the telephone. This works better when there are only a few questions involved, the questions are not open ended, and do not require a long answer to be written down verbatim. Probably ten minutes is the longest one can expect to hold the attention of the respondent on the telephone.

The type of question you can ask in a telephone interview is restricted. For example it is difficult to explain or demonstrate a new or unknown product clearly by phone. Have you ever tried to describe a process on the telephone, and found yourself drawing pictures in the air with your hands? We often speak in this way but of course the respondent on the telephone cannot benefit from your explanatory gestures!

In telephone interviews you cannot ask respondents to compare colours, or shapes or images; you cannot have long lists of alternatives from which the respondent chooses, as they will probably have forgotten the first item on the list by the time you have reached the fourth one. You may get a better response by sending information to the respondent in advance, warning them of your phone call so they are prepared for your questions when you ring. This may help to get cooperation in advance but it is no guarantee that the respondent can find your material at the time you call or will have read it in advance! Despite these problems, the telephone can be a very useful, quick and relatively cheap way of collecting information.

In most cases telephone interviews in this country are used for business-to-business research, where the telephone is an accepted part of the working process. Even then, there are some types of respondents where a telephone interview is not easy. If the telephone is on the shop floor, the respondent may have to stand at a wall telephone with considerable machinery noise in the background. If you are interviewing surgeons or dentists, unless you pick your moment carefully they might find it inconvenient to drop what they are doing and come to the telephone! Elsewhere, managers might be protected by secretaries who are reluctant to let you through to ask market-research questions.

However, in the UK, there is a widespread reluctance among consumers to give a market-research interview by phone, although it is used successfully in the USA and other countries. It can be seen as an invasion of privacy, especially as the telephone has been taken over for cold call selling of consumer goods and canvassing charity donations. This has made the general public less amenable to telephone information gathering. There are research agencies that do use the telephone to do market research, but they have to choose their respondents with care. If the permission of the respondent has been sought in advance the response may be better.

Activity 4.13

Think back to the questionnaire which you wrote for the face-to-face interview. How might you have to change this for a telephone interview?

Postal surveys

Another method of collecting information is by a questionnaire that is sent to respondents by mail. It has a number of advantages over both telephone and personal surveys. It overcomes the cost of having an interviewing field force all over the country, the travelling expenses and wasted time for repeat calls.

The postal survey has less restrictions on the number and type of questions than telephone interviewing. It can be used for consumer or business-to-business research; you can include samples of colours of the product or pictures with the material and you can include more sophisticated scaling or ranking questions on opinions and attitudes.

There are drawbacks of course, the main problem being getting people to fill in and return the questionnaire. It may be put to one side and forgotten; not all the questions may be completed; and in some areas there may be a literacy problem which leads to difficulties in interpreting the questions and later in understanding the written answers. It has to be accompanied by a letter which convinces the respondent that it is worth their while to fill in and return the questionnaire.

The major concern for the researcher is the non-response rate; this refers to the proportion of the sample that do not return the questionnaire. Response rates vary from 20 per cent to 75 per cent, depending upon the time of year, the type of respondent and the clarity of the questionnaire. The researcher must decide what is an adequate response rate for the survey and what to do about the non-respondents. The researcher must decide if the responses are biased in any way, or if they only represent one particular viewpoint.

It may be possible to increase the response rate by sending out one or two reminders, or to undertake a sample of those not responding by a telephone interview to see if their views match on one or two key points. Sometimes a free gift is included in the envelope, as an incentive or reward for their time. This might be a pen to help the respondent with their reply! The researcher might appeal to the respondent's need or desire to improve products, services or knowledge about the market for the industry or consumers.

Activity 4.14

Look again at your smoking-ban questionnaire. What other changes would you make if you were going to send it out by post? Try writing an accompanying letter which would encourage people to complete and return it. What type of incentive could you use to improve the response rate?

The collection of primary data takes time and is often relatively expensive. There are a number of ways in which the fieldwork and associated costs can be shared with other organizations.

An *omnibus survey* is one in which an agency sets up the vehicle – a large-scale personal interview survey, often for the consumer market. Organizations then pay for specific questions to be included in the questionnaire. It is rather like paying a bus fare to travel a few stops, instead of buying the whole bus!

These surveys can be used for an 'incidence' survey. This is where an organization wishes to find out the answers to such questions as:

- How many people use a particular type of product?
- How many people go to concerts?
- How many people own a personal CD player?
- How many households have had to claim on travel insurance in the past year?
- How many people smoke?
- How many people approve of a ban on smoking in restaurants?
- How many people have had a broken window in their house in the last six months and what have they done about it?

To the respondent these questionnaires may seem unfocused, because they ask about so many different topics.

9 omnibus surveys on Italian market
Representative samples of 2,000: males, females, families, special targets.
Beginning of fieldwork: Circled dates on calendar.
Last date for submitting questions: 2 weeks before start of fieldwork (see dates above).
Delivery: 6 weeks after beginning of fieldwork, except for holiday periods.
Price per question ranging from 650,000 Italian lira (2,000 respondents) onwards.
Fieldwork dates and price per question may be subject to slight variations.

Figure 4.19 *Advert for an Italian omnibus survey styled as a calender*

Another shared research method is the *consumer panel*, similar to the retail audit in that it attempts to track consumer buyer behaviour on a regular basis to discover trends in the market. Unlike the audit which deals in quantitative information by collecting the information from retail outlets, the consumer panel sets up a sample of households who agree to fill in a questionnaire about their weekly shopping and therefore can include the qualitative and classification information that the retail audits lack. Sometimes this is a pencil-and-paper activity; in some cases it is entered into a small electronic data machine which may work with a modem and send the information directly to the collecting agency.

It is vital that you have set the objectives for your research carefully and only collect data that is appropriate to solving the problem and helping managers to make decisions. Once you have collected the data, it is time to analyse and interpret the results.

Analysis and interpretation of data collected

Your analysis of the data collected in the fieldwork will usually need to take into account both quantitative and qualitative data. It is important that you plan how to analyse the data when you are designing the questionnaire so that all the necessary questions are asked. You need to know what type of information you are seeking, and this takes you back to the original objectives set for the research.

The analysis of quantitative data can take the form of percentages of respondents who say yes or no, or who own or don't own a piece of equipment, or do or don't buy or like a brand or service. Alternatively you can look at the frequency of responses to a certain category or value. You may also look at maximum values, minimum values, median values, modal values or arithmetic means.

The advent of the computer in the office has made analysis and interpretation of data easier, if only because it can overcome the tendency to make errors with lengthy calculations using a calculator, and it can speed up the process once the initial layout or package is decided.

Where the computer is networked, you may have access to more sophisticated statistical analysis packages. Alternatively you can use standard spreadsheet or database packages to help your analysis.

A *spreadsheet* can be used to produce a log sheet of responses, using rows for the questions and the columns for question responses. The spreadsheet can be used both for word responses and numeric data. In the latter case the formulae can be used to take the tedium out of calculating weighted averages and percentage responses, etc. The spreadsheet data can then be used to produce charts, bar graphs, pie charts and to do the cross analysis.

A standard *database* can be used to sort categories and for cross analysis. You can use them to pick out respondents from particular subcategories who have expressed an interest in a particular product or service.

All samples are selected to represent the total universe from which they are chosen. If you have used a random sample there are mathematical theories which allow you to calculate the range of error for each given prob-

COLD AND FLU REMEDIES

15165

	POPULATION '000	ALL USERS A '000	B % down	C % across	D index	HEAVY USERS A '000	B % down	C % across	D index	MEDIUM USERS A '000	B % down	C % across	D index	LIGHT USERS A '000	B % down	C % across	D index	NON USERS A '000	B % down	C % across	D index
ALL ADULTS	45350	28159	100.0	62.1	100	9125	100.0	20.1	100	9620	100.0	21.2	100	9414	100.0	20.8	100				
MEN	21899	13641	48.4	62.3	100	4350	47.7	19.9	99	4698	48.8	21.5	101	4593	48.8	21.0	101				
WOMEN	23451	14518	51.6	61.9	100	4775	52.3	20.4	101	4922	51.2	21.0	99	4821	51.2	20.6	99				
15-24	7436	4908	17.4	66.0	106	1399				1809	18.8	24.3	115	1700	18.1	22.9	110	4226	24.6	38.2	101
25-34	8915	5951	21.1	66.7	107	2021	22.1	22.7	113	2054	18.9	23.8	109	1874	18.1	21.0	101	1992	11.6	39.3	104
35-44	7516	4956	17.6	65.9	106	1522	16.7	20.2	101	1792	18.6	23.8	112	1366	14.5	18.2	88	1590	4.5	38.5	102
45-54	6948	4288	15.2	61.7	99	1245	13.6	17.9	89	1427	14.8	20.5	97	1366	14.5	19.7	95	1688	4.0	44.1	116
55-64		4743	16.8	53.4	86	1242	13.6	14.0	70	1475	15.3	16.6	78	2023	21.5	22.8	110	1837	19.1	36.6	97
55+	5890																	2245	15.3	36.4	103
																		2113	15.3	38.4	101
																		1069	6.2	34.8	92
																		381	1.6	43.8	116
AB	9275	5485	19.5	59.1	95	1697	18.6	18.3	91	1976	20.5	21.3	100	1812	19.2	19.5	94				
C1	12199	7548	26.8	61.9	100	2550	27.9	20.9	104	2671	27.7	21.9	104	2330	24.7	21.6	104				
C2	10813	7020	24.9	64.9	105	2294	25.1	21.2	105	2324	24.2	21.5	101	1642	17.4	21.2	102				
D	7398	4745	16.9	64.1	103	1555	17.0	21.0	104	1549	16.1	20.9	99	1253	13.3	22.1	106				
E	5666	3360	11.9	59.3	96	1030	11.3	18.2	90	1078	11.2	19.0	90								
ABC1	21473	11033	46.3	60.7	98	4246	46.5	21.4	98	4597	47.8	21.4	101	4189	42.5	19.5	94				
C2D	18211	11765	41.8	64.6	104	3849	42.1	21.1	105	3944	41.0	21.7	105	3972	42.2	21.5	97				
35+ 15-34	7454	4870	17.3	65.3	105	1579	17.3	21.2	105	1814	18.9	24.3	115	1505	16.0	20.2	97				
55+	6694	4525	16.1	67.6	109	1116	17.3	21.6	107	1635	17.0	22.3	105	1311	13.9	17.5	86				
C2DE 15-34	8897	5638	21.3	61.8	99	1816	20.5	16.7	83	2052	21.3	23.1	109	2069	22.0	20.5	112				
35-54	7812	4419	15.7	56.4	91	1270	13.9	16.2	80	1386	14.4	17.7	83	1394	14.8	19.5	108				
GREATER LONDON	5474	3395	12.1	62.0	100	1044	11.4	19.1	95	1293	12.4	21.8	101	1192	12.4	23.4	110	2245	12.3	38.0	101
SOUTH EAST/EAST ANGLIA	10437	6361	22.6	60.0	98	2086	22.9	19.7	98	2229	12.4	21.8	103	1098	12.4	20.4	104	1556	11.2	37.5	99
SOUTH WEST	3835	2250	8.0	56.7	94	669	7.5	15.4	87	739	7.6	19.2	90	855	10.3	19.1	92	1929	10.3	34.7	92
WALES	2347	1502	5.3	64.0	103	500	5.5	21.4	106	481	5.0	20.5	97	971	10.3	19.8	92	1776	10.3	34.8	92
EAST & WEST MIDLANDS	7526	4789	17.0	63.6	102	1458	16.0	19.4	96	1753	18.2	23.3	110	918	9.8	18.4	89	1902	10.1	38.1	101
NORTH WEST	5175	3204	11.4	61.9	100	1042	11.4	20.1	100	1103	11.5	21.3	100	1501	15.9	24.0	117	2768	16.1	38.0	100
YORKSHIRE & HUMBERSIDE	4027	2476	8.8	61.5	99	853	9.4	21.2	105	811	8.4	20.1	95	1101	15.7	24.2	117	1758	10.2	38.7	102
NORTH	2481	1541	5.5	62.1	100	489	5.4	19.7	98												
SCOTLAND	4048	2641	9.4	65.2	105	984	10.8	24.3	121	1386		20.1	95	2384	25.3	40.5	107	4030	23.4	40.5	107
LONDON	11060	6634	24.3	60.7	98	2145	23.5	19.4	96					718	7.6	18.6	89	1473	8.6	38.1	101
SOUTH	4131	2540	10.0	61.5	99	1065	21.7	19.0	104					966	10.3	18.8	90				
EAST OF ENGLAND	2540	871	3.1	65.5	101	208	8.0	19.6	97												
SOUTH WEST	1558	2734	9.7	62.6	101	855	8.4	19.9	98												
WALES & WEST	4369	5689	20.2	64.6	104	1728	18.9	20.2	100												
MIDLANDS	8976	3607	11.7	61.6	99	1161	12.9	20.5	98												
NORTH WEST	5851	3288	11.7	60.8	98	1537	12.9	20.4	102												
YORKSHIRE	5401	1618	5.7	61.6	100	724	7.9	20.5	102												
NORTH EAST	2627	2007	7.1	65.2	104	289	3.2	26.7	113												
CENTRAL SCOTLAND	3076	350	1.2	56.2	90	108	1.2	17.3	96					111	1.2	17.8	86	273	1.6	43.8	116
BORDER	623																				
H/D INCOME £35,000 OR MORE	3866	2392	8.5	61.9	100	774	8.5	20.0	99	1192	12.4	23.4	110								
£25,000 – £34,999	5145	3216	11.4	62.5	101	1041	11.4	20.2	101	1098	12.4	20.4	104								
£20,000 – £24,999	4480	2924	10.4	65.3	105	1005	12.7	22.7	113	1483	15.4	20.4	96								
£15,000 – £19,999	5096	3320	11.0	65.2	105	1157	12.7	22.7	113	1823	18.9	18.6	85								
£11,000 – £14,999	4992	3089	11.0	61.9	100	1073	11.8	21.5	107	1849	19.2	18.6	88								
£5,000 – £10,999	7286	4517	16.0	62.0	100	1534	16.8	21.0	105												
£4,999 OR LESS	4545	2787	9.9	61.5	99	1101	16.9	18.4	94												
NOT STATED	9942	5912	21.0	59.5	96	1679	18.4	16.9	84												

Column D. Index
An index based on the percentage in Column C. 22.7% of all adults aged 25-34 are Heavy Users. This is 13% above the average for all adults (20.1%) thus giving an Index of 113.

Column C. Across
The percentage of all 25-34 year olds (or whatever group is listed on the table side heading) who are Heavy Users.

Column B. Down
The percentage of all Heavy Users who are 25-34 year olds. The percentages in each demographic sub-group add up to 100% vertically (except ITV overlap, presence of children).

Column A. 000's
The projected number of people in thousands who are users in that sub group. Thus 2,021,000 adults 25-34 are Heavy Users of Cold and Flu Remedies.

Figure 4.20 *Example of data provided by TGI (Target Group Index) BMRB International*

ability level. This will allow you to indicate, for example, that in 95 out of a 100 cases your results will be accurate to within 3 per cent. If you have used a small sample or a quota sample, you cannot use statistical theory to calculate margins of error.

Even if you have used a random sample, and are confident of the degree of error, you need to remember that this has usually been calculated on the total sample size, and the more you look at the findings for subgroups of the data, the smaller your sample size becomes, and the less representative of the population as a whole.

The design of the questionnaire is a skilled task. There are a range of specialist software packages available for marketing research which can design the questionnaire, analyse and cross-tabulate the data and produce the desired charts and tables. There are also computer bureaux that will undertake the preparation, data entry and analysis for you.

Once your data has been analysed and tabulated, the important stage of interpretation has to be undertaken. This is an attempt to understand the material you have collected, and to judge its validity. You will need to cross-check your data analysis with your experience of the market, or the knowledge of those already involved in the market: your sales force, your distribution channel or other experts that you have consulted, and the trends already indicated in the desk research.

In presenting the report of your analyses and interpretation, you need to consider if you have met the original objectives of the survey, and if, on the basis of your report, the user can take the required decisions. You must consider the various audiences there will be for your report. The decision maker will either want clear action points, or information which will allow him or her to make those decisions. Other readers may only need a summary of the main points while those required to take action may also require the technical details of the survey and the basis of the analysis and interpretation. Preparing and presenting reports is considered further in Chapter 8.

CASE STUDY: THE NEWTOWN LEISURE CENTRE

Let us consider our survey of users of the sports centre discussed earlier and how that data might be interpreted and used to build a strategy for the development of the centre.

You may have tried to find out how much each facility has been used. The following table shows the results for the use of the badminton courts. Remember that the analysis should always give details of the base for the table – the number of responses that have been used.

Question: Did you use the badminton courts at the centre during the last month?

Use of badminton court	Number of responses	%
Yes	360	36
No	620	62
Don't know	0	0
No response	20	2
Total	1000	100
Base no:	1000	

This is a single response question, because the respondents either did or did not use the badminton court, they couldn't have done both!

You might wish to look at badminton court usage in greater depth by cross-analysing this question with details of the type of user, and thus analyse the question by age of user, sex, time of use, how close the user lives to the centre. All these details should be in the classification questions. If, however, you wish to cross-analyse this by standard of play, if they played with a member of their family or friends, if they made a special journey or combined it with a visit to town for another purpose, or if they are a member of a club at the centre, you would need to make sure these questions had been included in the questionnaire at the planning stage.

The breakdown of badminton court usage by sex might look like this:

Question: Did you use the badminton courts at the centre during the last month: by sex of respondent

Use of badminton court	Total %	Male %	Female %
Yes	36	30	45
No	62	58	55
Don't know	0	0	0
No response	2	2	0
Total	100	100	100
Base no:	1000	500	500

This table shows us that more females had used the badminton courts than males (45 per cent compared with 30 per cent) in the last month. If we were then to compare the times of play, we might find a daily pattern emerging; but if we were also to compare frequency of play, we might find in fact that although there were fewer men using the badminton courts, they used them more times than the women:

Question: How many times did you use the badminton courts at the centre during the last month: frequency of use: by sex of respondent

Use of badminton court	Total %	Male %	Female %
Once only	49	30	63
2–4 times	44	60	33
5–8 times	5	6	4
More than 8 times	2	4	0
Total	100	100	100
Base no:	360	150	210

To find out how many more times men use the courts than women, the question would need to be answered not in intervals, as shown above (i.e. 2–4 times) but in actual numbers of times. This might show, for instance, that while most men tend to play regularly once a week, most women tend to play only once or twice a month.

With this information the manager could then start planning their strategy. Should they concentrate on attracting more men to join the centre, as they are the most frequent users, or should they try to persuade the women members to use the facilities more often?

Sometimes in market research surveys you wish to use multi-response questions, where the respondent can tick any number of choices.

The users of the sports centre may respond as follows:

Question: Which extra facilities would you like the centre to provide:

Facilities	Positive response %
car park	60
fitness centre	55
snackbar	50
sauna	43
bar	10
private coaching	40
massage	25
creche	18
facials	10
whirlpool	5
Total	*
Base no:	1000

* multi–response

Again, the value of this analysis would be increased by cross-analysing it by sex and frequency of use. While overall the numbers wanting to use saunas, massages, facials, whirlpools and creches might be considered low, it might represent a high proportion of those women using the centre, and providing these facilities could be one way of attracting the women to use the centre more often.

When you are analysing qualitative data, you may have to deal with open-ended questions or scaled questions. With open-ended questions respondents are asked to give their own answer rather than respond to a set list of choices, and the interviewer writes these down verbatim. In theory, while there could be as many different answers as respondents, the answers do tend to follow a similar pattern and can be grouped into categories.

For example, we may have asked an open-ended question about how the service at the leisure centre could be improved. An analysis of the answers could come up with the following broad groups:

Opening hours	open longer hours
	open earlier in the morning
	open later in the evening
	open on Sundays
Access	have special hours for children
	have adult-only sessions
	have women-only sessions
	have singles nights
Booking facilities	allow more block bookings
	allow fewer block bookings
	allow booking a week ahead
	have a dedicated phone number just for bookings
Price	allow credit card payments
	allow discounts for regular bookings
	allow discounts for booking more than one facility at a time
Staff	have name tags for staff
	have a staff of the week award

There will also be an 'other' group where the comments that do not fit in anywhere else can go. It may be possible to pre-guess the categories and therefore use a closed question, but these may mean you miss some of the good ideas. It is a matter of balancing judgement against time taken to analyse the questionnaire. It may also depend upon how many questionnaires you expect to be returned.

A scaled question usually involves the respondent judging an attribute on a 5 or 7-point scale. A common scale would be:

> very good
> fairly good
> neither good nor poor
> fairly poor
> very poor

This can be analysed, as for the single and multiple response questions, by recording the percentage of scores in each category. However, if you wish to compare the ranking for a number of items, or against competitive offers, it helps to weight the factors and obtain a mean score. To do this you allocate a weight to each scale point, and multiply this by the number of responses in that scale point; this is divided by the number of responses to give the weighted average. This is shown in the table below:

Helpfulness of staff

Response	Weight	%
very good	+2	30
fairly good	+1	40
neither good nor poor	0	10
fairly poor	−1	15
very poor	−2	5
Total	1000	
Mean score	0.075	
Base no:	1000	

This is calculated by:

$$\frac{(30 \times 2 + 40 \times 1) - (15 + 5 \times 2)}{1000} = 0.075$$

The rating of 0.075 on its own means little, and it will only be of use in comparing this weighting with the rating of satisfaction for other service factors at the leisure centre.

Measuring, monitoring and improving customer service

Quality in customer relationships

Quality is about setting standards by which the organization can judge its output. Do the products and services it delivers meet the standards or goals or set of requirements that they originally set themselves as targets?

Quality standards and quality assurance methods have been discussed in Chapter 3, but it is important for organizations to consider quality in terms of customer relationships, where the emphasis is on the standards required to meet and satisfy customer needs.

Many organizations are concerned with customer-care programmes, but in reality they often stop at standards for customer service – how they interface with the customers. True customer-care programmes concentrate on satisfying the customers needs, rather than the efficiency with which they conduct interactions with the customers. It is not sufficient to meet targets for speed of answering the telephone or sending written replies to customers if those replies do not result in satisfying the customers' needs. For example, a local authority housing department may reach its quality targets by replying to a tenants request within five days (customer service), but if the letter says the council is unable to replace the broken window which is the subject of the request, the customer need has still not been satisfied (customer care).

Activity 4.15

Draw up a list of what quality means to you personally for a product and services you have used. Write it in two columns:

What quality is: *What quality is not:*

Now consider your own department at work. How does its output match your own quality list?

You may have included items such as good service, friendly service, politeness by the people who deal with your enquiries or complaints, service within acceptable waiting times, a clean environment for buying or consuming the service, products that fit the purpose.

Think through your list – were you looking for excellence or adequate service? Does this vary from product to product? Do you expect the same quality from your table salt as your car? Why and how are they different? Can you try to define good service?

For a quality programme to be effective it needs to be quantifiable, measurable and results oriented, and everyone has to know about it.

Loss of custom results from poor quality

Quality assurance systems aim to ensure that the right quality is delivered first time, thus avoiding future problems. The systems should be designed to assure that the appropriate quality is achieved. The 'cost of quality' can be related to the costs of prevention, appraisal and failure. The cost of failure may be far reaching – embracing not only loss of market share or reputation but in terms of the bottom line – a loss of turnover, profits, and perhaps ultimately, closure.

Poor quality may lead to the loss of the hard won trust of the customer. This may come from any of the measures of customer satisfaction.

The product or service is not fit for the purpose or does not meet the expectations raised; the quality is not consistent and cannot be relied upon, or it was not delivered to the time-scale agreed. This may cause downtime in a customer's production line, or loss of face with their customers. Some customers complain and give you a second chance; many others just drift away and are lost as they try competitive brands or alternative ways of satisfying their needs.

This table shows a somewhat lighthearted approach to why customers are lost, but is underpinned by a serious point:

1%	of lost customers die
3%	move away
4%	just naturally float
5%	change on a friend's recommendation
9%	can buy it cheaper elsewhere
10%	are chronic complainers
68%	go elsewhere because the people they deal with are indifferent to their needs

(*Source*: D. Bone and R. Griggs, *Quality at Work.*)

Figure 4.21 *Bone and Griggs customer loss table*

The government has attempted to set a good example in as far as the citizen's and user's charters attempt to embed the concept of customer service in legislation. The Social Charter has led to all public sector organizations issuing 'service promises' to their users. You can see these statements everywhere, and many organizations are making genuine attempts to transfer these promises into action.

A fundholding doctors' practice has recently taken on a Computer Manager, and issues a booklet setting out their aims and practice details and issues a regular newsletter for patients. Their slogan is 'Health for All' and their aim is 'within the limits of the resources provided by the health service to our practice, to ensure that each patient receives the best treatment in the shortest time possible'. A worthy aim, but one that remains unquantified and unspecific. It would be hard to measure achievement against this, and difficult for the patients to judge if the service is 'up to standard'!

The practice is, however, moving towards a customer focus and has set up a patients' suggestions' scheme. They provide feedback slips and a postbox in the waiting room and encourage patients to tell them about complaints on service or suggestions for improvement.

Figure 4.22 *Doctors' practice – a quality service promise which cannot be measured*

The British Gas Celsia
Customer Promise

The Celsia Customer Promise is our guarantee of the highest standards of service and workmanship. Order a Celsia system and here are just a few of the promises we make to you. We will:

∗

Work with you to design a heating system tailored for your home – using the very latest computer technology

∗

Explain exactly what will be done before the work starts, how long it will take, and the steps we will take to minimise disruption to your home

∗

Use only qualified engineers who carry official identity cards, so you can be sure who you are letting in to your home

∗

Stay until the job is completed as planned – *never* disappearing to work on another job and leaving you in chaos

∗

Clean up thoroughly afterwards and leave your home just as tidy as we found it

∗

Contact you within 48 hours of completion to make sure you are happy with everything, and that the system is working perfectly

Figure 4.23a *British Gas – customer promises*

Figure 4.23b *A mail photograph processing company uses this statement on its packaging*

Jobseeker's Charter
Standards of service from Jobcentres

Standards of service:

Average waiting time during the last quarter:

Interviews:	1–2 hours
Reply by phone:	5–10 seconds
Reply by letter:	1–5 days
Current vacancies:	99% available

Figure 4.23c *Jobcentre service standards*

The Commercial Union Customer Power Promise.

We aim to be accurate, helpful, timely and to keep our promises at all times. To underline our commitment to service excellence we will send you a Customer Power Voucher worth £10 against your next renewal premium (up to a maximum of £30 in any one period of insurance) if we fail to deliver to you the following standards of service.

1 We will issue written confirmation to you within two working days of any quotation given by telephone, if requested.

2 We will issue written confirmation of cover within one working day of acceptance, if required.

3 We will issue motor cover notes immediately payment is received.

4 We will issue policies no later than five working days after receiving all the information and payment of premium.

5 We will issue policy change documents no later than five working days after receiving all the information.

6 We will contact you at least ten working days before the renewal date of your policy.

7 We will send claim forms by 1st Class post within one working day of their request.

8 We will inspect your vehicle, if necessary, within two working days of it being made available at one of our Selected Repairers or at any other repairer of your choice.

9 We will respond to all correspondence from you in relation to any claim you may have, within five working days of receipt.

10 We will send out cheques within three working days of agreeing settlement of your claim.

Figure 4.23d *Commercial Union – customer promise*

Customer Power Promise.

At Commercial Union we have always placed great importance on our service to the customer. Now we have published the standards and timings we work to for handling claims, payments and other communications with our customers.

This means that you can now be sure of the standards of service you can expect from us – and of recompense if we fail to meet these standards.

We pride ourselves on our promise that 'we won't make a drama out of a crisis'. In the unlikely event that you should have a complaint in connection with your policy, we will respond within two working days of receipt.

If you feel that we have broken the Customer Power Promise and wish to claim a Customer Power Voucher in compensation, or if you have any other complaint about our service, you should first write to your Commercial Union Branch Manager.

Should the Branch Manager be unable to resolve the complaint to your satisfaction, please write to:
The Consumer Relations Executive,
Commercial Union Assurance Company plc,
St. Helen's, 1 Undershaft, London EC3P 3DQ.

If you are still not satisfied with the way your complaint has been dealt with, there are two further options open to you:
a) as a private policyholder, you may approach the Insurance Ombudsman Bureau at City Gate One, 135 Park Street, London SE1 9EA.
b) you may also approach the Consumer Information Department of the Association of British Insurers. Their London address is 51 Gresham Street, London EC2V 7HQ. They also have a number of regional offices, details of which may be found in your local telephone directory.

Law applicable to Contract.

The law applicable to this contract will be that of the country where the policyholder is usually resident, where this is within the UK, the Channel Islands or the Isle of Man. Otherwise English Law will apply.

Customer Power Purchase – practical, money-saving discounts.

In the course of a year our **Customer Power Purchase Discounts** could save you a large proportion of the cost of your policy. We have negotiated special discounts for you on purchases from major retailers and leisure companies.

The discounts vary from company to company but they are all worthwhile. To claim them, simply present your Customer Power Card.

Customer Power Promise – the standards you can expect.

The **Customer Power Promise** sets out in black and white the timings we work to in handling quotations, claims, renewals and changes to policies. So you will know exactly the standards of service you can expect when you deal with Commercial Union. And if we fail to meet those standards, we will offer you a Customer Power Voucher, which can be set against your next renewal premium.

The Customer Power Promise is printed in full later on in this booklet.
The following pages give full details of Customer Power services open to you. Customer Power is being constantly updated and we will keep you informed of new developments in our service.

Figure 4.23d *(continued)*

Commercial Union's slogan of 'we won't make a drama out of a crisis' has been well publicized in their promotions and advertisements. They are backing this up with published quality standards and have set up a 'Customer Power Promise' (see Figure 4.23d), which indicates the standards of service they intend to meet, including times taken to issue confirmations and policies, times of contact in advance of renewal dates, and dealing with claims, correspondence and complaints. They are so keen to achieve these standards that they are offering a cash discount if they don't achieve them.

Activity 4.16

Considering the above examples of quality service statements, see if you can find similar examples from your own personal experience or with the suppliers for your organization.

Have they made their service promise explicit? Is it quantified? Do they give you feedback on how well they achieve their targets?

Measuring and monitoring satisfaction of customer needs

Achieving quality in customer relations is about setting standards, goals and interpreting a set of customer requirements. These have to be in measurable terms rather than a vague expression of goodwill or doing your best for the customer. The organization needs to pay continuous attention to see that quality standards, once reached, are maintained, improved upon, and the results measured often and in an appropriate manner.

In adopting a quality approach it is necessary to define the quality required by the customers. At present many organizations are setting these standards by what they can achieve, without reference to customer needs. Those companies that are closer to overall quality start with customer expectations of quality.

These standards must be set in terms that are measurable, so that it can be seen how far the organization is achieving them. The next step is to plan the operations of the organization to achieve the desired quality and then to monitor progress and output against those measures, making corrections where shortfalls are found.

What do you measure? You measure what satisfies the customer – the things that your customer feedback tells you are important to them. There is no point in measuring qualities which have no value in the eyes of the consumer.

1 Identify customer needs:	what they need/want in terms of volume, value, specifications, quality level, augmented product, service implications tangible and intangible needs.
2 When do they want it:	delivery tolerances, speed and delay times, duration of services.
3 How will it be achieved:	what processes will the organization adopt?
4 Result and feedback:	how will you measure it – how will you know when you reach the goal?

Figure 4.24 *Steps in setting customer satisfaction standards*

Why live up to a promise to deliver all orders within 24 hours if the customer has no need for the items within seven days? You will probably be adding extra costs to your own organization for a speed of turnround that adds nothing to the satisfaction of this customer. The organization should save those efforts for the times when it really matters.

Why tell your customer that your labels will stick for 50 years when all they want is an adhesive label giving instructions for handling during delivery and installation, and which will be removed and discarded within ten days at the most.

Make sure that you are providing and measuring against standards of quality that are adequate and appropriate – if in the eyes of the customer that level is 'excellence' then adjust your policies and strategies to provide excellence. If, on the other hand, by quality the customer means adequate to do the job – set up a system that provides just that.

Utility
Does the product or service do what it claims to do for as often or as long as required?

Sales service
What level of pre- and post-sales service was given? Was it adequate in the eyes of the customer?

Delivery
Did the environment or experience of buying meet the customer's expectations?

Image
Did the product or service feel right for the customer – create the right image or status for the buyer? Did the customer feel 'cheated' or 'disappointed' or 'unhappy' that they didn't get what they were expecting?

Figure 4.25 *Measuring satisfaction*

To measure satisfaction levels the organization needs to set up formal methods of collecting the information regularly and acting upon it quickly.

The informal methods of feedback can often give the first clues that something is not quite right. Regular surveys can be used to track levels of satisfaction.

Responsibility must be allocated to someone for overseeing the feedback, collection and interpretation of the information, and organizing the regular and ad hoc surveys to track customer opinion and satisfaction.

This type of feedback is only effective if action is then taken on the issues raised, or the rationale behind why things cannot change either in the short term or long term, or sometimes why change is not desirable or possible, must be fed back to the clients. Customer feedback should always be a two-way communication.

When dealing with complaints and enquiries it is important to set up a process or mechanism for handling these. Responsibility should be allocated, and all employees and the customers informed of this. People need to know how and to whom they can complain. All employees then know where to direct such comments and feedback. Appropriate action needs to be taken within a specific time-scale and the customer kept informed of progress or the outcome. Quality standards here may be set in terms of the time taken to respond to the first contact, the type of action taken and how and when feedback is given to the customer. Schemes that merely measure the number of complaints handled do not add up to a satisfactory quality standard: it is only how they are handled and resolved, and how quickly that matters.

Once standards have been agreed, it is becoming the practice to publish these so that the customer can see how well they are achieving them – and how they are striving always to improve their performance. This is an important element of quality in customer relationships – communicating what you are doing and what you are achieving to the customer and to the community at large. A local job centre has posters informing clients of the standards of service they are trying to achieve; and each month they publish the figures to show how far they have achieved this.

Activity 4.17

Look at the system for handling complaints in your own organization.

- Is it clear how and to whom customers can take complaints?
- Does everyone in the organization know where to direct complaints?
- Is there a routine process established?
- Have people been allocated the responsibility of handling and solving problems?

- How often is the success rate checked?
- Is this part of the organization's quality standards?
- Do employees see it as an opportunity to improve quality standards by feeding back problems to appropriate departments?
- How could the process be changed to improve customer relationships?

A PROMISE TO OUR CUSTOMERS:

'If we have made a mistake we will put it right.'

- **Welwyn Hatfield Council is committed to providing good quality services at reasonable cost.**
- **We aim to satisfy our customers and to ensure everyone is treated fairly and efficiently.**

Even in the best run organisations, however, things sometimes go wrong.
We want you to let us know if you think we have done something wrong or failed to do what we should have done, so that we can put it right.
To be sure that we deal effectively with any complaints you may have and to improve our service to you the council has a formal procedure. This leaflet outlines how this works.

Definition of a complaint. The Local Government Ombudsman defines a complaint as being an expression of dissatisfaction about a council's standard of service, actions or lack of action.

Figure 4.26 *Welwyn Hatfield Council complaints procedure*

Organizations with a positive quality attitude go one step further, and feed back this information into their planning and review systems, and communicate the results to all staff concerned with customers and customer relationships and take positive action for improvement.

Monitoring and improving customer relationships

As customers become more sophisticated and demand satisfaction, and as markets become more competitive, organizations should remember that

---

PUTTING IT RIGHT

OUR **Customer Complaints Procedure** explains your rights and gives set times in which you can expect a response from us.

If you make a complaint to us about our service it will be acknowledged within three working days and we will aim to resolve the matter within 15 working days or tell you within 15 days the reason for the delay and when you can expect it to be resolved.

Our leaflet *Dealing With Your Complaint* which explains the procedure in full and what steps you can take is available from council offices or ring our Public Relations Unit (01707 331212 ext. 2228) for a copy.

FEEDBACK

If you have any comments and suggestions about our services please write to:

> **FEEDBACK**
> **c/o Public Relations Unit,**
> **Welwyn Hatfield Council,**
> **Council Offices,**
> **Welwyn Garden City**
> **AL8 6AE.**

Figure 4.27 *Welwyn Hatfield Council's 'Putting it right' procedure*

customers always have a choice – even if it is ultimately not to consume! The organization that takes care of its customers and builds good and long-lasting relationships with its customer chain will achieve a competitive edge.

Quality takes time and energy to achieve and maintain; the standards need to have commitment from top management but to be understood and agreed by all staff. They should be written, widely circulated and often repeated. The main reason for developing quality standards is to provide products and services for customers that satisfy their needs, and that do this within the profit or cost parameters of the organization.

Quality standards affect what organizations do, how they do it, when and how they meet customers' needs. Quality can always be improved, as can customer relationships. The two are closely linked.

Therefore, to improve customer relationships, the organization needs constantly to checkout what the customers' needs are, and if the organization's provision is meeting and satisfying those needs. Internally the processes can be improved by checking that quality standards are regularly updated. The standards that have been set should be prominent in the company's mission statement, and embedded in its objectives, policies and strategies. These must be communicated in a form that is readily understood, remembered and achievable by all employees. The achievement of these standards is then measured regularly and the results widely published within and outside the organization.

The Court Service provides a very important service to members of the public in circumstances which are often difficult and stressful. Most people coming to a court for the first time will be anxious about what to expect. We want to reduce these anxieties by making the court system as friendly and effective as possible. This first Charter for Court Users sets out some of the things we intend to do.

We will respond to your views and suggestions in setting future standards of service. In the first national survey of court users which we carried out during 1994, we asked for your views on a whole range of services. This Charter takes account of what you told us.

We are fully committed to maintaining and improving the quality of the service provided in the courts. Some changes can be brought about quickly. Others, often because they require full consultation with other agencies, will take longer. But it is our aim, with your help, to meet and improve on the standards set by this Charter.

Michael Huebner

M D Huebner
Chief Executive

Listening to you

So that we can continue to improve our service, we want to find out:
- how satisfied you are with the current levels of service and facilities we provide
- how do you think we can improve our service

We do this by:
- collecting and analysing the suggestions and complaints you send us
- commissioning independent national court user surveys
- carrying out local court user surveys

We will display information in the court waiting area on:
- complaints and suggestions that have led to improvements in the court
- the results of local and national surveys
- changes we plan to make as a result of those surveys

Figure 4.28 *Lord Chancellor's Department: extracts from the Court Services Charter for Court Users*

The contribution that staff make to maintaining and improving customer relationships is paramount. They are the people who have the first and continuing contacts with customers. First impressions really do count. Besides the staff who have direct contact with the customers there is also an impact from every other employee, even when they have no direct contact with the final customer. What they do have is contact with other members of the organization – the internal customer. Everyone has to think about 'what I am here for' and how their own contribution adds to achieving the overall company objectives.

Motivation and training are key points. Awareness of quality standards needs to be measured and then raised until all staff are aware of the standards and how well the organization is reaching them.

Activity 4.18

Make sure you have a copy of the mission statement and overall objectives of your organization. Think about the activities and objectives of your own job.

- How do you contribute to the organization's overall objectives?
- Who are the users or customers of the results of the work of your department?
- What sort of quality statements can you make about the work of your department?
- How do you contribute to this?
- How can you improve on the service and quality you offer your department's customers and the organization's end customers?

Summary

More organizations are recognizing the need to develop satisfactory relationships with their customers. They are adopting a customer approach and using marketing principles to identify their customers, their needs and wants. They can then adjust their services or products to meet those needs.

It is important to identify what need the customer is satisfying in buying a product or service. This performance specification is then used to write the design specification and develop products or services that satisfy those needs. In marketing the right product to the right customer you need to segment the market according to customer needs. You can then adapt your product or service and the marketing mix to suit the needs of specific target markets. One further stage is needed in identifying customer needs, this is an understanding of customer behaviour – how they choose which products and brands to buy.

Collecting information about customers and their needs is expensive, and it is important to set the objectives for any research. There are many sources of information available. Desk research can provide a good overview of a topic, despite its limitations. The results may not provide the whole answer for your purposes and often need to be supplemented with primary data from a field survey.

Organizations need to measure customer satisfaction against pre-determined standards for the quality of their products and services.

5 Interpersonal communication

Aims

By the end of this chapter, you should recognize the significance of effective interpersonal communications in managing people. The exercises here should help you to build effective working relationships and provide you with a toolkit of basic communication principles and techniques to handle interpersonal situations, either in one-to-one or group situations.

Key concepts

- Interpersonal communication;
- Purposes and uses;
- Barriers;
- Interviews;
- Structured questioning;
- Constructive feedback;
- Meetings;
- Meeting conventions.

Introduction

You will recall from Chapter 1 that communication is essentially a two-way process. The messages that we send to others either verbally or non-verbally will be interpreted and evoke a response. Whether that response will be exactly what we intended will depend on the other's perception. What does perception involve? Basically the use of our senses – eyes and ears – to convey messages to our brains which then interpret the signals received according to our previous experiences and the expectations we currently hold of a situation. Each individual's perception is unique and it is likely that a complex situation will be interpreted quite differently by different people. This is sometimes why witness statements of, say, a road traffic accident may vary quite drastically although the people involved appear to have viewed the same event. It is not necessarily the case that some people are lying (although of course this may sometimes be true!); it is often a genuine account of what the individual perceived. To illustrate the ambiguity of communication, you will find below just three sentences and a series of questions about them. Follow the instructions and complete the necessary feedback to demonstrate the point that some people will interpret the statements differently from you! If you are not studying this text as part of a course or programme of studies, ask friends or members of your family to complete the activity.

Activity 5.1 What does the story tell (source unknown)

Instruction: Each individual is to read the following short story and assume that everything it says is true. Read it very carefully because, in places, the story is quite vague. You need not try to memorize it because you can look back at it at any stage. Do not discuss the story with anyone else at this stage. When you have finished your reading, look at the numbered statements about the story and decide whether you consider each one true, false, or questionable. Circling the T means that you feel sure the statement is definitely true. Circling the F means you are sure it is definitely false. Circling the ? means you cannot tell whether it is true or false. If you feel doubtful about any part of a statement, circle the question mark.

Take each statement in turn and do not go back later to change any of your answers. Do not re-read any of the statements after you have answered them. When each individual has completed their answers, you should calculate the scores for each of the 13 statements.

Story: The owner of the Adams Manufacturing Company entered the office of one of his foremen where he found three employees playing cards. One of them was Carl Young, brother-in-law of foreman Henry Dilson. Dilson, incidentally, often worked late. Company rules did not specifically forbid gambling on the premises, but the chief executive had expressed himself forcibly on the subject.

Statements:

1 In brief, the story is about a company owner
   who found three men playing cards.   T   F   ?
2 The chief executive walked into the office of
   one of his foremen.   T   F   ?
3 Company rules forbade playing cards on the
   premises after hours.   T   F   ?
4 While the card playing took place in Henry
   Dilson's office, the story does not state
   whether Dilson was present.   T   F   ?
5 Dilson never worked late.   T   F   ?

6 Gambling on the premises of the Adams
  Manufacturing Company was not punished.   T   F   ?
7 Carl Young was not playing cards when the
  chief executive walked in.   T   F   ?
8 Three employees were gambling in a
  foreman's office.   T   F   ?
9 While the card players were surprised when
  the owner walked in, it is not clear whether
  or not they will be punished.   T   F   ?
10 Henry Dilson is Carl Young's brother-in-law.   T   F   ?
11 The chief executive is opposed to gambling
   on company premises.   T   F   ?
12 Carl Young did not take part in the card game
   in Henry Dilson's office.   T   F   ?
13 A corporation owner found three employees
   playing cards.   T   F   ?

    We are fairly certain that you will have found considerable differences in individual answers to the statements in the activity above. As another example of how perception may change, look at the illustration below.

Figure 5.1

What do you see? An elderly woman or a younger woman? Whichever image you see currently, keep looking at the picture and watch it change to the other image!

Now that you have had a chance to recognize the importance of differences in perception, you may well be realizing that effective communication is far from simple! It involves appreciation of the fact that others will perceive things differently from us. The way that you as a potential manager communicate with others is obviously of vital importance.

In Chapter 2, you encountered the concept of organizational culture, which can be defined quite simply as 'The way we do things round here' (Deal and Kennedy, 1988: 4). Part of an organizational culture – just as it is part of a national culture – will involve the way that people interact with one another including how they speak and the kind of jargon which is in common usage. As well as the notion of 'culture', there is another important variable, which although advanced some twenty years ago, has once again achieved some prominence. This is the issue of the psychological contract. Just as there is a legal contract between employer and employee which states who gives who what in return for a consideration, so there is a psychological contract between individuals and the organization. Such a contract implies a set of expectations on each side – on the employee side, what he or she expects to get out of the relationship in terms of individual needs in return for their workplace efforts – on the employer side, what they expect of the individual in terms of commitment and effort in return for payment and other benefits. Handy (1985) suggests that there are some important corollaries:

1   Most individuals belong to more than one kind of organization and will have different psychological contracts with each. It is not necessary, therefore, for one contract to satisfy all of an individual's needs.

2   A contract which is not perceived identically by both parties becomes the source of trouble, conflict or even litigation. If the organization's view is more all-embracing than the individual's, then the individual may experience a feeling of exploitation and the organization may experience a feeling of lack of cooperation by the individual.

Handy goes on to suggest that it is possible to categorize organizations according to the type of psychological contract which predominates:

1   *Coercive contracts*   The method of control is rule and punish. Power tends to be in the hands of a small group. The individual's task is to conform and to comply in return for which he or she will receive payment. Control can be reinforced through impersonality and lack of individual identity.

2   *Calculative contracts*   Control is normally retained by management of the organization, but is expressed mainly by their ability to give desired things to the

individual – not just money, but promotion, social opportunities and even work itself. Studies have shown that the vast majority of people would go on working even if they had no economic need to do so, so that the availability of a place to work, over and above the material rewards, is a desired reward.

3   *Cooperative contracts*   The individual tends to identify with the goals of the organization and to become creative in the pursuit of those goals. In return, in addition to just rewards, he or she is given more voice in the selection of the goals and more discretion in the choice of means to achieving them. Management relinquishes a significant amount of day-to-day control but retains ultimate control, partly through the right of selection of people, partly through the allocation of resources.

Activity 5.2

It has been said that the trend is for organizations to be moving towards this latter kind of contract. Do you agree? Can you identify different types of psychological contract that you have with different organizations?

The psychological contracts which operate are rarely clear cut. There may also be more than one type of contract operating in an organization. The variety can be confusing to the individual. Sometimes the contract changes as the nature of the task changes. Can you identify any examples?

Communication

As a starting point for this section, jot down a few examples of occasions, preferably from your workplace experience, when you feel that your manager did not communicate effectively with you. Now try to identify the reasons for that poor communication. Secondly, think of one or two occasions when you feel that you communicated your message clearly to others. What made it effective? How do you know? In the following sections, we will be exploring some of the components of interpersonal communication and identifying some of the workplace situations where it is critical to effective performance; we will also identify some of the barriers which may prevent its successful implementation.

CASE STUDY

You have already met Jean Harrison in Chapter 1. You will recall that she is anxious to secure a full-time post at Dillfield School where she is currently employed part-time as a Laboratory Technician. Jean has invited a friend, Pete Galloway (a tutor on her course) to come along and speak to the fifth-form general science class about his experiences as a Research Chemist for a large pharmaceutical company. Jean had of course got permission from the Head of Science and had also asked the fifth-form general science teacher, Suzy Leadbetter, if she would be happy with the arrangement and Jean added that she would be happy to supervise the class. Suzy had jumped at the idea, knowing that she would be having a particularly busy time on the day in question and was relieved to think that at least she would not have to teach the fifth form on that day and could get on with her marking in the staffroom.

On the day in question, Jean and the Head of Science, Jan Thornton, were waiting for Pete to arrive. It was 10.10 a.m. and Pete had been expected at 10 o'clock. The fifth form were noisy and restless. Jean left the room to go and look for Pete. At 10.15, Jean spotted him running towards her. 'I've been looking for the car park which you said was down a left turning after the school gates', Pete exclaimed crossly. 'No I didn't!' replied Jean, 'I said turn left inside the school gates and the car park was down there'. Jean and Pete arrived in the classroom at 10.20 a.m. The fifth form realized that they were now likely to be late for their mid-morning break and many of the pupils were looking sullen. After Jean had introduced Pete, he began by saying, 'I am particularly pleased to have been invited here today. My talk for the next 40 minutes will address some of the methodological problems that my team and I encountered in our studies and will look at the statistical implications for future research'. Although Pete's talk contained a lot of interesting anecdotes, much of it was lost on the fifth form who had switched off after the first sentence! As break time approached the class became increasingly restless and at the end, the only person who asked Pete any questions about his talk was the Head of Science. By 11.15, Pete had decided he would never agree to give a talk to another class of school children; Jan Thornton was feeling thoroughly embarrassed at the behaviour of the class and demanded to know why Suzy Leadbetter had not been there at the beginning of the lesson; Jean was practically in tears having upset Pete, Jan and Suzy.

So, what went wrong? Well, of course it would have been sensible for Jean to have given Pete a note and a map to confirm the exact time and location of the school and its car park. Even when Pete did arrive, he started off on the wrong foot with the fifth form by using inappropriate language. Both of these factors exacerbated the events of that morning. Tempers became frayed; people became restless and the total result was a pretty disastrous morning for Jean.

It is important to remember that the components of interpersonal communication skills may be both verbal and non-verbal. Remember our definition that communication was about the conveying or exchanging of information or ideas either by speech, by writing or by signing. Interpersonal communication must be two-way – either on a one-to-one basis or a group basis. It involves *reciprocity* and *feedback*. To illustrate what that means, consider the following:

'I'm going to pay you back for that!'

Reading the statement on its own, it could be interpreted as: 'I am going to repay you a sum of money for something which you have provided', or as: 'I am very annoyed with you and I am announcing that I intend to get even for a perceived injustice'. If an observer could see you respond with a smile and say: 'It's OK – I'm happy to treat you to a cup of coffee', he or she would know that the interaction probably related to the first interpretation. That conclusion would be based on your reciprocal statement and the exchange of information between you.

Interpersonal communication is a *dynamic* process. The interaction will rely on continuous interpretation and adjustment in the light of information exchanged between senders and recipients. The way in which our messages will be interpreted will depend to some extent on the appropriateness of the language, the tone we use and the pace of delivery, but will also involve, as we have seen, non-verbal signals or body language. In the foreword to Allan Pease's book, *Body Language* he notes that Albert Mehrabian found that the total impact of a message is about 7 per cent verbal (words only), 38 per cent vocal (including tone of voice, inflection and other sounds) and 55 per cent non-verbal. Professor Birdwhistell made some similar estimates of the amount of non-verbal communication that takes place amongst humans. Like Mehrabian, he found that the verbal component of a face-to-face conversation is less than 35 per cent and that over 65 per cent of communication is done non-verbally.

Activity 5.3

Write down what you think is meant by the term 'non-verbal signals'. Then, for each signal you have identified, try to think of an example of a situation where it might be used. Compare your lists with ours below and that of other students and then, over the next few days, spend about 10 minutes each day observing the non-verbal communication or body language of others. A point to mention here is that you should not just look for isolated signals – what is most illustrative are 'clusters' of signals. For example, an isolated gesture of someone standing with their arms locked tightly together could just be an indication that they are cold! But if this posture is observed along with perhaps a frown or a shake of the head, it may well be a defensive posture and it could indicate disagreement with something that is being said.

Non-verbal signals could include eye gaze, facial expression, hand and arm gestures, leg barriers, distance between people when they are talking.

Using body language to establish rapport and empathy

When you create empathy you develop a sympathetic understanding with another person. You show them that you can identify with their experience. This is the most important process in any interpersonal interaction. Without establishing empathy, you are unlikely to achieve what you want – particularly important in negotiation. Most of the time we create empathy or rapport between ourselves and others easily and naturally. There are occasions, however, when our intuitive ways of creating rapport do not work and it is at these times that we need to call on learned skills to create rapport consciously. Such skills are called mirroring or matching. By reflecting back to another person their own behaviour we can also signal that we are reflecting their way of thinking. There are five non-verbal ways of matching. You can match:

- voice tone and tempo
- breathing
- facial expression
- body posture
- rhythms of movement with a different movement.

In the business world, matching voice tone and tempo is probably the best way to establish rapport. People are usually unaware of how they use their voice and they will not notice you matching it. Thus it is an easy way to establish rapport and make a person feel understood. Try also matching voice tone and tempo on the telephone and discover how it helps you deal effectively with even the most difficult person, making life easier and more productive.

When we talk of establishing rapport, we tend to think of positive attitudes that are being matched. But you should also remember that we can be in rapport with a person who is in a negative frame of mind. They may be angry, anxious or unresponsive. By matching that person we are demonstrating that we are trying to identify and join them in their experience. In the matching process, we are joining them in their experience by 'pacing' them and we 'travel' along with them for a short way. If they match us in the pacing process and rapport is not lost, we can then 'lead' them – through deliberately mismatching the old behaviour. Matching breathing is another powerful way of establishing rapport. With practice it is easy to notice whether a person is breathing shallowly or deeply, rapidly or slowly. Matching movement rhythms is a more subtle way of establishing rapport. It is seldom noticed by the other person especially if you choose to match with a different part of your body. Someone who gesticulates a lot can be matched by head movements, foot jiggling or finger drumming. Matching facial expression may be a useful way of establishing rapport. Many people use their eyebrows quite rhythmically when they speak or frown or curl their mouths. They are usually not aware of making these movements. This means that direct matching of the movements can be used and is not perceived as mimicry. Matching body posture can be overdone if the matching becomes mirroring! It is important to be subtle. Very often, the matching occurs naturally and spontaneously. If it is used too obviously, people may think that you are making fun of them. Each person is different, with their own way of thinking and behaving. So each person has their unique set of behaviours that are apparent when they are communicating. Your aim is to minimize the difference between you and that other person.

Other skills that are needed include effective listening. You will recall the exercise that you carried out in Chapter 1 and know the importance of *active listening*. This requires considerable concentration and effort and it is a skill we need to practise. It's important to resist distractions and delay your evaluation. So often we jump to conclusions without really getting the full picture. Emotion often gets in the way of reason. Read the following interaction to illustrate the point.

CASE STUDY

Sanjit is a supervisor in the packaging department of a large china manufacturer. Joan has been a packer with the company for a number of years and is normally a good worker, though two days ago, Sanjit had cause to talk to her about her work. Joan had not been securing the 'bubble-wrap' sufficiently around the china and consequently a number of complaints had been received about chipped china. Sanjit is concerned that a large consignment has been delayed due to a problem with a supplier. However it is now finally ready for packing. Sanjit arrives at the factory and sees a cardboard carton lying on the floor with broken crockery strewn around. Joan is clearing up the mess.

'What the hell has happened here?' demands Sanjit, 'Don't you realize how important this consignment is? How could you be so careless? I warned you only a couple of days ago about not using sufficient bubble-wrap. If you had wrapped this stuff properly, most of it would have been OK – instead of which the whole lot's broken'.

'But' says Joan, 'I've only just arrived and...'

But Sanjit doesn't listen and interrupts, 'You've gone too far this time – I want to see you in my office as soon as you've cleared up'.

Sanjit storms off. In fact, Joan was trying to tell him that the cardboard container was actually full of rejects because one of the machines had not applied the pattern correctly and it wasn't Joan who had dropped it but one of the cleaners. Clearly Sanjit had allowed emotion to get in the way of reason. Had he stopped to think he would have realized that none of the china had any bubble-wrap around it and so it was unlikely to be a part of the consignment in question. His over-reaction has caused Joan to be upset. She had been trying extra hard to keep up to a tight time schedule and ensure careful packaging. She moves off towards Sanjit's office and is heard to say to the others 'Why should I bother? He hasn't noticed how hard I've been working and now he's accusing me of something that was nothing to do with me. I've had enough...'

Handling emotion

Emotional outbursts can be hard to handle, but the following steps will help:

- ■ Openly acknowledge the emotional behaviour, but remain calm yourself: 'I can see that you are getting upset...'
- ■ Explain the effect of the behaviour on you and the discussion taking place.
- ■ Show empathy and try to create rapport using the matching techniques of body language discussed above.
- ■ 'Pace' and lead the emotional behaviour towards more productive behaviour. Decide if it is possible to continue the discussion constructively or whether you should suggest that the meeting should be reconvened at a later time.
- ■ Suggest an alternative way if you can of refocusing on the issue.
- ■ Indicate your continued support for the employee.

Transactional Analysis

An important concept, linked with effective interpersonal communication, is the analysis of interchanges or 'transactions' between people. Dr Eric Berne (1964), a Swiss Psychologist, developed Transactional Analysis to help people understand and improve their communication with others. We can only give you a brief introduction to his work here, but, if you are interested in the subject, you will find some suggested further reading at the end of this chapter.

According to Transactional Analysis, it is possible to observe quite different and distinctive types of behaviour which appear to come from different sources within the individual. These are called our 'ego states' and Berne believed that there were three such states:

- Parent
- Adult
- Child.

In his view, we are all a mix of these, and different situations in which we may find ourselves may evoke a particular response from one of the three states. If we can recognize such behaviours in ourselves, we can perhaps start to understand why we get the reactions we do from our colleagues and friends and, if necessary, start to change or adapt our behaviour when it becomes harmful or ineffective.

In Berne's view our Parent behaviour comes from what we encountered as children in our parents and in other authority figures. It is the perception that parents are:

- Always right
- Powerful
- In charge
- Not subject to the same rules as children
- Not having to be fair
- Not having to explain.

The Parent ego state is subdivided into two parts – the Critical Parent and the Nurturing Parent. The Critical Parent can be seen during transactions between people when one or both of them is 'laying down the rules', hiding behind regulations or refusing to compromise – for example 'When I tell you I want something done, I mean I want it done now!' Typical words of this ego state are 'ought', 'should', or 'must'.

The Nurturing Parent can be identified when the caring, concerned person gives encouragement or support, perhaps shows warmth and affection, but is sometimes overprotective and eventually overwhelming. For example, 'Please don't worry about the situation, I'll sort it out and put things right'.

In the Adult ego state, the behaviour is reasonable, calm and assertive. Its logicality and rationality derive from an ability to think complex matters through clearly and arrive at a workable solution. Adult behaviour is typified by negotiating rather than steam rollering, responding reasonably rather than bullying. It involves the ability to recognize and direct feelings by not allowing them to interfere or explode; in addition it recognizes the needs, feelings and behaviour of others and assumes that their position is of equal importance.

For example, 'I recognize that the pressures on you are considerable and we must work together to meet your deadlines. I am also concerned for our quality standards and I would like to agree with you a schedule which will meet both our needs.'

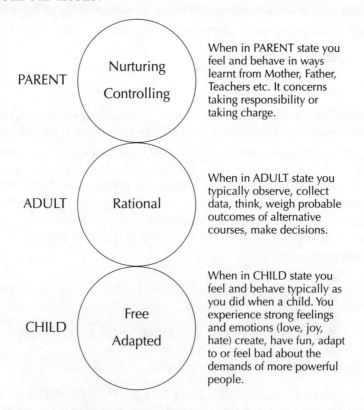

PARENT — Nurturing / Controlling — When in PARENT state you feel and behave in ways learnt from Mother, Father, Teachers etc. It concerns taking responsibility or taking charge.

ADULT — Rational — When in ADULT state you typically observe, collect data, think, weigh probable outcomes of alternative courses, make decisions.

CHILD — Free / Adapted — When in CHILD state you feel and behave typically as you did when a child. You experience strong feelings and emotions (love, joy, hate) create, have fun, adapt to or feel bad about the demands of more powerful people.

Figure 5.2 *The three ego states*

The Child ego state, like the Adult, is subdivided into two – the Free Child is the one where the behaviour is straightforward, uncomplicated and uninhibited. It may involve being loud and exuberant and 'letting off steam'. It is about the here and now and there is little thought for the future or for the consequences of our actions. There is often considerable enthusiasm and energy for the execution of new ideas.

In the Adapted Child, the individual has learned to adapt his or her feelings to others' norms. The resulting behaviour may be constrained and may reflect feelings of frustration or inadequacy. It is behaviour which has been learned in response to Critical Parent behaviour. It is often accompanied by a feeling of a lack of power and the individual may exhibit fear when speaking at meetings, or depression when criticized, or be excessively anxious when faced with deadlines.

With some practice it is not difficult to apply Transactional Analysis to events which occur both at work and in other situations. Once you start to identify your own ego strengths, it is easier to recognize those which others may be operating in. It is then possible to develop the ability to switch states in order to move from, say, a Nurturing Parent to a logical Adult or from a Free Child to a more rational Adult ego state. Flexibility is the key to effectiveness and the recognition that if one approach is not working, it is important to switch to another. The danger is that many people often operate in just one mode. For example, if you consistently approach every problem in Critical Parent mode, then you are likely to encounter the responses of Adapted Child and vice versa. In most organizations, the most effective ego state is that of Adult although other states can work effectively.

Workplace interaction

Now that we have identified some of the elements of interpersonal communication skills, we need to consider in more depth the kinds of workplace situation where effective interaction is vital.

Activity 5.4

Using an organization with which you are familiar, write down as many situations as you can think of where face-to-face communication was vital. Try to be as specific as you can and give examples wherever possible.

Your list probably included examples of meetings, presentations and interviews and also examples of one-to-one situations where information or advice was being passed to another person. Depending on the type of organization selected, you may have included examples of communication with other offices or with external customers and suppliers. Some interactions may be formal, others more informal.

An important area which we need to consider before moving on is that of interpersonal communication in the training situation. In almost every workplace, employees will need to be trained in how to do their work effectively. This may involve direct instruction, observation, coaching, mentoring or facilitating. The speed at which an employee learns a new skill is obviously of importance to any organization. The faster they learn, the more productive they can be, which in turn will save the organization time and money. Whatever type of training is involved there will be a need for the trainer or instructor to impart information effectively and encourage the trainee to ask questions where necessary and provide opportunities for them to practise in a non-threatening environment where self-confidence and skills can flourish. You should always remember that we have different learning styles and different speeds of learning. Some people like to learn by watching and listening to others; some will want minimal instruction and to be left to learn by themselves. Some prefer to learn by watching videos or CD ROM materials; others will prefer to learn from a book.

There are many barriers to effective interpersonal communication. Read the following extract:

> A foreign-born plumber in New York wrote to the Bureau of Standards that he found hydrochloric acid fine for cleaning drains, and did they agree? Washington replied: 'The efficacy of hydrochloric acid is indisputable, but the chlorine residue is incompatible with metallic permanence.' The plumber wrote back to say that he was mighty glad the Bureau agreed with him.
>
> Considerably alarmed, the Bureau replied a second time: 'We cannot assume responsibility for the production of toxic and noxious residues with hydrochloric acid, and suggest that you use an alternative procedure.' The plumber was happy to learn the Bureau still agreed with him.
> Whereupon Washington wrote: 'Don't use hydrochloric acid, it eats the hell out of the pipes!'
> (source unknown)

The above example serves to illustrate that we need to use appropriate language to convey our meaning which must take account of differing levels of knowledge and experience. We should avoid using unnecessary jargon and acronyms unless we are sure that others share our knowledge and experience. Read the following Case study and then answer the questions which follow:

CASE STUDY

Susan Moffatt is the Manageress of the administration section of a large after-sales warehouse. The warehouse attempts to hold in stock the most common parts that are needed for the electrical goods and equipment that they sell. Administration attempts to turn orders around in

24 hours on parts which they keep and operates a seven-day service on most other components. Under certain conditions, the seven-day service may be expedited to a 24-hour service if there is an urgent need for a particular part. Susan has six people working for her. She is a very efficient manager, though some of her staff find her rather cold and unapproachable. One day she walks over to Jasmine's desk. Jasmine's computer has been out of action for an hour and she is now frantically trying to catch up on the backlog of orders which have built up. In addition she has promised to help Neal sort out some old files later and to check some figures which Melanie has typed.

As Susan approaches, Jasmine's phone rings. Just as she picks it up to answer Susan says: 'Oh Jasmine, I'm going to be out for a couple of hours at a meeting on the main site. I'm leaving you in charge – OK?'

'Er... well, I'm not sure... I suppose so', replies Jasmine rather nervously.

'Of course you'll be able to cope' says Susan and disappears.

Half an hour later Jake walks in. He is the Sales Manager for the Eastern Region and wants to know where the order for one of his major customers is. Jasmine looks up her records and finds that although they have some of the components in stock, others have been ordered and should be delivered in three days' time.

'That's no good' says Jake, 'You'll have to do a special order and get them despatched up here today by courier.' Jasmine asks Jake to wait until Susan's return to which Jake retorts 'Surely you can make a simple decision like that can't you? I thought you said that Susan had left you in charge!' Jasmine reluctantly agrees to phone through the special order and says she will telephone Jake when the parts arrive later that day. Susan overhears Jasmine later telling Jake that the parts are now in the warehouse and she will see that they are despatched that evening.

'What on earth have you done?' says Susan, 'You had no right to authorize a special order without consulting either myself or Bob Truefoot.'

'But you weren't here', wails Jasmine.

'I am aware of that' replies Susan acidly, 'however, if you had bothered to read your office procedure manual, you would have known that you should consult Bob in my absence. I will see you later about this.' Jasmine is about to reply that nobody bothers to read the manual because it is virtually incomprehensible and impossible to find relevant parts quickly. However, her phone starts ringing again and Susan has moved away.

Questions

1   Whose fault was it that the special order was processed?
2   What barriers to effective communication can you identify?
3   How effectively did Susan delegate to Jasmine?

In the above example, you probably picked up the fact that Susan is not likely to be a very approachable person. One wonders if Jasmine has felt able to ask her previously about things which she did not understand. Susan's initial attitude towards Jasmine could be considered rather patronizing and the language that she used to delegate was perhaps inappropriate given that Jasmine was nervous. Jasmine was given no opportunity to clarify her understanding of what Susan expected her to do and she clearly had a heavy workload. There are also possible indications that she might not be too good at prioritizing her time. But what about the procedures manual? It is true that it sets out company policies and procedures, but its terminology is unclear, it is at least 5 cm thick and is not well indexed! Such documents are not uncommon in many organizations and can cause inertia because people spend considerable time trying to decipher their meaning and finally give up until they can find an appropriate person to ask.

What other barriers have you encountered in your communications at work? Sometimes there is personal animosity between colleagues which prevents them interacting effectively. Different personalities may hinder communications – for example, in meetings you frequently find that it is the same people putting forward their ideas and suggestions while others who may find difficulty in expressing themselves forcefully are neglected. As a consequence, many good ideas can be lost. There may also be important cultural differences of which we are unaware. For example, in some cultures it is considered rude to answer a question directly! But the perception of the questioner may be that the other person is being evasive in his or her answer. Words too may have different meanings in diverse cultures. To take an extreme example, the word 'snow' in English is pretty clear to someone born in the United Kingdom. However, to an Eskimo the word 'snow' is fairly meaningless. They have no fewer than seven different words which signify different types of snow. Weather conditions are so crucial to their way of life that they need a much more specific definition. Words which might be termed jargon are also sometimes used unadvisedly. For example, it is often found that people who design computer software are not the appropriate people to write the manuals. The designers, used to very complex jargon, may be too close to the subject and will not be able to perceive the needs of the user and write accordingly.

Activity 5.5

Identify three or more different situations requiring effective interpersonal communication by managers; then describe some of the communication barriers that they may encounter and how these might be overcome.

Making effective presentations

Having the confidence and skill to give a sound oral presentation is an important ability that every manager should develop. The key to giving a good presentation is to ensure that you have prepared thoroughly. As with so many other management issues, preparation begins with identifying *objectives*. In other words, you need to consider what it is that you, the speaker, wish to achieve; in doing so you must take into account the nature of the subject, the audience's familiarity with the topic and the time available. Once you have identified your objectives, it is often most sensible to start at the end and work backwards! This is not as silly as it sounds. Decide what your *conclusions* are and how you wish to present them to your audience so that they are comprehensive and memorable.

Once you have your objectives and conclusion sorted out, you can then break your subject down into logical *building blocks*. Don't try to put them in any sequence yet. Just jot down the main headings that you need to cover – preferably on separate cards. Once you have these, you can then put them into a logical sequence so that there is a natural flow to your presentation. Now consider the time-scale that you have available. Remember that most people have a very short attention span which will be unlikely to last for more than 15–20 minutes, unless your presentation is a very complex subject which the audience is already familiar with. Beware of trying to cram in too much detail in your presentation. Get your main messages over to your audience and give them the detail in a typewritten handout for later reference if appropriate.

The last step you need to take is to consider your *introduction*. You need to capture the attention of your audience right at the beginning – explain the objectives of your presentation and how you propose to deliver the topic. There is an old saying that you should 'Tell them what you are going to tell them; then tell them; then tell them what you have told them!' In other words, provide a clear structure, deliver your message and then summarize it in a conclusion.

You should also consider the likely questions that you may be asked; put yourself in the audience's position. What might you ask? Anticipate likely topics and make sure you have done your homework and appear to have been thorough in your preparation. Never try to fudge a question you cannot answer. Be honest and say so, but offer to find out the answer if you can and make sure you follow through with your answer.

What makes a really good presentation?

- *Control*. When your audience has settled, mentally count to three before you start. This short silence will signal that you are waiting for their full attention.
- *Introduction*. Design a really good transparency for your introduction – one which will engage the audience and provide them with an overview.
- *Timeliness*. Don't go rambling on and on! Put your watch on the table if necessary to ensure that you can keep an eye on the time.
- *Clarity*. This is where preparation is all. Try to practise your presentation either in private or with a couple of colleagues who can provide you with some constructive feedback.
- *Rapport with your audience*. Establish eye contact with your audience. Try to ensure that you look at all the people there – especially those at the back of the room – to ensure that your voice projects to them. Sound interested in what you are saying. Vary your tone and speed of delivery. The most interesting presentations will appear laboured if they are presented in a monotone.

Effective visual aids

One could say that the most important visual aid is yourself! The audience will be focused on you and it is therefore important that you prepare your own image as carefully as your illustrative materials. Wear clothes which are appropriate for the occasion and in which you feel comfortable. The other main types of visual aid include: overhead projector transparencies, photographic slides, whiteboards, flip charts, films and videos, and handouts.

The use of visual aids

These should hold attention and help the audience to recall what you have said. The old saying that 'A picture can speak a thousand words' has some salience here. If you show a pictorial representation of a key point as well as summarizing its content, research suggests that comprehension and retention will be six times greater than just saying the words.

The value of effective visual aids

■ They can increase your confidence; you can focus on them instead of wads of notes, which makes your presentation far more spontaneous and interesting.

■ Preparation of them forces you to think clearly and carefully in advance.

■ They can reduce confusion, add variety and clarify important concepts.

■ They can help create a lasting impression.

What is an effective visual aid?

Aids must be visible, accurate, appropriate, clear and any audible elements must be capable of being heard and understood.

Some golden rules when using visual aids

Always stand to the side of the aid so that you do not block its image.

■ Do not turn your back on the audience.

■ Do not talk to your aid – talk to your audience.

■ Write legibly.

■ If you are using an overhead projector, switch it off in between transparencies.

■ Make sure that you know how any necessary equipment works *before* your presentation.

■ Rehearse your presentation with the use of your visual aids.

Controlling nerves

It is well recognized that giving presentations is something which can cause considerable tension. Some nervousness is often felt even by the most experienced presenters. To minimize the effects of anxiety, we offer you the following tips:

■ Planning is all – prepare your talk, as we suggested earlier, in a structured and logical sequence.

■ Prepare all your visual aids well in advance.

■ Rehearse your whole presentation – but not more than once or twice, or you may lose spontaneity.

■ Check the venue in advance and make sure you are familiar with any equipment you will need to use.

■ Smile! – this may be difficult, but you'll feel better and so will your audience.

■ Maintain eye contact with your audience; it is often useful to focus your gaze for short periods of time on some people at the back of the room if you are using theatre-style seating. This will ensure that you don't bury your head so that your voice becomes inaudible.

Activity 5.6

1 Prepare an oral presentation which will provide colleagues at work with up-to-date information on a project with which you have been involved. Prepare all necessary visual aids. After the presentation, invite your audience to provide you with some constructive feedback.
2 Conduct a one-to-one interview with a colleague or your line manager for an agreed purpose, applying appropriate questioning and listening techniques.

Structured one-to-one interviews

Interviews are an increasingly important part of any manager's role and the way they are conducted will have a major bearing on how the manager is regarded both within and outside the organization. Consider for a moment the interviews you have experienced either as an interviewer or as an interviewee. How well were they conducted? Was there a beginning, a middle and an end? Were appropriate questions asked? What was the outcome? If you identified instances of unsatisfactory interviews, can you say why they went wrong?

Interviews may be either formal, as in the selection of new employees, or informal, as in day-to-day problem solving or information gathering. In this section, we are concerned with both types, but in either case there is a need for them to be *structured*. This implies careful planning and preparation. Interviewing is a skill which requires training and practice if managers are to get the best out of their people, and in the following pages we will be examining some of the techniques of good interviewing practice and giving you the opportunity to try them out.

Activity 5.7

As a starting point, write down what you consider to be the differences between a structured interview and a conversation.

Some of the differences should have included that an interview is planned in advance, that the interviewer should control the flow and pace, that it is conducted for a specific purpose, whereas a conversation is normally spontaneous, lacks a specific structure and is concerned with a free exchange of information or opinions. Do note though that both are two-way or should be! All too often the interviewer is too fond of the sound of his or her own voice and does not encourage or permit the interviewee to have their say.

Now jot down all the different types of workplace interview that you can think of. Our list included selection, appraisal or performance review, disciplinary and grievance. Additionally, you might have included fact-finding or investigative interviews, counselling, developmental and exit interviews.

Although different types of interview may require a difference in interviewing style, one of the common requirements is that they all involve the use of questioning techniques and this is the first area we shall consider.

Activity 5.8

You and a partner should identify a favourite hobby or sport in which you are involved. Tell your partner what your chosen subject area is. Each person should then spend five minutes jotting down a plan of the questions they will use to find out all they can about their partner's chosen topic. When you are ready you will each conduct 10-minute interviews with your partner. When you have both had a chance to conduct your interview, consider the following:

1 Do you now have a clear idea of your partner's subject area?
2 What types of questions did you use?
3 Which questions were most useful in providing the information you required?
4 Did you manage to establish a rapport with your partner?
5 Was there a beginning, a middle and an end in your interview?
6 Try to repeat back to your partner the main findings of your interview and then evaluate how accurate they were.

Questioning techniques

The types of question we use and the way in which they are asked will provide the main building blocks of any interview. The purpose of asking questions is two-fold – either to gather information (fact-finding) or to provide clarification.

It is important to recognize that there are two main types of question – open-ended and closed. The latter require only a 'yes' or 'no' answer. For example, 'Do you enjoy the work that you do?' A much more meaningful question would be, 'What do you enjoy most about the work that you do?'; even more useful might be, 'What do you enjoy least about the work that you do?' With either of these, the interviewee will not be able to give a one-word answer, but will have to provide at least some information. Even if the information provided is minimal, there will probably be an opportunity for the interviewer to use a *probing* question. For example, suppose the interviewee replies, 'I particularly enjoy working with other people'; the interviewer could respond by asking one or both of the following questions: 'How many other people do you work with?', 'What types of work is your team involved in?'

The open-ended questions are those which start with one of the following words – what, why, when, where, how. Look back at the interview you have just conducted with your partner. The questions which you identified as being the most successful were probably those which used one of these words.

Other types of question may be those which are 'leading', 'rhetorical' or 'reflective'. A leading question is one where the interviewer asks a question which invites a specific response. For example: 'I think that the shift time should be changed to start and finish half an hour earlier – don't you agree?' Such questions should usually be avoided. A rhetorical question is one to which no real answer is expected. An example would be: 'Is this really what you would call a good day's work?' Again, this type of question should normally be avoided. It is probably too general to be meaningful and is likely to evoke either an indignant or a resentful response. If you, as a manager, considered that an individual's performance was unsatisfactory, it would be far more constructive to discuss specific examples of poor work or behaviour. A reflective question is one which can be useful because the interviewer can use a previous response in order to seek clarification and move the discussion forward. For example, suppose an interview is being conducted on the shop floor to discuss how the current frequent breakdown of machinery can be avoided. Emotions may be running high because the team is prevented from carrying out its work efficiently and a variety of solutions are being offered. Here the use of specific, reflective questions can assist: 'Are you suggesting that we should try and carry out more maintenance during the holiday period?' or 'Are you saying that we need extra people on the shift?'

It was suggested earlier that one of the differences between an interview and a conversation is that the former is specifically controlled by the interviewer. The types of questions that an interviewer may use to maintain progress and control will vary – sometimes there will be a need for the use of many probing questions to encourage the interviewee to provide more information; sometimes the interviewer will need to use 'controlling' questions to keep to the subject matter and avoid digression. For example, 'What you are saying is very interesting, but I would like to return to the question of how you think we can improve the efficiency of order processing.'

Questions need to be prepared carefully for each interview situation and below you will find our suggested list of 'dos and don'ts'. Feel free to add to them if you wish.

1 Use open-ended questions rather than closed questions.
2 Avoid leading questions.
3 Do not use multiple questions. For example, 'Which is the biggest problem at the moment? The work scheduling? The maintenance programme? Or the administrative load? How do you think we should deal with them? Most people can only handle one question at a time and asking multiple questions can make things very complicated, so stick to asking one question at a time.
4 Ask relevant questions.
5 Do not ask ambiguous questions – make sure they are clear.
6 Decide on your order of questions in advance – general questions may help establish rapport at the beginning of an interview.

The following are some suggestions of the kinds of questions which may be useful:

Questions which invite an interviewee to talk about themselves

- How would you describe yourself as a person?
- How would your colleagues describe you?
- What kind of first impressions do you think people might have of you?
- What do you feel you have done particularly well during the past month?
- Can you describe the job or task which you carried out recently which gave you most satisfaction?
- What specific job or task do you feel you might have done better?
- What kind of training or development do you feel would benefit you most?

Questions which invite an interviewee to talk of their previous experience

- What problems have you had to face in your current/past job?
- What have you learned from past work situations?
- What kinds of people do you find most difficult to get on with?

- What were your exact duties in your past job?
- What skills have you learned from your past job?
- Can you describe an event or situation which you found difficult to handle and then say how you overcame the difficulty?
- How do you react to disappointments at work?

Questions which invite an interviewee to discuss their relationships with previous managers and colleagues

- Can you describe the manager who you feel you worked best for?
- What do you think are the characteristics of a good manager?
- What sort of person would you like to work for?
- What did your manager say about your work at your last appraisal?
- What do you think are the characteristics of good teamwork?

Questions which invite the candidate to talk about their motivation in applying for a job

- How does your previous experience match the job description?
- What difficulties can you foresee in the job as described?
- What similarities can you see between your current work and the work described in the job description?
- Why do you think you might like to work for this company?
- What particular qualities do you feel you can bring to the job?

Structured interviews

Earlier in this chapter, we identified the different types of interview that might take place in organizations. We now need to consider some of those situations in a little more detail, particularly their purpose and outcome.

Selection interviews

Here the purpose of the interview is to assess each candidate's capacity to undertake the specified job and also to provide candidates with the opportunity of learning more about the organization. Note therefore that the purpose is two-fold; it is not just about the organization's selection of candidates – the interview must also provide candidates with the chance to evaluate a potential employing organization. The manager's desired outcome will be the selection of the most suitable candidate who is motivated to perform a particular task or job to their mutual satisfaction. How can this be achieved?

First there will need to be detailed criteria against which each candidate can be assessed. Without these it is difficult to imagine how interviews can be conducted fairly. In the next chapter you will cover the design of job descriptions which set out the duties and responsibilities of a specific role, and personnel specifications which consider the necessary skills, qualifications and attributes of likely candidates. Most candidates will have completed application forms prior to interview which may have been used by the manager to draw up a short list of candidates for interview.

Once the short list is agreed, the manager should draw up a plan of how he or she proposes to conduct each interview, including the subject areas to be covered and the types of question which will be asked of each candidate. During the introduction to the interview, the manager should attempt to put each candidate at ease. Most people are fairly nervous, especially at the start, and it is sensible to start by asking very general questions. It is often helpful for an interviewer to tell candidates the topic areas that will be covered in the main body or middle of the interview so that they are not trying to anticipate what may happen next! Also the interviewer should stress that there will be an opportunity for the candidate to ask questions so that they can learn more about the job and the organization. This is often done towards the end of the interview in the winding-up phase. Once the interviewer and the interviewee have completed their questions, it is the responsibility of the interviewer to close the interview. The manager may briefly summarize what has been discussed and reiterate key points. He or she should tell the candidate what the next step will be – perhaps that they will be notified in writing within seven days of the outcome, and if a further interview is offered, the form that this would take.

It is worth mentioning that the interview, although the most common, is not the only selection method. Nowadays there is frequent use of psychometric testing where candidates may be asked to complete questionnaires in order to provide a more detailed picture of their aptitudes; in addition, assessment centre techniques may be employed. These do not describe a place! They are a method of selection where each candidate undertakes a variety of tasks – often consisting of case studies, presentations, role plays and group work.

Even if the interview is the main selection method, it may take a variety of forms. Here we have been concerned with one-to-one interviews, but there may also be panel interviews where several people are involved in asking questions of the candidates, or there may be two or more interviews involved – often a fairly informal one at the beginning, moving on to a final formal selection interview.

Finally, it should be remembered that after the selection interview, inevitably some candidates are going to be very disappointed if they are not offered the position. However, they should certainly feel that they have been given a fair hearing and been treated courteously. So the selection interview should be regarded as an occasion when the organization is particularly vulnerable to scrutiny and its dealings with any potential employees must be beyond reproach.

Appraisal or performance review interviews

The purpose of an appraisal interview is firstly to maintain and improve job performance and also to identify any training or development needs of the interviewee. The interviewer should also seek to discover the aspirations of the interviewee with regard to work in the organization. If there is trust and a healthy rapport established, then the outcomes should not only be improved performance, but also improved relationships and increased motivation.

In most organizations, both the managers and his or her subordinates will have completed some preparatory documentation and the manager should ensure that they have read the appropriate material, looked at the records of previous appraisal interviews and drawn up a plan of how they will conduct the current interview. It is rare that a thorough appraisal could take much less than one hour and it is quite common for them to take considerably longer than this. It is not a job that can be rushed and the manager must ensure that sufficient time is allowed in his or her schedule. At the start of an appraisal interview, it is wise for the manager to concentrate on the positive aspects of individual performance – recognition and praise of good work will improve motivation and encourage employees towards greater achievements. It is also important to invite the person being appraised (the appraisee) to comment on what they see as their most significant achievements during the period under review in order to establish two-way feedback.

The manager may also have identified areas where he or she believes that improvements are needed. In order for constructive feedback to be given, there is a need for this aspect to be handled sensitively. Most people want to know how they are doing, but will still react negatively when any criticism is offered. Why should this be so and how can we try to avoid such adverse reaction?

Activity 5.9

Think of a specific occasion when you received some criticism of your performance at work. Write down the circumstances as you recall them. What was said? Who said it? If you can remember the dialogue, try to write it down as accurately as you can. What was going through your mind when you listened and responded to the criticism? What do you think was going through the mind of the other person as they were saying it?

Your response above may have included phrases such as 'You're not being fair!' 'It wasn't my fault!' 'If I had been told what to do, then it would-n't have happened!' If you managed to write down the actual dialogue, you may have realized that the other person was perhaps viewing the situation very differently from you. Think back to what we said about perception at the beginning of this chapter and you should realize that it is quite possible for two people genuinely to 'see' things differently and that they are not just being rude for the sake of it!

If you as a manager are to provide people with constructive feedback, it is important that you should be as objective as possible – focus explicitly on the behaviour or performance that you have observed – not on the person. Provide clear detail and specific examples and then invite the appraisee to give their views. A comment such as 'You need to improve your attitude' is not constructive. When you have listened to their viewpoint, ensure that you check your understanding using paraphrasing and the open-ended questions identified earlier to repeat back what you have heard. If you believe that training or development needs have been identified, these should be discussed openly with the appraisee. Ask them what they feel could be of most benefit to them. It is vital that the manager ends an appraisal interview on a positive note with clear performance targets identi-fied with the appraisee. A plan of action should be mutually agreed with common understanding of any developmental activities that will be taken and the time span before further review.

An appraisal interview should be an opportunity for the mutual exchange of constructive feedback. If a manager has performed effectively, there should not be any major surprises in store for the appraisee because he or she will already have dealt with specific situations as they have arisen.

You will find below a checklist which you may find helpful when you are called upon to provide constructive feedback to members of your team.

Giving constructive feedback – some basic rules

- Ensure that you have planned what you want to say and have all necessary paperwork to hand.
- Give praise and recognition of good performance using specific examples.
- Be sure of the facts – not opinions – about individual performance.
- Provide specific examples of where you believe perfor-mance is not satisfactory.
- Ensure that the interview is performance oriented – that it concentrates on behaviour not on personality.
- Avoid moralizing or giving feedback which is judge-mental or prescriptive.
- Invite and listen to the response to your feedback.

- If performance needs improving, ask the individual for suggestions as to how they think their performance could be improved.
- If necessary, offer your own suggestions.
- Summarize appropriately what has been said and check mutual understanding.
- Express support and ensure you follow up on any agreed action.

Investigative or fact-finding interviews

The purpose of the interview is to establish objectively what has happened, including perhaps the sequence of events and what occurred on each occasion. The purpose is *not* to allocate blame. The outcome should be a statement of facts including a record of where there may still be disagreements which need to be resolved and an action plan of what is to happen next.

Conclusions

Whatever type of interview the manager is conducting, planning and preparation is all. Using those key words identified at the start of this chapter, we need to consider the following:

1   *Where* will the interview be held?
    Physical arrangements: for example, has a suitable venue been selected? Does it need to be booked? Is the room layout appropriate? Are refreshments available if required? Has the manager ensured that there will be no interruptions? Do all participants know the exact location – is a map needed?

2   *When* will the interview be held?
    Has the time of day been chosen that is most appropriate for all parties? What will be the sequence of interviews if there are several?

3   *Why* is the interview being held?
    What is its purpose? What are the desired outcomes? How can we best ensure that they will be achieved?

4   *What* will happen at the interview?
    Personal preparation: for example, has the manager read all relevant documentation prior to the interview? Is all the necessary paperwork available? (For example, if a selection interview is being held, does each interviewer have the appropriate application forms and rating forms available to record their assessment of each candidate? If an appraisal interview is being held, are the necessary records available for completion?)

Conducting the interview

Whatever type of interview is carried out, there are some general rules which should be observed:

1. Ensure that there is an introduction, a middle and a wind-up, leading to a close.
2. Plan your main questions in advance.
3. Keep to a logical sequence.
4. Observe the interviewee's body language as well as listening carefully to what they are saying.
5. Summarize at appropriate stages to check mutual understanding and confirm that there is agreement on what has been said to date.
6. Beware of halo effects – if an interviewee gives a good impression at the start and answers questions lucidly, the interviewer may make an early favourable judgement and overlook or not listen adequately to later answers which may not be so positive.
7. Avoid stereotypes – that is making judgements about candidates on the basis of scant information and 'categorizing' people unfairly.
8. Do not make moral judgements or show bias.
9. Pay particular attention to an interviewee's difficulties or dislikes in their work – discussion of these is likely to be more revealing than communication centred around tasks which they perform well and find relatively easy.
10. Never terminate any interview without giving the interviewee the chance to ask further questions or raise outstanding issues.
11. At the closure stage ensure that there is common understanding of what the next step will be.
12. Keep records and note down your findings or observations immediately an interview has terminated.

Work group meetings

As a starting point for this section we need to be clear about the definition of a work group meeting. What does it mean to you? It is in fact quite hard to define because meetings can occur in many forms. They may be formal or informal gatherings; they can be of any size; they may be regular or irregular occurrences. Why are they held? Again their purposes may be diverse. Some may simply be for exchanging information or reviewing and reporting on progress; some may be for planning and decision making; others may be called to solve problems and some may be called for no clear reason! In fact, one of the main grumbles frequently heard in organizations is that 'too much time is wasted in attending meetings'. Why should this be so?

Activity 5.10

List the main types of work group meetings which you have attended. How effective do you consider each one was in achieving its purpose or objective? What do you consider are the main consequences of ineffective meetings? Provide examples if you can.

We suspect that your list will have included things like boredom, frustration, low morale, lack of commitment, resentment. All very negative feelings – the complete antithesis of what we would like to occur. Precisely because meetings can generate such emotions and do take up a considerable amount of time in most organizations, it is vital that they are adequately prepared for, that the objectives or purposes are clear and that they are run efficiently.

Meeting preparation

Assuming that you are given the task of conducting a work group meeting, what are the first things you need to consider? The first question that should be asked is 'Do we actually need a meeting?' Remember that they are very costly in terms of time and therefore money. If you have decided that there is a need for a meeting, then you should know the reason and that will identify the purpose of the meeting. For example, is it to gather information, is it to make a decision? From the answers to these questions, you can decide on the type of meeting that will be necessary. Will it be formal or informal? Who will be the key participants? Will it require extensive documentation? Where should it be located? What time will suit most people? Once you have answered these basic questions we can move on to more detailed planning.

Activity 5.11

Read through the agenda below and identify as many faults as you can. Try to suggest ways in which it could be improved.

Agenda
We will be holding a section meeting tomorrow at 12 noon.

We wil be discussing the following items. Please attend if you can.

1 Revised advertising and promotion campaign
2 Staff holidays for next summer
3 Sales figures
4 Temporary closure of canteen facilities
5 Coverage of stand at autumn exhibition

Circulation: June, Lesley, Peter, John, Andrew

You should have identified that there was no location or date specified, no indication of who was to lead the meeting, no time for any preparation by participants, the subject items were not related, insufficient information was provided on agenda items, no idea was given of the proposed length of the meeting; there was no item of any other business to allow further discussion of other areas if considered appropriate.

The order of your agenda needs careful consideration. Try to include at the beginning those items which you believe can be dealt with quickly, thus allowing you more time for the more complex items which might need considerable discussion. Also group similar items together; in the example above, there was constant switching between external matters such as sales and internal matters relating to employees. You might find it helpful to try to remember four key questions when communicating your proposed agenda to participants – What is to be discussed? Where is the meeting to be held? When? Why?

Activity 5.12

As well as drawing up an agenda make a list of all the other things you might need to do prior to running a work group meeting.

We hope that your list included the necessity of circulating the minutes of previous meetings and informing participants of the input expected from them; identifying any other documents which might be needed for the meeting and circulating pre-meeting documents if appropriate; ensuring that refreshments are available if necessary; checking that equipment such as projectors or flip charts are available; deciding on the layout of the room. This last point may not seem terribly important but it is one which should not be ignored. If you are leading a formal meeting then it may be appropriate for the chairperson to sit at the head of the table with other participants on each side. However that type of layout is certainly not conducive to an informal meeting where you may want to encourage participation and discussion. For the less formal meeting it is more appropriate to have a circular or square arrangement so that no participant can occupy a 'dominant' seating position. Finally, before you conduct the meeting itself, you should spend some time anticipating what you think might happen. What questions or issues are likely to be raised? Do you have available all the information that might be required and what authority do you or the group have to take any decisions which may be necessary?

Meeting conventions

The conventions required for running effective meetings will now be investigated in more detail.

Chair – This is the person who is responsible for the conduct of the meeting and as such their role is critical to its success. He or she must be quite clear about the meeting's objectives and should then decide on their own role. This could be as a leader in the case of a formal meeting or as a coordinator or facilitator in a less formal meeting. The interpersonal skills required in each role should be carefully considered. For example, the style used in a formal setting such as a boardroom meeting may well be more *autocratic* than that which is needed on less formal occasions when a more *democratic* or even *laissez-faire* style could be adopted. If you need clarification of these terms, look back to Chapter 2 where different management styles are discussed. It is the role of the chair to make clear at the outset the style of the meeting. This is where careful agenda planning is so important because an appropriately written agenda will provide the model to be followed.

Secretary – This role is again a vital one in most workplace meetings, their main function being to record the discussions and outcomes and circulate these after the meeting as *minutes*. The secretary may also be responsible for other administrative arrangements such as circulation of the agenda, liaison with participants. One of the first items that should be present on most agendas is *apologies for absence*. This provides an opportunity for anyone who is unable to be present at the meeting to inform the secretary accordingly and the fact can then be recorded in the minutes.

Agenda – Several important points have already been covered earlier in this chapter including the fact that there should be room towards the end of the agenda for *any other business*. This is to allow any other items which may be relevant to the meeting to be raised. The final item on most agenda should be the *details of the next meeting*, so that participants can agree on a suitable date and time. Before we leave the question of the agenda, there is one further issue which should be considered. It is sometimes appropriate to put a time limit or *guillotine* on the meeting. This could be included in the agenda headings or possibly in an accompanying memorandum which may provide further detail of the agenda items. It is a useful device in that participants then know exactly how much time they need to allocate in their diaries and it is also useful for the chair so that he or she can move the meeting on at appropriate points. There is of course the downside though that a guillotine may prevent proper discussion of key items.

Minutes – These may be narrative minutes where the content of the discussion under each agenda item is recorded or, more likely, brief minutes which record the items discussed, the outcomes and the action that needs to be taken with an appropriate date for action. A suggested format is provided in Figure 5.3 below.

Item	Action to be taken	Who	When	What
1 Exhibition	Organize staff rota	Sarah	By 1 October	Circulate agreed rotas
	Investigate prices of local hotels	Mike	By 10 October	Book rooms

Figure 5.3 *Suggested format for minutes of a meeting*

Running the meeting

If you are leading a meeting, it is important that you set the 'ground rules' at its commencement. You will have already considered your style as we discussed above, but whatever type of meeting is involved you need to state clearly to the meeting participants:

- WHAT the meeting is for – the reason that it has been called, the objectives that you are hoping to achieve (e.g. solve a problem, report on progress or make a decision).
- WHAT will be covered – the areas to be discussed which should be in line with the agenda.
- HOW it will be run – whether participants are free to join in discussions at any appropriate time or whether they should only speak when invited to do so by the chair.

As leader, it is your job to ensure that everyone at the meeting has a fair chance to 'have their say' either formally or informally. Keep the meeting firmly focused on the agenda items to ensure that contributions are relevant to the subject in hand. Encourage participants to be concise – don't allow them to draw on lengthy anecdotes which may divert attention away from key issues. It is often thought that conflict in meetings should be avoided.

This is not necessarily the case. Conflict can be very useful in airing controversial subjects provided it is *constructive* and not *destructive*. What do we mean by this? Constructive conflict is where participants are able to put forward their viewpoints and listen to their opponents' viewpoints, but personal issues are kept out of the way. Read the following exchange:

'Well, I think we should scrap the whole idea of putting on an exhibition. It's just too expensive and...'

Before John could continue, Derek interrupts him. 'Don't be so stupid, you want it scrapped just because you're too lazy to organize your staff to run it!'

'That's not true,' shouts John and a heated exchange follows.

What has happened here is that emotion has got in the way of reason. Derek might be right in his assertions about John, but he hasn't even given John a chance to explain his reasons for scrapping the exhibition. It is difficult for any progress to be made while personal insults are being traded! Mullins (1989) quotes the following passage:

> From a survey of practising managers, who reported that they spend approximately 20 per cent of their time dealing with conflict situations, Schmidt (1974) records a number of both positive and negative outcomes of conflict.
>
> *Positive outcomes include:*
>
> ■ better ideas produced
> ■ people forced to search for new approaches
> ■ long-standing problems brought to the surface and resolved
> ■ clarification of individual views
> ■ stimulation of interest and creativity
> ■ a chance for people to test their capacities.
>
> *Negative outcomes include:*
>
> ■ some people felt defeated and demeaned
> ■ the distance between people increased
> ■ a climate of mistrust and suspicion developed
> ■ individuals and groups concentrated on their own narrow interests
> ■ resistance developed rather than team-work
> ■ an increase in labour turnover.

What are the potential sources of conflict in your organization? The most common that we have encountered include:

■ Allocation of resources: in most organizations *all* resources – people, money, information and time are limited.

■ Concerns over job roles: in many organizations, people are being expected to take on a greater variety of roles and responsibilities. With increasing pressures on all of us, if it is felt that some people are not pulling their weight and that others are being overburdened as a result, resentment and tension can set in.

■ Goals or objectives: different functions, departments and individuals may well have conflicting objectives. What is perceived as a priority by one individual may not be similarly viewed by others.

Activity 5.13

Write down two examples of conflict which you have encountered in work group meetings. Then try to identify the causes of the conflict.

Your list may have included points such as the participants' unwillingness to be open-minded and listen to the other's viewpoint; different objectives; personality clashes; a desire for a different course of action.

Dealing with conflict effectively depends to some extent on your ability to anticipate what may happen. If you know that two participants are likely to clash head on, don't let them sit opposite one another which can encourage confrontation. If you find that the conflict is becoming excessive, try to remember the following points:

■ Refer back to the meeting's objectives and ensure that participants have a common understanding.

■ Make sure that participants keep to facts and leave excess emotion out of the issues.

■ Summarize the views of opposing participants, but do not refer to individual names; use terms such as 'On the one hand we have the view that... and on the other the view is...' rather than 'John is saying... whereas Peter's view is that...'

■ If appropriate offer an alternative viewpoint which may encompass part of each side's arguments, but do not reach compromise just for the sake of peace and quiet! A genuine consensus though may be appropriate where all participants feel that they have at least had the opportunity to put forward their views even if the final decision is not to their liking.

As a leader you also need to ensure that the information being given by participants is accurate and reliable. Supposing for example that at a meeting to discuss sales of your organization's product in the South-East, one of your field sales representatives makes a statement that 'Sales of our product are 75 per cent higher than those of our competitors in part of my area.' That sounds pretty good, but when the leader of the meeting asks for clarification, it turns out that the information has come from one store manager who sells both rival organizations' products. In addition, that particular outlet only sells a tiny number of the products anyway. When the sales figures are examined for all retail outlets in the representative's area, it turns out that sales are in fact down by 10 per cent on the previous year's figures. If you are ever in doubt as to the precise meaning of a participant's contribution, ask for clarification and, if necessary, repeat your understanding of what is being said.

We have talked briefly of the need to manage conflict effectively, but you should also anticipate other potential problems. Some people seem to make a point of being aggressive in order to coerce others to their viewpoint. Ensure that their viewpoint is listened to, but then move the discussion on; bring in others and do not allow them to be interrupted. Sometimes people say nothing at meetings. Is this because they are bored or is it due to nervousness? If it is the former, then perhaps you need to check your handling of the meeting. If it is the latter, you can invite them specifically to contribute and again ensure that there are no interruptions. Ask 'open-ended' questions such as 'How do you feel about this...?' 'What do you think we might do next...?' Summarize the discussions regularly and invite feedback from other participants. At appropriate points you should summarize the discussions and then invite the secretary to record details of decisions made and details of the action to be taken in the minutes.

Follow-up arrangements for a work group meeting

After all agenda items have been dealt with, the leader should thank all participants for attending and agree with the secretary the time when the minutes will be completed. The circulation list needs to be drawn up identifying exactly who is to receive the minutes. This will obviously include the participants, but it may also involve other managers or departments.

Activity 5.14

Arrange to observe a work group meeting in your organization in which you do not normally participate. Then write a report describing the usage of meeting conventions, the identification and encouragement of effective contributions, the handling of any conflict which may occur and the agreement of follow-up arrangements.

Summary

In this chapter we have studied some of the theory and practice of effective interpersonal communication. We have considered the importance of the psychological contract and the theory of transactional analysis and their significance in application to the workplace. We have also looked at some of the techniques involved in the practice of workplace interviews and oral presentations.

References

Berne, E. (1964). *Games People Play*. New York: Grove Press.
Deal, T. and Kennedy, A. (1985). *Corporate Cultures*. London: Penguin.
Handy, C. (1985). *Understanding Organisations*, 3rd edn. London: Penguin.
Mullins, L. J. (1989). *Management and Organisational Behaviou*r, 2nd edn. Pitman.

Suggested further reading

Harris, T. (1973). *I'm OK – You're OK*. London: Pan.

6 Employment, recruitment and development

Aims

By the end of this chapter, you should be familiar with patterns of employment in the UK workforce, including the role of employee organizations. Within employing organizations, you should be familiar with workforce utilization and employment policies. You will consider the role of the First Line Manager in the recruitment and selection process, as well as general principles for good practice. The increasing importance of training and development will be considered, and how organizations can benefit from such activity. Finally, you will gain an appreciation of the rights of employees in the workplace.

Key concepts

- Employment patterns: deployment, flexibility, utilization; pay and reward systems.
- Recruitment and selection context: job roles; workforce planning; legal requirements; equal opportunities.
- Recruitment and selection process: job descriptions; person specifications; advertisements; applications, shortlisting, selection methods, interviews, assessment centres, validation.
- Training and development: identification of needs, induction programmes, assessing performance, delivering training, evaluation.
- Employee rights: contractual, statutory, non-statutory.

Introduction

In recent years, employment has been subject to considerable change: the way people are employed, who is employed and in what type of organization. This has been reflected by significant changes in the way organizations utilize their workforce, and major shifts in attitudes to jobs and careers. Many of the rules, structures and practices of the past that were referred to as 'industrial relations' have changed completely since the early 1980s. Some of these changes have been driven by structural changes in the economy, while others are the consequence of a number of new pieces of legislation.

The simple employment relationship whereby the employee works for the employer and receives payment in return implies a straightforward financial/legal transaction. While this can be used as a basis, the reality is much more complex than this. For many people the notion that one should expect to remain in employment for the whole of one's working life has simply ceased to exist. Similarly, many people entering a career in banking, engineering, local government or the Civil Service in the 1970s could confidently have expected a 'job for life'. Employment at the end of this century is therefore characterized by the need for a flexible workforce, prepared to accept retraining or non-traditional patterns of employment. At the same time, there continue to be regional variations in both the levels of employment, and employment opportunities. However, at the time of writing the UK continues to have the longest working week in the European Union, with UK employees working on average five hours more per week than their contemporaries in France, Germany or Italy.

Activity 6.1

Consider the employment characteristics of your own geographical area:

- Who are the local employers?
- Which are declining or growing?
- Is the employment rate increasing or decreasing?
- How does this compare with the national picture?

In August 1995, according to official statistics, 8.3 per cent of the UK workforce were unemployed, compared to 9.3 per cent one year previously. The term 'full employment', once widely used by politicians, is now recognized as more or less an impossibility, principally due to technological advances and structural changes in the economy. Nevertheless, it remains a sensitive political issue. In the interwar years, mean unemployment had been 14 per cent; from 1945 to 1970 it was 1.5 per cent. In the 1980s, it was back up to 10 per cent. The patterns of unemployment within the work-force are discussed below. It is worth remembering that the causes of unem-ployment (the cyclical nature of the economy, structural factors, technological change, skills shortages, the difficulty of re-employment for the long-term unemployed, and so on) have been recognized for many years, as have some of the potential remedies. There have been a variety of mea-sures by central government, aimed at reducing unemployment, or provid-ing training opportunities for vulnerable groups such as young people. The calculation of the measure of unemployment has also changed. What has happened, as you will have recognized in Activity 6.1, is that there has been a decline in full-time employment, and a trend towards what has been called the 'casualization' of the labour force.

Finally, the UK is not alone in having to deal with unemployment: almost 10 per cent of the EU's workforce is presently out of work. This is an incredible waste of human resources in one of the most productive and tech-nologically advanced parts of the world. In Europe, Finland (16.2 per cent) and Spain (15.3 per cent) have the highest rates of unemployment (August 1995), with some countries in central Europe such as Poland (15.2 per cent) also experiencing difficulty.

Full-time or part-time employment?

While our expectations of work have traditionally been based on the notion of full-time, permanent and relatively stable employment, there are many features of alternative forms of employment that are attractive to both employer and employee, although for different reasons.

A pool of part-time employees is attractive to a manager of a unit where skill requirements may not be high, but where there is the need for work at weekends, in the evenings, or at peak periods during the week. The Advisory, Conciliation and Arbitration Service (ACAS) add that other advan-tages include lower total wage costs if the employee is below the earnings limit that attracts National Insurance contributions; higher productivity and lower absence rates than full timers.

As an illustration, most large retail outlets will have relatively few full-time, permanent staff, often only those on the most senior managerial grades, as part-time staff can have some supervisory responsibility. For the employee, part-time work remains an option to integrate the opportunity to earn money with other activities, such as study or domestic responsibilities. However, ACAS point out that: 'Part-time employees may find that pay, training and career prospects are proportionately poorer than for full-time workers.'

To illustrate this, in a survey of 4000 employers by the Reward Group, almost half admitted that they offered poorer terms and conditions to part-timers. During 1993, the number of men in part-time jobs increased by almost 10 per cent, while the number of women increased by just 3 per cent. Only 29 per cent of the companies in the Reward Group survey stated that they intended to harmonize terms and conditions of employment in the near future.

What do you think will happen to the relative pay and conditions of service of full-time and part-time workers over the next few years? What reasons can you give for this?

For the manager, part-time employees must be recognized as a key resource. They should be thoroughly trained to ensure that they are fully competent. To the customer, using this term in the widest sense, they are members of staff from whom certain standards of service are expected.

Activity 6.2

Prepare an organization chart for an organization with which you are familiar, indicating the distribution of full-time and part-time staff.

- What are the reasons for this organization employing part-timers?
- How many hours per week do they typically work?
- How is the staffing allocation varied during the week?
- What is the reason for this?

What are the other alternatives to permanent, full-time work?

Traditionally, employees have expected the security and continuity of earnings that go with full-time, permanent employment. It can affect the standard of living, and the ability to obtain a mortgage or other finance. For the employer, the reliability of an employee who has made a long-term commitment and who may be working towards career goals is an invaluable asset. Other advantages to the employer can include the employee accumulating skills and knowledge of systems, procedures and customers.

Despite the various advantages of permanent employees, it is often illogical for an organization to maintain a full complement of permanent, full-time employees in the face of varying workloads and competitive pressures. The recession of the early 1990s increased the use of temporary employees, often agency-based. Although this may have reduced costs and enabled them to meet short-term needs, the recruitment of temporary staff, or the need to deal with a number of agencies is often frustrating for managers. To counteract this, some organizations use the concept of 'partnership sourcing', where a smaller number of agencies, often a single supplier, provide a block of temporary employees for a particular function on a long-term basis. Companies that use this approach include Hewlett Packard and Glaxo. The company therefore has just one contact; the person from the agency coordinates the supply of all clerical and secretarial 'temps' throughout the country.

There have been sometimes optimistic predictions about the growth of homeworking for the managerial or professional employee. There is some evidence that the practice is spreading. For the organization, there are clear advantages. Barclays Bank claim improved productivity, where employees can control the times at which they perform the job, and IBM claimed a productivity increase of 200 per cent from one site in the US. Employers can also make savings on expensive office space. Members of the Business Design Group at the Basingstoke offices of Digital Equipment work primarily from home. When they visit the office, they occupy one of six desks allocated to the group, or occasionally move to a desk elsewhere in the building.

To make such arrangements work, several factors are crucial. Meetings at the office become much more of a focus for interaction, and attendance becomes more important. The clerical support service at the head office becomes a lynchpin operation, relaying messages where appropriate, or redirecting telephone calls. For someone managing 'teleworkers', trust is essential. Anecdotes from the US tell of managers checking employees computer activity in the evening to see who was still working.

Working from home does not suit everyone. Some employees will miss the interaction of the office environment. There can be a reluctance to call someone at home about a work-related matter, and there is the need to transport documents to and from the office.

Activity 6.3

Using the information prepared in the activities above, identify the key issues for First Line Managers associated with managing those who are not employed full-time, who work on an irregular basis, or who work from home. What are the particular skills that will be needed to get the best from such employees?

Women in the part-time workforce

It is widely recognized that while there has been a decline in employment in full-time, traditional occupations, there has been a growth in the part-time workforce. Women make up almost 90 per cent of the part-time workforce, with over 50 per cent of women being economically active. The UK percentage of working women is higher than the European average, coming second only to Denmark. Conversely, unemployment among women is significantly below most other European Union states, with Spain, Italy, Ireland and Belgium having the highest. Women made up most of the increase in the labour force in Europe in the 1980s, yet in the UK manual women employees earned only about two-thirds of their male counterparts' gross earnings, and almost half in the case of non-manual employees, the second widest gap in the EU.

Despite this less than encouraging picture, many organizations have adopted flexible working arrangements to encourage the employment of women, which are discussed below.

'We're all getting older...'

The UK, in common with most Western economies, has an ageing population. This will become more evident in years to come, as the 'baby boomers' age, and form an increasingly numerous elderly population. Even now, the more mature members of the workforce are still numerous, and there is increasing recognition of the reality of age discrimination. The Institute of Personnel and Development (IPD) have a voluntary code on age discrimination, but a survey of 1140 personnel managers revealed that 80 per cent of them thought that this was not going far enough, and that the government should either introduce its own voluntary code or enact legislation. However, it must be pointed out that many more enlightened organizations now include age as a dimension of their equal opportunities statements.

The growth in early retirement combined with high levels of unemployment have led to a huge withdrawal of men aged between 55 and 65 from the labour force. Unfortunately, older workers are also under-represented on training courses, largely due to employers' views about entrenched attitudes and poor performance. In *The Empty Raincoat*, Charles Handy presents a more positive view, where the 'third age' is a time after the demands of a conventional career, and after the greatest demands on an individual's earning capacity. It is when individuals can engage in fulfilling activities which may fall outside the boundaries of what we regard as traditional employment. A further dimension of this so-called 'grey demographic timebomb' will be the future pressure on pensions.

How can employers keep up?

There is nothing new in the revelation that in the broad area of training the UK lags behind the rest of Europe. The problem is largely historical – a combination of an insular culture, an education system that was not attuned to the needs of industry, and a view in industry that training was a soft target for cost cutting in times of economic adversity. These combined to produce a workforce that, as recently as 1993, was described by the National Institute of Economic and Social Research as 'underqualified and undertrained'. Fewer than 30 per cent of the UK workforce holds vocational qualifications compared with 60 per cent in the former Western Germany. At school, the mathematical abilities of 13 to 16-year-olds lag behind those of their Japanese equivalents by up to three years.

Much is now being done to improve the vocational skills of the workforce. A variety of government initiatives over the years ('A New Training Initiative', 'Investors in People', and more recently 'Modern Apprenticeships') have been matched by reforms in vocational qualifications. The establishment of the Training and Enterprise Councils has also contributed to an increase in training activity. The recent combination of the Institute of Personnel Management and the Institute of Training and Development into the Institute of Personnel and Development may be further evidence of the growth, at last, of a UK 'training culture'. Increasing participation in higher education is also seen as an encouraging sign for the future. However, there is no room for complacency, and a long way to go to make up for the shortfalls of the past.

All change in the 1990s

The recession of the late 1980s introduced a much greater competitive spirit into business in the UK. In particular, organizations began to look at their staffing structures, and again at the layers of management hierarchies that they had acquired over the years. 'Restructuring', 'delayering' and 'downsizing' became terms used to describe the evolution of flatter hierarchies with more autonomous work teams. Organizations came to be seen as flexible delivery mechanisms rather than permanent bureaucracies. Privatization has created a range of new corporations, with contracted-out services operating in new marketplaces. These were among the driving forces for the flexibility in the workforce that is described earlier in this chapter, and which has forced an acceptance of a change culture on many organizations and their employees. For the First Line Manager, this has often meant accepting the role of 'change agent', with a requirement not only to stimulate change, but also to manage it and motivate staff at the same time – a challenging role! What is certain is that the rate of change in the business environment is increasing, and that there is a growing requirement on organizations to be flexible and responsive to cope with this.

Within the above framework, organizations remain under pressure to ensure that they have the right number of employees, with the right level of talent and skill, to meet their future human resources needs. Many are operating within tight financial constraints. This is not just about cutting costs – nor is it about paying artificially low salaries – that will have an impact on motivation and labour turnover. Controlling costs is also about making the best use of the human resources available, and about eliminating waste. Very often this can be achieved through effective control of absence and labour turnover.

High absence levels can increase costs through overtime payments to provide cover, and business commitments can suffer. Similarly, labour turnover can increase pressure on recruitment and training budgets, and can have knock-on effects on the motivation of other employees, and the effectiveness of the firm.

Activity 6.4

You are to take on the role of a First Line Manager in a medium-sized manufacturing company. The company has high levels of sickness absence among the manufacturing operatives, with an average of 15 days per year in the main group of 400 employees. Labour turnover is also high, with annual levels of 60 per cent in the warehouse, and 55 per cent in the production area. What measures will you use to establish the exact scale of the problem, and to identify the causes? On the basis of the limited information avaialable, what measures should the company consider to tackle these problems? Finally, what do you see as the likely consequences if they do nothing?

The impact of technology

In the early 1980s the Banking, Insurance and Finance Union (BIFU) produced a booklet called 'New Technology in Banking, Insurance and Finance' that outlined what they saw as some of the future consequences of the advances in technology in their sector of employment. Their predictions included the spread of the use of Automated Teller Machines (ATMs), the installation of ATMs in retail outlets, the centralization of management structures away from the bank branch level, delayering, and the corresponding decrease in staffing levels. By any standards, their predictions were remarkably accurate, accepting the difficulty of accurately quantifying the scale of the changes. At one time, redundancies in this sector of employment were unthinkable, but media items in recent years have revealed the scale of staff reductions that have taken place.

The impact of technology is to require new work patterns and new attitudes towards change. For employees, it means an acceptance of the need for occupational mobility and training and retraining as an ongoing process. There is also an impact on the amount of discretion exercised by the individual worker, which in turn will have an impact on job satisfaction and attitudes to work.

Models of workforce utilization

The above sections were intended to set the scene in terms of the context of changes in patterns of employment in the workforce as a whole. We can now consider how the individual organization can respond to these trends, and the associated issues for practising managers.

The core/peripheral workforce

It is often possible to identify a core group of permanent full-time employees who have made a long-term commitment to their employing organization. Companies will have made a training investment in these employees and therefore have an interest in protecting that long-term investment. Continuity of employment will also protect the build-up of skills over a long period of time, which will allow those employees, in the long term, to carry out a wider variety of tasks, thus creating a multi-skilled workforce. This is known as achieving functional flexibility – the ability of employees to break down rigid demarcations, and move between departments and jobs.

Beyond this, the focus for many organizations in the 1990s is switching to employees who may be called the 'peripheral' workforce. These workers give the organization numerical flexibility, where they may be subject to laying-off and rehiring as required, as their skills are easily obtainable in the external labour market. The peripheral workforce is therefore made up of employees who have little prospect of secure, continuous employment. It is made up of part-time, temporary, or casual workers, and distance workers such as outworkers or subcontractors who supply their labour under contracts for services rather than contracts of service. They will tend to be more subject to market forces than core employees, and will also serve to protect the security of the core, by acting as a buffer to the uncertain, changing world outside the organization. Figure 6.1, adapted from Bramham (1990) illustrates the overall picture.

Employers derive a number of benefits from this approach, including reduced wage costs, the ability to vary the size of the workforce more easily in response to demand levels, increased productivity from the core workforce, and greater control.

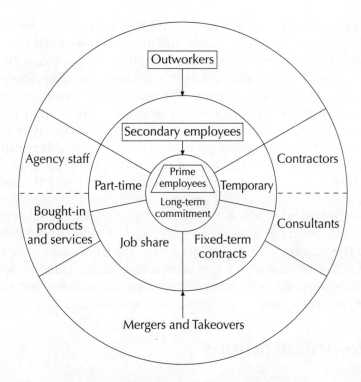

Figure 6.1 *The Flexibility Map* (From *Human Resource Planning*, John Bramham, IPM, 1989. Reproduced with permission)

What are the issues for managers of the flexible workforce? Potential problems may include: low morale among peripherals often due to lower levels of benefits and higher turnover; communication difficulties, particularly the overload on the core employees who may be dealing with a number of peripherals; the fact that peripherals may not be able to handle everyday crises without the help of core staff; and conflict between the core and peripheral groups. Clearly many of these are training issues, and it must be recognized that effective training is essential for the peripheral employees to avoid undue pressure on the core.

Activity 6.5

Earlier in this chapter you prepared an organization chart showing full and part-time employees for an organization with which you are familiar. Now attempt to interpret this chart in terms of the 'flexible firm' model illustrated, and produce another chart based on the illustration. To what extent do you think this model applies to the organization you have chosen? Do organizations really think about their workforce patterns in this way, or can you identify other reasons for the growth in part-time, temporary employment?

Sometimes an employer may not fill a vacancy with just one person. Job sharing involves sharing a single full-time job between two people who share the pay, responsibility and the benefits. It need not be an exactly equal split, as a 60:40 arrangement is not uncommon. Employees can share on a daily basis, with one working afternoons and another mornings, or 'alternate week' arrangements can also be used. The benefit of job sharing to the employer is that it allows them to recruit skilled employees who may be unable to work full time, perhaps due to domestic responsibilities, or who simply may not wish to do so. If one of the sharers leaves, it can provide an element of continuity, as is the case if one is absent. For job sharing to work effectively, it may be necessary to arrange for an 'overlap period' to allow the sharers to communicate. Ideally, however, the situation where two people occupy two desks each for half of the time should be avoided! Potential problems include the incompatibility of job-share partners that may emerge after appointment, that workload for the partners is more than is actually given to one job incumbent, and communication difficulties for subordinates where the job sharers have managerial responsibilities.

Employee organizations

Trade unions

Once, trade unions were seldom out of the media, and tended to evoke very strong emotions, depending on one's political viewpoint! Today, the industrial relations climate is somewhat different, and while their powers may have been curbed, their basic functions remain the same. The principal aim of trade unions is to promote the interests of their members, which can best be served by ensuring that the undertakings in which their members work prosper. An important basic fact to remember, however, is that unions are responsible to their members first and foremost and not to managers or to the government.

Traditional approaches to employment relations laid down rules (procedural agreements) through which the unions could work in a regulated and orderly manner towards the substantive agreements that make up remuneration and compensation packages, or to develop procedures for health and safety, joint consultation and other workplace matters. The discussions on substantive and procedural matters are generally referred to as collective bargaining, and can take place at a variety of levels, from the level of the whole industry, down to the individual workplace or group of employees.

In addition, many employees are members of organizations called staff associations. These exist primarily to serve the social interests of the members. This is not always the case, however, as some staff associations acted as employee representative bodies. In the 1970s, for example, staff representation in the National Westminster Bank was split between the National Union of Bank Employees (NUBE), and the National Westminster Staff Association (NWSA). The bank was faced with negotiating with both bodies. In the social sense, staff associations fulfil a very valuable role, as such events can help to foster team spirit among the employees, and to build a sense of 'belonging'.

What is meant by union recognition?

When an employer agrees to negotiate with a trade union or other organization then that organization is said to be 'recognized' by the employer as being representative of the workforce. There is a long history of trade union-ism in the UK, and the industrial relations framework developed in a very fragmented way. In some organizations a number of unions came to be 'recognized' as representing the employees. This produces a rather difficult situation for managers, particularly where multi-unionism means that negotiations relating to one group of employees involves having to deal with a number of unions. These may not necessarily agree among themselves. In Germany or Finland the model taken is quite different – here, 'industrial unions' (discussed below) are the norm. Many UK organizations are moving this way.

Changes in business practices, not least those relating to employ-ment, sometimes introduce new words or phrases into the language. 'De-recognition' is one such phrase, and it refers to the practice of an employer refusing to participate in the collective bargaining that may have been 'custom and practice' in an organization for many years, and simply seeking to determine conditions of employment. Clearly this requires a situation where the employer is confident that the union will not be able to do any-thing about this, and falling union membership has produced exactly this situation in a number of instances.

What different types of union are there?

General unions

These are unions that draw their membership from a wide range of occupa-tions, and therefore have the potential to be very large and powerful, for example the Transport and General Workers Union (TGWU). Their member-ship will typically be either 'blue collar' (i.e. manual, skilled, or semi-skilled), or 'white-collar', which is further described below. Very often they may be the result of mergers of a number of smaller unions at an earlier stage in their history.

Unions for professional people

The image promoted by the popular press in the strike-prone days of the 1970s was of a cloth-cap wearing, banner-waving trade union member, referring to colleagues as 'brothers and sisters', and doggedly resisting the march of change. In the changed world of the 1990s, there has not only been a decline in the traditional occupations, there has also been a growing trend towards professional people joining some organization that will do more than provide professional networks and a monthly journal. BALPA, the British Airline Pilot's Association, is one such body.

White-collar unions

By far the biggest growth area in trade-union membership in recent years has been among technical, professional and administrative workers – the so-called 'white-collar' sector. Examples include USDAW, for employees in retailing, the Banking, Insurance and Finance Union, and UNISON, princi-pally for employees in the public sector. 'White-collar' employees may not be naturally politically inclined towards union membership – they are more likely to see their membership as a sort of 'insurance policy', especially as their type of employment has not been immune to redundancies, and has often been affected by technological change.

Industrial unions

The rather ad hoc structure that has developed in industrial relations in the UK, where a number of different unions may operate for similar employees within one industry, and even within one company, is clearly less than ideal. There are alternatives which have clear advantages. After the Second World War, when Germany's devastated economy was being rebuilt, their union structure was remodelled on industrial lines – workers in one industry tend to be members of one union. Similar examples exist elsewhere in Europe – for example employees who are union members who work in engineering in Finland are members of their Metal Industry Union. Such unions have been very strong in the past – Finland was characterized by many strikes in the late 1980s when the country was among the most prosperous in the world. In their severe recession of the early 1990s unemployment rose to nearly 20 per cent, and the unions' power diminished accordingly. Industrial union organization does tend to produce a 'tidier' industrial relations structure generally, and certainly leaves no room for the multi-unionism that has his-torically been so problematic in the UK.

Changes in membership, structure and power of trade unions

In the 1980s, however, union membership declined dramatically, as traditional industries declined and the kind of changes in the makeup of the workforce described earlier in this chapter meant a shift away from traditional occupations in highly unionized work environments towards an emphasis on part-time, temporary and casual work, where union membership is almost non-existent. Nevertheless, some of the growth areas of employment in the service sector and clerical and administrative occupations have seen continuing growth in union membership. A further factor has been the extensive legislation enacted in the 1980s by the Conservative governments which has had the effect of considerably limiting the power of trade unions, particularly in situations when normal relations have broken down.

Structural changes in the economy have not been the only factor to undermine their power. Shifts in public attitudes and political influence have meant that a much more favourable climate now exists for managers wishing to change working practices. Workers in the new industries are not so interested in joining unions, and managers have successfully resisted recognition claims where there has been union activity. Membership of TUC-affiliated unions has fallen to around nine million whilst the employed workforce has increased. Against this, the perceived influence of unions by the public has fallen substantially.

Professional organizations

At this point it should be mentioned that there are other organizations that represent people at work, although not necessarily within the context of collective bargaining. Professional organizations fulfil a valuable service for their members. A primary role is to provide professional accreditation and recognition, often through the completion of examination-based qualifications, although there is also a trend towards the use of professional diaries and portfolios of competence based evidence, sometimes linked to NVQs or SVQs (National or Scottish Vocational Qualifications). Through regular branch meetings at local level, professional organizations can provide a valuable local support network, and a forum for discussion and the sharing of expertise. Examples include the Institute of Management and the Institute of Supervision and Management. Others may be occupation-specific, such as the Chartered Institute of Purchasing and Supply. Through their professional journals and other publications they extend professional knowledge in their field, and provide an opportunity for practitioners and academics in the field to publish their work. They may also act as pressure groups, lobbying the UK or European parliaments on issues of concern.

Some of them fulfil a dual role, as in the case of the British Medical Association, where they also act as the employee representative body, particularly for those members in NHS Trust employment. They may also operate at an international level, providing links to related organizations in other countries.

Reward systems

Some organizations may have a policy on performance-related pay. Here this term is used to relate to those payment schemes more commonly known as 'appraisal-related pay', where increases in pay are wholly or partially based on the systematic assessment of performance, as opposed to payment by results or piecework, which are referred to below. The value of appraisal-related pay is to emphasize the importance of effective job performance, and it may have a motivating effect on employees by strengthening the link between pay and performance. However, it is essential to base this on a sound and fair payment system, and that the basis for the reward is clearly understood by all concerned. Properly introduced, it can be a mechanism for strengthening employee commitment and involvement, as well as improving staff retention.

Pay related to appraisal is not the only way in which employees can be paid according to how well they perform in the workplace. Traditional piecework bears a rather more direct relationship to the amount of work produced. Here, the employee is paid a specific price or rate per unit of output (or per piece). This is a very simple form of individual payment by results, and has been in use for hundreds of years. The standard time or piecework basis time rate system is similar in principle, but here a standard time is allowed to do a particular task. The employee is then paid the allowed time for the task completed. Piecework is enduringly popular in some industries, such as knitwear, footwear and hosiery. It is generally considered that individual payment by results is more suited to production work but not exclusively so – the commission paid to sales staff is a form of individual payment by results.

In a pay policy, what other ways of paying employees might be incorporated? One method is to use one or more of a range of time rates, normally expressed as an hourly rate, a weekly wage, or an annual salary. Hourly pay is often used in relation to part-time employees, and may be used in conjunction with a form of payment by results. For the employer, time rates are relatively simple and cheap to administer, and facilitate the forecasting of labour costs. They are also easy for employees to understand, and consequently are the source of fewer disputes. However, they have little incentive value. They are appropriate where the volume or quality of work is difficult to measure, workflow is uneven, where the volume or pace of work is outside the control of employees, or where considerations other than the volume of work are paramount.

Salaried staff

Normally this term is used to refer to the situation where pay is expressed on an annual basis. It has historically been applied mostly to clerical and managerial staff, although some organizations have used it as part of schemes to introduce what is called 'staff status for manual workers'. Another approach is the notion of 'annual hours', which is a form of flexible contract where account can be made of varying workloads during the course of the year by paying staff for a certain number of hours on an annual basis, although this may actually manifest itself as a fixed regular monthly salary. Again, the annual salary may include some element of appraisal-related pay. Whatever scheme is used, it is essential that the pay policy is clearly understood and communicated, and based on an agreed method of job evaluation.

Some employees may be fortunate enough to receive bonuses at work. Bonuses can take a variety of forms, such as an annual profit sharing bonus which may be expressed as a percentage of gross annual salary. They may also be one-off *ex gratia* payments made to an individual employee in recognition of outstanding effort or attainment. In some situations, they may become an expected part of the normal remuneration package, at which point the motivational value may become somewhat diluted.

Share ownership

Sometimes bonuses can take the form of share-ownership schemes, where employees are either credited with a certain number of shares, or have the option to buy shares at a special rate. These schemes can be very attractive, especially when the company is doing well or the share is under-priced! An anecdotal example is the sale of shares in the National Freight Corporation, the former nationalized road haulage organization, to the employees. While many employees such as drivers or mechanics were able to buy a few hundred pounds worth of shares, some senior managers bought several thousand pounds worth. The shares increased in value twenty times over. One cannot help but feel sorry for those employees who missed out! Clearly not all examples are that spectacular, but the feeling that one has a stake in the company does have some motivational value.

Perks

'Perks' is a colloquial term used to refer to 'perquisites', which can cover a range of benefits from company cars to luncheon vouchers. As with all the benefits described above, once these are embedded into the reward structure they can be very hard to remove, and reward policies may require a major rethink in the future. As a comparison, a manager in the United States would be surprised to receive the range of 'perks' expected by their

UK counterpart, but would expect to receive a much higher salary. A variation from the USA is the 'cafeteria' benefits package, where the employee may choose from a range of benefits which may include a company car (of varying values) or medical insurance, actually choosing themselves how the package is made up. Clearly this is a very attractive proposition as individual priorities differ.

Individual contracts

Strictly speaking all employees have an individual contract, although the terms and conditions are more than likely to have been collectively negotiated. The term above is used to refer to individually negotiated contracts, which is an increasingly popular part of many organizations' remuneration policy. Clearly this reflects the individual ethic prevalent today, but it also strengthens the hand of the employer. The employer is free to determine the organization of work, the level of payment, and the duration of working time.

Activity 6.5

Using the job vacancies sections from several copies of your local newspaper, compare the remuneration packages being offered for say three different jobs. How effective do you think the packages will be in motivating, rewarding and retaining the staff recruited?

Collective or Individual agreements?

Clearly in the face of such trends it is a very attractive proposition for an employer not to be bound by the procedural rules of traditional collective bargaining, and it is a reflection of the flexibility entering every aspect of the employment relationship that, particularly for those with technical skills or managerial responsibilities, individual contracts agreed on appointment are becoming more widespread.

Activity 6.6

Consider the following statements and attempt to identify arguments that support *both* points of view expressed here. Can you provide examples to support your statements?

> Organizations have to be efficient. If that means that some individuals lose their jobs, then that is worthwhile if it

enhances the profitability of the enterprise. We can always buy-in the skills we need later.

Lean organization has gone too far. Many organizations have removed jobs and layers of management without really thinking the process through – they are just copying others in their field. Surely it is better to live with a little inefficiency, but still have an effective team and a willing workforce?

Human resource planning, recruitment and selection

We will now consider the staffing of organizations, and the role of the First Line Manager in areas such as workforce planning, recruitment and selection.

Human resource planning

This term refers to a variety of techniques that can be used to ensure that the organization has the human resources that it requires to meet its current and future needs. By looking into the future to assess their requirements, organizations can consider how the deployment of their current workforce needs to change to meet trends or patterns that can be identified. This in turn will affect recruitment, training, the minimization of redundancies, promotion and career development policies, succession planning, and the control of staffing costs. The kind of changes that may affect organizations include the introduction of new technologies, organizational restructuring, closures or relocations of premises, changes to work methods, or new markets, products and services.

Human resource planning can be seen as a process that involves reviewing and forecasting, developing and implementing strategies, and finally monitoring, evaluating and replanning. In the first stage, organizations will seek to assess the likely future impact of the business environment on their operations, then analyse forecasts of internal and external labour supply. Finally organizations will seek to analyse the unit labour costs of their competitors, and their productivity.

Demand forecasting involves the examination of business plans to assess the impact on the numbers and skills of employees, the analysis of unit labour costs and productivity, and the production of a qualitative and quantitative forecast of staffing requirements. An assessment of the supply of labour will be based on an analysis of the existing employees on the basis of age, length of service, training and so on; the impact of early retirements, turnover and wastage; and from this the development of a forecast of the future availability of people. The benefits of workforce planning should include a better trained and more flexible workforce, better employment stability for the 'core' employees, improved succession planning, better staff retention, improved employee relations, and more reliable attainment of organizational goals. Planning is therefore a key role of the human resources management function. For the human resources specialist there is a great deal more to the process than this, with complex statistical techniques being employed. For now, it is sufficient to consider how the First Line Manager will be affected, and what their input into workforce planning will be.

In the short term, workforce planning is likely to focus on the First Line Manager's level. Here an individual manager is likely to be balancing short-term staff availability in the light of immediate contingencies such as absences, emergencies or 'rush jobs'. Clearly this kind of 'seat of the pants' situation is the normal state of affairs in many organizations, and the term 'planning' is something of a misnomer here. Even so, the information being collected at this stage will prove to be very valuable later on. In this kind of environment the flexibility of the workforce is crucial, not only by recruiting temporary staff quickly from an agency but also in terms of skills, and the ability to switch staff from one job to another, often within the course of a day. It is important at this level that staff are aware of the standards of performance expected of them – communication and 'hands-on' management are important here.

Medium-term planning

In the medium term, say from six months to one year, the human resource planning specialist should be able to consider the information given to them by the First Line Managers and develop a response. In this kind of time-scale we will also be able to take greater account of the long-term planning, and also the long-term impact of the business environment and labour market. On the supply side, for example, information will be available on entrants from training programmes, on recruitment, on wastage and turnover, or on longer term contracts for the supply of temporary or agency staff. The manager will have a better idea of unit labour costs, and will be able to incorporate these into the staffing levels and allocations. At First Line Manager level, their input at this stage will include the consideration and identification (possibly through appraisal) of the training and development needs of staff, and the regular monitoring of employee performance with feedback to the human resources specialist.

Long-term planning

The longer term goals and strategies of the organization will account for other trends identifiable within the workforce, for example turnover, retirement and training completion, as well as an assessment of the external labour supply over the next few years. It is essential at this stage to ensure that the human resource implications of long-term plans have been expressed in terms of action plans, and that strategies are in place to ensure that quantitatively and qualitatively the organization can meet its future needs. Much greater account will need to be made of technological updating, of changes in working methods, while at the same time opportunities can be created to build a greater level of flexibility into the workforce. This will assist managers operating in a medium to short-term framework in the future. One thing that is certain in the long term is greater uncertainty, and the plans drawn up now need to be flexible enough to accommodate this.

Activity 6.7

Consider the above in the context of an organization with which you are familiar.

1   What factors would affect this organization in the short, medium and long term?
2   What do you consider would be appropriate responses at an organizational level?
3   What input would a First Line Manager have at the various levels of activity?

Equal opportunities

Equal opportunity issues arise throughout employment, but especially in recruitment and selection. Recruitment practices in the UK are less regulated than in some other European countries, but the law is an important consideration none the less. As a concept, 'equal opportunity' can be taken to relate to three levels:

1   'Equal opportunity as equal chance' where, in recruitment terms, everyone should have the same opportunity to apply for and be considered for job vacancies. Discrimination is a reality at this level, however, as we will see below.
2   At the second level, once the barriers of recruitment have been passed, there may well still be barriers to onward progression and training.
3   Finally, in an ideal world, we would see equal representation of all groups at all levels of the organizational hierarchy.

The following sections look at the specific areas where legal requirements have equal opportunities implications in recruitment.

Sex discrimination

The Sex Discrimination Act 1975 makes it unlawful to discriminate against a person on grounds of sex or marriage. There is not yet legislation relating to sexual orientation in the UK. The Act covers three types of discrimination:

1 Direct discrimination, where a woman is treated less favourably than a man or vice versa, or a married person is treated less favourably than a single person.
2 Indirect discrimination, where a man or woman cannot comply with an unjustifiable requirement which on the face of it appears to apply equally to men and women (or to married and single people), but can only be met by a smaller proportion of one sex – for example a requirement that clerical workers must be over six feet tall may only be met by men, and is practically impossible to justify.
3 Victimization of someone who has made a complaint under the Act, or under the Equal Pay Act is also prohibited.

Race discrimination

Under the Race Relations Act 1976, direct and indirect discrimination and victimization are also unlawful on the grounds of colour, race, citizenship, nationality or ethnic origins. The Act is framed in very similar terms to the Sex Discrimination Act. The UK was the first country in Europe to have legislation in this field, and continues to place greater emphasis on this area than any of our European neighbours.

Sex and race discrimination in recruitment

Both the acts above specifically refer to discrimination in recruitment and selection. The scope of this therefore includes advertisements, interviews, selection arrangements and the terms offered as well as the actual offer or refusal of the job. Individuals can complain about any aspect of these practices, except in the area of advertising, where only the Equal Opportunities Commission or the Commission for Racial Equality can initiate action.

Where an individual considers that they have been the victim of discrimination, they must complain within three months to an industrial tribunal. An Advisory, Conciliation and Arbitration Service (ACAS) conciliation officer will contact both parties to attempt to bring about a voluntary settlement before the matter reaches the tribunal stage.

Sex or race discrimination can be allowed where it is specified as a 'genuine occupational qualification' or 'GOQ'. Examples of situations where

GOQs may apply may include in the recruitment of employees for women's refuges, for some positions in counselling, for actors or for models.

The rehabilitation of offenders and recruitment

The provisions of the Rehabilitation of Offenders Act 1974 enable offenders who have received sentences of 30 months or less, to be 'rehabilitated' and their convictions 'spent'. This means that after a specified length of time they can reply 'no' when asked if they have a criminal record. It is illegal for an employer to discriminate against them on the grounds of a spent conviction. The 'rehabilitation periods' vary according to the age on conviction, the nature of the offence, and the sentence imposed, and can be between six months and ten years.

What is observable is that ex-offenders make up a significant proportion of the workforce, with over 20 per cent having some sort of criminal record. The percentages are even higher in inner-city areas. Many employers are unaware of the records of their employees, while on the other hand some occupations, such as teaching and medicine, are excluded from the provisions of the Act.

Discrimination against the disabled in recruitment and selection

The UK has historically been relatively weak in protecting the rights of disabled people in recruitment and selection. While there has been some legislation, this was widely ignored. Recent governments have sought to respond to a growing lobby in this area by improving the situation, and by the passing of the Disability Discrimination Act 1995.

Age discrimination in recruitment and selection

According to the IPD: 'Arbitrary age discrimination can be both overt and covert and occur directly and indirectly at all stages of the employment cycle.' By the year 2000 it is estimated that one person in three in the potential labour force will be aged over forty. The United States is enacting legislation relating to older workers, yet age discrimination remains a reality in the UK.

Recruitment implications of equal pay legislation

The Equal Pay Act 1970, as amended by the Sex Discrimination Acts of 1975 and 1986, provided for women to have a right to equal treatment with men in employment: 'on work of the same or broadly similar nature to that of a man, or where the work although different, has received equal value under a job evaluation scheme.' The act also gave the same rights to men in relation to women.

The Equal Pay (Amendment) regulations 1983 provide for a man or woman to seek equal pay with a named person of the opposite sex on the grounds that the work done makes similar demands on the postholder.

The implications for recruiters are that it is essential to ensure that all jobs have been properly evaluated, and that the job evaluation system used is free from bias. The pay structure similarly may need to be reviewed. The point at which a vacancy arises is of course a good opportunity to look closely at the job and the job description to see if updating is required.

Promoting equal opportunities

Many organizations rely on interviews being carried out by line managers whose knowledge of the law and good practice in general may well be superficial. This may be the case where the main responsibility for recruitment interviewing has been devolved to the line manager, but without proper preparation and training. Training is crucial, in interviewing skills and in the legal requirements. There are pragmatic reasons for this, the cost of a tribunal award against the company in the event of discrimination being proven may be very high!

Often job applicants are required to complete a questionnaire requesting information on their ethnicity, gender and so on. This 'monitoring' information provides valuable feedback to the human resources specialists. The numbers of ethnic minority, female or disabled applicants responding to the advertisement can be recorded. Over time the proportion of responders to appointees, the extent of the success of targeted recruitment (see below), and whether the response rates and appointment rates accurately reflect the makeup of the local population can be monitored.

Sometimes monitoring information may reveal that there are shortfalls or discrepancies in the makeup of the workforce, for example in terms of gender or ethnicity. Here 'targeting' may be employed to attempt to rectify this, by focusing the recruitment effort on a particular section of the community in the hope that they will apply. Traditionally, such adverts might have been phrased like this:

> Women/ethnic minorities/the disabled are under-represented in this area of the organization's activities and are therefore positively encouraged to apply.

Some organizations have attempted to break down traditional barriers in employment through access to training provisions. One example is in encouraging young women to take up places on a youth training scheme for entrants to the building trades, a strategy used by Leicester City Council in the late 1980s.

One term that the manager may encounter in this context is 'positive action'. This term is normally taken to mean specific initiatives that are used by organizations to achieve the kind of balance they are seeking within their workforce. For example, a company may present positive images of women in non-traditional roles (such as that of an engineering technician) in its recruitment literature. Similarly recruitment literature that showed ethnic minority employees in managerial positions would be seen as providing a positive role model to potential applicants.

The recruitment and selection process

The role of job descriptions and person specifications

The following sections describe the main steps in the actual process of recruitment and selection. We have already considered in previous sections the organizational, environmental and legal context in which the recruiter operates. According to the IPD Recruitment Code:

> Successful recruitment depends upon finding the applicants with the appropriate level of skills and qualifications who will identify with the objectives, values and aims of the organization and will see themselves as making a positive and innovative contribution towards them.

Does the vacancy need to be filled?

Once a member of staff resigns there is an opportunity to assess whether the post really needs to be filled. The manager should take this opportunity to determine whether the job needs to be filled at all. Perhaps the post could be done away with altogether, as the work it once did may have disappeared, or maybe the work can be reallocated among other members of the team, or perhaps the job could be done on a seasonal basis, by temporary staff on an ad hoc basis, when required, or even be technologically updated or contracted out.

The job description

The process above will mean that the manager has started to think about the vacant post in some considerable detail. The systematic examination of the job can start here by deciding what the main objectives of the job are, how it has changed, and the main duties and responsibilities. In short, job descriptions should be:

- As brief and factual as possible, to a maximum of two sides of A4.
- Provide an understanding of what the job entails by describing its key features only.

■ A true and accurate description of the job as it currently is.
■ Possible to update if substantial changes occur in the future.

Job Description

Job title: Grade:

Section: Post number:

Department:

Responsible to:

Responsible for:

Job purpose:

Main duties and responsibilities:

Prepared by... Date.........................

Signed (postholder).. Date.........................

Figure 6.2 *An outline job description*

Job title and job purpose

Some organizations may include a statement of job purpose, as follows:

> Buyer: To purchase a range of raw or packaging materials to required standards of quality and performance at lowest achievable cost.

One of the purposes of the job description is to identify the main responsibilities and duties associated with the post. This section will also cover the extent of personal responsibility involved, key contacts, and any special conditions. Some organizations may include a measure of the financial impact of the job, such as budgetary responsibility, which can also be framed as authority over assets and spending.

A more 'results-orientated' way of writing job descriptions is to phrase them in terms of the results the postholder is expected to achieve rather than simply a list of duties or tasks. Each statement is written so that it is seen to 'do something – to something – for some reason' (see Figure 6.3).

do something	*to something*	*for some reason*
e.g.: provide interpretative analysis	of the market for 'x' product	to ensure marketing and commercial decisions are made to the company's advantage
(Market analyst)		

Figure 6.3 *A results-orientated way of writing job descriptions*

Key questions to ask are:

- What are the outputs of this job?
- Why is this output done, i.e. in order to..., to allow..., to ensure...?

The statements should explain the results which have to be produced to achieve the purpose of the job. When the job description is actually produced it will not appear in three columns as above, this is simply an *aide-mémoire* to assist preparation. Such a job description would normally be written in draft form by the line manager of the vacant post, and then a final version produced by a human resources specialist. If producing a job description for an existing postholder, it is common practice to ask them to agree the contents, and sign it.

> ## Activity 6.8
>
> Using the above information as a guide, write a job description for work that you have undertaken, either paid or unpaid. Imagine that someone you do not know was reading it – would they understand the nature of the work described?

Person specifications

The next stage is to use the information gained so far to evolve a picture of the ideal candidate to fill the vacancy. This is referred to as the 'person specification' or 'candidate specification'. This involves specifying the minimum requirement as well as the ideal person specification. This is to avoid appointing someone who does not meet the minimum criteria.

Essential and desirable characteristics

A common practice is to structure the person specification as in the example provided. Here, the minimum requirement forms the 'essential' column. Use of a proforma such as the one illustrated (Figure 6.4) is likely to ensure that specification writers do so reasonably consistently, in a house style, with hopefully systematic and fair results. The desirable characteristics are those which would enhance job performance if possessed by the candidate.

Recruitment advertising

A good recruitment advertisement will successfully attract an appropriate number of candidates of suitable calibre and qualifications at reasonable cost. Ideally the job requirements stated should be based on the person specification, fairly reflecting the requirements of the job. A concise, attractive advertisement is likely to be more effective than a long involved statement about the job. Most will contain the following items:

- The organization: history, location, aspirations
- The job: duties and responsibilities
- The rewards: pay, allowances, job grades, 'perks'
- Action: a named person, how to apply, closing date.

You should also consider:

- The media: is it appropriate – local newspaper, national newspaper, professional magazine, radio?
- Is it a national or local labour market for this job?
- Past response rates balanced against the cost

Person specification

Job title: **Grade:**

Attributes	Essential	Desirable

Educational qualifications
School:
Further/Higher:
Professional:

Training
Occupational:
NVQs:

Experience/skills
Type of work:
Level of work:
Duration:
Skills:

Aptitudes
General Intelligence:
Literacy:
Numeracy:
Spoken English:
Other languages:
Manual dexterity:
Ability to drive:
Special interests:

Personal characteristics
Flexibility:
Career ambition:
Motivation:
Stress Tolerance:
Self-reliance:
Attitudes:
Leadership skills:
Influencing skills:
Empathy:
Colleague relationships:
External contacts:

Physical characteristics
Appearance/presentation:
Height/build:

Personal circumstances
Mobility:
Other:

Other
Post-specific:
Major attributes of previous successful postholders:

Figure 6.4 *An outline person specification*

- Lead times: longer for monthly publications
- Nature of audience: homogeneity, distribution
- Can applicants 'select themselves out' to avoid getting inappropriate applications?

Activity 6.9

1 Gather examples of recruitment advertisements from a range of sources, including:
   - your local newspaper
   - a broadsheet national newspaper
   - a professional publication.
   Identify what you believe to be the good and bad features of these advertisements.
2 Using the 'good and bad' criteria you have identified as a guide, design a job advertisement for a job you have done or are familiar with.

Employment agencies

So far in this chapter, there has been considerable discussion of the 'casualization' of the workforce in a variety of occupations and industries. There are some areas of employment where agencies have traditionally supplied staff, for example temporary clerical and secretarial staff, production workers, and heavy goods vehicle drivers. In these cases the staff concerned have skills that are readily transferable into a new employment situation. This area, however, is one of the key parts of the 'contracting out' of specialist aspects of the personnel function. It looks set to grow even further.

Traditionally, employment agencies, due to the 'success only' nature of their fees, would tend to be limited in the amount of time they would devote to one vacancy. It would often be unlikely that one agency would have the person you were looking for. Agencies would often attempt to offer candidates who would fall slightly outside the stated criteria – your response, as the prospective employer, would be to specify the criteria more tightly in future! An agency that can produce a limited but relevant response to your request is generally to be preferred to one which responds with frenetic activity, but of little relevance to what you actually need. Some organizations are now adopting the 'partnership sourcing' approach whereby a closer and more reliable relationship with a smaller number of agencies is developed.

The term 'selection consultant' is normally used when one is dealing with more senior vacancies. Such organizations are useful in their use of the 'executive grapevine', allied to 'headhunting' if necessary. It may also be that anonymity is desired by the recruiting organization, or that the vacancy may be in a specialist area that requires specialist recruiters not retained by the employer. Because selection consultants are very expensive, it is often helpful to find a client referee to give you an idea of how they will handle your vacancy. This area can also encompass 'search consultants', who will carry databanks of likely candidates, and 'outplacement consultants', who are retained by companies shedding staff (which can be at any level, not just executives) to try to find them alternative employment. To their clients, they offer access to the 'hidden jobs market' – vacancies that are not advertised or may be arising in the future.

Internal advertising

In large organizations it will be common practice to advertise vacancies internally – indeed it may well be a mandatory part of the procedures for recruitment in large public sector organizations. They will often have a vacancies bulletin that is circulated among existing employees, and may well be available in public libraries or other public buildings. The advantages include the fact that your existing employees may well act as recruiters themselves, to let others know of the vacancy, there will be an opportunity for all internal staff who have aspirations to the post to apply (with some motivational value arising from a perceived opportunity for internal promotion), and there will be a shorter familiarization period for an internal appointee.

The drawbacks include the disadvantages that may arise from the possible perpetuation of existing practices, a limited 'pool' of candidates, and the fact that there may be no opportunity to compare these to 'outsiders'. A further point is that some organizations see internal-only advertising as poor equal opportunities practice, as it will do little to introduce 'new blood' to address the inequalities that exist within the existing workforce. Note too that some organizations will simply appoint from within as a matter of course, without ever advertising promotion posts.

Application forms

If you are going to have to deal with a large number of applications, or if you wish to have the applicants structure the information presented to you in a particular way, then it is worth asking them to complete an application form. Done well, it can facilitate screening (see below), as well as forming the heart of the employee record. If you are designing an application form, it is worth considering the job requirements, the likely characteristics of the candidates, and the needs of the organization.

It is worth asking candidates to complete the form in their own handwriting. For one thing, this will assure you that they actually completed it themselves (which can be cross-checked by careful questioning at interview), and for another it will give the committed and well-motivated candidate the opportunity to take time and care over their application, to structure their information well, and to emphasize their positive qualities, but in the framework that you have determined. Finally, some application forms include biographical questionnaires (also called biodata) to add to the picture given of the candidate.

Assessment of applications

Also referred to as 'sifting', 'screening' or 'shortlisting', this term refers to the process of deciding who to interview from a range of applications. Here one is reducing a relatively large number of applications to a number manageable enough to take through the next stage of the process.

When screening application forms it is generally considered to be good practice to involve a minimum of two people to avoid bias, and ideally all those involved in the selection process. The criteria used for shortlisting should be based on the person specification and should be applied equally to all candidates. At this stage it is important to begin keeping a record of the reasons for decisions made, as you will need to be able to produce these in the event of a complaint being made that your decisions have been discriminatory.

Interviews

Interviews have been covered extensively in Chapter 5. Here, we focus on the role of the generalist manager in recruitment interviewing. It is worth remembering that interviews are generally seen as poor predictors of performance in the real work situation and that quite 'average' candidates can benefit from grooming and interview skills training. It is also worth remembering that despite a proliferation of training materials on the subject, more people still think they are good interviewers than is actually the case. In spite of these reservations, interviews are the single most common way of selecting candidates for employment.

Tests

There are often strong feelings for and against the use of tests in selection. Those in favour will point to the unreliability of interviews and the perceived greater accuracy of test data. Detractors will point to the implied objectivity of test results which may not actually be true, and the fact that the interaction of the interview is a valuable process in itself. Tests should not be used lightly, and only if your employing organization retains the services of an accredited tester, either internally or externally. The science of test design is complex, and the use and interpretation of tests must be carried out with great care. What is certain is that whatever test or other selection method is used, it must follow a careful consideration of the job itself, and of the kind of person you are looking for. One final point is that tests should be both valid: do they actually do what they claim to do, and reliable: will they repeatedly give the same result for the same individual so that you can have confidence in them as a predictor of performance?

Assessment centres

So far we have tended to talk about selection techniques on an either/or basis. There is no reason why a battery of selection techniques cannot be used, given a sufficiently large budget, and a suitable venue. Candidates carry out a range of activities in a very intensive situation (often where they will carry on to the point of exhaustion). You will find out a great deal about their ability to cope in a pressured work situation. An assessment centre therefore is the application of a range of techniques, within a limited period of time, assessing a range of skills and aptitudes. One example of their use is in graduate recruitment, where you have high-calibre individuals often from a variety of academic subject backgrounds, about whom you know very little as to their ability to function in a work environment. They may be asked to carry out group exercises, face interviews, complete tests and make presentations; during all of which their performance will be observed. The activities will typically start early in the morning and carry on until late at night, and the observation will continue when they are in the social and 'off duty' hours just as much as when the candidates are 'performing'.

However, assessment centres are expensive, not only because of the activities undertaken, but also because of the personnel specialists' or consultants' time taken in assessment, the cost of the venue (often a large company training centre or hotel), and so on.

Training and development

It is unfortunately true to say that training has been a low status function in many organizations in the UK. However, given the extensive changes to the workforce and to the nature of employment that have been considered so far, there is an increasing recognition of the importance of training. Training should not be seen as a one-off exercise undertaken shortly after the recruitment of an employee. Often new recruits do not possess all the skills and knowledge that are required. A flexible, dedicated and well-motivated workforce, capable of meeting the demands of the changing roles expected of them, will need ongoing training throughout their working lives. In this section we will consider the various aspects of training in which a manager may be involved, the methods used, and how these can be evaluated.

Induction programmes

It is hoped that the recruitment process we have considered already will have produced a well-motivated employee who is keen to prove themselves in their new surroundings. A good induction programme, followed by effective job-related training should have the effect of capturing that initial enthusiasm, of projecting it forward into the future, and of realizing an effective contribution sooner rather than later.

For a new employee, the induction process begins during selection, when they will begin to form impressions of the organization and the people who work there. A good reception on the day of arrival is crucial – for employees new to the organization it is often a good idea to plan their arrival when the organization is 'up and running', thus avoiding the nervous wait on the doorstep.

A manager needs to:

- Help the new employee 'settle in'
- Start to recoup the outlay on recruitment
- Induct the new employee into the organizational culture
- Provide a basis for the job-specific training
- Generate a sense of 'belonging' to the organization
- Foster long-term commitment
- Introduce, in younger employees, a positive attitude to work and a sense of the 'work ethic'
- Prevent early labour turnover
- Minimize the cost of errors and the disruption to working groups
- Get them to understand workplace rules.

Activity 6.10

How can a First Line Manager use the following to stimulate interest and motivate a new employee?

- Meeting key people in the organization?
- Employee handbooks?
- Logbooks or records of achievement?
- Visual aids?
- Activities, group work and problem solving?
- Peer support?
- Open learning materials?
- An individual, negotiated, programme?

What are the particular needs of:

- Younger employees and school or college leavers?
- Employees changing job roles?
- Transferred or promoted employees?
- New appointees to First Line Managerial positions?
- Women returning to the workforce after a career break?

What else should an induction programme cover?

New employees will also want to know about:

- Terms and conditions
- Hours of work including overtime
- 'Clocking in', breaks, holidays
- Notice periods
- Payment – and does a younger employee need to open a bank account?
- Health and safety, hygiene, housekeeping, fire drills
- Smoking, eating and drinking
- Sickness certification and notification
- Employee representation
- Pension arrangements
- Organizational values and culture
- Organizational policies and plans
- Discipline and grievance procedures.

As much of the above material will be 'standard' for almost all entrants, it is often set out in an Employee Handbook, which can be updated easily.

The identification of training needs

Organizations need to ensure that they have a trained workforce to achieve their goals. A starting point is to identify exactly what the training needs are, in a number of specific areas.

Historically, the training that an employee would receive on entry to an occupation would equip them with a range of skills that would carry them through their working lives. What is important now is the acquisition of transferable skills, which can be converted into different work situations, and which can be updated. The current flexible approach to jobs requires employees who are multi-skilled, and whose day-to-day work is not necessarily confined by traditional demarcations between what were formerly specialist areas. This flexibility also requires flexible approaches to learning and development, and some techniques for delivering this are discussed below.

Training in practice

The term 'on-the-job training' refers to those training methods which are actually carried out in the workplace, often involving learning while the job is being performed. This is different from 'off-the-job' training, where the learning takes place away from the immediate work environment, such as in a company training centre, or in a hotel or conference venue.

By far the easiest form of training is simply to show new employees how to do the job. At one end of the scale is the method known as 'demonstration', historically, 'sitting by Nellie', where the trainee simply observes an experienced operator doing the job, then acquires the skill through practice. There is nothing wrong with this method of instruction – it has been the traditional method of training probably since the word was first thought of! At a more sophisticated level, demonstration can encompass the operation of new machinery or complex technical tasks.

Despite its widespread (and continuing) use in higher education, the traditional lecture is a fairly limited and often very boring means of delivery, really only suitable for the simple dissemination of information. Even then there are much more stimulating and effective methods. What is certain is that good visual aids can help the process immensely. The problem with lecturing is that it is tutor-centred – the trainee is passive. For effective learning to take place the training sessions should be made as participative as possible. This does mean that the numbers of participants needs to be restricted.

What did we learn today?

Learning, however, is not just confined to training events – it goes on all the time, whether we are at work or not. If we were to ask ourselves 'what did we learn today?' a little more often, we would be maximizing the value of our learning experiences through reflection.

What have you learned in the past week – at work, or on your course of study?

Coaching and mentoring are often applied in management development and refer to the situation where the trainee develops a one-to-one relationship with a tutor or counsellor, often a more experienced manager. There are regular interactions between the two to ensure that the individual's development is going according to plan. Very often these approaches place great emphasis on the self-assessment of learning needs, which can be carried out as a four-part cycle, namely self-assessment, diagnosis, action planning, and monitoring and review.

Sometimes individuals may not be able to participate in formal training programmes, or their organization may wish them to undertake the training either at home or in their own place of work. Here, there may be scope for the technique known as 'open learning'. To be successful, open-learning materials need to be designed with thought and care, as the learner or trainee is often working through the material themselves. It is therefore important that the materials are easy and interesting to use. A wide variety of occupational training can be carried out using open-learning materials, from refrigeration engineering to accountancy. The widespread use of video, including interactive video, has brought about an increase in both the quality and the quantity of materials available.

Finally, the latest type of computer-based training incorporates the use of on-line interactive open-learning materials, so that staff in a branch of say a retail or financial services organization can undergo training, linked to their head office, without actually having to leave the place of work.

Training and development for individuals

As we have seen above, where an individual is identified as having particular training needs, there are ways of catering for that individual trainee. An individual may also be the recipient of an ongoing programme of on-the-job training, which may be personalized for them, devised by their training department, and monitored and controlled by the line manager. Many management training programmes operate in this way, the programme may be spread over one or two years, principally at the operational unit level, where the individual will have the opportunity to sample a range of job roles. During this time they gain the experience to equip them for a managerial position. With a programme like this, it is a good idea to incorporate a conventional 'grouped' training course (and review sessions) from time to time, and it is essential to monitor the ability of the operational unit to deliver the programme.

Training and development for groups

Sometimes the organization may wish to develop the teamwork skills of individuals, and sometimes they may wish to develop the skills within an existing team. Under these circumstances some kind of group or team development activity is appropriate. The more ambitious programmes may well incorporate a range of 'outdoor pursuits' type of problem-solving activities, often in a residential context. Some companies have their own facilities which can be used to good effect in this way, the National Westminster Bank has an excellent venue at Heythrop Hall, their training centre in Oxfordshire. Other programmes may be provided by specialists, and are popularly located in the Lake District, Peak District or the more mountainous areas of Wales or Scotland. Consideration needs to be given to the safety aspects, and especially the nature of the activities undertaken in relation to the fitness of the participants. It may be a good idea to mix 'indoor' and 'outdoor' exercises, to develop a range of skills – after all, we are trying to develop managers, not just physical fitness!

Such courses can be both motivating and intimidating; it is a question of the individual's preferred learning style and other abilities. The secret is in getting the balance right, without compromising safety at any time.

In-house or external courses?

If an organization has the staff and facilities, it may prefer to run its own courses for the majority of staff. This can be done in a number of ways – retail organizations may have a 'training room' in their branches where training can take place. Responsibility for this may be shared between the branch personnel officer (if there is one) or line manager, and a mobile trainer, who will travel around the branches in a particular region. Alternatively, there may be an area or regional office, where training staff are based, and employees from other offices can travel there to participate in the programme. Some large units, such as the Vauxhall Motors Ellesmere Port plant, have excellent training facilities on-site, rather like a mini-college, equipped to deliver technical skills, clerical and computer skills, and NVQs. There may be cost advantages to the in-house approach arising out of economies of scale. The organization also has ownership of the programme.

For any external course, the organization needs to ask itself whether the cost of the programme is matched by the benefits received, including motivational benefits. Unfortunately, some organizations have taken the cynical view that external courses benefit the employee more than the employer. An alternative view is that if organizations care about their employees, then they should contribute to their continuing development.

Appraisal

The assessment of employee performance in the workplace, more generally known as appraisal, is at the heart of the training and development process. It is a key part of the identification of training needs, and of the evaluation process in determining the effectiveness of the training.

An appraisal therefore is a means of regularly reviewing and recording an employee's performance and development needs. This is linked to their long-term development. It is also an opportunity to review workload, work content, relationships, to give the employee an opportunity to make an input into the process, and to agree objectives for the future.

Goals and targets

The main aims of the appraisal discussion are usually to review performance over a time period and to set goals and objectives for the next. These will relate to the team, group, section or department, and it is most appropriate that the review should be carried out by an employee's line manager. The discussion will focus on strengths and also shortcomings, and will include a consideration of ways in which the shortcomings can be overcome. The use of the word 'weaknesses' has been avoided because a poor performance may result from organizational rather than individual deficiencies.

Many organizations use six-monthly appraisals, but three, four and twelve month intervals are also common. Obstacles to achievement, both individual and organizational, can be identified, as well as steps to overcome these. Training undertaken can be reviewed, and new objectives identified. Both the appraisee and the manager usually sign the document summarizing the discussion.

A First Line Manager needs to consider the objectives set for the individual employee in the context of their section or department as a whole, which in turn must be congruent with the objectives of the wider organization.

CASE STUDY

Libra plc are a large retail clothing company who have traditionally had a strong high street presence in most major towns and cities in the UK. Their products are well known for their high quality, although they tend to be a little conservative in their approach to current fashions. Most of the staff in the retail stores are part-time, and there has been a long tradition of the company 'growing their own' managers from staff who joined them as school or college leavers. The company has the reputation of being a good place to work, especially for part-timers. The company organization and culture tends to be very formal, which is seen by long-serving members of staff as being part of the way in which traditional standards of quality and service are preserved.

Three years ago the company reinstated a graduate training scheme – there had been a scheme in existence up to the late 1980s, when it had been withdrawn principally due to over-staffing in the company as a whole. The new scheme has met with mixed success, as the turnover of graduates has tended to be high, most leaving in less than two years. Recruitment for the scheme is handled by the head office personnel department in Liverpool, who use assessment centres and a variety of techniques in their selection process. There are normally several hundred applicants nationwide each year for the scheme, who are then reduced to about twenty appointees. Personnel then allocate the Graduate Management Trainees to the retail stores, where they spend twelve months gaining general experience before they move on to a management role. The initial twelve-month period is quite pressurized – the intention is to see if they can acquire a range of experience in a short period of time, to handle the pressure of the retail environment, and to acquire some staff-management experience.

This case study is set in a medium-sized branch in a city centre location, where there are just five full-time staff including a Staff Manager and a Graduate Management Trainee. All the rest of the staff are part-time, and most of these have worked for the company for some time. The Graduate Management Trainee at this branch was appointed six months ago, replacing the previous trainee who left after one year to return to higher education to study for a master's degree.

Questions

1   Try to identify the reasons behind the problems Libra have experienced with this scheme. You might find it helpful to start with a consideration of the company's objectives in reinstating the scheme, and the ambitions, skills and knowledge possessed by the new recruits. To what extent is there a match between these two factors? Do you think that the problems experienced here are widespread ones for Graduate recruitment?

2   For a First Line Manager in this company, who may have joined them through a more conventional route, what sort of issues might be raised by the existence of a Graduate Management Training Scheme?

In organizations where the emphasis is on teamwork, or where one may be in a leadership role with a well-defined group of subordinates, there is scope for peer review to be incorporated into the appraisal process. This uses input from colleagues of a similar level within the team, or subordinates from within the section or department. Openness and honesty are crucial for this process to succeed. The participants need to be able to give and receive constructive feedback, and to reflect constructively on it. The use of peer review will depend to a large extent on the culture of the organization, as it is likely to work best where the managers are seen as 'first among equals', rather than a traditional, hierarchy-based organization.

Self review and peer review can be incorporated into a wider appraisal framework – it is unlikely that they will be used as a stand-alone process. For example, by filling in structured questionnaires the appraisee can ensure that they are fully prepared for their side of the appraisal discussion.

The peer review can either be fed back to them directly, or via the appraiser who is likely to be the line manager. Self review is an important part of the career planning process, and while accepting that the demise of the traditional career is one of the phenomena that goes hand in hand with many current patterns in the workforce, the 'where am I now – where do I want to go – what do I need to do to get there' discussion can be a useful motivator and will certainly focus an employee's efforts, hopefully along a line that fits with the aims of their employer!

Reward review

Here, salary increments, incentives and bonuses are awarded on the basis of the employee's performance. These may be linked to the appraisal process although it is generally considered to be good practice for them to take place separately. Some schemes may be based on fixed incremental scales with limited flexibility, others may be an individual remuneration package, or a one-off lump sum, not consolidated into the employee's salary. Whichever system is used, it must be based on a sound payments system and introduced with great care. The performance criteria should be based on objectives that are actually within the control of the employee being appraised. Systems that are used to 'shore up' ineffective pay structures will certainly cause discontent and may well fail.

Evaluating the effectiveness of training and development

How can we evaluate the effectiveness of training and development? Some indicators, such as the number of:

- hours spent training
- NVQs attained
- course 'completers'

don't actually tell us very much about any improvement in performance or changes in behaviour. What is needed is:

- The ability at First Line Manager level to recognize training needs.
- The flexibility to free staff up for training in spite of operational constraints.
- Sufficient resources for training or the ability to buy it in.
- A careful review of training activity – was it worth the effort and cost?

The review process can be carried out in a number of ways. For skills-based training, 'post-testing' can be a quantifiable solution, as can questionnaire responses, supported by structured group discussions or feedback sessions. 'Diagonal slice' review groups take employees from all levels in the organization, and from different functional areas, thus giving a broader view.

Overall, accepting that investment in people is fundamental to the success of the organization's long-term strategies means actively facilitating the long-term growth and development of individual employees. It ensures that staff can deliver products and services to the quality our customers expect. A starting point for a training and development strategy must therefore be an assumption that continuous training and updating is the norm, that for most employees learning will be a life-long process. Employees need to be multi-skilled to cope with change. Finally, the employee needs to appreciate the significance of their continuing development to themselves as well as to the organization, and to be able to make constructive inputs into the process.

Expenditure on training and development is a calculated investment, where the pay-off is in business performance. Specifically, this includes employee motivation, managerial competence, less waste, fewer mistakes, fewer accidents, better customer relations, lower staff turnover and greater flexibility in the workforce – as well as the development of a 'learning culture' where continuous training and development is seen as normal activity, as part of the process of organizational development, and as a necessity rather than a luxury.

Employee rights

This section relates principally to the relationship between the employer and the employee, the rights of the employee, and the role of the manager in this relationship. Some workers are in fact not employees at all, but are self-employed. The rights and duties covered in this section do not apply to these workers. Finally, due to the dynamic nature of employment law and the rights of employees at work, care should be taken to ensure that reference material used is current, and for this purpose it is recommended that you keep a file of information from a range of sources in this area, (e.g. ACAS and Employment Department Leaflets) which can be regularly updated.

The relationship between an employer and an employee is a contractual one, based on common-law principles. This relationship gives rise to a number of contractual rights. The contract of employment exists when an employer and employee agree on the terms and conditions of employment. This may be shown to exist when the employee starts work for the employer. Both parties are bound by the agreed terms, although the contract need not be in writing.

There are also statutory rights established by Acts of Parliament, giving employees a number of rights arising out of their employment. These are now contained in the Employment Protection (Consolidation) Act 1978 and the Trade Union Reform and Employment Rights Act 1993, as amended by various Employment Acts; and in certain other pieces of legislation. The rights of employees and obligations of employers are also affected by statutory provisions for health and safety, taxation, data protection, insurance and so on, some of which are referred to below. Parliament is not the only source of statute law in the UK, there is also law from the European Parliament. The 'UK Law' will always follow 'European Law'.

The EPCA is a very significant piece of legislation. One of its provisions is that an employee must be given a written statement of the key terms of their contract of employment (the contents of the statement are discussed more fully below). The statement is not a contract in itself, but it provides evidence as to what has been agreed in the contract of employment: written, oral or implied.

Written or oral terms are sometimes together referred to as 'express' terms, that is, they are spelled out for you. 'Implied' terms are not spelled out; they may be obvious, or custom and practice in the industry. Statutory terms are those imposed by law, such as the right not to be discriminated against on the grounds of race or sex. There may also be 'incorporated' terms, which may arise from within the organization (and may be found in the company handbook if there is one), or from a collective agreement.

Activity 6.11

Obtain a copy of a statement of terms and conditions of employment from a local organization. If you have not already done so, obtain copies of the relevant Employment Department leaflets (obtainable from your local job centre). Using these, prepare a file of resource material which can be regularly updated. These leaflets do change from time to time as legislation changes – ensure that yours are up to date!

Employees' contractual rights

Most employees' contractual rights will be in a written statement. According to the Employment Department handbook, the written statement includes:

- The names of the employer and the employee
- The date when the employment (and the period of continuous employment) began
- Remuneration and the intervals at which it is to be paid
- Hours of work

- Holiday entitlement
- Entitlement to sick leave, including any entitlement to sick pay
- Pensions and pension schemes
- The entitlement of employer and employee to notice of termination
- Job title or a brief job description
- Where employment is not permanent, the period for which the employment is expected to continue or, if it is for a fixed term, the date when it is to end
- Either the place of work or, if the employee is required or allowed to work in more than one location, an indication of this and the employer's address, and
- Details of the existence of any relevant collective agreements which directly affect the terms and conditions of the employee's employment – including, where the employer is not a party, the persons by whom they were made.

The Trade Union Reform and Employment Rights Act 1993 added a number of items to the list:

- The place of work
- The existence of any collective agreements which directly affect the employee's terms and conditions
- Certain matters relating to employees who are working outside the UK for more than a month, which are:
  - the period for which the employment abroad is to last
  - the currency in which the employee is to be paid
  - any additional pay and benefits, and
  - terms relating to the employee's return to the UK.

All employees are entitled to receive a written statement covering the above, although there are exceptions to the entitlement to a statement of particulars, such as where an employee works wholly or mainly outside the UK. Sometimes there will be no details to include against one of the statement items – where there is no pension provision, for example, then this must be indicated. The statement must also include a note giving details of the employer's disciplinary and grievance procedures, and stating whether or not a pensions contracting-out certificate is in force for the employment in question.

In some cases, there are details which do not have to be in the main statement itself, but can be in some other document (e.g. an employee handbook) which the employee has 'reasonable opportunities of reading' in the course of their employment. Such items include:

- Entitlement to sick leave, including any entitlement to sick pay
- Pensions and pension schemes
- Disciplinary rules, and
- any further steps that follow an application to the employer's disciplinary or grievance procedure.

Details of the entitlement of the employer and employee to notice of termination of the contract may be given by reference to provisions of the relevant legislation or to the provisions of any collective agreement.

The rights of part-time workers

These have changed recently illustrating the relationship between the legal framework in the UK and the European Union. Briefly, these changes include:

- Extending the statutory employment rights of full-time workers to part-timers
- Subject to their having two years' continuous service (previously five), regardless of the number of hours worked per week.

The ruling arose because the previous position was found to be discriminatory against women, 87 per cent of part-time workers being women.

Disciplinary procedures

Above, we made reference to disciplinary rules and procedures. This is an area worthy of particular attention. Many First Line Managers may feel tempted to overstep their authority when dealing with disciplinary situations at work. They can very quickly get themselves and their employer into serious difficulties unless they clearly understand what they should do, and the limits of their authority.

A disciplinary procedure is essentially a series of rules relating to behaviour at work. By establishing rules for minimum acceptable standards of conduct an employer is making it clear to employees what is acceptable and what is not. For pragmatic reasons, clear rules ensure consistency, and so should indicate what action will be taken if the rules are broken. They should be in writing, and clearly communicated to all employees.

Broadly, unacceptable conduct at work falls into two categories:

Misconduct: 'Offences' in this category may include persistent lateness, unauthorized absence, and failure to meet known work standards. It is conduct which requires disciplinary action; dismissal is not likely in the first instance, although it may be a stage on the route to dismissal.

DISCIPLINARY PROCEDURE

(1) Purpose and scope

This procedure is designed to help and encourage all employees to achieve and maintain standards of conduct, attendance and job performance. The company rules (a copy of which is displayed in the office) and this procedure applies to all employees. The aim is to ensure consistent and fair treatment for all.

(2) Principles

a)   No disciplinary action will be taken against an employee until the case has been fully investigated.

b)   At every stage in the procedure the employee will be advised of the nature of the complaint against him or her and will be given the opportunity to state his or her case before any decision is made.

c)   At all stages the employee will have the right to be accompanied by a shop steward, employee representative or work colleague during the disciplinary interview.

d)   No employee will be dismissed for a first breach of discipline except in the case of gross misconduct when the penalty will be dismissal without notice or payment in lieu of notice.

e)   An employee will have the right to appeal against any disciplinary penalty imposed.

f)   The procedure may be implemented at any stage if the employee's alleged misconduct warrants such action.

(3) The Procedure

Minor faults will be dealt with informally but where the matter is more serious the following procedure will be used:

Stage 1 – Oral warning
If conduct or performance does not meet acceptable standards the employee will normally be given a formal ORAL WARNING. He or she will be advised of the reason for the warning, that it is the first stage of the disciplinary procedure and of his or her right of appeal. A brief note of the oral warning will be kept but it will be spent after . . . months, subject to satisfactory conduct and performance.

Stage 2 – Written warning
If the offence is a serious one, or if a further offence occurs, a WRITTEN WARNING will be given to the employee by the supervisor. This will give details of the complaint, the improvement required and the timescale. It will warn that action under Stage 3 will be considered if there is no satisfactory improvement and will advise of the right of appeal. A copy of this written warning will be kept by the supervisor but it will be disregarded for disciplinary purposes after . . months subject to satisfactory conduct and performance.

Stage 3 – Final written warning or disciplinary suspension
If there is still a failure to improve and conduct or performance is still unsatisfactory, or if the misconduct is sufficiently serious to warrant only one written warning but insufficiently serious to justify dismissal (in effect both first and final written warning).

Figure 6.5 *A disciplinary procedure* (ACAS: reproduced with permission)

A FINAL WRITTEN WARNING will normally be given to the employee. This will give details of the complaint, will warn that dismissal will result if there is no satisfactory improvement and will advise of the right of appeal. A copy of this final warning will be kept by the supervisor but it will be spent after . . . months (in exceptional cases the period may be longer) subject to satisfactory conduct and performance.

Alternatively, consideration will be given to imposing a penalty of a disciplinary suspension without pay for up to a maximum of five working days.

Stage 4 – Dismissal
If conduct or performance is still unsatisfactory and the employee still fails to reach the prescribed standards, DISMISSAL will normally result. Only the appropriate Senior Manager can take the decision to dismiss. The employee will be provided, as soon as reasonably practicable, with written reasons for dismissal, the date on which employment will terminate and the right of appeal

(4) Gross Misconduct

The following list provides examples of offences which are normally regarded as gross misconduct:

> theft, fraud, deliberate falsification of records
> fighting, assault on another person
> deliberate damage to company property
> serious incapability through alcohol or being under the influence of illegal drugs
> serious negligence which causes unacceptable loss, damage or injury
> serious act of insubordination
> unauthorised entry to computer records.

If you are accused of an act of misconduct, you may be suspended from work on full pay, normally for no more than five working days, while the company investigates the alleged offence. If, on completion of the investigation and the full disciplinary procedure, the company is satisfied that gross misconduct has occurred, the result will normally be summary dismissal without notice or payment in lieu of notice.

(5) Appeals

An employee who wishes to appeal against a disciplinary decision should inform .... within two working days. The Senior Manager will hear all appeals and his/her decision is final. At the appeal any disciplinary penalty imposed will be reviewed but it cannot be increased.

Figure 6.5 *(continued)*

Gross misconduct: 'Offences' here may include theft, unauthorized possession of company goods, fighting, or serious breaches of health and safety rules. It is conduct which may lead to dismissal without notice, or 'summary dismissal'. Much will depend on the circumstances of the offence and consideration must be given to the reasonableness of the outcome. In some cases a final warning may be appropriate. 'Summary dismissal' is not the same as 'instant dismissal', a strategy so beloved of the 'macho manager'.

To 'instantly dismiss' an employee implies that it has been done without a proper investigation or a consideration of all the facts, or without following the proper procedures. This will certainly count against the employer if the case should go before an industrial tribunal.

Experienced managers know that employees can be very creative in breaches of discipline, and it is unlikely that one list can be exhaustive. Organizations will evolve their own procedures to suit their own circumstances and the particular nature of their operations. Generally, any procedure should allow matters to be dealt with quickly. No disciplinary action should be taken until the case has been thoroughly investigated. It is important to specify the levels of manager who have the authority to take the various forms of disciplinary action. An employee's immediate superior should not have the power to dismiss without reference to senior management, they may tend to overstep the mark! Individuals should have the opportunity to state their case before a decision is reached, often at a disciplinary hearing. Only in the case of gross misconduct should an employee be dismissed for a first breach of discipline. Employees usually have the right to be accompanied by a trade union representative, or a fellow employee of their choice. Finally, the procedure should provide for a right of appeal and specify the procedure to be followed. While procedures won't be exactly the same – they will have common features.

An example of a generally applicable disciplinary procedure is included here as Figure 6.5 extracted from the relevant ACAS handbook.

Activity 6.12

Obtain a copy of the disciplinary procedure of your organization, or an organization with which you are familiar.

■ What are the main stages of the procedure quoted?
■ What are the outcomes that are specified?
■ What does the procedure say about the circumstances under which these will be used?
■ What are the unique features of this procedure that relate to the nature of the organization, the product or the market?

There are some basic principles for dealing with disciplinary situations. The following guidelines may be helpful.

The aim of a disciplinary procedure is to improve future performance, not to punish: it is often best to try to solve the problem informally. A constructive two-way discussion can often reveal the real reasons why the problem arose in the first place and can assist in agreeing the solution.

If an 'offence' is believed to have taken place, the first thing to do is to gather all the facts. Sometimes, in serious situations, it may be appropriate to get the offender/s off the premises while this progresses. The employee should always have a chance to give their side of the story. If a breach of the rules took place, did the employee know about the rules, or was the standard clearly communicated to them?

A preliminary investigation will establish the facts and give you an idea of the action to take. An informal talk, possibly in 'counselling mode' rather than 'ticking-off mode', may well get at the reasons behind the undesirable behaviour, and may reveal that this is not a disciplinary situation at all. Examples may include where lateness may be due to domestic, personal or health problems. However, if there is no such explanation for the poor performance or behaviour problems, the manager will need to make it clear that they are dissatisfied with the employee's conduct, and the steps to be taken.

In the case of a minor offence the outcome may be a formal oral warning. A written warning may be used in the case of a more serious offence, or for persistent problems. A final written warning may result from further misconduct, or may be used for serious offences. Employees should be clear that 'final warnings' mean just that – if the behaviour continues, dismissal will follow. Employees should be made aware that all written warnings will be recorded – most procedures will allow for organizations to keep warnings 'on file' for a certain period of time, after that time they are deleted rather like 'spent convictions' – subject of course to the employee's behaviour being satisfactory. Very often the fact that the employee has been through a formal disciplinary hearing, with a line manager, personnel officer and employee representative all present, will leave them in no doubt that their conduct has been unacceptable.

CASE STUDY: EASTWELL ENGINEERING

In this case study you are a Personnel Officer. John Gordon is the Engineering Workshop Manager. There are thirty trained staff under his supervision, and the company has recently taken on two trainees. Generally, they have both made good progress, although one of them, Chris Geary, has had two warnings in respect of his lateness, and his work has sometimes been of a poor standard. John recently witnessed a rather surprising incident involving Chris and his friend, Aman Patel, who had an excellent record until the time of the incident, and John has asked you for your advice.

Chris had already arrived at work and was putting on his overalls when Aman arrived. Aman rushed over, shouting abuse at Chris, and punched him to the ground. Aman was then restrained by his workmates, and Chris was taken to the first aid room.

He wasn't seriously hurt, and was interviewed by John later that morning. First, though, he called Aman in, who by now was genuinely very remorseful about what had happened. At first he was very reluctant to talk about the matter, even when John made it clear to him that he was in serious trouble. Fighting is clearly identified as Gross Misconduct in the company disciplinary procedure. Eventually, however, he did reveal a reason for his behaviour. He had had a relationship with a girl called Julie, whom they had both known at school. They had even considered an engagement, but the night before the incident Aman had seen Julie out with Chris. He hadn't been able to do anything about it at the time, as Chris and Julie had been with a large group of people, but by the following morning his anger and jealousy had built up, and he had been unable to restrain himself on his arrival at work. John noted all this down carefully, advised Aman he was going to investigate the matter further, told him to go home, and informed him that he would be advised of a decision at 8.00 a.m. in the morning on his arrival at work.

Chris, also interviewed by John, appeared relatively unshaken by the incident. He too was reluctant to talk about what had happened, but eventually revealed that yes, he had been out with Julie, but that they were old friends, that they had been with a group of former school mates, and that Aman had over-reacted. Chris was then sent back to work.

It is now mid-morning and John has just told you about the above incident and how he has handled it. He came to you asking for your advice – what will you say to him? How do you feel he has handled the case so far? Provide a long-term as well as a short-term solution.

You may use the Disciplinary procedure (Figure 6.5) for further reference.

A written warning should be signed by the employee or their representative, and they may then keep a copy. If they refuse to sign it, it is a 'rejection of disciplinary action', in which case grievance procedures (see below) may be called into operation. It is useful to define the time by which, for example, the employee must reach an acceptable standard; again, this will clarify exactly what is expected. If the employee is unrepentant, or doesn't improve, action may also be specified.

Overall, disciplinary procedures must be fair, and consistently applied, by managers who know how to use them and understand the limits of what they can and cannot do. Having looked at the situation where the employer is unhappy with the employee – what about when the employee is unhappy about their treatment by the employer?

Grievance procedures

A grievance procedure should provide an open and fair means by which an employee can complain about an employer's actions. The employer can consider the complaint, and if necessary something can be done about it with the minimum disruption to work. Like a disciplinary procedure, a grievance procedure should be in writing and clearly communicated to all employees. The 'procedure' here will give the employee a series of levels in their organization through which to address their complaint, until it is either resolved or it is determined that the grounds for complaint were invalid.

In the first instance, the issue should be raised informally with the employee's immediate superior. If there is no agreement, then the employee should have recourse to a higher level of authority within the organization and may wish to be represented or assisted by a friend or colleague, or an employee representative. Some grievance procedures in large organizations may take the matter to a third level, but in smaller organizations ACAS recommend (in their handbook for small firms) that there should be no more than two levels, and that it is a good idea to try to resolve matters within seven days.

The type of issue likely to be raised through grievance procedures are pay, bonus calculations, overtime payments, complaints concerning the allocation of holiday periods. Finally, areas where there may be a lack of clarity or precedent such as discretionary benefits like unpaid leave of absence can also be a source of complaints.

Operated well, a grievance procedure can be a means whereby staff can raise genuine problems without fear of victimization. They can also be a means by which staff can pursue individual disputes or conflicts. Spotting when this is the case is not always easy, and it is important to ensure that genuine grievances are addressed and the causes and sources of the rest identified.

Other contractual rights

Pensions

The Social Security Act 1986 brought about major changes in the pension arrangements in the UK, and covered flat rate (old age) pensions, which are subject to a minimum contribution level; state earnings-related pension supplement; occupational pensions, and personal pensions. Employers and managers should ensure that all employees are aware of the legislation, as well as the company's own pension scheme and the options that are open to them as individuals. While some employers provide pre-retirement courses, pension provision is an important consideration for younger employees, particularly in the light of the demographic effects discussed earlier in this chapter.

Periods of notice

Under statute law, both employer and employee are entitled to a minimum period of notice of termination of employment.

Sick pay

The employee handbook may well include a statement about the employee's eligibility for sick pay, as well as statements on more general health matters – such as, for example, the right of the company to insist on an employee having a medical examination if appropriate. The statement will also include rules on notification of illness to the employer (e.g. by the end of the first day or a certain time), and make reference to the state certification procedures in relation to statutory sick pay. The employer may also make some statement about long-term sickness.

Payment intervals

Finally, an employee handbook or similar document will include information on the payment of wages and salaries. Staff paid on a monthly basis will often be paid on a certain day each month, or a specified working day near to it, this again will be clearly stated. The statement will also include reference to action that may be taken in the case of overpayment, or where an employee feels there has been a 'misunderstanding' about the amount paid.

Statutory employee rights

Here, consideration will be given to the rights of employees arising from statute law, such as the 1978 Employment Protection (Consolidation) Act. Many of the rights carry a 'qualifying period' of continuous employment, and often of the hours worked per week.

Activity 6.13

Try and find out what are the current maternity provisions, and how these affect the rights of pregnant employees. What are the responsibilities of the employer and employee, and what are the time-scales involved?

   If possible try and find the comparable provisions in other European countries – Finland, Germany, for example. How have these differences arisen? How and why may the position in the UK change in the future?

Maternity

Although the UK compares very poorly to the rest of Europe in general, there are maternity rights, subject to qualifying conditions. These cover maternity leave and protection against dismissal on maternity-related grounds, and certain maternity-related health and safety protections.

Redundancy

This section will look at the various areas of employee rights in relation to redundancy, following the chronological sequence through. The Employment Department handbooks should also be used for current source material, while your portfolio can also be complemented by cuttings from newspapers describing how redundancy situations are being tackled in your area.

Prior to redundancies, an employer who recognizes an appropriate trade union has responsibility to consult the union about any proposed redundancies. This applies whether or not the employee concerned is a union member. When ten or more employees are to be made redundant, there is a minimum time for this consultation, and the employer must also notify the Secretary of State for Employment by a specified advance date. (Employment Protection Act 1975, part iv).

Under the EPCA, employers are required to make a lump-sum compensation payment, called a 'redundancy payment', to employees dismissed because of redundancy. The exact amount of the payment is related to the employee's age, length of continuous service with the employer, and weekly pay up to a maximum amount. The figures are subject to annual review. The employer must also give the employee a written statement showing the payment calculation, at or before the time the redundancy payment was made.

Employees who have less than two years continuous employment with the same employer, or who have reached age 65, have no entitlement to a redundancy payment. Service under 18 does not count, and the maximum length of service used in calculations is 20 years.

There are also provisions concerning the offer of alternative work by the employer. If an employee unreasonably refuses this then no redundancy payment will be due. Disputes in this area are handled by industrial tribunals. There are also rules regarding employees whose remuneration under their contract of employment depends on their being provided with work, and those who are laid off or are on short time. In addition, there are also rules in circumstances where the employer is unable to pay, or is insolvent.

CASE STUDY: REDUNDANCY PAYMENTS

You are a First Line Manager with Scorpio Insurance Services, a high street financial services organization, presently undertaking a six-month placement in the Regional Personnel Department as a Personnel Officer. Due to a range of factors, including increasing competition, technological advances, a reorganization of the management structure, and a drive throughout the company to achieve more flexibility in the utilization of labour, some redundancies are to take place in the near future.

Using the information you have collected, and the current formula in the guidance leaflets:

■ Calculate the redundancy payment due to each of the following employees (statutory minimum)

Arthur Rockwell	age 46	28 years service	£26 500 pa
Madeline Smith	age 37	21 years service	£13 917 pa
Gerry Dixon	age 65	44 years service	£23 955 pa
Dorothy Jewson	age 55	30 years service	£28 650 pa
June Riding	age 23	6 years service	£8480 pa
Tessa Hart	age 42	13 years service	£17 985 pa
Richard Jones	age 38	16 years service	£27 868 pa

■ Is redundancy the most cost-effect solution in the above cases? What alternatives are there?

Employee rights in relation to health and safety

The main rights of employees at work in relation to their health and safety arise through the Health and Safety at Work Act 1974. This also placed a duty on all employers with a total of five or more employees to produce a written health and safety policy. The rights arise through the duties of employers, which include the following:

■ To provide and maintain safe plant and work systems.
■ To ensure safe use, handling, storing and transporting of articles and substances.
■ To provide information, instruction, training and supervision.
■ To provide a safe working environment without health risks.
■ To provide adequate welfare facilities.
■ To ensure that the public are not exposed to risk as a result of the employer's main enterprise.

- To make no charge for anything provided for the employee's safety which is required by a specific law (e.g. safety equipment).
- To provide a safety policy and bring it to the notice of employees.
- To consult safety representatives and establish safety committees.
- To prevent noxious or offensive fumes entering the atmosphere.
- To give information in the shareholders' report.

In addition, the employees have certain duties, which include:

- To take care of themselves and others.
- To cooperate with the employer.
- To refrain from intentionally or recklessly interfering with anything provided for their health, safety or welfare.

There has also been a growing interest in the general health of employees and provisions for this. In addition, there is growing concern among human resources professionals about stress levels among employees in the UK, and a trend to seek redress from employers for the effects of stress-related illness.

Unfair dismissal

Employees have the right not to be unfairly dismissed. Those who think that this has happened to them may seek a remedy by applying to an industrial tribunal, usually within three months of the date of termination. Before a claim for dismissal can be heard, the tribunal will want to establish that dismissal has actually taken place. Dismissal has occurred when:

- The employer terminates the contract with or without notice.
- A fixed term contract expires without being renewed.
- The employee resigns with or without notice because the employer by their conduct is in breach of the contract of employment and has shown an intention not to be bound by its terms ('constructive dismissal').

An easier way to consider constructive dismissal is to say that, by their behaviour, the employer has made it impossible for the employee to carry on working for them.

There are qualifying periods for unfair dismissal, normally two years service, although there are rules in relation to maternity, retirement, or trade union activities. Remedies for unfair dismissal include reinstatement, re-engagement or compensation.

Health-and-safety-related victimization

The 1993 Act gives all employees, regardless of their length of service or hours of work, the right to complain to an industrial tribunal if they are dismissed for example for:

- 'Leaving their work area in the face of serious and imminent danger', or
- 'Bringing a reasonable health and safety concern to the attention of their employer'.

Non-statutory conditions of employment

There are a number of circumstances under which employees may be subject to other conditions of employment, which do not arise through employment law, but which nevertheless are part of their conditions of employment. These conditions may well be specific to a particular employer or field of employment, and will suit the circumstances or the nature of the organization.

One example is the requirement on staff in domestic banking (i.e. high street banks) for confidentiality in relation to the affairs of their customers. New recruits to the organization will be required to sign a 'declaration of secrecy', which states that they will not disclose information relating to customers of the bank or their financial affairs. This is very important – a school-leaver new to this area of employment may well find that they have access to sometimes sensitive financial information about family, friends, relatives or their former teachers! Similarly, new entrants to the Civil Service Agencies are required to sign the Official Secrets Act, which although arguably statutory, has a similar effect in this context.

Rights of employees in relation to holidays and time off are largely a matter for the employment contract; the agreement on bank holidays and so forth may well be a matter established by custom and practice. There is no legislation relating to employee holiday entitlements. However, the Sunday Trading Act, which came into effect on the 26 August 1994, provided for shop workers not to be dismissed, made redundant or 'subject to any other detriment' for refusing to work on Sundays. With the exception of 'Sunday-only' workers, these provisions apply to all employees of organizations open to serve customers on a Sunday irrespective of age, length of service or hours of work, and even if employees have previously agreed to a contract requiring Sunday work. Existing employees (i.e. prior to the Act) are automatically covered, while new employees (from the enforcement of the Act onwards) have to give their employer notice that they wish to 'opt out' and then serve a three-month notice period.

It should be noted that there is no general right to extended leave without pay. This is a matter for agreement between the employer and employee, as are agreements relating to sick-pay payments over and above the statutory minimum, and overtime payments, although these will normally be covered by the employment contract.

There are rights to time off in relation to public service such as jury service, trade union duties and activities, antenatal care and to look for work if declared redundant with at least two years service.

Many employers will have further non-statutory conditions which may be contained in their employee handbook. Some of them may well be amplified by their own codes of practice, or by codes published by ACAS, employer organizations, employee organizations or the Institute of Personnel and Development. These seek to inform good practice.

Summary

In this chapter we have looked at some of the patterns of employment in the UK workforce. We have looked at recruiting, selecting and training the workforce, pay and other reward systems. Finally, you should now have an appreciation of the rights of employees. Many of these areas are continually changing, particularly with new legislation and you should aim to keep up to date.

References

Advisory, Conciliation and Arbitration Service (ACAS) (1990). *Employment Handbook*.

Advisory, Conciliation and Arbitration Service (ACAS) (1992). Code of Practice, *Disciplinary Practice and Procedures in Employment*. London: HMSO.

Banking, Insurance and Finance Union (1982). *New Technology in Banking, Insurance and Finance*.

Beardwell, I. and Holden, L. (eds) (1994). *Human Resource Management, a contemporary perspective*. Pitman.

Bramham, J. (1989). *Human Resource Planning*. Institute of Personnel and Development.

Handy, C. (1994). *The Empty Raincoat*. Arrow Business Books.

Harrison, R. (1993). *Employee Development*. IPM.

Merrick, N. (1993). *Flexible Work Comes of Age*. Personnel Management Plus, October, pp. 22–23.

7 Managing financial resources

Aims

By the end of this chapter you should have a clear understanding of the importance of managing financial resources. You will have considered some of the theory behind the preparation of budgets and accounts as a means of providing financial information. You will have examined some practical worked examples of typical problems faced by managers which require an understanding of these subjects. You will appreciate the importance of proper planning and control in organizations, and will have acquired some of the tools and techniques to enable you to answer many of the financial questions with which managers are faced.

Key concepts

- Cost classifications;
- Cost ascertainment;
- Costing systems;
- Purpose and use of budgets;
- Budget types;
- Decision-making techniques;
- Financial accounts;
- Profitability;
- Liquidity;
- Solvency.

Introduction

Financial information is used by a wide variety of people interested in an organization. It is used as a means of measuring performance, controlling resources and planning for the future. Managers commonly have to answer the following questions:

- How much does a product or service cost?
- How much will a product or service cost in the future?
- Are the results obtained, or to be obtained, satisfactory?

■   Have we got sufficient money to continue in the way we want to?

You are aware that money is an extremely important and useful unit of measurement in our lives, but the management of financial resources does not rely solely on money as a basis for decision making. More stable units of measurement such as time, quantity, area or weight are used, especially when calculating costs and preparing budgets.

You might feel that managing financial resources is of interest only to accountants; this mistaken view is one which frequently leads to misunderstanding between managers, resulting in arguments, friction, mistrust and lack of goal congruence. The importance of, and techniques for managing financial resources should be understood by *all* managers, as financial resources affect decisions made in all areas of an organization, from product design and development, through production control, marketing and customer service, human resource management and finally accounting and finance departments. Decisions made in individual areas of an organization eventually affect the organization as a whole – and can determine its success or failure.

Consider a marketing manager wanting to develop and promote a product which is going to make a loss for the organization – and imagine the arguments and repercussions which could result from a decision to go ahead with such a product! The marketing manager needs an understanding of the theory and practice of cost measurement, monitoring and control to obtain details about the cost of the product, to determine the selling price, and to ensure that any decisions made are in line with company policy.

Profit and cash

It is commonly accepted that an organization should be profitable – or at least not make a loss. But in recent years, the number of organizations falling by the wayside has increased dramatically and yet many of them were profitable. Their problem was cash – or rather lack of cash. Consider the following situation:

> George buys in materials for £10, paying in cash. He pays Moyra £5 cash to fit them together. He sells them to Julia for £23. His profit is £8. That's good isn't it? But Julia doesn't pay for three more weeks. George has had to pay out £15, so he has an overdraft at the bank. What's more, next week he has to pay for more materials and wages for the next order, and then the next, and then the next – and still no cash has come in. So a profitable business acquires an overdraft, until the bank manager refuses to honour George's cheques – and then his suppliers refuse to supply him. Of course, Julia pays up eventually, and perhaps the other customers do too – but by then it might be too late. And if

> the customers are unable to pay (because their customers
> haven't paid them) the business fails.

You can see that proper planning and control of costs, profits and cash is vital for the survival of the modern business. That is what this chapter is about.

Costing

Costing is a collection of techniques used to assist managers in making decisions. There is no legislation governing costing information – an organization can produce as much or as little as it likes – but the decisions then made by the managers might be ill-informed. Costing information comes mainly from internal data.

The techniques used by an individual organization will depend very much on its products, its methods of making or acquiring those products and the costing data available to it. For example, you cannot accurately calculate the cost of a single peanut but you can probably calculate the cost of a bag of peanuts. On the other hand, if you were building an estate of a hundred houses you would need to determine the cost of building a single house.

What are costs?

Costs can be classified in many different ways. You can classify your own personal costs into essential and non-essential. Some costs are for permanent or long-lasting items, others are for things which are quickly used up. Some costs remain the same whatever happens – for example your car tax and insurance have to be paid whether you drive much or not. On the other hand, the more driving you do the more petrol you use up. Organizations can classify their costs in different ways too, depending on the information they are trying to obtain.

The elements of cost

One way of classifying costs is to group them according to the three elements of cost which are:

- Material costs
- Labour costs
- Overhead costs.

Material costs are the components: fabrics, liquids, etc. which an organization uses. This category would include raw materials, partly-made or bought-in goods, packing materials, stationery, cleaning materials, etc.

Labour costs are the costs of employing the staff of the organization, including overtime, holiday pay, national insurance, pension costs, etc.

Overhead costs are all other costs not classed as materials or labour, for example:

- Heat and light, rent and rates, insurances
- Supporting services such as maintenance, personnel and training, administration costs
- Sundry costs such as finance charges, depreciation of equipment.

Direct and indirect costs

This is another important way of classifying costs. *Direct costs* are those that can be identified with a specific unit of sales, e.g. to a particular product, batch of products, or to a service. In practice, it is difficult to identify costs with individual units of sale, therefore often only materials and labour are regarded as direct costs. Some overheads such as royalties payable, import duties, etc. can be classed as direct costs.

Indirect costs are costs which cannot be identified with a specific unit of sales. This category would include overheads, but also some materials and labour. For example, indirect materials would include stationery, cleaning materials, etc. which do not form part of the finished goods; indirect labour would normally include supervisors' wages – even though they may work in the factory supervising the production of goods, they are not actually producing themselves so they cannot be regarded as direct costs. Some organizations regard all indirect costs as overheads dividing them into factory and administrative or office overheads.

Cost behaviour

Costs can be said to behave in different ways at different levels of output. Variable costs are those which change in direct proportion to the level of output – i.e. if output doubles, so do variable costs; if output decreases by 5 per cent, so do variable costs. Variable costs are also direct costs. For example, if material costs £1000 to produce 1000 units, then 1020 units will cost £1020.

Fixed costs are those which do not change in this way, but may increase or decrease for other reasons, e.g. due to inflation or price reductions for bulk purchases. For example, the cost of car tax is fixed each year by the government and will not alter whether the car travels 500 miles or 50 000 miles in a year.

Some costs change only if the level of activity alters by a large amount; these costs are called stepped costs. For example, a factory supervisor will be paid the same wage for supervising 1000 units as for supervising 1020 units. If, however, production rises to 1500 units they may ask for extra pay; if production rises to 2000 units then two supervisors might be needed.

Semi-variable costs are costs which contain both a fixed and a variable component. An example is an electricity bill, which comprises a fixed quarterly charge and a variable cost per unit of electricity consumed.

Labour costs involved in production are often regarded in theory as variable, even though in practice they are not. Many workers are paid a fixed weekly wage even though production might vary slightly. But, for costing purposes, the wage is regarded as variable.

Activity 7.1

Rule up a table with the headings:

Materials/labour/overheads   Direct/indirect   Fixed/variable/semi-variable

and determine which classifications each of the following items would fall into in a company which manufactures shoes:

Leather	Cobbler's wages	Pension contributions	Telephone costs
Shoe laces	Foreman's wages	Advertising costs	Rent of premises
Cleaning costs	Oil for machinery	Salesman's salary	Insurance

How costs are measured

Costs arise in various ways. Some arise by being bought in from outside the organization, and hence there are invoices to confirm their cost. Some arise from within the organization and may or may not have set values attached to them.

Material costs

In the first instance, materials will be bought in from outside, so there will be invoices containing details of quantities and prices. But unless materials are used at once for a specific job, they will probably be placed in store along with other materials of the same kind but bought at different times and prices. The problem is to determine which price to use when the materials are used in production.

Good storekeeping normally involves using up old stock first, but with some materials this is not important, and stock is simply used as required. Even if old stock is used first, it is not normally necessary to know the exact quantity and price of each item used – if this were done then every production run would result in a different cost merely because of the order of materials used. Instead, most organizations are happy to use assumptions when determining the cost of stock used.

There are four common methods of calculating the cost of stock used, and at the same time the cost of stock remaining. These are:

1 First in first out (FIFO) – which assumes that stock received first is issued first
2 Last in first out (LIFO) – which assumes that stock received last is issued first
3 Average cost (AVCO) – which uses an average value revised every time a new delivery is received
4 Standard cost – which uses a predetermined rate designed to take account of price changes over the coming year.

LIFO is little used nowadays, especially as it is not acceptable to the Inland Revenue. The other three methods are widely used.

Example

Your organization has the following details regarding stocks of material X:

1 April	Stock on hand:	10 units, cost £1 each
3 April	Purchases:	15 units, cost £1.20 each
5 April	Issued to production:	14 units

We will now work through this example using both FIFO and AVCO methods.

The FIFO method of stock valuation

The FIFO method assumes that the stocks which were purchased first are issued first (first in, first out). Here is the store's record card using this method:

Stores record card		FIFO				Material X		
Date	Reference	Received		Issued			Balance	
		Qty	Cost	Qty	Value	Qty	Value each	Total value
			£		£		£	£
Apr 1	Balance in stock					10	1.00	10.00
Apr 3	Purchases	15	1.20			15	1.20	18.00
Apr 5	Issues			14=				
				10@	1.00			
				4@	1.20	11	1.20	13.20

The card starts off with a Balance in stock of 10 units valued at £1.00 each. On 3 April purchases of 15 units at £1.20 each are added to stock, so there are now 25 units at two different prices. On 5 April, 14 units are issued, oldest first. Thus, all of the 10 units of stock at 1 April are issued, plus 4 units of those purchased on 3 April. This leaves a balance of 11 units at £1.20 each. The value of stock issued during April is £14.80.

The AVCO method of stock valuation

The AVCO method is slightly more difficult. Each time a new purchase is made, it is added to the previous balance, and a new total of Quantity and Total Value is found. A new Value Each is then calculated by dividing the Total Value by the total Quantity. The store's record card for the above transactions using AVCO would be as follows:

Stores record card		AVCO				Material X		
Date	Reference	Received		Issued		Balance		
		Qty	Cost	Qty	Value	Qty	Value each	Total value
			£		£		£	£
Apr 1	Balance in stock					10	1.00	10.00
Apr 3	Purchases	15	1.20			15	1.20	18.00
	New average					25	1.12	28.00
Apr 5	Issues			14	1.12	11	1.12	12.32

Again, we started with 10 £1 units in stock. On 3 April, purchases of 15 units at £1.20 each are made, and a new average is calculated. The total value of goods after the purchase is £28.00 and the total quantity is 25 units, giving a new average of £1.12 per unit. This average is then used for the issues on 5 April, giving a value of stock issued during April of £15.68.

Using the AVCO method, in times of rising prices, the issues are valued at a slightly higher amount (£15.68 as opposed to £14.80), so increasing the costs of the organization, but the materials still remaining are valued at a slightly lower amount so that future costs will be reduced.

Activity 7.2

Using the following information about the movements of tubs of margarine, prepare the stores record card using both the FIFO and the AVCO methods. Calculate the value of the materials issued in each case, and state which would provide the lowest cost to the restaurant.

1 May	Stock of margarine: 23 tubs at £1.40 each
4 May	Issued 12 tubs
7 May	Purchased 6 tubs at £1.50 each
18 May	Issued 10 tubs
19 May	Issued 3 tubs
23 May	Purchased 6 tubs at £1.60 each
24 May	Issued 5 tubs

Labour costs

These are determined by the organization and consist not only of normal wages, but also overtime rates, bonuses, national insurance, pension contributions, commissions, etc. as well as support costs such as personnel, training, canteen facilities, sports facilities and so on.

It might be necessary to calculate an average rate of pay in order to calculate the cost of individual products produced by different workers at different times.

Overhead costs

Many of these are bought in from outside the organization and hence have an invoice value. Some overheads are time-based, e.g. salaries, rent, rates, insurance, car tax. Some overheads are usage-based, e.g. gas and electricity, telephone. Even so, these overheads are not variable costs because they do not vary in direct proportion to the level of activity.

One overhead cost which needs special consideration is that of depreciation of fixed assets. A fixed asset is an item which is bought with the intention of being used in the organization for .a long period of time. Examples include land and buildings, plant and machinery, office equipment, furniture, motor vehicles, etc. The cost of the fixed assets is not all consumed in one period, but needs to be spread in some way over the life of the asset. This estimate (or provision) is called depreciation. There are three common methods of calculating depreciation of fixed assets.

1   The 'straight-line' method. This takes the cost of the asset (less any expected sale proceeds) and divides it by the expected useful life to the organization. The result is the annual depreciation which is the same for every year. This annual depreciation is an overhead cost for the year. The value of the asset goes down with each year's depreciation – the new, decreased value is called the 'net book value'.

Example

A car cost £1200 and expects to be sold in 5 years time for £200. The annual depreciation is:

(1200 – 200) divided by 5 years = £200 per year

The net book value after 1 year will be £1000; the net book value after 3 years will be £600, and after 5 years it will be £200, which is what it is expected to be worth.

2   The 'reducing-balance' method. This takes the asset's cost and charges a fixed percentage as depreciation in the first year. This depreciation is taken off the cost to give the net book value. The second year's depreciation is the same fixed percentage of the net book value; this is also deducted to give another net book value on which the third year's depreciation is based. The net book value goes down each year, so the depreciation also goes down each year.

Example

A machine costs £2000 and the fixed percentage depreciation is 40 per cent per annum. The depreciation would be:

Year 1:   40   per cent of £2000 = £800 (and the asset value goes down to £1200)
Year 2:   40 per cent of £1200 = £480 (and the asset value goes down to £720)
Year 3:   40 per cent of £720 = £288 (and the asset value goes down to £432)

3   The machine-hour method. This takes the original cost and divides it by the estimated number of hours usage to give a depreciation rate per hour. It is particularly suitable for machinery and can be adapted to assets such as cars (based on number of miles) etc. The actual number of hours for which the machine is used is multiplied by the hourly rate to give the amount of depreciation.

Example

A machine costs £5000 and is expected to perform 5000 hours of work. The depreciation rate is £1 per hour. If in the first year, the machine works for 1200 hours, the depreciation will be £1200.

Activity 7.3

A new oven costing £2400 is bought at the beginning of 1996. Calculate the depreciation to be charged to the kitchen during 1998 (year 3) by each of the following methods:

■   The straight-line method, assuming the oven will last for 10 years and be scrapped.

- The reducing-balance method, using a percentage rate of 25 per cent per annum.
- The machine-hour method, assuming the oven is usable for 24 000 hours and during 1998 it is used for 5000 hours.

How costs are ascertained

Cost units

In order to determine the cost of a unit, we first need to decide what is meant by a cost unit. A cost unit might be a single product or service, a number of products produced together, a job or a process. Examples include a washing machine, an hour of a solicitor's time, a passenger-mile, a barrel of beer, a gallon of petrol, the rewiring of a house or the production of a quantity of sheet metal.

Cost centres

Before we can calculate the cost of a unit, costs need to be collected together; this is done by creating a number of cost centres. A cost centre is a location, function, activity, type of expense or asset whose costs may be attributed to cost units.

In some instances the cost centre might be a cost unit, particularly for direct production costs. In other cases, costs will need to be gathered elsewhere before being allocated to cost units. Examples of such cost centres include:

- a production department
- a production machine
- a team of workers
- a maintenance or service department
- an administration department
- a sales region or a salesperson
- premises costs, e.g. heat and light, insurance, rent.

Cost allocation and apportionment

Costs are allocated to cost centres often by using a coding system which ensures that as costs arise they are coded to their respective cost centre so that a total for each cost centre can be obtained.

Shared costs such as premises costs, etc., might be allocated to cost centres and then apportioned between other cost centres on some basis (e.g. product sales, floor area).

Example

An organization has the following sales for July:

Product A   £50 000
Product B   £20 000
Product C   £5000

The total costs of the marketing operation for July were £6000. To apportion these costs on the basis of sales of each product, the formula is:

> Cost of marketing operation to be apportioned/total sales × sales of each product

So the apportioned marketing costs will be:

Product A   6000/75 000 × 50 000 = £4000
Product B   6000/75 000 × 20 000 = £1600
Product C   6000/75 000 × 5000 = £400

Activity 7.4

A college has the following floor areas:

Classrooms: 8000 square feet
Teaching restaurant: 3000 square feet
Student refectory: 2000 square feet
Library: 1000 square feet

The heating and lighting bill for January was £6300. Apportion the heating and lighting bill on the basis of floor area.

Costing systems

There are four main costing systems. These are:

- absorption costing
- marginal costing
- activity-based costing
- standard costing.

Absorption costing

This is based on the assumption that the cost of a unit should include not only the direct costs associated with that unit, but also a proportion of the overheads incurred. Direct costs will have been allocated directly to the production cost centre/cost units concerned; indirect costs (overheads) will by now have been apportioned in various ways to the same cost centres. They now need to be absorbed into the individual products, jobs or processes.

The problem lies in determining what proportion of overheads should be absorbed by individual products, jobs or processes. The most common methods of overhead absorption depend on the time and effort which have gone into making the product or completing the job or process. Therefore, common absorption rates are based on direct labour hours, machine hours, number of units produced, etc. Each production cost centre is likely to have a different basis for the absorption of overheads.

Example

The budgeted overheads for cost centre 1234 are £12 000. The direct labour hours of cost centre 1234 should amount to 6000 for 1998. The overhead absorption rate is therefore £2 per direct labour hour.

If product X takes 4 direct labour hours to produce, then as well as the cost of materials and direct labour, the product will also be charged with £8 for overheads.

Absorption costing is usually used to determine a selling price which will cover all the costs incurred. In the above example, if direct materials and direct labour cost £18 per unit, and overheads are absorbed at £8 per unit, it is assumed that the selling price must be over £26 per unit in order to make any profit. If the selling price is £30 a unit then the profit will be:

Sales revenue (1500 units × £30)	£45 000
Direct materials and labour (1500 units × £18)	£27 000
Overheads	£12 000
Total costs	£39 000
Profit	£6 000

Activity 7.5

An advertising consultancy prices its jobs on the expected number of executive hours. It therefore apportions its overheads on the same basis. Overheads for next month are budgeted at £10 000 and the total expected executive hours amount to 400. A particular job is expected to take 20 hours. The job will also incur direct materials of £350, and executive hours are costed at £45 per hour. Calculate the selling price necessary to make a profit of £600.

Over/under absorption

If the value of overheads or the budgeted hours, units, etc., are different from the actual amounts, or if the quantity sold is greater than budgeted, then there might be under or over absorption of overheads.

Example

Using the same overheads as in the previous example, of £12 000, if we expect to produce 1500 units of product X, then we expect to absorb overheads at £8 per unit. If only 1200 units are produced then only £9600 of overheads will be absorbed. However, if actual overheads amount to only £10 000 then an underabsorption of £400 has occurred.

If absorption is on an hourly basis and 6500 hours are worked, then £13 000 of overheads will be absorbed. Again, if actual overheads amount to £10 000 then an overabsorption of £3000 has occurred.

It is tempting to think that overabsorption is a good thing – you are covering the overheads and making profit. But it could result in you setting a selling price which is higher than it need be – a lower selling price could have resulted in a greater quantity being sold, and hence even more profit.

Valuing stock using absorption costing

Because all overheads are absorbed into the cost of a unit, then stocks are valued at that 'fully absorbed' cost. It follows, therefore, that unsold stock carried forward to the next period includes its proportion of overheads. This means that not all overheads have been charged against profits in the period in which they were incurred; only those overheads included with the stock which has been sold have been charged against profits. In the example above, if only half the stock is sold, then half the overheads are carried forward in the stock valuation.

Marginal costing

This is based on the assumption that the cost of a unit should include only the additional or incremental cost of producing that unit. In effect, this means that the marginal cost includes only variable costs as these are the only ones which are an additional cost. In making decisions, such as whether to make extra units, fixed costs should be ignored as they are not affected.

Marginal costing relies on each unit sold making a contribution to the organization. Contribution is the difference between selling price and marginal cost. It is the amount which is available to go towards the fixed costs, or, if these have already been covered by previous sales, it goes towards profit.

Example

(using the same figures as in the absorption costing example above)

1500 units of a product take £9000 of direct materials and £18 000 of direct labour per year. Each unit sells for £30, and fixed costs amount to £12 000 per year. If all units are sold, the profit is £6000.

> The variable or marginal cost of a unit is only £18:
> Direct materials = £9000/1500 units = £6
> Direct labour = £18 000/1500 units = £12

The profit can therefore be calculated as follows. The contribution which each unit makes is the selling price less the variable cost, i.e.:
£30 – £18 = £12 per unit.

Total sales	£45 000 (1500 units × £30 each)
Less variable cost	£27 000 (1500 units × £18 each)
Contribution	£18 000 (1500 units × £12 each)
Less fixed costs	£12 000
Profit	£6000

In marginal costing, the contribution which a unit makes is the most important factor in deciding on a selling price. A selling price which gives any contribution at all is often considered acceptable – some contribution is better than none! Obviously, the higher the contribution the better, but the following example using the same figures as above shows the point.

Example

A new customer offers to buy 100 units for £20 each. Normal selling price is £30. The absorption cost of a unit is £26, but the marginal cost is only £18. Should the offer be accepted?

Answer: yes, because it will bring in extra contribution:

Selling price	£20 per unit
Variable cost	£18 per unit
Revised contribution	£2 per unit

Additional contribution = 100 units x £2 each = £200.
Thus extra profit of £200 will be made (or £200 less loss, if the organization has not yet sold enough to cover its fixed costs). Would you refuse £200 extra profit?

Even if the fixed costs have not already been covered, extra contribution is worth having.

Example

Using the same figures again, suppose only 800 units have been sold to date at the full price of £30. The contribution received so far would be 800 × £12 per unit, i.e. £9600. This falls short of the £12 000 fixed costs by £2400. The organization needs to make a further £2400 contribution or it is in trouble.

Suppose a customer offers to buy 500 units at £22. Should you accept?

Answer: yes again.

This price makes a contribution of £4 per unit, so £2000 extra contribution will result from this decision. This is still not quite enough to cover all the fixed costs – but we're nearly there. So the order is worth having.

Activity 7.6

Calculate the profit, using the marginal costing method, and showing the amount of contribution clearly, from the following information regarding 5000 products made and sold during March:

Direct materials cost	£25 000
Direct labour cost	£20 000
Fixed costs	£15 000
Selling price	£15 per unit

Calculate the extra profit to be made if an additional 20 units are sold at the same selling price.

If an order is received for an additional 500 units at a selling price of only £10 each, should this be accepted? What would the extra profit be?

Marginal costing and the break-even point

The break-even point is the point at which no profit (and no loss) is made. Using marginal costing terminology, it is the point at which the contribution from products exactly equals the fixed costs to be covered.

Example

In our earlier example, the contribution of a unit was found as follows:

Selling price   £30
Variable cost   £18
Contribution per unit   £12

The fixed costs for the year were £12 000, so the firm needed to sell enough units contributing £12 each to raise £12 000 in order to break even. The break-even point therefore is 1000 units, i.e.:

Fixed costs/contribution per unit = £12 000/£12 = 1000 units.

Each unit up to 1000 contributes towards the fixed costs. Once the break-even point has been reached, then each additional unit contributes entirely to profit.

Activity 7.7

Calculate the break-even point from the following information regarding 5000 products made and sold during March:

Direct materials cost   £25 000
Direct labour cost   £20 000
Fixed costs   £15 000
Selling price   £15 per unit

Activity-based costing (ABC)

This is a fairly new costing technique which is very similar to the absorption costing technique except that it is based on a more precise allocation of costs to cost centres or 'cost pools'. The costs collected in these cost pools are then apportioned to products according to many different 'cost drivers' rather than just on the basis of volume of production or hours taken. A cost driver is an activity which causes costs to be incurred. For example, if a purchase order needs to be placed for every production run, the cost of that activity will be the same whether the production run is large or small – thus both jobs should be charged with the same amount of purchasing overheads. If the small run requires several orders, it should be charged more than a large run requiring only one order. In other words, the activity drives the amount of overhead cost to be charged to production.

Standard costing

Standard costing is a system of costing using planned costs for a unit of production. It is prepared in advance of the start of the period, and is an estimate of the expected costs for the next period. It is particularly suitable for large production quantities of the same type of product. It will consider estimates for:

- material usage and cost
- labour times and rates
- overheads consumed and their costs
- the level of activity.

The estimates assume that there are clearly defined working methods, good quality materials and an efficient workforce. All of these must be capable of accurate measurement for a single unit of production.

Once the standards have been determined, they are used to calculate a standard cost and a standard selling price per unit, and hence expected profit can be ascertained. When the actual results are known, they must be compared with the standards and the differences (known as 'variances') should be calculated and investigated.

The standards used are often those determined when the budget is prepared. See later in the chapter for more on budgeting.

Activity 7.8

Consider two different types of organization, from manufacturing, service, voluntary and local government organizations.

For each of your chosen type of organization, identify the various cost centres and cost units which might exist. What are the various classifications of cost for each type of organization, e.g. fixed and variable, direct and indirect, etc.

Are the following costing techniques appropriate to each organization:

- stocks valued using FIFO or AVCO
- marginal costing or absorption costing
- activity-based costing
- standard costing.

Budgets

A budget is a plan for the short-term future. Longer-term plans are called forecasts. A budget is usually quite detailed and is prepared with a considerable degree of precision; forecasts cannot be so precise because much of their content is uncertain.

The purpose of budgets

Budgets perform many different functions. Perhaps the most important is to provide a system of control, i.e. the comparison of actual results with the budget so that managers can determine whether or not the organization has performed adequately. But there are other purposes of budgets:

- To ensure that the objectives of the organization are met
- To force managers to plan and look ahead
- To set targets for performance
- To act as a motivating force
- To encourage the communication of ideas and plans for the future
- To coordinate activities so that there is no duplication of activities and no important areas are omitted
- To establish areas of responsibility
- To provide a system of comparison and control.

If the business is a complex one, then budgets should be prepared for each segment of the business so that people can identify with their particular area.

The psychology of budgets

For a budget to perform any of the functions above, it must be acceptable to those who use it. This means that it must have been discussed and agreed with those who are going to be responsible for its implementation. Preferably, those people should be actively involved in its production.

The targets set by the budget should be fair and achievable. Budgets which are out of reach only act as demotivators. On the other hand, budgets which are easily attainable do not encourage efficiency. Following on from this, budgets must be amended in the light of changing circumstances. An out-of-date budget is of no use.

The budget must be used. A budget, however carefully prepared, is of no use if it is filed away and forgotten. It must be compared with the actual results on a regular basis and seen as an important tool of control.

Those using the budget must understand fully how it is made up, what it contains, and what its purpose is. They must appreciate its importance and the benefits of achieving the budgeted levels. It follows that the budget must be expressed in terms which users understand, backed up with additional information where necessary. Budgets are often prepared in summary form, but there must be the facility to provide further detail and breakdown as required.

The budget must not be seen as a straightjacket, to be adhered to at all costs, irrespective of the circumstances. If additional expenditure is required which will produce a reduction in unit costs, then it should not be dismissed purely because it has not been included in the budget.

Comparison of budgeted figures with actual should not be seen as an exercise to apportion blame, otherwise people will be afraid of the budget. It should be seen as an opportunity for control and adjustment, so as to improve performance. Variances from budget should be properly investigated so as to avoid incorrect assumptions being drawn.

Gathering data for budgets

Much of the data for budgets is internal to the organization. For example, data on production, sales, marketing, personnel, research and development will come from the organization's own costing and financial systems. Not all of the data will be in written format; some will be held electronically or visually, some will be informal, e.g. held in people's minds. External data will be required to some extent, even for short-term budgets, such as data on the economy, competitors, the extent of the market, etc.

The planning cycle

Budgets are commonly prepared annually, covering a twelve-month period broken down into individual quarters or months. The exact budget period depends on the type of organization, but most organizations operate on an annual cycle, as being a reasonable period over which to measure performance, and to compare with other organizations and previous periods.

Organizations which deal in long-term projects, such as construction, aeronautical engineering and shipbuilding, will have a longer planning cycle.

The principal budget factor

It is possible to produce a detailed budget for almost every area of an organization. Such budgets are known as subsidiary budgets and often they have to be produced first before other budgets can be produced. However, in most organizations the starting point for the preparation of budgets is to determine the *principal budget factor* or *key factor*. This is the item on which all the other budgets are based and take their figures from. The most common principal budget factor is sales, but it is not always the case that sales are achievable – it might be that productive capacity, or shortage of materials or skilled labour can restrict the level of sales.

The sales budget

If sales is the key factor, then the sales budget is the first to be produced. It will be based on the number of units to be sold, and the expected selling price. Ideally, it should be broken down into individual products or product categories, and perhaps also into geographical areas. It should consider the timing of sales, e.g. seasonal variations, and should be broken down into short periods rather than whole years.

It is important that the starting point for budget preparation should be carefully thought out. To simply use last year's budget and add a straight 5 per cent to everything is totally inappropriate and unreasonable. It is likely that some market research will be needed to produce a realistic sales budget.

Example

The sales budget for your firm for next year contains the following figures for January, February and March:

	Jan	Feb	March	Total for quarter
Number of units	1200	1400	1000	3600
Sales at £40 each	£48 000	£56 000	£40 000	£144 000

Production budgets

These usually follow the sales budgets, and are also prepared by product and period. There will be individual budgets prepared for materials used, materials purchased, labour and overheads, as well as budgets for machine utilization. These budgets will consider the level of output, materials usage and cost, labour efficiency, wage rates including overtime and bonuses, and the absorption of overheads. You are not going to cover these budgets in this book as their preparation is mainly undertaken by cost accountants, but you should appreciate the importance of and difficulties of preparing budgets.

The production volume budget and the flow of production

Some organizations like to maintain an even flow of production, i.e produce the same quantity each week/month. This makes production planning easier and is more acceptable to the workforce. However, if the level of sales is not even, then it does mean that there will be stocks of finished goods on hand at the end of some months, and the firm will need to make sure it does not run out of goods.

Example

Let us say that your firm has an uneven pattern of production, as follows:

	Jan	Feb	Mar	Total for quarter
No. of units	1300	1200	1150	3650

and commences on 1 January with 150 units already completed. The production budget will be as follows:

Production budget (units)

	Jan	Feb	Mar
Opening stock of finished goods	150	250	50
Production	1300	1200	1150
	1450	1450	1200
Sales	1200	1400	1100
Closing stock of finished goods	250	50	100

You can see that the stock falls to 50 at the end of February. Management need to consider if this is sufficient and, if it isn't, to increase production in either January (but that will give a very high level of stock at the end of January) or in February (which would appear more reasonable).

Using the sales figures for your firm above, you can see that 3600 units are required for the whole of the first quarter. But if you produce an even flow of 1200 units per month, you will be 200 units short in February. Therefore you will need to produce more than this or keep a stock on hand.

Alternatively, if the firm can produce different amounts each month, by paying overtime or engaging part-time staff, the production can more easily mirror the sales level, perhaps with a smaller amount of stock on hand for emergencies.

Activity 7.9

Produce a production budget for KK Ltd for the months of January, February and March. Opening stock of finished goods is 300 units. Production will be 800 units per month, and sales will be 700 units in January, 600 units in February and 650 units in March. Comment on your results.

Administration budgets

Separate budgets will be prepared for areas such as marketing, office salaries, heat and light, depreciation, personnel and training.

Capital expenditure budgets

These are prepared to show planned expenditure on capital items, e.g. plant and equipment, motor vehicles, office machinery, etc.

Cash budgets

The cash budget shows receipts, payments and expected balances at the end of each month. It is usually prepared for a year, broken down into individual months or quarters. The purpose of a cash budget is to forewarn of cash shortages and excesses so that plans can be made in advance.

With cash shortages, it might be necessary to raise temporary, short-term finance via an overdraft; or it might be possible to reschedule existing or future commitments to avoid a shortage altogether. Encouraging payment by customers might involve offering discounts and other incentives for prompt payment. Or it might be possible to raise additional funds by the issue of shares or to take out long-term loans.

If there is a cash surplus, this should be invested for a period to suit the surplus. Money which is left in bank current accounts generally earns little or no interest and should be channelled elsewhere even if only on a temporary basis.

Cash receipts include monies from:

- Cash sales, i.e. sales for immediate payment
- Credit sales, e.g. one month after sale (these are payments from debtors)
- Sales of fixed assets
- Issue of new shares
- New loans taken out

■   Interest, dividends, rent, etc., received.

Cash payments include:

■   Cash purchases
■   Credit purchases (payments to creditors)
■   Wages and salaries
■   Other expenses
■   Dividends
■   Interest and bank charges
■   Purchase of fixed assets
■   Loan repayments
■   Taxation, including VAT (value added tax).

It is important to realize that making a profit and having sufficient cash do not necessarily go hand in hand. This is due to:

■   Items affecting cash but not profit
■   Items affecting profit but not cash
■   Items affecting both cash and profit but at different times.

Example

An organisation has the following budgets for the first three months of next year:

	Jan £	Feb £	Mar £	Total £
(a) Sales (£1 per unit)	1000	2000	3000	6000
(b) Variable costs (40p per unit)	400	800	1200	2400
(c) Fixed costs	300	300	300	900
Profit	300	900	1500	2700

But you are also told that:

 (i) Customers pay half on sale and half a month later.
(ii) Variable costs include 15p per unit for labour, payable at once and 25p per unit for materials paid one month later.

In addition the stock of materials is to be increased by £150 each month.

(iii) Fixed costs include 10 per cent annual depreciation on a machine bought and paid for on 1 January, costing £12 000.
(iv) Other fixed costs are paid one month in arrears.
 (v) Additional share capital is received on 1 February, of £19 000.

An example of a cash budget is as follows:

Example

Cash budget for the three months to 31 March

	Jan £	Feb £	Mar £
Receipts			
Sales – cash	500	1000	1500
– credit	–	–	500
Share capital issued	–	10 000	–
	500	11 000	2000
Payments			
Variable costs – labour	150	300	450
– materials	–	250	500
Materials for stock	–	150	150
Fixed costs	–	200	200
Machine purchase	12 000	–	–
	12 150	900	1300
Opening balance	nil	(11 650)	(1550)
Receipts	500	11 000	2000
	500	(650)	450
Less payments	(12 150)	(900)	(1300)
Closing balance	(11 650)	(1550)	(850)

Activity 7.10

A painter and decorator has the following budgets for the first three months of next year:

	Jan £	Feb £	Mar £	Total £
(a) Sales	6000	8000	9000	23 000
(b) Variable costs	2400	3200	3600	9200
(c) Fixed costs	1000	1000	1000	3000
Profit	9400	12 200	13 600	35 200

But you are also told that:
 (i) Customers pay one quarter on sale and the rest a month later.
 (ii) Variable costs consist of half materials and half labour. The labour is paid for at once, but the materials are paid for one month in arrears.
  Additional stock valued at £400 is to be purchased in January to provide a 'buffer stock'. Payment is to be made at once.
(iii) Fixed costs includes 10 per cent annual depreciation on a motor van paid for on 1 January, costing £9600.
(iv) Other fixed costs are paid one month in arrears.
 (v) An old van is sold for £500 on 15 February, paid for at once.

Prepare a cash budget for the 3 month period.

The master budget

All the subsidiary budgets are brought together in a set of master budgets which will include a budgeted trading and profit and loss account and balance sheet. These two important statements are discussed in more detail later in the chapter.

Budget changes

A budget is not a rigid structure, but exists as a guideline for monitoring and action. If circumstances change, then the budget should be changed accordingly. Actual results should be compared with a budget which reflects the same level of activity and set of circumstances otherwise the exercise is meaningless. It is rather like comparing your own expenditure with that of a millionaire – there is no comparison!

Some areas of a budget are more sensitive to change than others. Those which reflect variable activities, e.g. variable costs, are sensitive to changes in the level of activity; interest payable is sensitive to changes in national interest rates; wages are sensitive to national insurance contribution changes. These areas must be reviewed regularly to ensure that they are still accurate and representative of the current situation.

Using budgets for monitoring and control

Budgets should not be produced and forgotten, but they are there to be used to monitor the actual performance of the organization, and to take action wherever necessary. To assist in this, various budgetary control reports are likely to be produced for every area of the organization, to show the budgeted and actual results, and the variance, both for the current month and for the year to date. As well as monetary values, percentages are often also included. These reports need to be prepared on a regular basis, so that action can be taken before too much time has elapsed; on the other hand, reports which are prepared too frequently can be misleading.

Once the budgetary control report has been produced, the variances identified should be investigated further to determine their causes.

The purpose and use of management accounts

Management accounts are accounts and records produced by organizations for internal use. They often contain more detail than the accounts which have to be published by law, particularly about the manufacturing and costing operations of the organization.

They are used in conjunction with additional information and with the published financial accounts in order to measure the performance, liquidity, profitability and stability of the organizations' operations. They are also used as an aid to decision making. Some examples of the uses of management accounts follow.

Measuring productivity

Reports can be produced showing the efficiency or usage of materials, machinery and labour.

Labour reports can be used to examine the number of hours worked, the number of units produced, and reasons for over or under performance. Time sheets can be used to identify how individual workers have spent their time; it is important to allow time for changeover of jobs and shifts, training, waiting for additional materials and so on.

Poor productivity might be due to faulty materials, ill-maintained equipment or unmotivated workers. Lack of training can results in wastage of materials, slow speeds and poor quality. Slow speeds by one employee can result in another employee having to wait for work. It is important that all these areas are adequately investigated.

Determining selling prices

This is perhaps a job for the marketing department, but they will need accurate costs on which to base their decisions. It is important to understand the different costs obtained by different methods of costing – i.e. absorption costs include a proportion of overheads. If these have already been covered by previous sales, is it fair to include them again in determining the selling price of additional products?

The same problem applies to deciding whether to accept or reject orders which are for selling prices lower than normal. Marginal costing is based on the assumption that a product is worth making and selling at any price which provides a contribution towards fixed costs and/or profit. However, the manager must consider not only costs and the immediate effect on profit, but also other factors such as the attitude of existing customers if they discover that goods are being sold at a lower price than they are paying. If they insist on the same lower price, then profits could be in jeopardy – quite apart from the reputation of the firm!

Activity 7.11

How would you fix a selling price for a product which your company has just started to produce, using new machinery. Assume that other companies have already been producing this item for some time.

Make or buy decisions

It is sometimes possible to buy in products rather than make them internally. This kind of decision is most common when the firm has already filled its existing productive capacity and needs to compare the costs of expanding its own operations or contracting with other firms for the supply of those items. The costs can easily be compared, but there are other factors which might make one more advantageous than the other. The advantages of making products are:

- Work is provided for employees, whereas buying-in might entail dismissing workers, or reducing their hours. Once dismissed, they may not return if the firm reverses its decision to buy in.
- The firm has some control over the costs.
- The firm has control over supply too.
- There are no problems with product security.

The disadvantages of making products are:

- Overtime rates might need to be paid if the workforce is already working to capacity; workers might then resent losing this extra money if the contract is only short-term; furthermore, workers might be unhappy to work overtime at all.
- Additional fixed costs might need to be incurred, e.g. machinery, premises rental, etc. If the contract is only for a short period, these costs might be difficult or impossible to avoid when the demand falls.
- Additional fixed costs involve additional capital investment which might be unavailable.

The decision is somewhat more clear cut if there is existing productive capacity which will be utilized by the additional production, or if the new production is completely separate from the existing production and involves a different set of customers.

Making decisions regarding short-term working or shutdown of operations

This type of decision is often emotive and involves skills in human resource management; such decisions affect people's attitudes and even their lives, and can have long-term effects on an organization. If you consider purely financial factors, then you should remember that some fixed costs will remain at that level even if short-term working is operated. Some costs might need to be reclassified – for example, variable labour might become a fixed cost if employees are paid fixed weekly wages instead of piecework rates. And some of the firm's operations might be less efficient in smaller quantities.

Activity 7.12

If shutdown is being considered, then you should be aware of extra costs which might be incurred. Can you think of any?

Activity 7.13

Budgets are used to monitor and control business activities. What are your views on the following statements:

1 Budgets are no use if costs change due to inflation, because that is beyond your control.
2 Some managers set their own budgets without consulting with others; if that is the way they like to operate, then why shouldn't they continue in that way?
3 Once a budget has been prepared, there is no point in worrying if the actual results are different.
4 It is pointless to prepare a cash budget because you can never be accurate about the timing of receipts and payments.
5 A firm should always make its own products if possible, because buying them in is more expensive.

Using financial accounts

Accounts which are needed for day-to-day use by the management team are called management accounts and consist of cost accounts and statements such as those you have already seen in this chapter. Many of these are expressed in terms such as 'units', 'metres', 'direct labour hours', 'machine hours', etc.

Financial accounts are prepared primarily to serve the needs of those not connected with the day-to-day management of the organization but who require a periodic picture of the organization's activities. Financial accounts are records of the monetary transactions of an organization, and the resulting summaries of the effects of those transactions during and at the end of an accounting period.

The financial accounts are normally produced annually, and are summarized into two main statements:

■   The profit and loss account
■   The balance sheet.

Some organizations are owned by the government or are owned by trusts and charities, such as hospitals, prisons, schools and colleges. These are known as 'not-for-profit' organizations. These organizations produce different kinds of statements. Charities and local authorities, for example, produce an income and expenditure account rather than a profit and loss account, because they do not generally make profits.

The profit and loss account and balance sheet are discussed in more detail in the next few pages, but first you should be aware of the main purposes of financial accounts.

The purposes of financial accounts

The three main purposes of financial accounts are to assess profitability, liquidity and solvency. Later in this chapter, you will look at ways of doing this, but here is a brief explanation of what these purposes are.

Profitability

This measures the extent to which the organization has increased its wealth by its ordinary activities (i.e. has made a profit) over the period concerned. An organization which does not make profits does not grow; continued losses usually lead to an organization ceasing to exist. Therefore it follows that the level of profitability must be sufficient to enable the organization to pay its way and provide something for future growth.

Profit is used in a variety of ways in order to determine how well the organization has performed. You will look at some of these later.

Remember that some organizations are not primarily profit-making; some aim to provide services at a cost to the government (e.g. health, education) although nowadays many of these services provide income too. The level of profit is obviously different in such organizations, and other measures are used to assess the success of the organization.

Liquidity

This is to do with the organization's ability to pay its way on a day-to-day basis. An organization needs to have sufficient funds available at any time to pay the demands made on it. The concept of liquidity can be applied to your own financial situation – if you need money for your bus fare to college or work, you need liquid funds with which to pay it. Offering to sell your stereo system next week is no use to the bus driver – he wants cash, and now.

Organizations have a little more leeway than an individual on a bus –

they can usually manage to defer payments for a short time until funds are available. Often this is simply a case of waiting until customers pay up; if the situation is more difficult than that, perhaps stock can be sold a little more cheaply than normal in order to bring in extra income quickly. Alternatively, it might be possible to take out a short-term loan to pay particular debts. So the organization might still be in a liquid position, even if it has to take measures to improve the situation which it would rather not take.

Solvency

An organization can often manage to reorganize its liquid funds on a temporary basis, but if it continues to have a liquidity problem for any length of time, then its long-term solvency might be affected. If it makes continual losses, and spends more than it has available, then it could become insolvent. If it has to start selling its stock at knock-down prices or if it has to sell long-term assets in order to pay off debts, it will eventually find that it has insufficient assets to cover its liabilities. This is insolvency.

The users of financial accounts

It is impossible to name all the possible users of financial information, and the types of financial information they require. There are four main groups of users of financial information, outside the management team. These are:

- The owners of the organization
- Employees of the organization
- Those who provide goods, services or money to the organization
- The tax authorities and government departments.

Let us look at each of these in turn, and the types of financial information which they might need.

Owners (also called investors)

They put money into (invest in) the organization, in the same way as you might put money into a building society. They usually want a return on their investment. A return on an investment is the amount of money which the investment makes for the investors. Therefore they are primarily interested in the organization's profitability.

This means they want the organization to make a profit, which they might be able to have paid to them. They will want to compare this 'return' with the amount invested. If an owner invests £1000 for a year, and only gets a £1 return, this is poor. He or she might get £50 from a building society for the same amount invested. Most owners need to know the return on their investment on an annual basis – things change so often from day to day that it is not realistic to check too frequently on this information. Many organizations only calculate their profits annually, or perhaps quarterly, so the information is not available any more often than this.

There are different kinds of owners in different kinds of organization. In small businesses, such as corner shops, there might be only one owner, called a 'sole proprietor'. The sole proprietor provides all of the money (the capital) for the business and therefore is the sole owner. In slightly larger organizations there might be a few owners who provide the capital, and this organization is called a 'partnership'. In bigger organizations, there might be hundreds or thousands of owners, each owning one or more 'shares' in the organization – these are 'limited companies', and the majority of our well-known businesses are of this type.

Point of interest: Anita Roddick, who is now managing director of the Body Shop, started off as a sole proprietor. As the business grew, she joined forces with other investors, and formed a Public Limited Company, where she is only one shareholder among many.

Activity 7.14

Make a list of organizations near your home, workplace or college. Find out whether they are owned by sole proprietors, partnerships, limited companies or government bodies. Try to find at least one of each type. You can probably guess at the ownership of some of them, or you can find out the ownership by examining their stationery.

Employees

Employees are interested in almost all areas of the business. Obviously, they are concerned with the company's overall profit and whether any of it can be directed towards increasing their pay. But they are also interested in the longer term prospects of the organization, so they will look at the liquidity and solvency of the organization.

Providers of goods, services and money

These are people who lend money to the organization. They include banks, building societies, finance companies, and also people who sell goods or services to the organization who are not paid at once. The amounts owed to these providers are called liabilities.

Some providers are long term, i.e. they are repaid over a long period of time, maybe many years. Some providers are short term or 'current', which means they are paid fairly soon, perhaps in a few weeks. The majority of suppliers of goods on credit (creditors) are current liabilities.

Activity 7.15

Think of four different situations where an organization might need to borrow money. Include at least one long-term and one short-term borrowing.

Providers are interested in knowing that the organization has enough cash or money in the bank to pay them back when they are due to be paid. In other words, they are interested in knowing what assets the organization has. Assets are things which an organization possesses.

Like liabilities, assets can also be divided into two types. *Current assets* consist of things which the organization owns which could easily be turned into cash, without damaging or altering the nature of the organization. Current assets include cash and bank balances, stocks of materials, etc. Current assets also include money owed to the organization by its customers – debtors. It might seem strange to imagine money which is owing to you as an asset, but really the money belongs to the organization – it is simply being kept for the time being by the debtors.

Fixed assets consist of things which the organization intends to keep for a long time, and which, if sold, would damage or alter the nature of the organization. Fixed assets include land and buildings, equipment and machinery, furniture and fittings, etc.

Activity 7.16

Look at your college or place of work. What assets can you find there? Which ones are fixed assets and which are current assets?

The tax authorities

There are two main authorities requiring financial information of an organization. These are the Inland Revenue and the Customs and Excise. The Inland Revenue want to know how much profit has been made, so as to charge the correct amount of income tax or corporation tax. Customs and Excise want to know what the organization has bought and sold so that it can collect or refund the appropriate amount of value added tax.

The management team

Although primarily interested in internal management accounts, the management team will scrutinize the financial accounts in order to gain an overall picture of the activities of the organization. However, in most cases, management will need access to the more detailed cost and management accounts in order to investigate problem areas and exercise control.

The financial accounts do provide management with an overview of the financial health of the organization, and can sometimes provide reassurance or warnings of the state of the organization.

Characteristics of limited company accounts

A limited company is one whose capital is divided into shares (small units), enabling individuals or groups of individuals to own one or more shares. For example, if a company requires a million pounds in capital it could be divided into one million shares of £1 each, or ten million shares of 10p each. People can buy as many or as few shares as they want (within certain restrictions).

Each person is then a shareholder or member of the company. Shares are like money – they can be passed around to other people, bought and sold, left to people in wills, etc.

What 'limited liability company' means

A limited liability company gives the owners limited liability for its debts. The shareholders must pay for the shares which they own, but if the company fails, they will not be called upon to pay towards the company's debts. Sole traders, and most partners, do not have this limit on their liability and can be forced to sell their own private assets to pay the debts of their businesses. Because of this limited liability for limited companies, they are obliged to publish their accounts each year so that anyone can examine the results of the organization.

Private limited companies

These are frequently owned by families. Shares in a private limited company can only be sold if the other members agree. Often if one member wants to sell his or her shares, the other members buy them.

Public limited companies

Shares in these companies can be bought by, and sold to, almost anyone, without the need for any agreement. Many are quoted on the stock exchange

– you can see them listed in the financial pages of many daily and weekly newspapers.

Activity 7.17

Obtain a copy of the financial pages of a quality newspaper. Make a list of the main categories of company shown there. Pick out ten companies whose products or services your family might have used in the last two years.

Running a limited company

In many limited companies, the shareholders have nothing whatsoever to do with the running of the company. Directors are appointed for that purpose, and they are employees of the company just like any other employees. In some limited companies, shareholders do work in the business – this happens in many small, private limited companies where family members own and run the business. It also happens in many larger companies, where directors are also shareholders.

Types of shares

In a limited company, the profit belongs to the shareholders. They receive a share of the profits according to how many shares they own and the type of share. This share of the profits is called a dividend. However, it is not normal for the whole of the profits to be paid out as dividends – if a company did that, it would not grow. The directors decide how much is to be paid out as dividends.

Preference shares

These are shares which have preferential treatment in the payout of dividends and on the closure of the company if that ever happens. They receive their share before any other shareholder. The dividend is a fixed, fairly low percentage rate, e.g. 5 per cent, and if the company closes, they simply receive back whatever they paid for their shares. Even though the dividend is fixed, it is possible for the directors to decide not to pay it. Only if they pay a dividend to the ordinary shareholders, can the preference shareholders insist on their's first.

Ordinary shares

These are shares with no special treatment, but the rate of dividend can be anything which the directors decide – from very low to very high. They are considered to be the main shareholders of a company, and they own everything in the company apart from the portion owned by the preference shareholders. They are also known as equity shareholders and the amount they own is called the equity capital. If the company closes, the ordinary shareholders share out the wealth of the company (after paying out the preference shareholders).

As with preference dividends, if the directors decide not to pay a dividend, then the shareholders do not get one.

Share prices

When the company raises capital by issuing shares, the shares are given a nominal or par value, e.g. £1 or 10p.

The shares might be popular enough for the company to ask more than the par value when it issues shares. Any extra is called the share premium. For example a £1 share issued for £1.50 includes a premium of 50p.

Shareholders can sell their shares to anyone else, for whatever price they wish. The company has nothing to do with such a deal. For example, shareholder A can sell his £1 share (for which he paid £1.50 to the company) to shareholder B for £10. This is known as the market price and it is the price you see quoted in the newspapers. This is a private deal, and shareholder A makes a gain on his sale. The company makes nothing.

Activity 7.18

The *Financial Times* offers a service whereby you can telephone to order copies of the accounts of companies marked with a symbol in their newspaper. Obtain copies of five companies. Make a note of the market price as quoted in the *Financial Times* on the day you order your account. When the accounts arrive, use them to find out the par value of an ordinary share (you will find this in the section headed 'Notes to the Accounts'). Compare the two figures you have for par value and market price.

The profit and loss account

The profit and loss account is used to calculate the profit for the period. Profit is the difference between the revenue earned during a period, and the expenses incurred in earning that revenue.

In a manufacturing organization, the revenue is earned from selling finished goods to customers. It does not matter whether the customers pay up at once, the revenue is earned as soon as the contract to supply the goods has been fulfilled.

The expenses incurred in earning that revenue will include the cost of materials, labour and overheads used up. It will *not* include the cost of goods not yet sold, or stock not yet turned into finished goods. But it might include goods and services not yet paid for – it is the point at which these are used up in earning the revenue that determines whether they are included in the profit calculation, not the point of payment.

The profit and loss account can consist of up to three sections, depending on the type of organization and its owners. In the business of a sole trader who does not make and sell things, for example a solicitor, there is only need for one section – the profit and loss account itself. In the business of a sole trader who buys and sells things, a trading account is needed as well. And in a partnership or a limited company, an appropriation account is needed too.

Organizations who manufacture goods from raw materials or components will probably also prepare a manufacturing account, but this is an internal statement, not published, and is a summary of the cost accounts of the period. This textbook does not cover the preparation of manufacturing accounts.

The trading account

This shows the sales revenue earned from selling goods and the costs incurred in making those goods fit for sale (the cost of goods sold). It does not include the cost of selling or delivering goods, administration costs or other costs not connected with making goods fit for sale. But it would include the cost of materials and labour, and perhaps some overheads.

The end result of the trading account is the calculation of gross profit – sales revenue less cost of goods sold.

Example

At the beginning of 1996, JKL Ltd has a stock of goods for sale which cost £2000. During the year, they buy in more goods costing £12 000 and at the end of the year they value the closing stock at £3000. Sales for the year amount to £18 000 (of which £1500 is still owing by customers).

The trading account for the year would appear as follows:
JKL Ltd trading account for the year ending 31 December 1996

	£	£
Sales revenue		18 000
Less cost of goods sold:		
Opening stock	2000	
Purchases	12 000	
	14 000	
Less closing stock	(3000)	
		11 000
Gross profit		7000

Activity 7.19

Coglan Clothes Ltd sold goods for £180 000 during the year ending 30 June 1997. Opening stocks of clothes were valued at £8000 and closing stocks at £9500. Purchases during the year amounted to £143 500. Draw up a trading account for the period.

The profit and loss account

This is the section which calculates the net profit – the profit after all revenues earned and expenses incurred during the period have been included.

As well as revenue from sales, an organization might have revenue from fees, commissions received, royalty income, bank interest earned, etc. – and in non-trading organizations all of the income will come from sources such as this, as there will be no sales as such.

In addition to the cost of goods sold, an organization might have expenses incurred in selling, advertising, delivering, administration, research and development, loan interest, etc. – again, non-trading organizations will have all of their expenses in this category as they do not incur costs in selling goods.

Example

As well as making £7000 gross profit, JKL Ltd also earns £500 from renting out part of the premises, and there are various expenses which have been used up during the year, and corporation tax of £400. The profit and loss account would appear as follows:

JKL Ltd profit and loss account for the year ending 31 December 1996

	£	£
Gross profit		7000
Rent received		500
		7500
Less expenses:		
Selling and delivery	1300	
Administration	2200	
Research and development	300	
Directors' fees	400	
Depreciation	600	
Finance costs	200	
		5000
Net profit before tax		2500
Corporation tax		400
Net profit after tax		2100

What are expenses?

The profit and loss account should contain all expenses incurred during the period – that means expenses used up. It does not contain expenses not used up, such as stationery which is left over to the next period, or rates paid for part of next year as well as part of this year. Only the portion relating to the current year is included.

Depreciation

We have mentioned depreciation before. The cost of fixed assets is normally spread over their expected useful life. The proportion which is used up in a year is the depreciation for the year. This is an expense used up in earning the revenue for the year, so it is included in the profit and loss account.

Corporation tax

This is a tax on companies, and is deducted from the profits as an expense would be, but after the profit for the period has been calculated. It is only deducted if it is corporation tax. The personal income tax of sole traders and partners is never deducted from the profits.

Wages and salaries

Wages and salaries includes all payments made to paid employees of the organization. They are normal business expenses and should be charged as expenses against profit. Payments made to owners simply because they are owners (whether they are sole traders, partners or shareholders in a limited company) are *never* treated as wages and salaries (see Drawings below).

Confusion can sometimes arise where a person is an employee in a limited company and a shareholder as well. It is important to realize that people who do paid work in a limited company are employees and people who own shares in limited companies are shareholders. If a person is both of these, then any payments received as an employee must be regarded differently from any payments received as a shareholder. As an example, consider a director who is also a shareholder. Any payments made to the director in return for work done is a payment of salary and is a normal business expense. You will see how payments to shareholders are treated when we look at dividends.

Drawings

Drawings are amounts of money taken out of a sole trader or partnership business by the owner or owners for their own private use. They are exactly the opposite of putting money into the business – you would not regard an owner putting money in as 'revenue earned' and so you should not regard money taken out as a business expense either. Some owners like to pay themselves a regular wage or salary, and they often include this with the salaries they pay to their employees. However, this is not correct – owner(s)' drawings should never be charged as expenses in the profit and loss account, but should be deducted from the owner(s)' capital on the balance sheet (which you will look at shortly).

Activity 7.20

Coglan Clothes Ltd also had expenses during the year to 30 June 1997, consisting of advertising costs £3500, distribution costs £8300, administration costs £4000, and loan interest £1500. Corporation tax for the year amounted to £3700. Draw up the profit and loss account for the period, starting with the gross profit you calculated in the previous task.

The appropriation account

The net profit (after tax in a limited company) belongs to the owners of the organization (or to the members/trust holders in a not-for-profit organization).

Appropriating a sole trader's profits

In a sole trader's business, everything belongs to the one trader, so there is no need to appropriate it in any way, and therefore no appropriation account is required. The whole of the profit is available to the owner, and is added to the amount of capital invested in the business by the trader.

Appropriating a partnership's profits

In a partnership the profit belongs to several partners, and so the appropriation account is used to show how it is shared out. In a simple division, the profits might be divided equally between the partners. The following example illustrates this.

Example

Suppose the partnership has a net profit of 12,000 for the year, and there are three partners (A, B and C) sharing profits equally. The appropriation account would look like this:

A, B and C appropriation account for the year ending
31 December 1996

Net profit		<u>12 000</u>
Profit share:		
A	4000	
B	4000	
C	4000	
		<u>12 000</u>

In many partnerships, the division of profits is not so straightforward. Some partners are allocated more than others because of the work they do, because they have provided more capital, or because they have withdrawn monies from the business. So the appropriation account can be more complex than the example given.

Appropriating a limited company's profits

In a limited company, all of the profits belong to the shareholders, but not all are distributed. Some are distributed as dividends but the remainder are kept in the business as retained profits.

The retained profits can be built up in the business over the years, to enable the business to grow. Alternatively, they can be used in future years to enable the company to pay out dividends even though the profits of that period might be too low. The balance of profits available for this purpose is recorded as a profit and loss account balance carried forward. If the company has such profits retained from previous periods, they are added to the profits for the current period.

Part of the retained profits can be 'earmarked' for specific or general purposes, e.g. to replace fixed assets. These are known as 'reserves'. A company is not allowed to pay out dividends if it has no profits for the current or previous years, and no general reserves available.

Example

The appropriation account of JKL Ltd might appear as follows:

	£	£
Net profit after tax		2100
Profit and loss account balance brought forward		6500
Profits available for distribution		8600
Dividends	2000	
Transfer to general services	3000	
		5000
Profit and loss account carried forward		3600

The final balance on the profit and loss account is added to the shareholders' capital on the balance sheet, which we will look at in the next section.

Activity 7.21

Coglan's Clothes Ltd proposed a dividend of 5p per share to the ordinary shareholders for the year, and decided to transfer £10 000 to general reserves. The profit and loss account had a balance brought forward of £7000. There were 100 000 ordinary shares in issue during the year. Starting with the net profit you calculated in the previous task, draw up the appropriation account for the year.

The balance sheet

The balance sheet is a statement which shows the position of the organization at a particular point in time – some people describe it as a 'snapshot' of an organization. Whilst the profit and loss account covers a period of time, say a year, the balance sheet is prepared at the end of that period. It is rather like describing to someone what you have been doing over the past year (the profit and loss account), and what position you are now in (the balance sheet).

It shows the assets, liabilities and capital of the organization at a point in time, and is used by those who need details of the security of their money, such as lenders. You have read about assets, liabilities and capital earlier in the chapter, but just to refresh your memory, here is a brief reminder as to what they are.

Assets

Assets are things which an organization possesses. There are two main categories of assets:

- *Fixed assets* are assets which are intended to be used for a long period of time. Examples include: land, buildings, equipment, furniture, furnishings, motor vehicles.
- *Current assets* are assets which are intended to be used for only a short period of time, or are expected to change frequently. They include stocks of raw materials and finished goods, stocks of stationery, bank balances.

Current assets also include amounts owed to the organization by other people. These people are called debtors and they are customers who buy goods or services 'on credit', which means they do not pay for their goods or services at once; instead they pay later, perhaps at the end of next month. The amount they still owe when the balance sheet is prepared is shown as a current asset because the organization owns money which is still held by these debtors.

Activity 7.22

Name some of the assets you would find in the following organizations, and label them either 'fixed' or 'current':

- a hospital
- a public sports centre
- a football club
- a used car dealer
- a stationery supplier.

Liabilities

Liabilities are amounts owed by the organization to people who have provided it with money, goods or services. There are two main categories of liabilities too:

■ *Current liabilities*. These are amounts which the organization expects to repay in a short period of time. A bank overdraft is usually a current liability.

Current liabilities also include amounts owed by the organization to other people. These people are called creditors and they arise if the organization buys goods or services 'on credit', which means it does not pay for the goods or services at once; instead it pays later, perhaps at the end of next month. The amount they are still owed when the balance sheet is prepared is shown as a current liability because the organization owes money to these creditors. (Do not confuse creditors with debtors who are mentioned above under 'Current assets'. Creditors are people who are owed money by the organization; debtors are people who owe money to the organization.)

■ *Long-term liabilities*. These are amounts which the organization has borrowed which do not require repayment in the immediate future. Examples include mortgages, loans, etc.

Capital

Capital is the money put into or left in the organization by its owner or owners. In a limited company, it consists of:

■ The par value of shares issued (both ordinary and preference)

■ Share premium (where shares have been issued for more than their par value)

■ Reserves (amounts of profit retained in the business), including the balance carried forward from the profit and loss account.

The reserves are increased by profits, and decreased by losses. Here is an example of a balance sheet for a limited company:

Example
JKL Ltd balance sheet as at 31 July 1996

	£	£	£	Author's comments
Fixed assets:				
Land and buildings		100 000		
Furniture and equipment		60 000		
			160 000	(A) Total of fixed assets
Current assets:				
Stocks	3000			
Debtors	1500			
Bank and cash	11 000			
		15 500		(B) Total of current assets
Less current liabilities:				
Creditors		3900		(C) Total of current liabilities
Net current assets			11 600	(D) Current assets less current liabilities
			171 600	(E) Fixed assets plus net current assets
Less long-term liabilities:				
Loan			43 000	(F)
Net assets			128 600	(G) All assets less all liabilities
Financed by:				
Ordinary shares of £1 each			100 000	
Share premium account			22 000	
General reserves			3000	
Profit and loss account balance			3600	
			128 600	(H) Equals total above

Note that the two totals (G and H) of £128 600 are equal. If this does not happen, then a mistake has been made in preparing the balance sheet.

The balance sheet is based on the 'accounting equation'. The accounting equation states that:

Assets minus liabilities = owners' capital.

In other words, the assets of the organization (what it owns), less its liabilities (what it owes) equals the value of the organization to the owners.

In the balance sheet above, the assets are those figures labelled A and B:

A (fixed assets)	=	£160 000
B (current assets)	=	£15 500
Total assets	=	£175 500

and the liabilities are those figures labelled C and F:

C (current liabilities)	=	£3900
F (long-term liabilities)	=	£43 000
Total liabilities	=	£46 900

Therefore assets minus liabilities = £175 500 – £46 900 = £128 600 and we can compare this with the capital figure (H), which is also £128 600. So the above balance sheet proves the accounting equation.

Net current assets (working capital)

Net current assets are shown on the above balance sheet. Another name for net current assets is 'working capital'. Working capital is current assets minus current liabilities, and it tells us how much 'ready-money' the organization has for immediate use.

The current assets can all be easily turned into cash without destroying the organization, and after paying off the current liabilities the working capital will be left over to run the organization on a day-to-day basis. In the above balance sheet, working capital is:

B (current assets) minus C (current liabilities)

= £15 500 – £3900
= £11 600

It is very important to control the amount of working capital an organization has. If it has too little, it might be unable to pay its immediate debts, with the result that its suppliers refuse to supply it, or the bank starts to dishonour (bounce) its cheques. If it has too much, then that is wasteful – the excess should be invested to earn money for the organization.

Activity 7.23

Draw up a balance sheet for Coglan's Clothes Ltd from the following information as at 30 June 1997:

Plant and machinery	£45 000
Furniture	£8000
Office equipment	£5900
Bank balance	£7200
Stocks	£9500
Owing by customers	£6500
Owing to suppliers and others	£10 400
Loan for plant and machinery (repayable in 5 years)	£10 000
Ordinary shares at 50p each	£50 000
Share premium	£2700

Profit and loss account balance – from the previous task.

The balance sheet of a sole trader

The 'top portion' of a sole trader's balance sheet is the same as that earlier for a limited company – it shows assets less liabilities. The 'bottom portion' or 'financed by' section is slightly different because there is only one owner who provides all of the capital, is entitled to all of the profits, and can withdraw amounts from the business at will. Therefore this section shows the capital which the business commenced with at the beginning of the period, plus the profit (or less the loss) made during the period, less any drawings made by the owner.

Example

Freda put £20 000 of her own money into the business. During its first year, it made a profit of £12 000 and Freda withdrew £8000 for herself. The capital of the business will be:

	£
Opening capital	20 000
Add net profit for the year	12 000
	32 000
Less drawings	(8000)
Closing capital	24 000

This total will equal the total of the top half of the balance sheet – the Net Assets.

The use of ratios to interpret financial results

A ratio is a comparison of one item with another. The comparison can be shown in several ways, for example:

- As a 'straight' comparison, e.g. £4000 compared with £2000 is 2 : 1
- One as a percentage of another, e.g. £2000 as a percentage of £4000 is 50 per cent
- One as a fraction of another, e.g. £2000/£4000 is ½ (a half)

or in other ways as appropriate.

Values on their own are of interest, but they do not give a full picture of the results of an organization. Look at the following results for three businesses for a year:

	A £	B £	C £
Sales turnover	12 000	14 000	16 000
Net profit	2760	3010	3360

It is almost impossible to say which of the above businesses has the 'best' profit for the year. What do we mean by 'best'? If we mean the highest, then C has the highest profit and A the lowest. If we mean the greatest amount of profit per pound of sales turnover, then we need to compare the profit with the turnover, for example in firm A, the profit per £ of turnover is £2760/£12 000 = 23p. This is a ratio – a comparison of one item with another.

Activity 7.24

Calculate the net profit per £ of turnover for the other two firms. Which would you say is the 'best' now?

Firm A has the highest net profit per £ of turnover, and firm C the lowest. This still does not tell us conclusively which firm is the 'best' but you can see that the use of ratios gives us an additional means of analysing the financial results of an organization.

Ratios should be compared with other ratios to be of maximum use. In the above example we compared three different companies. We need to know whether they are of the same kind, in the same line of business, of similar sizes, with similar markets, etc. If they are, then we might be able to draw some conclusions from the ratios we calculate. Comparison should be made with ratios from:

- other companies
- other periods
- budgets/expectations
- in order to get as full a picture as possible.

Types of ratio

You can calculate a ratio using any two figures, as long as the result means something to the user. The full range of ratios is far too large to be included in this book, but we have included some of the more common ratios. They are divided into four main categories:

- profitability (or performance) ratios
- liquidity ratios
- asset utilization ratios
- investors' ratios.

The ratios we are going to calculate here are based on the accounts for JKL Limited which we looked at earlier. They are reproduced here (in a shorter form) to save you having to turn back in the book:

Example

JKL Ltd balance sheet as at 31 July 1996

	£	£	£
Fixed assets			
Land and buildings		108 000	
Furniture and equipment		60 000	
			168 000
Current assets			
Stocks	3000		
Debtors	2500		
Bank and cash	2000		
		7500	
Less current liabilities			
Creditors		3900	
Net current assets			3600
			171 600
Less long-term liabilities			
Loan			43 000
Net assets			128 600
Financed by			
Ordinary shares of £1 each		100 000	
Share premium account		22 000	
General reserves		3000	
Profit and loss account balance		3600	
			128 600

Profitability ratios

These ratios are used to measure the profit made by an organization.

1 Gross profit percentage

This is gross profit as a percentage of sales. It is also called the gross margin.

$$\text{Margin} = \frac{\text{Gross profit}}{\text{Sales}} \times 100 = \frac{7000}{18\ 000} \times 100 = 38.9\%$$

There is no way of telling whether this is good or bad without comparing it with the margin for other periods and companies.

2 Net profit percentage

This is net profit as a percentage of sales.

$$\frac{\text{Net profit}}{\text{Sales}} \times 100 = \frac{2500}{18\ 000} \times 100 = 13.8\%$$

Note that the net profit figure is taken before deducting tax. This is because the tax payable by companies is not always in line with their profits for the year; if we take the net profit after tax, we might distort the ratio.

Compared with the gross profit margin, it shows how much has been 'swallowed up' by administration costs, etc. Again, it should also be compared with other periods and companies.

3 Return on capital employed

$$= \frac{\text{Profit}}{\text{Capital employed}} \times 100$$

This shows us how much profit has been earned compared to the money invested in the business. The consideration here is whose capital has been employed in making the profits? We could take the view that only the shareholders' funds (ether equity capital or total shareholders' funds) have been employed in making the profits, because they are the main providers of capital. Or we could include the funds provided by long-term lenders as well. Shareholders are the main people interested in profit, so we normally calculate the return based on shareholders' funds only.

Shareholders' funds includes all reserves: share premium account, general reserves, profit and loss account balance, etc. The profit which is available to the shareholders (in theory) is the net profit after tax. Therefore, for JKL Ltd:

$$\text{Return on capital employed} = \frac{2100}{128\,600} \times 100 = 1.6\%$$

Again, comparison with previous periods and other companies is essential.

Activity 7.25
Calculate three profitability ratios from the accounts you have prepared from previous tasks for Coglan's Clothes Ltd.

Liquidity ratios

These measure the ability of a firm to meet its debts. 'Liquidity' is the value of cash and near-cash assets, less current liabilities. The two main liquidity ratios are:

- the current ratio
- the 'acid test' (or 'quick') ratio.

1 The current ratio
This compares current assets with current liabilities and measures the

ability of the company to pay its current liabilities out of current assets. The ideal ratio is around 2 : 1, i.e. for every £1 in current liabilities, there is £2 of current assets. In recent years, it has become acceptable to trade with a lower ratio than this, say 1.7 : 1. Too high a ratio means that the firm has money 'sitting' in current assets unnecessarily. The ideal ratio is different in different types of industry – in a cash-based industry (e.g. supermarkets) a much lower ratio is acceptable.

$$
\begin{aligned}
\text{Current ratio} \;&=\; \text{Current assets : current liabilities} \\
&=\; 7500 : 3900 \\
&=\; 1.92 : 1
\end{aligned}
$$

There is £1.92 in current assets for every £1 of current liabilities.

2 The acid test ratio

In a firm with stocks which cannot be sold quickly for their balance sheet value or more, the current ratio might be misleading. If stocks are excluded from the current assets figure, a more realistic comparison of assets which can be readily converted to pay the current liabilities can be made.

$$
\begin{aligned}
\text{Acid test ratio} \;&=\; \text{Current assets less stock : current liabilities} \\
&=\; 4500 : 3900 \;=\; 1.15 : 1
\end{aligned}
$$

There is £1.15 in liquid assets for every £1 of current liabilities. The ideal ratio is around 1 : 1, so the firm can comfortably pay its current liabilities quickly if they so demand.

Other liquidity ratios

Activity 7.26

Calculate the current and acid test liquidity ratios from the accounts you have prepared from previous tasks for Coglan's Clothes Ltd.

Activity 7.27

Try and obtain the accounts of a range of organizations, such as:
- manufacturing companies
- utilities, e.g. electricity and water
- service industries, e.g. hotels, travel companies
- local government, e.g. your own borough or county council.

Questions for Activity 7.26

1. Who do you think might be interested in the various items of information contained in the accounts?
2. What do you understand by the profit and loss accounts and balance sheets contained in the accounts?
3. Calculate a range of ratios for each organization and compare them. Can you draw any conclusions from your comparisons?

Summary

This chapter should have given you a clear understanding of the importance of managing financial resources. We looked at the importance of budgets and accounts, and how they provide financial information. You have also had the oportunity to work through some examples typical of the types encountered by managers. We hope you can now answer the often asked question: 'How much does this product or service cost?'

8 Handling information

Aims

This chapter looks at the information flows within an organization; the reasons why information is collected; who collects and disseminates it and its usage. Information helps the manager in planning, implementing, controlling activities and decision making. The chapter also considers the organization's needs for information and how the First Line Manager can use it effectively.

By the end of the chapter you will:

■ Understand the flows of information, both internal and external to the organization
■ Understand the types of information and their sources
■ Be able to write an information brief and decide how and what to collect
■ Recognize quality criteria for information
■ Understand how information is handled, stored and retrieved using various media.

Key concepts

■ Use of information by managers;
■ Collection, analysis, storage in paper and electronic formats for retrieval and communication;
■ Written presentation;
■ Quality, information flows, data protection.

Introduction

Organizations have vast amounts of information circulating internally and flowing both in and out. Some is discarded rapidly, other information needs to be stored for long periods: maybe for reference; as evidence of activities; or records of meetings, decisions and action points; or notes of decisions. Some information may be retrieved regularly while other information may never be retrieved but must be kept for legal reasons. An organization's information system has to be able to cope with all these types of information and the different demands made upon it.

The more information and paper that circulates the more confusing it can become. Like time management, good information management is crucial to effective management. It is not necessary to collect and store everything. Deciding how much and what information to collect is one of the arts in setting up effective management information systems.

Information is not prescriptive, it does not make the decisions or dictate action. Information must be interpreted and analysed and managers must apply judgement to make the decisions. Information is an aid and not an end in itself.

Types of information

There are many different types of information held and used within an organization. Information can be qualitative or quantitative; formal or informal; transferred orally, in written format or electronically. It may be produced for regular organizational reporting procedures or for external requirements. It may be sent to a single recipient or circulated widely within and outside the organization. It can be in the form of correspondence, documents, invoices and orders, published sources, cuttings, memos, notices, forms, notes and minutes of meetings or conferences; procedure manuals, published statistics...the list goes on.

Information may come internally from managers, team members and other departments, and externally from customers and clients, official organizations, government departments, trade associations and other external stakeholders. Information may be numerical or textual, regular or ad hoc.

Information versus data

The problem for the manager is often too much information, much of which is still in its raw data form. It requires interpretation, or sorting and verifying before it becomes information which is comprehensible and relevant to the manager.

Activity 8.1

As you go through your in-tray next week classify the items into internal and external, formal and informal, regular and ad hoc items. Then ask yourself:

- How much of it is relevant to your current job?
- How much can you use immediately?
- How much of the information has a clear objective that is appropriate to your work?

■ How could it be improved?

At the same time you might like to apply this Activity to the information you send out to other people inside or outside your organization during the week.

■ Is the information you send out 'more useful' than the information you received?
■ Does everyone on your circulation list need to see it?
■ What will they do with it?
■ Is everything you send out necessary?
■ Can you provide it in a better format so that it will be more useful to the recipients?

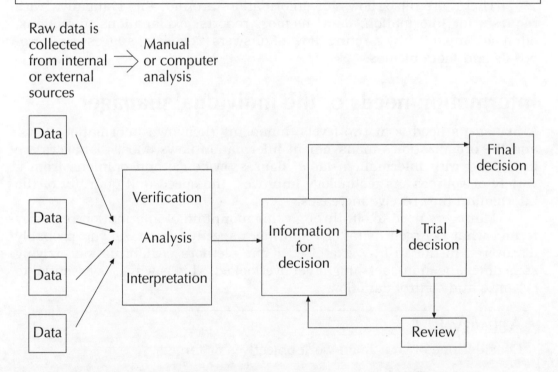

Raw data is collected from internal or external sources $\Longrightarrow$ Manual or computer analysis

Figure 8.1 *Data–information–decision making*

Charles Handy (1996) cites a senior manager who complained bitterly about the excessive efficiency of his company's information systems which were drowning in voice mail, Lotus notes and general e-mail. The executive complained:

> They are responding all the time now – they have stopped thinking. We are losing the initiative. Knowledge is important, but there are all sorts of knowledge. Knowing how is as important as knowing what, and then there is knowing who

and where, which can be crucial ingredients in any project, not to mention knowing why, which can be the most important of all. We need all sorts not just the first.

Information flows

An organization has information flowing both inwards and outwards. The organization disseminates information to outside bodies and receives information back. Information may be sent to customers and potential customers, shareholders, suppliers, trade associations, and to government departments. This type of information includes annual reports, technical information on products or services, sales brochures, price lists, publicity, sales pitches, direct mail, delivery notes and invoices.

There are also flows of information around the company, with requests for information, data, memos, reports, explanations, directions, often accompanied by a return flow of answers, requests, suggestions, proposals and more memos.

Information needs of the individual manager

A manager's need is at two levels: managing their own information flows, and the organization's management information flows. Most managers are inundated with information, facts, figures, evidence and opinions from a variety of sources. As technology improves, the speed and quantity of the information they receive increases.

Managers need to sift through this mountain of information regularly to find what is urgent, vital or requiring a speedy return. As you probably discovered in the 'in-tray' exercise, in the plethora of information arriving sometimes the main facts might get overlooked. This is why it is essential to organize and control data flows.

Activity 8.2

Consider one of your main work objectives or targets.

- ■ What information do you need to make the routine decisions to meet that objective?
- ■ What information would be ideal?
- ■ How regularly would you like it?
- ■ How up to date must it be?
- ■ How accurate?
- ■ What format would this take?

Now look at the paperwork you listed in the in-tray exercise at the beginning of this chapter. How much of it matches the ideal list you have just made? Are there any gaps? What could you do about these?

A manager's own information control system

First Line Managers need to set up systems suitable to their own information needs. This is done by deciding their daily, weekly, and monthly targets.

The role of information

First Line Managers are likely to need information for planning, setting targets, implementing plans, and controlling and monitoring activities.

In planning activities and setting targets a First Line Manager needs to know the department's targets, the resources available, the quality standards of, and the demand for the product being made or the service being offered. If the product or service relies on outputs from or supplies other departments then the First Line Manager needs information on these departments' workloads and schedules.

To implement, control and monitor activities a First Line Manager needs regular information on the actual supply of resources, the actual operating and time schedules from their own and other departments, and the quality of the product or service being produced. This will enable him or her to compare actual performance against targets and take any necessary corrective action. All this information needs to be fed back into the review process and the planning of future activities.

Activity 8.3

Look again at your list of information needs. Which of these are essential and you cannot do without, and which are useful? Are there any which are just for interest?

Look again at the 'useful list', what do you do with this information. Do you need to consult it regularly or only occasionally, or do you just need to know where it is in case you need to use it? Perhaps, knowing this, you could take yourself off the circulation list, going to consult it at source only when the need arises.

You could try putting such information in a separate file and seeing how many times you have to consult it over the next month. If, at the end of the month, you used it only infrequently or not at all you could think about discarding it entirely.

Now go back to your first list, the information which is 'essential to your job'.

- ■ Does it actually match what you really need?
- ■ If not, in what way could it be improved?
- ■ Could the producer reorganize the way the information is produced to better meet your needs?

■ What do you do with the information once you have it?

■ Do you need to interpret it, to make it usable?

■ Does this require complex manipulation, reorganization or representation by hand, using a calculator, or perhaps even using a statistical package on a computer?

Sources of information

Having decided what is needed, the next step is to think about who, or what source, might provide this information. The information may already be available within the organization from records already collected or held elsewhere. Alternatively it may be available from external published data. If not it may even require original research.

A vital element which must be considered is the cost of collecting and interpreting the data. It needs to reach the required level of accuracy and detail at a cost which is within the department's budget. If this means that the data takes longer to collect, leaving insufficient time to interpret and use the data a compromise may be needed.

Requesting information from another department, may increase their costs either by the production of another copy or by changing the format. As an alternative, is the information really needed in paper form? It might be possible to use it in a different form, either electronically, or by access to a central database, providing a more effective storage and retrieval process.

An organization's information needs

The process of determining an organization's information needs will echo the procedure for the individual, although in this case, there may be an information manager who is responsible for asking similar questions but on an organizational level. First it is necessary to find out who requires information and for what purpose.

Once again information is needed to plan, monitor and control activities, but this time within the whole organization. It may take the form of an overview, or show trends, or detailed information about markets, sales, production or performance against targets. More detailed information is needed for planning, schedules and operations, and for control purposes – checking actual outcomes against forecasts. Again this allows corrective action to be taken.

Information is used to analyse performance at two levels: for short-term comparison of actual performance against targets, and for strategic decisions which may have implications for changes in direction.

Who needs it?	Decision makers
What for?	Decision making in planning, implementation and control
Why?	More informed decisions
Using:	People, equipment and procedures
How?	Gather, sort, analyse, evaluate, distribute
Quality controls:	Relevant, timely, accurate, complete

Figure 8.2 *The effective management of information*

The information manager may request the following types of information from information users in order to design a suitable management information system.

1 What types of decision are you regularly called upon to make?
2 What types of information do you need to make these decisions?
3 What types of information do you regularly get?
4 What types of special studies do you regularly request?
5 What types of information would you like that you do not get now?
6 What information do you want

    daily?
    weekly?
    monthly?
    quarterly?
    annually?

7 What magazines and journals do you see regulary now?
8 Which of these do you read regularly?
9 Which ones do you refer to regularly for information?
10 Which additional magazines would you like to see regularly?
11 What specific topics do you want to be informed about?
12 What types of data analysis program would you like to be made available?
13 Which improvements could be made in the information you receive?
14 What internal information do you receive that is vital?
15 What information do you receive that you don't use?

Figure 8.3 *Determining information needs*

The 'management information system' (MIS) is a system for transforming data into information that can more readily be used by managers in their decision making. MIS managers must first find out what information is required by the various departments, then they need to determine the most effective way of collecting it. Once collected the data has to be converted into the information desired, and in an easily accessible format. They also need to control the flow of information so that it goes only to those managers who need it.

The requirements of departments vary, depending on the decisions they need to make. An organization's MIS has to take account of the needs of the different departments for what might appear to be the same information from the same source but provided in a different format.

Problems with information

Relevant information may not be reaching everyone – managers often assume that colleagues have the same information or have been on the circulation lists. Some organizations specify who, or which levels should be on the circulation list for different types of information.

Information should flow vertically through the organization from top to bottom via channels illustrated in the organization chart. Often information gets bottlenecked, perhaps at supervisor level or middle management level. These managers receive information from above and below, and have to collect, analyse and decide, not only if any action needs to be taken, but also if the information needs to be passed on again.

Sometimes information flows break down and the information is not disseminated – this can happen either accidentally or intentionally.

The effectiveness of an MIS should be evaluated against its capacity to assist managers in taking decisions, particularly through enabling the comparison of various possibilities in new and meaningful ways. The information must be understandable, a bad information system is one that passes on every bit of information, without interpretation or summary. That summary must be in a format that is relevant and useful to the user.

Activity 8.4

You have considered what types of information are needed by your organization and for your own job. You have compared this with the information you receive and looked for gaps. Now think about the quality of the information you receive:

- ■ Is it accurate?
- ■ Is it complete?
- ■ Is it up to date?
- ■ Is it in the right format?
- ■ Do you need further analysis to use it?

If the answer is 'no' to any of the first four questions, or 'yes' to the last question, try talking to the department which produces it to see if it can be adapted to meet your needs more closely.

A number of factors need to be taken into account in assessing the quality of the management information system and the information it provides to managers.

Quantity: There should not be more information than the manager can use or usefully absorb. The 'Goldilocks' principle for information should apply: not too much and not too little. Too often it is tempting, when collecting information or preparing it for a report, to be enticed along lines of enquiry that are interesting rather than necessary to the objectives at that time.

Completeness: The information should be as complete as possible. Occasionally there are managers who keep some information to themselves, because information is seen as power. Each manager should ensure that sufficient information is passed on so that decisions are not biased by a distorted picture caused by incomplete information. Sometimes decisions need to be made based on incomplete information because cost or time factors make it impractical to wait until all the information is available. In these cases some contingency plan or interim report might be needed as more information becomes available, which might alter plans or implementation.

Accuracy: Information needs to be sufficiently accurate for the intended purpose, but exact information is not always required. If you are considering entering a new market, information about the trends and the approximate positions of competitors may be sufficient for you to decide whether or not to look further at the market. When it comes to making a go/no go decision for entry to a new market, when capital will be committed to the development process, and equipment and resources acquired, more detailed information will be required. When looking at cash flows or setting up budgets for a potential project, managers will work in rounded figures, but the invoicing department or accounts need to be correct to the last penny!

Currency: It is important to ensure that the information is up to date, especially when using information from published data sources. Statistical information published regularly by government departments takes time to collect, process and publish.

Timeliness: Information needs to be communicated at the appropriate time. Perfect information too late is worse than incomplete information on time. Information which becomes available after a decision has been made may be of little use, or merely used to confirm the action taken.

Frequency: Information needs to be provided regularly, as the decision-making pattern dictates. If a decision or control point occurs monthly, then the information should be provided monthly. The frequency with which information needs to be provided may depend upon the level of management and the function for which it is required. A senior manager considering strategic decisions may be concerned with trends, while the middle and first line managers implementing the plans on a daily basis will need the information in more detail.

The frequency with which information is required may differ from time to time. In times of rapid change in a market, or when entering a new market, the manager may require daily information to control progress; once the market is established information may only be required on a monthly basis.

Reliability: The user departments need to have confidence in the information they receive. It needs to be clear that the information has been collected in a systematic way; that published sources of information have been validated, and that reasonable care has been taken to eliminate bias or error (both statistical and human) in the collection and processing of the data.

There is, however, a tendency for people to believe what they see in print, especially if it has been provided by a computer. Computers can generally provide information more quickly than people can, which may make it more timely. It is generally expected to be accurate; however there can be human error in inputting the data, or in the computer programme. Sometimes this may be a matter of asking the programme to do something for which it was not designed, or an incorrect interpretation of the process concerned. The manager should always look at the information provided rationally and consider if it makes sense.

Suitability for intended audience: This should include the level, depth, layout and presentation style. The information should be communicated in a clear format that is likely to be understood by the users, without inappropriate jargon.

A poor information system may impede decision making, and affect productivity if the right information is not available at the right time. It may lead to lost orders, particularly if reports or proposals cannot be produced at the right time. It may alter schedules and mean that there is more wasted waiting time or downtime for staff and equipment. It is like the 'domino effect', one fault in the information system may adversely affect motivation, product or service quality, production, productivity, sales and profitability.

The gathering, interpreting and presentation of material

The information brief

The information received and its interpretation is only as good as the brief given to the provider of the information. If the brief is given to an outside organization it is even more important to get it right.

An information brief should identify and define the objectives and characteristics of the information required, accuracy levels and time-scales.

It should identify the precise information required, specifying what is essential and what would be useful or just interesting. Limitations of time and cost of collection may preclude these latter items. It is also necessary to specify the format, depth and degree of accuracy required.

Interpreting data

Once the data is collected and organized, it has to be analysed and then turned into information in a format that can be used to make decisions. If you have understood the data you will be able to communicate the message or meaning of the numbers generated by the collection process as your role becomes one of communicator. When analysing information, it is important to distinguish between facts, evidence provided to support the facts, opinion and inferences.

CASE STUDY: THE NET BOOK AGREEMENT
A fierce price war is looming in Britain's book shops with the old price fixing agreement in tatters
A book price war involving some of the world's best selling authors is set to break out following the decision by Britain's biggest bookseller, W H Smith, to sell blockbusting novels on the cheap.

The move follows the announcement made by more publishers, Harper Collins, Random House and later Penguin, to abandon the Net Book Agreement which sets the price of most works of fiction and non fiction.

With the supermarket chain Asda too promising to better any reductions made by Smith's, the agreement now looks dead and buried.

With a quarter of the book market, W H Smith, which owns Waterstones, has the power to force the collapse of the Net Book Agreement and that in effect is what it has done. In the most significant move in the book trade for years, Smith's is to discount some of its best selling titles from Sunday by around 25 per cent.

The books initially involved are published by Harper Collins, responsible for Jeffrey Archer, and Random House which publishes Ruth Rendall. Both firms are voluntarily leaving the agreement this weekend, which means retailers can legally discount their titles.

In the past hour, a third publisher, Penguin, said it would be quitting as well. With few supporters left, the agreement which has survived for a century will no longer apply to most mass market fiction.

Harper Collins' spokesman Adrian Borne: 'There could be promotions; there could be cheaper books, but we are not necessarily looking to see total discounting of books across the nation. What we want to do is to be able to offer better value books to the public, and we believe we can do that.'

W H Smith will be discounting a typical hard backed novel costing £15 by around £4.

Waterstone's Managing Director Alan Giles said 'The book trade now accepts it has to try harder to attract the hard pressed customers. What it does do is to allow the book industry as a whole to start to compete more effectively against other categories of goods, video, music and other sources of discretionary spend. One of the consequences of recession is that even the most committed book lovers are looking for a deal and from next Sunday we'll be able to provide them with it.'

Smith's insists it hasn't started a price war but that's undoubtedly what has happened. The company is partly reacting to pressure from city investors worried by the group's falling profits. Many insiders in the book trade believe when faced with competition from the supermarkets – it's a war Smith's can't win.

Today's development has received a mixed reaction. For some who see the Net Book Agreement as nothing more than a mechanism for keeping prices artificially high, the advent of market forces into the world of books has been welcomed. Others have predicted it could mean the end of the small bookshop and so less choice for the consumer.

What are the consequences? Defenders of the Net Book Agreement say that by banning discounts it ensured that the widest possible range of books was published because full price best sellers subsidize sales of less popular titles.

The retailers who have been pressing to end the agreement say book buyers will now benefit because books will be cheaper.

Alan Priest of the supermarket chain Asda says 'big book chains like Smith's and Dillons will have to start competing on price. We think that if you are going to come into the real world, and into the competitive world, you have to make a price statement…that is to make sure you are offering great value and are selling more and more books to your shoppers. We are certainly going to beat any prices offered by any other retailer and that will be a guarantee in our stores as of Sunday.'

But the Booksellers Association, which today conceded that the agreement is effectively dead, said prices of only a few books will be cut. It also predicted a tough time for independent booksellers who have been protected from competition from larger price cutting rivals.

John Murray Brown runs the Angel Bookshop in London: 'I foresee a very bloody price war, when the small independent bookshop will be squeezed. Those who survive will not necessarily be the good booksellers or even the most profitable booksellers but the ones with the longest pockets.'

The Net Book Agreement has been facing a review by the Restrictive Practices Court even before today's developments. The Publishers Association is due to discuss on Thursday whether to defend the agreement before the court. Not all publishers are in favour of abandoning the agreement. Cutting prices of best sellers means lower margins and less profit at a time when the book trade is struggling.

Hodder Headline, which opted out of the agreement at the end of last year, this week has warned of lower profits in 1995 due to what it called exceptionally difficult trading conditions in the book market. The company's stock market value has dropped by a third as a result.

Activity 8.5

1 Sort the information into the following categories:

- ◼ assertion
- ◼ facts
- ◼ evidence
- ◼ opinions.

Based on these, write a summary for a small bookseller on a university site, who specializes mainly in textbooks, who wants to identify what impact it might have on the business.

You may have identified a number of assertions in the case including:

'the public will have more choice'
'there will be a book price war'
'book prices will go down'
'independent booksellers will suffer in the face of competition from the chain shops and supermarkets.'

To decide if this interpretation is valid you need to look for facts and evidence presented. There are a number of facts given, not all with evidence, and if this were information to be used in a presentation to the bookseller, you might wish to verify these facts from a second source.

Facts	Evidence
A number of book publishers are abandoning the Net Book Agreement	Statements by the publishers
Retailers can legally discount the books of these publishers	Statement, can be checked
A number of booksellers are planning to discount books	Statements by the sellers

Facts	Evidence
W H Smith has 25 per cent of the market	Statement, no evidence given in text
Some books will be cheaper	Statement by W H Smith; £15 book to sell for £11

Opinions	Source
'Customers will get better value'	Statement by Adrian Borne
'Books will need to compete with other consumer goods'	Statement by Alan Giles
'The NBA (is) a mechanism for keeping prices artificially high'	Reporter's interpretation, not attributed
'Big book chains...will have to start competing on price'	Statement by Alan Priest
'Small independent bookshops will be squeezed'	Statement by John Murray Brown

A different interpretation of the piece could be that customers will be able to buy lower priced books in a wider range of outlets. It is too early to say if this will affect the sales of lesser known authors and specialist books such as textbooks, by increasing the price or decreasing the market. This would need further research. It may well stimulate the book market by giving a wider potential audience access to lower price popular books.

Communicating quantitative information

Managers often need to pass on quantitative data in an understandable form: to support an argument, to prove a point. It is important to pass on the interpretation of the figures as well as allowing the reader/audience to make their own. This is where a manager becomes a communicator.

Many people find it easier to grasp the essential nature of quantitative information, mathematical relationships and trends more easily from a chart or diagram than an elaborate written explanation. However, each diagram should be accompanied by a brief explanation in the text. A key should be added to help the reader to recognize any special symbols.

Tables

A table is the most commonly used form for presenting quantitative data and results, but it is not always the most effective. Therefore, when tempted to include a table in a report or presentation always ask 'why a table and not some other format such as a graph?'

A table holds a lot of data; it can point to three things simultaneously, i.e. the variable at the top of the table, the variable at the side of the table, and the number in each cell. For example, average numbers of people unemployed may be shown by age and gender at the same time. Graphs cannot do that because they normally only use two dimensions.

Liking for work among employees at XYZ plc

	Do you like your work?		
Age	Yes	Indifferent	No
under 21	296	73	14
21–30	387	63	17
31–40	158	92	27
41–50	362	37	45
51–60	259	57	10
over 60	184	12	19

Figure 8.4 *Example of table*

This characteristic makes it an excellent device for sorting and manipulating data. It is possible to compare, look at averages, add and subtract columns and rows, or look for indexes and deviations.

However, this is analysis and not presentation or communication. For presentation of this data, in either written or oral form, it will require further interpretation. The results should be presented as clearly and simply as possible.

Formidable tables with a mass of numbers, particularly original computer printouts, probably will not be looked at at all. Readers may avoid reading tables which are difficult to understand. If the message conveyed is too complex it will not be remembered, or it may be interpreted incorrectly.

The following case study shows how quantitative data can be presented to give a clear indication of possible actions.

CASE STUDY: MILK DELIVERIES*

The main challenge to the milk industry is that the costs of daily doorstep delivery are becoming prohibitive. Yet if milk distribution is transferred to supermarkets, the risks will be heavy. When this was done in Holland, for example, milk consumption per head fell by one third. The marketing solution is to improve the profitability of milk rounds by selling other goods as well as milk.

To help identify the potential for this, a survey was conducted, using a structured questionnaire, of homes that did not buy goods other than milk, such as eggs and potatoes, from their milkman. The survey covered the characteristics, behaviour and attitudes of these two groups. See Figure 8.5.

The first table shows a printout from the survey, including raw data and percentages; in all there are over 200 figures.

[*data provided by Alan Wolfe.]

Activity 8.6

Look at the printout and present it as a table that is easy to understand and shows three main points about the market.

A possible suggestion is shown below in Figure 8.6. It has been reduced to 40 figures. The categories have been reduced, and the raw figures suppressed.

It is now much easier to see the facts; these are that homes with the highest expenditure on milk are large households, and that these buy the most goods from their milkman. The data that has been left out can be summarized in one sentence: 'most of the small households who spend little on milk are older, poorer people, such as old-age pensioners.'

To make the results even more relevant to the marketing manager who has to use these figures, the data can be interpreted as profiles. Now the chart is about *people* rather than *milk bills*. Now it can be used to answer the question: 'Who buys goods from their milkman?' The answer becomes: 'Households who buy most goods from their milkman are the large households that also buy most milk. This is the target market, and there is still apparently potential in this market.' This finding could be the key to a promotional strategy.

	Total	Age			Class			Household size			Does customer buy other goods from milkman?		
		16–34	35–54	55+	ABC1	C2	DE	1–2	3–4	5+	Regularly	Occasionally	Never
Total	544	144	163	237	212	182	150	260	200	84	110	109	325
Spent	100%	100%	100%	100%	100%	100%	100%	100%	100%	100%	100%	100%	100%
Up to 50p	58	2	3	53	20	10	28	55	2	1	6	8	44
	11%	1%	2%	22%	9%	5%	19%	21%	1%	1%	5%	7%	14%
50p–99p	176	28	33	115	63	60	53	137	29	10	21	40	115
	32%	19%	20%	49%	30%	33%	35%	53%	15%	12%	19%	37%	35%
£1–£1.49	142	49	42	51	61	49	32	47	84	11	33	27	82
	26%	34%	26%	22%	29%	27%	21%	18%	42%	13%	30%	25%	25%
£1.50–£1.99	89	37	38	14	32	36	21	13	55	21	23	20	46
	16%	26%	23%	6%	15%	20%	14%	5%	28%	25%	21%	18%	14%
£2–£2.99	61	24	36	1	33	18	10	4	26	31	23	10	28
	11%	17%	22%	*	16%	10%	7%	2%	13%	37%	21%	9%	9%
£3+	10	–	7	3	3	4	3	–	2	8	2	2	6
	2%	–	4%	1%	1%	2%	2%	–	1%	10%	2%	2%	2%
None/dk	8	4	4	–	–	5	3	4	2	2	2	2	4
	2%	3%	2%	–	–	3%	2%	2%	1%	2%	2%	2%	1%

(percentages are expressed to the nearest whole number; Source: A. Wolfe

Figure 8.5 *Operation Round Up: Weekly amount spent by households on milk bought from their milkman (base: all private households)*

	Total	Family size			Buying goods		
		1–2	3–4	5+	Reg	Occ.	Never
Sample size	544	260	200	84	110	109	325
	%	%	%	%	%	%	%
Up to 50p/None	13	23	2	5	6	9	15
50p–99p	32	53	15	12	19	37	35
£1–£1.99	42	23	70	38	51	43	39
£2 and over	13	2	14	47	23	11	11
	100	100	100	100	100	100	100

Figure 8.6 *Weekly household milk bill – Summary table (all percentages have been rounded to nearest whole number)*

Figure 8.7 *Weekly household milk bill – Summary chart (percentages)*

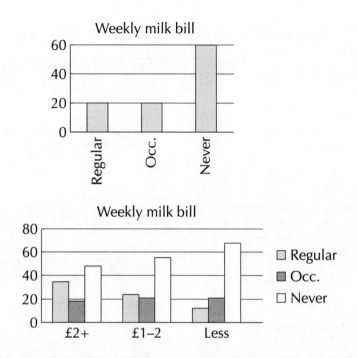

Figure 8.8 *Weekly household milk bill – Buyer profile (percentages)*

Graphs

Graphs can be more effective in communicating results when the reader is not expected to examine the data in depth. They can be used to communicate trends, qualitative results, relative sizes, or relationships between two variables; for example, price changes over time compared to the rate of inflation, sales of different brands of the same goods, or the relationship between actual and forecast sales. They can show that the sales of Brand A are higher than those of Brand B, and perhaps a lot higher than Brand C; or that there is a strong relationship between the sales of ice cream and July temperatures. Graphs show general relationships.

Graphs can still be vitally important. They come into their own when they can communicate a recognizable shape: a straight line, a simple curve, or even a dramatic change in one of the variables at a particular point. This is because the human brain can process shapes better than numerical figures. Think how one remembers a face even if you have not seen the person for many years. You would tend to recognize the face from hundreds of other faces in your memory bank. If it was presented as a numerical data string, the analysis of the data would probably be beyond your technical skill – unless of course you are a computer! Yet we process and recognize shapes instantly and without even understanding how we do it. Therefore, the use of familiar shapes is a powerful communication tool. However, if a shape is unfamiliar it can be as bewildering as the original raw data.

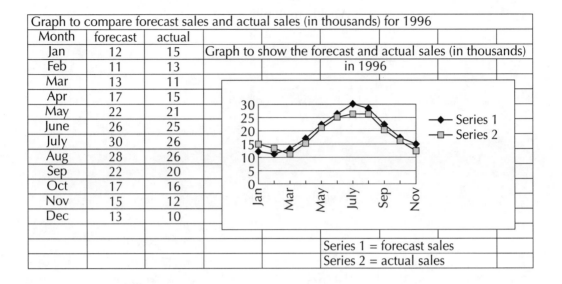

Graph to compare forecast sales and actual sales (in thousands) for 1996								
Month	forecast	actual						
Jan	12	15	Graph to show the forecast and actual sales (in thousands) in 1996					
Feb	11	13						
Mar	13	11						
Apr	17	15						
May	22	21						
June	26	25						
July	30	26						
Aug	28	26						
Sep	22	20						
Oct	17	16						
Nov	15	12						
Dec	13	10						
					Series 1 = forecast sales			
					Series 2 = actual sales			

Figure 8.9 *Graph example*

Graphs are not good at expressing the amount by which one thing is different to another. If something is 29 per cent bigger than something else, then it may be better communicated by saying so. They must be drawn to tell a single story and cannot be conveniently used to encourage further exploration of the data by the readers.

Other presentation formats for quantitative information

There are other visual pictures that can be used, including pie charts, bar graphs and histograms. They all have two thing in common: they are a way of improving the communication of information and they all take time and effort to plan and produce. Most computer graphics packages will provide both the analysis and top-quality presentations.

A *pie chart* is used to illustrate the relative sizes of the components of a whole. Do not use more than five components and, because the eye is used to measuring in a clockwise motion, position the most important segment at 12 o'clock (see Figure 8.10).

The *bar chart* is used to illustrate the comparative sizes of various quantities (see Figure 8.8). A compound bar chart, two or more bar charts combined into one, shows how two or more similar items vary with respect to each other as well as in some other dimension (see Figure 8.7).

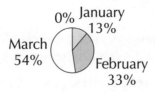

Figure 8.10 *Example of a pie chart*

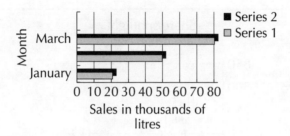

Figure 8.11 *Example of a bar chart*

The *histogram* represents relative frequency or occurrence of a particular event or characteristic.

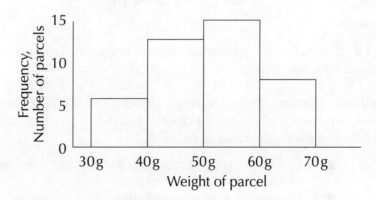

Figure 8.12 *Example of a histogram*

Activity 8.7

Look critically at the presentation of numerical information in the financial section of this weekend's broadsheet newspapers.

■   What techniques have been used to present the
     information?
■   Is it clear to the reader?
■   How could you improve the presentation?

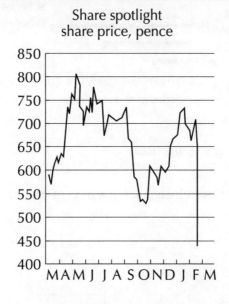

Figure 8.13 *Example of financial data presented in a newspaper
(Independent, 12 March 1997)*

Not all information is quantitative; sometimes it will include opinions
and attitudes, and even statements about 'feelings'. In this case you may
use some of the following techniques:

■   Bullet points – of main ideas that are echoed in the text
     or in your oral presentation
■   Positioning maps and diagrams – as in product or
     brand positioning
■   Profiles of main products or your competitors
■   Quotes backing up main points
■   'Thought bubble' drawings or illustrations.

The written report

Report writing is an important aspect of effective management. Reports are written for a specific readership and are probably intended to be kept as a record. A report will present facts and findings which usually form the basis of a set of recommendations.

Activity 8.8

Jot down some of your ideas as to what makes a good written report.

Probably 'easy to read' appears near the top of the list. Yet often main reports fail to meet this criteria. Writers often choose long words to make the report seem more authoritative. It is preferable to use familiar, short words wherever possible.

Successful writers always plan their report, they think about its purpose and its intended readership, what to put in, and, probably more importantly, what to leave out.

The purpose of the report

It is important for all managers to establish at the outset the exact purpose of the report. This will determine its nature and style. It may be a factual report to inform the readers about a new product or programme of work, or to report an incident. Or it may be written to explain a new procedure which is about to be introduced. Alternatively it may be written to persuade the reader to take a particular course of action.

Identifying the reader

Two common mistakes in report writing are to overestimate or underestimate your readers' knowledge. If possible try to discover how much they know already and then write the report to that level of knowledge. It can be difficult to establish this, especially when writing for a wide readership. In such cases aim for the reader whom you consider to be the most important. Some people are only on the circulation list for prestige, and some because no one remembered to cross them off!

The structure of the report

Many organizations use a common house style for their reports; however, they will normally include the following:

- *Title page*: this normally includes the author's name and sometimes the circulation list as well as the report title.
- *Summary*: this is often found at the beginning of a report, although it cannot be written until the whole report is finished.
- *Terms of reference*: these set out who requested the report, its objectives, its limits and the time-scale of the investigation.
- *Procedure*: this section describes the way the investigation was carried out, and who was consulted.
- *Findings*: these should be presented clearly and objectively. It can help the reader if this section contains graphs and other diagrams.
- *Conclusions*: these should flow from the previous section, following an analysis of the findings.
- *Recommendations*: here the writer can set out their preferred course of action, having, of course, considered the alternatives.
- *Appendices*: these should not be just a dump for extraneous material. The material presented here should be pertinent to the report and clearly referenced and referred to in the main body of the report.
- *Bibliography*: a clear list of any publications used, each giving the author, title, name of publication, date, publisher and place of publication.

Language and style

Reports are generally written in formal language and in the third person. The report needs to be objective, based on facts rather than opinions. There must be a clear distinction between facts and inferences drawn from facts. As mentioned earlier the wording must be concise and technicalities either explained or limited to the readers' knowledge.

Storage and retrieval of information

Techniques for information storage

Various techniques are used to organize information storage: content listing; catalogues; cross references; key words; indexing; classifying. The important factor is to find a simple and efficient method which enables you to retrieve information quickly. In some ways, because you cannot see information held on computers, it becomes easier to remember that an efficient retrieval system is needed.

Location of storage systems

Information may be stored centrally, in a computer mainframe which is networked for all authorized users, or in a manual central filing system.

Some documents need to be kept in a secure archive. This may be located outside the organization. A manager must take into account the difficulty and cost of replacement of documents and information in case of accident, fire or damage. Storage location and its accessibility will depend on how often the materials will be needed and how easy or fast this access should be.

Media for storage of information

Information may be stored in hard copy, in computer files, on a mainframe or in separate tapes or floppies; as microfiche, or in audio or video format.

The benefits of using computers rather than paper file formats is that, once the task reaches a certain level, it is usually quicker and more accurate to allow the processing to be undertaken by machine than by hand. This also leads to the ability to undertake more complex analysis and quicker processing. Where the computers are networked (where a number of computers are linked to the same system) the exchange of information can be more efficient.

Centralized systems occur where most of the processing is done in one location, using a mainframe computer and a central database. In *decentralized systems* each location within the organization decides upon its own needs, including physical equipment, programs, databases, and personnel. It may then become impossible for different departments or locations to share information as the programs and systems can be incompatible.

Networks are becoming increasingly important; allowing customers within a department or across an organization to exchange information from several different locations. A computer network is a group of interconnected computer systems that can exchange information among several locations. The computers may be linked on a department, organization, national or international level. This latter would be a *wide area network* (WAN), where communication may be by satellite. A *local area network* (LAN) is usually an internal network which would operate through cables or dedicated telephone lines. The computers in the network share processing systems, software, storage areas, data and access.

An example would be an emergency control room for a public service, where several telephone operators would receive details of the emergency or breakdown from the public or site engineers. They would then choose a member of staff with the appropriate skills to deal with the problem, based on who is working rather than off duty, sick or on holiday, and who is not currently occupied elsewhere. The central database would contain data on the staff, their capabilities, a roster of when they are on duty or on call, their current location if already on a call-out, and a contact telephone number. This database would allow the system to operate on a day-to-day basis as well as provide records of jobs completed or in progress, for performance analysis. Some ambulance services have now adopted 'criteria based dispatch'. This is a radical approach to handling 999 calls. The traditional system is that all 999 calls have the same target response rate, irrespective of the nature of the emergency. 'Criteria based dispatch' tailors the resource to meet the need. On receipt of a 999 call a member of staff in the control room asks the caller a set of predetermined questions. The call can then be prioritized according to clinical need into immediately life-threatening, serious and minor emergencies, and ambulance responses dispatched accordingly. An eight-minute response performance target has been set for immediately life-threatening emergencies. Calls in the other two categories get the same response rate target as they did before.

The next generation of computing technology will offer further help to managers in collecting, manipulating and controlling information and in aiding business decisions. Advances in telecommunications, information technology and artificial intelligence will continue to contribute to the ability of managers to gather and use information quickly and efficiently.

In the recent past it has been the miniaturization of computing facilities, combined with an increase in computing power, that has been the exciting aspect. This has enabled smaller and more powerful computers to move from mainframe and central locations to the desktop, laptop and pocket! Computing power has become portable, fast and easier and cheaper to use. This has given access to more people, with less formal training in computer technology, and wider applications. As the cost has decreased, such facilities have become available to smaller organizations and an increasing number of individuals.

Inter-office communicating is already paperless with electronic mail (e-mail). This electronically transmits data and information in letters, reports and documents between computers. E-mail communication may be internal to an organization, national or international. This system is becoming increasingly available in many organizations and is worldwide.

These systems have speeded up the response times between organizations, between customer and supplier, and between invoice and payment. They have also made access to information easier and faster. The problem that still remains is that of the individual manager who needs time to decide which information is important and how it needs to be manipulated in order to use the information, improve decision making and still meet deadlines!

The Data Protection Act 1984

All organizations or departments holding or processing data about (living) people have to register with the Data Protection Registrar. The Data Protection Act was passed because of the growing concern felt by some people about the use of personal data and the increased use of computer technology in all areas of public and private life.

If a department intends to hold details on computer, its manager needs to ensure that the registration held by the organization allows this to be done.

The following extract from the Data Protection Act Guidelines explains the coverage and exemptions of the act:

> Computers are in use throughout society – collecting, storing and distributing information (processing). Much of that information is about living people (personal data). The Data Protection Act 1984 places obligations on those who record and use personal data (data users). They must be open about the use (through the data protection register) and follow sound and proper practices (the Data Protection Principles).

The Data Protection Principles state that personal data shall be:

- collected and processed fairly and lawfully
- held only for specific and lawful purposes
- used only for those purposes and only disclosed to those people described in the register entry;
- adequate, relevant and not excessive in relation to the purposes for which they are held;
- accurate and, where necessary, kept up to date;
- held no longer than is necessary for the registered purpose;
- protected by proper security.

An organization can keep employees' names on the computer for the purposes of calculating and paying wages and pensions without being registered, but if they are to be used as a personnel record then this use must be registered. Similarly details of customer names and addresses for accounting purposes or as records of purchase can be kept without being registered, but not for marketing purposes.

Summary

This chapter considered who uses information and for what purposes; the information flows within an organization; the information requirements of the individual manager and the different departments within an organization. The quality of information was discussed with regard to its fitness for purpose, timeliness, accuracy and completeness.

Managers need to develop an information brief to give them information suitable to help them plan and take decisions; they need to know the sources of information, and how to interpret and present information within organizations on a regular and ad hoc basis.

Information needs to be organized and stored so that it may be retrieved efficiently. Organizations must be aware of and work within the Data Protection Act to protect the privacy and confidentiality of information retained on computer systems within the organization.

Index